Just Housing

Urban and Industrial Environments

Series editor: Robert Gottlieb, Henry R. Luce Professor of Urban and Environmental Policy, Occidental College

For a complete list of books published in this series, please see the back of the book.

Just Housing

The Moral Foundations of American Housing Policy

Casey J. Dawkins

The MIT Press
Cambridge, Massachusetts
London, England

© 2021 Massachusetts Institute of Technology

This work is subject to a Creative Commons CC-BY-NC-ND license.

Subject to such license, all rights are reserved.

The open access edition of this book was made possible by generous funding from the MIT Libraries.

The MIT Press would like to thank the anonymous peer reviewers who provided comments on drafts of this book. The generous work of academic experts is essential for establishing the authority and quality of our publications. We acknowledge with gratitude the contributions of these otherwise uncredited readers.

This book was set in Stone Serif and Stone Sans by Westchester Publishing Services. Printed and bound in the United States of America.

Library of Congress Cataloging-in-Publication Data
Names: Dawkins, Casey J., author.
Title: Just housing : the moral foundations of American housing policy / Casey J. Dawkins.
Description: Cambridge, Massachusetts : The MIT Press, 2021. | Series: Urban and industrial environments | Includes bibliographical references and index.
Identifiers: LCCN 2020053009 | ISBN 9780262543071 (paperback)
Subjects: LCSH: Housing policy—United States. | Housing—Moral and ethical aspects—United States.
Classification: LCC HD7293 .D33 2021 | DDC 174/.936355610973—dc23
LC record available at https://lccn.loc.gov/2020053009

10 9 8 7 6 5 4 3 2 1

publication supported by a grant from
The Community Foundation for Greater New Haven
as part of the **Urban Haven Project**

I dedicate this book to Mom and Dad, who made our house a home, and Erin, who gave my heart a home.

Contents

Preface   ix
Acknowledgments   xi

I   **Foundations**

    Introduction   3
    1   **The Materials of American Housing Justice**   13

II   **Context**

    2   **The Natural Right to a Homestead**   35
    3   **Housing for the Common Good**   61
    4   **Modern Housing and the Homeownership Republic**   89
    5   **Homes without Foundations**   121

III   **Structure**

    6   **The Architecture of Housing Justice**   159
    7   **Private Property and the Injustice of Tenure Insecurity**   193
    8   **Taking Housing Justice Seriously**   215
    Conclusion   243

Notes   249
References   259
Index   291

Preface

As I began to proofread the final draft of this book, the world changed. In March 2020, the COVID-19 pandemic forced everyone into their homes. The housing justice community mobilized for action on behalf of those without homes and those facing housing insecurity. Several local, state, and federal government agencies in the United States responded with policies that granted temporary relief from rental and mortgage payment obligations. In May 2020, George Floyd's brutal death at the hands of the Minneapolis police catalyzed a nationwide reckoning with the durable legacies of America's racist past and present. These events, combined with the disproportionate burden of COVID-19 borne by people of color, brought attention to structural injustices that are deeply embedded within America's institutions. A variety of proposals for reform that were only in their embryonic stages in summer 2020 will likely come into full view by the time this book hits the shelves. I hope that this book offers lasting advice to US housing policymakers seeking to incorporate the lessons from 2020 into policy reforms that will chart a path toward justice. As this book goes to press, these lessons have only begun to be revealed.

Acknowledgments

Most of my previous work dwelled in the realm of empirical housing and land-use policy evaluation. This book is a departure from that. The idea for the book originally came from my work in the fair housing arena, where advocates are currently engaged in a spirited debate about the scope of the Fair Housing Act's mandate to affirmatively further fair housing (Fair Housing Act of 1968, § 808). I quickly learned that this debate was one among many that could not be resolved with additional empirical data on the consequences of policy alternatives. The most interesting debates to me are those that boil down to disagreements over the moral foundations of housing policy that test the limits of consequentialist reasoning.

This book is my attempt to bring clarity to these debates. It would not have been possible without the support and encouragement of friends, family, and a large community of scholars. I am particularly grateful to my friends and family, without whom it would not have been possible to write a book about home's special meaning and significance. In addition to providing emotional support throughout the writing process, Erin Riley gave several constructive editorial suggestions. Kyle Dawkins offered valuable artistic advice on the book's cover. I am also indebted to my academic home, the University of Maryland School of Architecture, Planning, and Preservation (MAPP+D). I offer a special thanks to our current dean, Don Linebaugh, and former deans, David Cronrath and Sonia Hirt, for providing the resources and support to bring this book to completion. Gerrit Knaap and the National Center for Smart Growth were instrumental in helping me secure funding to support the development of several of the book's ideas.

This book is the culmination of numerous spirited conversations about the moral foundations of housing and land-use policy. These conversations have included too many scholars and advocates to list, but my doctoral advisor and coauthor, Chris Nelson, deserves special recognition for his support and encouragement over the years. My ideas have also been shaped by many conversations and engagements with the ideas of Andrew Aurand, Michael Bader, Howie Baum, Ariel Bierbaum, David Bieri, Raphael Bostic, Karen Chapple, Michael Elliott, Lance Freeman, George Galster, Ed Goetz, Andrew Greenlee, Sonia Hirt, Derek Hyra, Keith Ihlanfeldt, David Imbroscio, Dan Immergluck, Seema Iyer, Larry Keating, Gerrit Knaap, Ted Koebel, Rob Lang, Willow Lung-Amam, Brian McCabe, Kirk McClure, Myron Orfield, Kurt Paulsen, Rolf Pendall, Jessie Richardson, Bill Rohe, Barbara Samuels, Tom Sanchez, Ben Scafidi, Jenny Schuetz, Lisa Schweitzer, and Ron Sundstrom. I owe a special debt of gratitude to my students, who added the right amount of seasoning to the uncooked versions of the ideas expressed in this book. Others, too numerous to mention, have shaped my ideas through their written work. Their influence can be found in the book's citations. I thank the MIT Press editors and anonymous reviewers for numerous suggestions that greatly improved the book. I also owe a debt of gratitude to Laurie Prendergast, who prepared the index. The words on these pages are my own, but countless conversations about housing policy and justice have given the words meaning. This book is derived in part from material previously published in the following journal articles:

- Dawkins, Casey J. 2017. Autonomy and Housing Policy. *Housing, Theory and Society* 34 (4): 420–438. Published online January 8, 2017. Copyright IBF, The Institute for Housing and Urban Research, available online at https://doi.org/10.1080/14036096.2016.1274679.
- Dawkins, Casey J. 2017. Putting Equality in Place: The Normative Foundations of Geographic Equality of Opportunity. *Housing Policy Debate* 27 (6): 897–912. Copyright Virginia Polytechnic Institute and State University, Metropolitan Institute, available online at https://doi.org/10.1080/10511482.2016.1205646.
- Dawkins, Casey. 2018. Toward Common Ground in the U.S. Fair Housing Debate. *Journal of Urban Affairs* 40 (4): 475–493. Published May 19, 2018, Copyright Urban Affairs Association (https://urbanaffairsassociation.org/), reprinted by permission of the publisher (Taylor & Francis Ltd, http://www.tandfonline.com), available online at https://doi.org/10.1080/07352166.2017.1310595.

Acknowledgments

- Dawkins, Casey. 2020. Realizing Housing Justice through Comprehensive Housing Policy Reform. *International Journal of Urban Sciences* 25 (S1): 266–281. Copyright Institute of Urban Sciences, University of Seoul, available online at https://doi.org/10.1080/12265934.2020.1772099.
- Dawkins, Casey. 2020. The Right to Housing in an Ownership Society. *Housing and Society* 47 (2): 81–102. Copyright Housing Education and Research Association, available online at https://doi.org/10.1080/08882746.2020.1722055.

I Foundations

Introduction

I do not believe the American economy is strong when home foreclosures are now the highest on record, turning the American dream of homeownership into a nightmare.
—Bernie Sanders (2007, 1:17)

America is not so much a nightmare as a non-dream. The American non-dream is precisely a move to wipe the dream out of existence.
—William S. Burroughs, "From the Job" (1998, 289)

For the growing number of Americans who are homeless, lack safe shelter, or spend the majority of their monthly paychecks on rent, the American dream of home is a mirage. On a single night in 2019, nearly 568,000 people were homeless. Homelessness has risen for the third year in a row, following a six-year decline, because of increases in the number of people living on the streets or in unsheltered locations (Henry et al. 2020). The number of households experiencing severe housing problems has increased by 36 percent since 2001 (Watson et al. 2020).[1] For nearly one-quarter of all renters and more than half of renters with very low incomes, housing costs now account for more than half of household expenditures, yet only one-quarter of those eligible for federal housing assistance actually receive it (Watson et al. 2020).[2]

The problems of homelessness and housing insecurity are manifestations of two broader trends: rising housing inequality and a growing shortage of affordable homes. Since 1970, the price gap between the most and least expensive American homes has grown, in part because of increasing housing market segmentation within cities (Albouy and Zabek 2016).

Although housing production outpaced household growth between 1982 and 2010, completions and placements of new housing units barely kept pace with household growth between 2011 and 2018. Since 2011, the number of homes renting for less than $800 per month has declined by 4 million units (Joint Center for Housing Studies of Harvard University 2019). Today, those earning below 30 percent of their area's median income face a shortage of 7 million rental homes that are affordable and available for rent (Aurand et al. 2020).

The housing affordability crisis comes on the heels of a foreclosure crisis that erased years of accumulated home equity and forced 7.8 million households into foreclosure (CoreLogic 2017). The foreclosure crisis hit Black and Hispanic families particularly hard. Between 2007 and 2009, nearly 8 percent of homes that had been recently purchased by Black and Hispanic homebuyers were lost to foreclosure. During the same period, only 4.5 percent of homes recently purchased by white families were lost to foreclosure (Bocian, Li, and Ernst 2010). Racial and ethnic differences in foreclosure rates have exacerbated the racial and ethnic wealth gap. Between 1983 and 2013, median Black household wealth fell by 75 percent, and median Hispanic household wealth dropped by 50 percent. Over the same period, median white household wealth rose by 14 percent. By 2013, the median white household wealth of $116,800 was 58.4 times larger than median Hispanic household wealth and 68.7 times larger than median Black household wealth (Asante-Muhammad et al. 2017). In the same year, 5.5 percent of white homeowners owned homes worth less than the value of the outstanding mortgage principal owed, while 14.2 percent of Black homeowners and 12 percent of Hispanic homeowners owned homes with negative equity (Wolf 2014).

Matthew Desmond's *Evicted: Poverty and Profit in the American City* (2016) paints a vivid portrait of the human costs of housing insecurity. For Scott and Patrice, two protagonists in Desmond's ethnography, housing is more than four walls and a roof; housing is the key to economic stability. After Scott secured a bed in the Guest House, an 86-bed homeless shelter in Milwaukee, he was finally able to receive regular methadone treatments for his narcotics addiction. Eventually, Scott became a resident manager of the Guest House and received a subsidy to offset the cost of renting a unit at the Majestic Loft Apartments. The stability of his new home life enabled Scott to develop and pursue a five-year plan that culminated in a return to the nursing profession. After years of living in "rat holes," Patrice secured stable housing, earned her GED, was named Adult Learner of the Year, and went on to enroll in a local community college to pursue a career in law enforcement. The key to Desmond's stories is the chain of causality. Housing (in)security fosters employment (in)stability, not the reverse.

In addition to providing a platform for economic stability and mobility, housing enhances human health and well-being. Those who are homeless are more likely to fall ill, require hospitalization, and die at a much younger age than the general population (Maness and Khan 2014). While finalizing this book, I was reminded of these connections daily, as the COVID-19 pandemic required me to stay at home to protect myself and my loved ones from exposure to a deadly virus. I was also reminded of the health risks facing those without homes, who were asked to "shelter in place" despite having no place to call their own.

The US Congress first acknowledged the intimate links between housing and human well-being and prosperity in 1937, when in the Housing Act of 1937 it adopted legislation designed to "promote the general welfare of the Nation" by eliminating "the unsafe and insanitary housing conditions and the acute shortage of decent, safe, and sanitary dwellings for families of low income" (Housing Act of 1937, 42 U.S.C. § 1437). Twelve years later, the Housing Act of 1949 established the national goal of providing "a decent home and suitable living environment for every American family" (Housing Act of 1949, 42 U.S.C. § 1441). Today, many are calling for fundamental reform of the federal housing policies enacted during the first half of the twentieth century. One recent poll found that 60 percent of Americans view housing affordability as a serious problem in the places where they live (Badger 2019). Some consider the housing affordability crisis America's next big political issue. In the race to secure the Democratic Party's nomination for the 2020 presidential election, several candidates offered bold proposals for sweeping reforms of America's federal housing policy infrastructure (Schneider 2018b).

An emerging "housing justice" coalition views America's inability to deliver on its 70-year-old promise as a moral failing. In cities across America, grassroots advocates carry signs that read "cancel rent," "save our homes," and "housing is a human right" to draw attention to exorbitant rents, gentrification-induced displacement, and home evictions. Applying a twist to the NIMBY (not in my backyard) acronym given to affordable housing opponents, a new generation of YIMBY (yes in my backyard) advocates is calling for fundamental reform of local and state laws that constrain the supply of affordable housing. Other housing justice advocates demand PHIMBY (public housing in my backyard). The contemporary housing justice movement is a big tent that provides shelter to a loose coalition of right to the city advocates, housing rights advocates, civil rights advocates, and human rights advocates who believe that the government has a moral obligation to provide adequate housing to everyone living on US soil.

Behind the unity veil, housing justice advocates remain divided over the question of means. Some housing advocates seek judicial remedies to housing injustices, while others pursue statutory reforms. Some call for an expansion of subsidies for affordable housing production in the neighborhoods where low-income households live (Goetz 2003), while others favor tenant-based rental subsidies that enable low-income households to move to different neighborhoods (DeLuca and Rosenblatt 2017). Virtually all fair housing advocates endorse the goal of eliminating unfair forms of housing market discrimination, but some question the spatial objective of integrating neighborhoods by race and ethnicity (Goetz 2018).

Two recent events highlight these divisions. In response to the growing housing affordability crisis in the state of California, state senator Scott Wiener introduced Senate Bill (SB) 827 in 2018, which would have granted the state authority to override local zoning to permit the construction of high-density affordable housing near transit stations. YIMBY advocates offered their full support for the bill, while tenants' rights organizations and PHIMBY advocates opposed it. Tenants' rights organizations argued that removing regulatory impediments to private-sector housing development would only foster gentrification and displace low-income residents of color. In their opposition to SB 827, tenants' rights organizations found themselves politically aligned with the same NIMBY opposition groups they had previously opposed (Schneider 2018a).

Now consider another battle in the city of Houston. For years, the state of Texas has been under the national spotlight for violating federal fair housing laws in its Low-Income Housing Tax Credit (LIHTC) program. In January 2017, nine days before the inauguration of President Donald Trump, the US Department of Housing and Urban Development (HUD) notified the city that its rejection of a permit for a subsidized housing project in a majority-white neighborhood violated federal civil rights laws by maintaining existing patterns of racial segregation and giving too much weight to the racially motivated concerns of white neighbors. In March 2018, HUD and Houston agreed on a residential mobility and housing assistance plan coordinated with the city's Hurricane Harvey recovery efforts. Housing justice advocates objected to the plan, citing the agreement's weak enforcement provisions, which would not have reversed the city's historical policy of siting affordable housing in segregated neighborhoods. Attorneys for the Texas Low Income Housing Information Service later filed a lawsuit against HUD and Houston in a federal district court, threatening to block Houston's receipt of federal disaster recovery funds (Elliott 2018).

Conflicts such as these threaten the unity of the housing movement at a time when the more significant threat to housing security is America's historical opposition to government-sponsored low-income housing programs. Since the nation's founding, Americans have been suspicious of government actions that tread on private property rights. Conservative critics opposed the New Deal–era public housing program and have consistently rejected bills funding it. The objections of conservatives gained steam during the 1970s, following reports of rampant corruption in HUD-administered mortgage subsidy programs (Welfeld 1992). During the 1980s, President Ronald Reagan slashed HUD's budget authority, and the agency still has not recovered (Schwartz 2015). Today, libertarians argue that government regulations and housing subsidy programs that restrict and crowd out the supply of private-sector housing are to blame for the housing affordability crisis (Glaeser and Gyourko 2008).

Conservatives are not the only opponents of government-sponsored low-income housing programs. Many progressives who fought for social justice and environmental causes during the 1960s now lead grassroots NIMBY campaigns against affordable housing (Fisher 1994). In Seattle, one of America's most progressive cities, residents objected to a proposed tax that would have funded the provision of services for the city's homeless population. Homeless people and their representatives were verbally chastised during a public discussion of the tax proposal (Hobbes 2019). NIMBY opposition to affordable housing is a bipartisan issue, and the language of social justice has been appropriated both to support and to oppose policies designed to address the affordable housing crisis.

To offer a compelling rebuttal to the critics of low-income housing policies, housing advocates must do more than simply assert that housing is a human right or a matter of justice. If the content of the right to housing is left unspecified, and no one is responsible for satisfying the right through the provision of shelter, the right to housing becomes an empty "manifesto right."[3] The idea that housing occupies a separate sphere of moral concern raises several questions. How is housing any different from other goods distributed by economic institutions? If housing is not "special" in some morally significant way, why modify "justice" with the word "housing?" If housing is special, how does housing justice relate to other spheres of moral concern? Is housing justice right based? If housing justice requires the recognition of a right to housing, how does this right relate to the right to own private property? Is housing "just" if everyone has a roof over their head, or does housing justice also require the elimination of housing inequality?

This book is for those who seek answers to these questions, including advocates, policymakers, scholars, and anyone seeking to understand and critically evaluate the moral arguments that inform American housing policy. I draw on the moral and political philosophy literature to advance the thesis that the solution to contemporary housing crises lies in reform of the very institution that creates those crises. Property rules foster housing insecurity by legitimizing the exclusion of nonowners, but the institution of private property offers a distinctive solution to the problem it creates. I argue that housing justice does not require abandoning private property or rejecting private property's liberal philosophical foundations, but it does require distributing rights to the occupancy and use of residential property more broadly while simultaneously limiting the right to earn income from the ownership of residential property. Progressive Era critiques of private property foreshadowed new hybrid tenure arrangements that can be part of the solution to contemporary housing injustices, but progressive reformers' aim of elevating the common good over individual rights blinded them to the possibility that the solution to housing crises lay hidden within the very institutions they rebuked. In this book, I defend a right-based conception of housing justice that combines elements of liberalism, republicanism, progressivism, and pragmatism to offer a justification for, rather than an objection to, private property.

Overview of the Book's Organization

The contemporary quilt of local, state, and federal housing policies cannot be understood apart from the inherited legacy of generations of policy experimentation, shaped by evolving social conceptions of housing and property. This book weaves a history of ideas with interpretive policy inquiry and philosophical analysis to make sense of the intellectual traditions that have shaped American housing reforms. The book's historical investigation sets the stage for a philosophical analysis of the moral foundations of housing policy.

Chapter 1 explores the application of the "materials" of justice—conceptions of value, principles, grounds, and bases—to normative questions pertaining to the distribution of housing. I argue that certain contextual conditions influence housing's distribution and valuation, and these conditions call for an approach to justice that considers housing's distinctive qualities. I also examine the American home's social meaning, particularly as embodied in the ideal of the owned single-family detached home. I argue that while the social meaning of housing provides insights into the moral foundations of housing policy reform, social meanings are not monolithic. A conception of housing justice should be robust enough to accommodate a variety of social meanings.

Part II of the book explores the historical evolution of the American housing reform tradition, emphasizing the social meaning of housing and property as interpreted by America's liberal and republican political traditions. Although reformers did not view housing as a separate policy domain until the late nineteenth century, America's founders believed in the sanctity of home and the natural right to landed property. The framers enshrined these ideas in the US Constitution, despite holding different views of how to distribute property to promote republican values.

Housing reformers assembled the patchwork quilt that is America's federal housing policy apparatus from layers of housing and land-use policies enacted over time. During the nineteenth century, radical land reformers proposed policies designed to foster a more egalitarian distribution of landed property. As America's economy transitioned from an agricultural to an industrial base, the separation of home from work elevated the importance of land devoted to residential uses. Rapid urbanization during the late nineteenth century created a shortage of safe and sanitary working-class housing, and social reformers responded with various strategies designed to improve housing conditions and promote homeownership. During the Great Depression, housing construction and mortgage credit came to a grinding halt, and President Franklin D. Roosevelt wrapped housing into a package of economic stabilization and stimulus programs known collectively as the New Deal. By the 1960s, a new generation of right-based reformers fought to dismantle the legacy of decades of discriminatory housing policies that had segregated urban neighborhoods and concentrated urban poverty. Since the 1970s, the US government has been slowly dismantling its New Deal–era housing welfare state, and housing advocates have responded with appeals to housing justice.

The evolving sociocultural understanding of housing and property shaped each of these reform traditions. Social reformers responded to housing crises with solutions that challenged conventional understandings of property and housing while introducing new roles for government in the production and distribution of housing. Despite changes in American conceptions of housing and property, the owned single-family detached home has endured as the physical embodiment of American values. Thomas Jefferson's yeoman republic, nineteenth-century land reforms, Progressive Era housing regulations, and the New Deal–era federal housing policy apparatus were all designed in part to promote and protect the ideal of the owned single-family detached home. The American embrace of a single housing type has been both a blessing and a curse. Advocates have appealed to the ideal of the owned single-family detached home to expand access to middle-class housing while simultaneously denying housing to low-income persons of color.

While America may be exceptional in its love affair with private property and detached housing, American conceptions of property and home are the product of an international exchange of ideas. America's founders studied British political philosophy, and Europeans saw America as the blank canvas on which to paint European Enlightenment ideals. As John Locke wrote in the late seventeenth century, "Thus in the beginning all the World was *America*" (Locke 1980 [1690], 29; italics in the original). During the early twentieth century, American progressives borrowed European ideas, and the US government exported American homeownership strategies to developing nations during the Cold War era (Kwak 2015).

The historical discussion in part II sets the stage for an exploration of housing justice in part III of the book. Chapter 6 defends a right-based conception of housing justice that is grounded in the ideal of civic equality, understood as an ideal where every citizen is treated as an equal in accordance with a shared understanding of what citizens owe one another and what the government owes its citizens. Chapter 7 explores the implications of civic equality for the injustice of tenure insecurity. I argue that an acceptable defense of private property must appeal to the interests of those whose tenure is made insecure by the institution of private property. I propose that a "secure tenure" property regime, structured to extend the right to secure tenure to everyone, responds to this challenge.

Chapter 8 completes the circle by demonstrating how to extend the right to secure tenure to everyone in a way that is consistent with civic equality and social justice more broadly. I argue that civic equality justifies housing policy reforms that guarantee housing security and reduce housing inequality in a manner that is tenure neutral. My proposed "negative housing tax" is designed to achieve these aims by altering the income tax treatment of housing to fund a guaranteed housing allowance. After describing the justifications for and complications that arise from the negative housing tax proposal, I examine additional issues raised by the spatial geography of housing affordability. I also explore the relationships between housing justice and social justice writ large, bridging the gap between housing justice and racial justice while exploring the complementarities and conflicts between the right to housing and the right to the city. The final chapter summarizes the book's main arguments and offers concluding observations.

1 The Materials of American Housing Justice

He is all pine and I am apple orchard.
My apple trees will never get across
And eat the cones under his pines, I tell him.
He only says, "Good fences make good neighbors."
—Robert Frost, "Mending Wall" (1917, 12)

Humans live best when each has his own place, when each knows where he belongs in the scheme of things. Destroy the place and destroy the person.
—Frank Herbert, *The Great Dune Trilogy* (1979, 133)

What is housing justice? Although most US housing advocates generally agree that more should be done to address the affordable housing crisis, advocates do not hold the same or even similar views of what housing justice entails. For fair housing advocates, housing justice is a housing market free from discrimination. For tenants' rights advocates, housing justice is a legal system that protects renters from arbitrary evictions and gentrification-induced displacement. Human rights advocates often agree with many housing advocates that everyone should have a legal right *to* housing. Still, there are many ways of interpreting this right, and the Supreme Court has denied the existence of a constitutional right to housing.

This chapter introduces several ideas that are developed throughout the book. I begin by discussing the relationship between housing justice and justice writ large. I argue that housing justice is an application of distributive justice that defines what citizens owe one another and what the government owes its citizens in terms of housing provision. I explore how to assemble the "materials" of justice—conceptions of value, principles, grounds, and bases—into a conception of housing justice that accounts for the normative significance of housing and the institutional setting within which housing is produced and distributed.

The chapter then explores the question of whether housing exhibits special features that call for a housing-specific conception of justice. If not, then presumably there is no need for a book titled *Just Housing*. I argue that certain contextual conditions influence housing's distribution and valuation, and these conditions call for an approach to justice that considers housing's distinctive qualities. I also examine the question of whether housing occupies an autonomous distributive sphere with unique moral principles revealed by housing's social meaning. I argue that while the idea of home is deeply rooted in the American tradition, the social meaning of home has been contested throughout history. Furthermore, social meanings do not tell us everything we need to know to determine how housing should be distributed. At the same time, the social meaning of the American home, particularly as embodied in the ideal of the owned single-family detached home, has shaped the moral arguments offered in defense of American housing reforms. To understand the moral foundations of US housing policy, we must first understand what housing means to those who wish to see its distribution altered.

The Idea of Housing Justice

What is justice? While some equate justice with morality writ large, most theories of justice pertain more narrowly to what "we owe to each other" (Scanlon 1998, 7), particularly as these obligations are instantiated in actions taken by the nation-state or its agents to distribute goods, resources, and opportunities. Moral and political philosophers have offered a variety of conceptions of justice that appeal to fundamental moral principles or values derived from a conception of right behavior or the good served by treating everyone in a particular way. As most contemporary philosophers assert, any plausible conception of justice, even those not explicitly recognized as egalitarian, demonstrates a basic commitment to the fundamental value of human equality (Kymlicka 2002). According to Ronald Dworkin (1978, 272), "Government must treat those whom it governs with concern, that is, as human beings who are capable of suffering and frustration, and with respect, that is, as human beings who are capable of forming and acting on intelligent conceptions of how their lives should be lived." The question of what we owe to one another as moral equals underlies all housing policy debates, even if formal theories of justice are not explicitly referenced to justify policy alternatives.

I interpret housing justice to be a particular understanding of *distributive justice* that addresses moral questions about the production, distribution, occupancy, and ownership of housing. A conception of distributive justice provides answers to questions about the rightness or wrongness of a given distribution of goods or a given procedure for distributing them. Theories of distributive justice also typically address the government's role in distributing goods, including whether and under what conditions the government's role as distributor can be justified in the first place. Social contract theorists maintain that the reasons offered in support of a given distribution of goods must satisfy certain principles of "public justification," which Stephen Macedo (1990, 41) defines as the idea that "the application of power should be accompanied with reasons that all reasonable people should be able to accept." A public justification may require that everyone actively consent to a given distribution of goods, have no reason to reject their distributive shares, or be compensated for unjust allocations.

A distributive conception of housing justice should be robust enough to address relevant nondistributive moral concerns. For example, historical injustices that constrain the current generation's housing opportunities may call for a conception of housing justice that accounts for intergenerational obligations. Similarly, the distribution of housing may shape or be shaped by nondistributive injustices, such as oppression, discrimination, or misrecognition (Fraser and Honneth 2004). If members of some groups are denied housing because of racism, or if those without homes are socially stigmatized, a conception of housing justice should provide an account of housing policy's role in alleviating these injustices.

Theories of justice can be distinguished from one another according to how each organizes certain basic "materials," which define the nature and priority of moral statements about a good's distribution. The first material is a *conception of value*, a property that makes a good something that someone would have reason to want and that possibly obligates some other agent to respond to those reasons in some way. In this chapter, the term *value* refers primarily to prudential value, or the *good for* a person that benefits that person in some particular way (Tiberius 2015). I leave questions of moral values, or those values governing norms of social obligation, to later chapters. Market prices may or may not capture all a good's prudential values. I argue in the next section that prices are often poor proxies for housing's prudential value to inhabitants.

Principles of justice are propositions about the just distribution of goods across a population of interest or about just procedures for allocating goods. Principles of justice are associated with distinctive *grounds* and *scopes*. According to global justice theorist Mathias Risse (2012), the scope of justice refers to the population for which principles of justice apply, and the grounds of justice are the conditions that make it the case that principles of justice hold for that population. Put more simply, the scope defines the relevant population of interest, and the grounds provide the reasons for upholding justice. Risse distinguishes between *relational* and *nonrelational* grounds of distributive justice. Relationists hold that shared participation in some social practice, such as friendship or membership in a nation-state, grounds distributive principles, whereas nonrelationists ground principles of justice in something other than shared practices, such as humanity's intrinsic moral qualities or prepolitical rights.

The grounds of housing justice provide the reasons that individuals or government agents should support institutions that distribute housing in particular ways. As I argue in this book, American housing reformers have appealed to two distinct and often conflicting grounds of justice. The ground of *human status* is based on the idea that human beings are intrinsically valuable and that certain human qualities or conditions that contribute to humanity's intrinsic value, or without which human life would have no value, provide the grounds for principles of justice that all human beings have a duty to uphold. Those appealing to the ground of *citizenship* derive principles of justice from the relational obligations that arise from shared membership in a nation-state.[1] These two grounds may come into conflict if citizenship entails relational obligations that conflict with citizens' obligations to noncitizens or if human status creates rights or obligations that are thwarted by the actions of nation-states.

The *basis* of justice refers to what is morally fundamental or ultimate in a theory of justice.[2] Dworkin (1978) identifies three bases of justice: goals, rights, and duties. Goal-based theories assume that some aggregate or collective outcome provides the foundation from which to derive principles of justice, rights, and obligations. Right-based theories treat individuals as the most basic unit of justice and derive obligations and principles from individuals' fundamental rights. Duty-based theories also treat individuals as the most basic unit of justice but derive rights and principles from fundamental obligations.[3] To Dworkin's three bases I add a fourth, virtue, which takes some human excellence to be fundamental. Virtues may or may not ground duties to behave virtuously or promote virtue. As I discuss in the next several chapters, nineteenth-century land reformers appealed to right-based approaches grounded in a conception of human beings' natural rights to private property. Things changed during the Progressive Era, when collective goals and civic virtues played a more prominent role. Right-based approaches to housing reform, stripped of their natural rights foundations, returned with renewed force during the civil rights era.

A conception of housing justice should provide practical answers to questions such as: Why is housing something that individuals have reason to value, who should respond to those reasons, and how? Is it morally wrong if some are unhoused, and if so, why? Do government agents have a responsibility to house everyone? Do individuals have a right to be adequately housed? Is housing inequality wrong, and if so, why? What does a just distribution of housing look like, and what institutions support just housing arrangements?

Justice theorists approach questions such as these in one of two ways. Proponents of *ideal theory* derive principles of justice from an abstract conception of a perfectly just society, given certain minimal assumptions about human behavior. For example, John Rawls (1971) develops his theory of justice as fairness from a conception of the social contract that individuals would rationally accept if asked to choose the rules governing the "basic structure of society" from behind a veil of ignorance that shields individuals from knowing what interests and endowments they will have in the society created. Rawls further assumes that all individuals are willing to comply with the social contract and that social conditions enable compliance.

Proponents of *nonideal theory* argue that ideal theories of justice such as the one offered by Rawls are too abstract and too divorced from reality to guide action in an unjust world. John Dunn (1990) argues that principles of justice should account for what is feasible in a given society considering its unique historical circumstances. Basic facts about human nature may also affect the feasibility or stability of just institutional arrangements (A. Mason 2004). Amartya Sen (2009) argues that ideal theories often begin from the wrong starting point. He maintains that it is more important to alleviate severe injustices, such as homelessness or famine, before worrying about the features of a perfectly just society. David Rondel (2018) makes a similar argument in his comparison between ideal (or "perfectionist") theories and "meliorist" theories. He offers a medical example to describe the latter: "Just as a physician can effectively treat a patient's broken arm, say, without a regulative ideal of 'perfect overall health' in view, . . . so too can egalitarians address this or that inequality without consulting as a benchmark the 'perfect equality' sought by perfectionists" (Rondel 2018, 32).

The critique of ideal theory has several implications for housing justice. First, if housing has unique material characteristics or is distributed in distinctive ways, these properties may point to the need for a "local" (good-specific) theory of justice (Elster 1992). Most local concerns can be addressed without entirely abandoning an ideal theoretic framework, as long as it is possible to clearly identify and account for all a good's morally relevant distributive properties. A second implication of the ideal theory critique is that principles of justice should be sensitive to a society's historically determined culture, values, and political environment. Social context may affect the practical details of how principles of justice are interpreted or implemented through policy, or social context may justify the principles themselves. A third implication is that theories of justice should be attuned to the reality of injustice as experienced by those in the real world. These observations provide support for a meliorist approach to justice that is oriented toward improvement rather than perfection.

Michael Walzer argues that not only are ideal principles of justice impractical guides for action in the real world, but the very idea of justice has no meaning apart from society's conception of the greater good that defines a good's purpose. In his Tanner Lecture on Human Values, Walzer provides a useful example to illustrate this point that has direct relevance to housing justice:

> Away from home, one is grateful for the shelter and convenience of a hotel room. Deprived of all knowledge of what my own home was like, talking with people similarly deprived, required to design rooms that any one of us might live in, we would probably come up with something like (but not quite so culturally specific as) the Hilton Hotel. With this difference: we would not allow luxury suites; all the rooms would be exactly the same; or, if there were luxury suites, their only purpose would be to bring more business to the hotel and enable us to improve

all the other rooms, starting with those most in need of improvement. But even if the improvements went pretty far, we might still long for the homes we knew we once had but could no longer remember. We would not be morally bound to live in the hotel we had designed. (Walzer 1985, 14–15)

Throughout American history, social reformers have proposed utopian housing solutions resembling Walzer's Hilton Hotel that have ignored the diverse meanings of home and failed to adapt to evolving ways of living. Walzer's critique implies that a conception of housing justice should be constructed from a grounded appreciation of the home's social purpose rather than from an abstract utopian ideal that is divorced from social practices.

Sen's (2009) conception of "comparative justice" provides one way of navigating between the concrete world of injustice and the abstract realm of principle. According to Sen (2009), principles of justice can be context dependent but still be justifiable to an "impartial spectator" who is from a different social context but is still capable of impartially evaluating reasons for action.[4] Sen argues that a comparative justice perspective turns questions of justice on their head by asking not "What is a just society?" but rather "Is society X more just than society Y?" This approach permits both an internal critique of each society considered in relation to its own professed values (Does society X achieve justice according to X's conception of justice?) and an external critique of each society considered separately (Does society X or Y do a better job of promoting the value Z?).

The problem orientation of American pragmatism offers a useful way of interpreting nonideal theorists' concerns with practicality. According to Rondel (2018, 8), "Problems unsettle previously settled habit or belief, and are identified as problems in virtue of their disruptive, unsettling effects. When genuine problems rear their heads, it is no longer possible to carry on as usual." Elizabeth Anderson (2010, 6; italics in the original) argues that when faced with problems such as racial inequality, distributional ideals "embody imagined solutions to identified problems in a society. They function as *hypotheses*, to be tested in experience."

A pragmatic orientation has several advantages. First, pragmatism is broadly consistent with the American housing reform tradition's emphasis on problem solving and social improvement. Second, pragmatism takes the plurality of prudential and moral values seriously (Rondel 2018). As I argue in this book, individuals value housing for a variety of reasons, and an approach to housing justice that respects human beings as moral equals should respect this diversity. Third, pragmatism offers an approach to justice that considers how social relations shape the contexts of justice and the moral obligations that individuals have to one another. Although the conception of housing justice offered in this book draws on a variety of intellectual traditions, the spirit of American pragmatism informs the book's orientation toward actual housing problems as understood by American housing reformers.

Is Housing Special?

Curiously, most contemporary theories of distributive justice treat goods as abstract quantities and ignore the materiality of goods altogether. For example, Rawls's (1971) theory of justice is concerned with the distribution of "primary goods," which are abstract goods that every rational person would reasonably want. Other theorists emphasize the distribution of resources (Dworkin 2000) or opportunities (Sen 1985; Nussbaum 2000; Roemer 1998). Robert Nozick (1974) is more concerned with the procedure for distributing goods, including whether rights are protected, than with the final distribution or physical qualities of the goods themselves.

According to Rawls (1971, 29), "The correct regulative principle for anything depends on the nature of that thing." What is the nature of housing, and what makes housing "special" from the standpoint of distributive justice?[5] I argue that housing is special for three reasons. First, several contextual (e.g., physical, market, and institutional) conditions uniquely influence housing's distribution and valuation. Certain contextual features (e.g., heterogeneity and durability) are fixed and essential qualities of housing, whereas others (e.g., building technology and legal context) change over time. Second, individuals value housing for a variety of incommensurable prudential reasons. Third, individuals value housing, in part, for reasons that appeal to its social meaning, but social meanings are plural and contested. These conditions suggest that housing justice is best understood in terms of local, rather than global, principles of justice (Elster 1992).

The Contexts of Housing Justice

Private property rules are arguably the most important contextual conditions shaping the production and distribution of American housing. To see this, compare housing with virtually any other consumer good. Take a pencil, for example. Someone who purchases a pencil enjoys the right to use the pencil, destroy the pencil, temporarily lend the pencil to someone in exchange for money, or sell the pencil to someone else. One need not consult a pencil law treatise to determine what to do with a purchased pencil. The rights of housing consumers, on the other hand, are defined first by the nature of the exchange. Lease contracts define renters' rights, and lease terms are in turn shaped by contract and landlord-tenant laws. If a home is purchased fee simple, the owner may enjoy the same bundle of rights as the pencil owner, but a variety of laws and contracts define and constrain the elements of the bundle. Zoning regulations attenuate rights to use and modify homes; homeownership associations and occupancy codes constrain rights to lease homes; and a complex web of local, state, and federal real estate laws, tax laws, estate laws, and contract laws govern the sale of homes. With the rise of securitization and the vertical disintegration of the mortgage industry, ownership of any given home is also dispersed between homeowners and investors, with various intermediaries playing a role in mortgage payment collection, home insurance, and compliance with local, state, and federal laws. Importantly, residential property and contract laws are always in flux, and the meaning of private property itself has changed over time.

Housing's close connection to the institution of property implies that inhabitants understand the meaning of home partially in terms of the legal rights that are assigned to it. For some, a rented house is not a home. The rental lease limits the duration of occupancy, and landlords retain the right to enter rented property to perform routine inspections and maintenance. Temporary tenure arrangements such as a bed on a friend's couch or a hotel room provide the inhabitant with so few rights that most would be hesitant to refer to the places secured by these arrangements as the inhabitant's home. Those who sleep on park benches are labeled "homeless" persons, not persons whose home is a park bench, because those sleeping on benches lack secure rights to the spaces they inhabit.

The allocation of housing through markets and market-based institutions implies that its value is at least partially revealed by its exchange value, or market price. Exchange values reflect the simultaneous determination of what individuals are willing to pay to consume housing and the costs that producers are willing to incur to deliver it. In equilibrium, the market price is equal to the marginal social value of an additional housing unit.

There are three problems with understanding the value of housing purely in terms of revealed exchange values. First, housing markets rarely satisfy the assumptions of perfectly competitive markets. Second, housing is a heterogeneous, durable good. Third, housing is often valued for reasons that transcend exchange values. I explore the first two issues in the remainder of this section and then turn to a consideration of the third issue in the following section.

Housing markets are riddled with imperfections. The value of a home to an occupant is determined in part by a variety of actions taken by neighboring property owners and residents. If property rights to these externalities are poorly assigned, and there are costs to delineating and enforcing property rights, the price that individuals pay for homes may not capture the benefits that they receive from housing consumption or the costs that producers bear to deliver housing (Coase 1960). Informational asymmetries also make it difficult for buyers to assess the market values of individual housing units. The seller of a home has more information about the home's quality and may extract rents from prospective buyers who have incomplete information about a home's condition. Housing transactions are also time consuming and costly. Buyers and sellers engage in lengthy negotiations that can fall apart at any stage of the housing exchange. Moving also entails costs, which implies that housing choices, once made, are irreversible in the short term and will have long-lasting impacts on a housing occupant's well-being. If transaction and moving costs are high enough, otherwise mutually beneficial housing transactions may go unrealized.

Unlike most consumer goods, housing is a heterogeneous bundle of goods that includes physical space, architectural attributes, natural amenities, and local public goods. Because of variability in home styles, physical condition, and location, no two housing units are alike. If households exhibit different preferences for different components of the housing bundle, it is nearly impossible to compare the benefits that one person receives from the purchase of a given home with the benefits that someone else receives from a different home. Advances in hedonic econometric models have improved our ability to translate the value of individual housing units into homogeneous units of the "housing services" that housing units deliver, but hedonic techniques are still fraught with theoretical and empirical challenges, and government agents rarely rely on the most sophisticated hedonic methods to evaluate policy alternatives.

Housing's durability influences its distribution among inhabitants over the short term. Once constructed, homes can last for tens or hundreds of years if well maintained, as any visit to a historic town will reveal. Related to the issue of durability is the inelastic short-term supply of housing. Homes take several months to construct or retrofit, and regulations and public approval processes can add months or years to the process. Durability and housing supply inelasticity reduce the responsiveness of housing producers to changing consumer needs and preferences. Because the distribution of housing is essentially fixed over the short run, residential relocation and financial compensation are often the only feasible ways to alleviate short-term housing injustices.

Distinctive Sources of Housing's Value
Even if housing markets are perfectly competitive and in equilibrium, individuals evaluate their willingness to pay for housing in distinctive ways and value housing for prudential reasons that transcend their willingness to pay for housing. Exchange values reflect a utilitarian conception of value where the goodness of a thing is defined in terms of its beneficial consequences for human states of affairs such as happiness, desire fulfillment, or welfare. Lumping all these beneficial consequences into the general category of "well-being" masks the many distinct pathways through which housing enhances human well-being. Housing provides comfort, privacy, safety, and aesthetic pleasures to the inhabitant. Housing also enables occupants to satisfy larger life goals, such as raising a family or building a social network. Those without housing are socially stigmatized, marked as homeless, and may experience a diminished sense of self-respect and human dignity as a result.

Housing's contribution to human well-being is distinctive for three reasons. First, housing is a positional good. The well-being that individuals receive from the consumption of positional goods is evaluated in a relative sense, which implies that one's perceived ranking in the distribution of consumption is at least as important as the absolute amount of the good consumed. The positionality of housing explains the "keeping up with the Joneses" phenomenon, where households evaluate their level of residential satisfaction through comparisons with neighboring homes (Frank 2007; Dawkins 2017b). Positionality calls for an appropriately weighted metric of well-being that accounts for individuals' relative well-being compared to others (Brighouse and Swift 2006).

Second, for those who own housing, housing directly enhances well-being while also indirectly expanding the owner's opportunities to enjoy additional well-being in the future, because owned housing is a source of wealth.[6] A house's direct contribution to well-being through consumption may conflict with its contribution to household wealth. For example, prospective homeowners may avoid homes with garish external features even if they prefer them, because such features may compromise the home's "curb appeal," making it difficult to sell the home at a later date. Those planning to live out their lives in one place can enjoy their pink flamingoes, yard gnomes, and lawn art without worrying about a prospective buyer's taste for these accoutrements.

Third, housing satisfies certain basic human needs. At the most fundamental level, needs such as warmth, rest, security, and safety must be satisfied before pursuing the higher-order needs of psychological fulfillment and self-actualization (Maslow 1943). Needs are distinct from well-being because they arise whether or not someone wants to have them, and their alleviation is not necessarily associated with an increase in well-being (Raz 1986). For example, the ascetic denies basic needs in order to attain spiritual fulfillment. Because needs are biological constraints imposed independently of one's will, some argue that housing should not be allocated according to exchange values, because individuals should not have to choose whether to have their basic needs met (King 2003).

One implication of the discussion so far is that a metric of housing's contribution to well-being should be robust enough to account for the multiple pathways through which housing enhances well-being. Amartya Sen (1985) and Martha Nussbaum (2000) offer a metric of well-being that incorporates needs and human dignity while avoiding some of the common objections to utilitarian measures of well-being. Their "capabilities approach" is based on the idea that because individuals exhibit varying abilities to convert goods into well-being, it is more important to quantify what individuals are able to be and do with goods rather than the amount of subjective utility that individuals receive from the consumption of goods. According to Nussbaum (2000), housing's connection to well-being derives not from the passive conveyance of utility through housing services but rather from the conversion of housing services into valuable functionings, such as being sheltered or raising a family. Functionings are a more robust metric of well-being than utility and can be understood in terms of either the satisfaction of basic needs or the attainment of higher-level achievements. In addition to enabling functionings directly, housing enhances the capability to function in other domains. Housing provides spatial access to employment opportunities, social networks, natural amenities, and local public goods and services, for example. The capabilities approach departs from utilitarianism by shifting the *distribuendum* of justice from goods and the utility from goods consumption to the freedom, or capability, to function.

Regardless of how well-being is defined, individuals also value housing for reasons that transcend its beneficial consequences. For many, housing has "constitutive" value because it is an aspect of the good life from the standpoint of the individuals leading that life (Raz 1986). Goals and plans often refer to a life lived in a particular place. Many people organize their life plans around the eventual purchase of a dream home, for example. Furthermore, individuals modify and personalize housing in accordance with their goals and plans. My flower garden is an expression of my love of nature, and the care that goes into my gardening reflects my commitment to environmental stewardship.

Housing is also an aspect of an individual's identity, or personhood. According to Margaret Radin (1993, 35), "To achieve proper self-development—to be a person—an individual needs some control over resources in the external environment." She argues that "one may gauge the strength of significance of someone's relationship with an object by the kind of pain that would be occasioned by its loss. On this view, an object is closely related to one's personhood if its loss causes pain that cannot be relieved by the object's replacement" (Radin 1993, 36–37). The trauma of eviction, for example, arises in part from the loss of a vital material dimension of one's personal identity.

By enabling individuals to be the primary author of their own lives, housing plays a role in the cultivation and exercise of personal autonomy, a feature of human lives that has intrinsic value because "it is intrinsically good for people to take charge of their affairs and run their own lives" (Wall 1998, 149). Housing and autonomy are linked in a variety of ways. To the extent that a person lacks housing sufficient to satisfy their biological need for safety, warmth, and protection from the elements, that person is unable to devote their energies to the pursuit of larger goals and projects. By satisfying health and safety needs through the provision of housing, the inhabitant is liberated from biological necessity, freeing up time for the formulation, evaluation, and pursuit of long-term goals. Housing also enhances autonomy directly through the spatial privacy that it affords. Housing provides an undisturbed spatial realm within which inhabitants may formulate and pursue plans, meditate, or simply relax. Within the privacy of the home, individuals can evaluate and accept or reject their preferences and beliefs, free from the criticism of others (Dawkins 2017a). As Gaston Bachelard (1969, 6) writes, "The house shelters daydreaming, the house protects the dreamer, the house allows one to dream in peace."

Housing's contribution to well-being, personhood, and autonomy arises in part from the close connection between housing and leisure. Housing provides a private realm where human beings can enjoy leisure on their own terms, apart from the active world of work. As Josef Pieper (2009, 46) writes, "Compared with the exclusive ideal of work as activity, leisure implies (in the first place) an attitude of non-activity, of inward calm, of silence; it means not being 'busy,' but letting things happen." As I discuss in chapter 7, the connection between housing and leisure has interesting implications for the justification for the right to own property. If private property's contribution to leisure justifies a person's right to own private property, those who labor to acquire property have no special rights to their ownership claims, as John Locke (1980 [1690]) asserts. Furthermore, inequalities in the distribution of property are harder to justify, particularly if leisure is something that everyone has a right to enjoy.

In general, these different sources of prudential value are incommensurable, or not directly comparable in terms of a single metric. Furthermore, different individuals have different conceptions of what the good life entails, and different conceptions of the good life rank prudential values in different ways. Since there are many reasonable conceptions of the good life, there will generally be reasonable disagreement among individuals about the relative importance of different prudential values. Some prudential reasons for valuing housing, such as privacy and social affiliation, may be in tension with one another. Prudential value pluralism does not necessarily imply value relativism, because many prudential values are universally shared, at least among those who share a common cultural tradition (Crowder 2002). Furthermore, nothing I have said so far about prudential values necessarily implies a pluralism of *moral* values.

Prudential value pluralism has two important implications for housing justice. First, prudential value pluralism points in the direction of a plurality of distributive principles that may be in tension with one another. For example, the positionality of housing suggests that, all things considered, an equal distribution of housing delivers a higher level of aggregate well-being than an unequal distribution does (Brighouse and Swift 2006). Other reasons for valuing housing may ground distributive principles other than equality. If housing's value originates from the satisfaction of basic human needs, the moral urgency of these needs may call for a *sufficientarian* distribution of housing that guarantees minimally adequate housing to everyone but nothing more (Dawkins 2017b; Frankfurt 1987). I return to the tension between egalitarian and sufficientarian distributive principles in parts II and III of the book.

Second, value pluralism implies that any conception of housing justice derived from a publicly justified set of principles will likely appeal to a minimalist morality that, to the extent possible, respects the diversity of values that individuals assign to housing. Some interpret this requirement as implying that governments should remain neutral in their justifications for actions and not appeal to a controversial conception of the good derived from some ranking of value (Rawls 1993). Others interpret value pluralism as implying that the state should directly promote the diversity of values (Galston 2002). The conception of housing justice offered in this book is more consistent with an emphasis on state neutrality than with the active promotion of value diversity, but I argue in chapter 6 that value diversity may be instrumentally important in societies that value personal autonomy.[7]

The Social Meaning of Housing

A house is more than just a delivery mechanism for housing services. A house is a home. Some homes record the histories and identities of inhabitants, while other homes are merely places to hang hats. A home derives its meaning from a personally recognized way of life, a shared relationship with one's co-occupants, and an engagement with the socially constructed practice of domestic life. The terms "household" and "family" refer to the shared, intimate social relationships formed within the home, and those without homes are marked by society as "homeless." The phrase "American dream," which James Truslow Adams (1932, 404) originally coined to describe equality of opportunity, has been co-opted by real estate professionals to describe particular housing styles.[8] One's ability to take part in the social practice of living an American dream is determined in part by the social availability of that option. Individuals may choose to accept or reject a particular characterization of the American dream, but they leave the dream intact while doing so.

Walzer (1983) argues that the social meanings of goods have radical implications for distributive justice because "distributions are patterned in accordance with shared conceptions of what the goods are and what they are for" (Walzer 1983, 7). He argues that goods are first conceived and created before they are distributed, so to understand the appropriate principles governing a good's distribution, we must first understand why the good being distributed was conceived in the first place, within the historical context of the good's purpose in a particular society. Walzer presents a compelling case for a housing-specific approach to justice because if the social meaning of housing defines its distributive principles, it is impossible to know how to distribute housing without first understanding its social function.

This book draws on Walzer's social meaning idea to understand and interpret the historical arguments offered in defense of particular housing policy proposals. Still, as I argue here and throughout the book, one must be careful not to assign undue moral significance to housing's prevailing social meaning, because social meanings often conceal unjust social practices. For example, in the early twentieth century, racial zoning ordinances and racially restrictive covenants legally constrained housing options for people of color. An inquiry into the social meaning of American housing during this era would no doubt reveal that racial hierarchies governed the distribution of housing. To critique unjust social practices such as these, one has to step outside existing practices and critique those practices not only from the standpoint of prevailing social meanings but also from the perspective of more fundamental moral values.

Another concern is that dominant social meanings are often contested. First-wave feminists rejected the domestic ideal tied to the American home because it relegated women to an inferior social position (Hayden 1984). Nineteenth-century communitarians objected to the wastefulness of the single-family home and its tendency to isolate families from communal obligations (Jackson 1985). As America has become more diverse, different groups have interpreted the social meaning of home in ways that often clash with prevailing social meanings. Willow Lung-Amam (2017) describes how Asian Americans in Silicon Valley adopted the American love of the "McMansion" but interpreted this ideal in ways that clashed with their white neighbors' interpretation of the same ideal. Local planners in Silicon

Valley marginalized Asian Americans' interpretation of the social meaning of home through planning processes, development standards, and design guidelines that institutionalized the dominant white interpretation of the social meaning of home. Just as housing is valued for many reasons, the home has a variety of social meanings, and public policies that favor one meaning over another fail to show respect for those whose social meanings have been marginalized.

Although housing's sphere of justice need not be as self-contained as Walzer suggests, his recommendation to ground moral theory in a materialist understanding of a good's social function has merit, even if the conception of justice that emerges from the inquiry draws on principles that transcend the good's prevailing social meaning. Social meanings provide a place to begin a housing justice inquiry and help to ground principles of justice within a realistic social and political context. Social meanings also help us understand and evaluate the arguments advanced by reformers fighting for social change. It is impossible to make sense of normative statements such as "housing is a human right" or "everyone deserves to be adequately housed" without some understanding of what housing means to those who wish to see its distribution altered. If housing's social meaning assigns an elevated social status to some members of society and not others, social meanings provide a basis for social critique. An understanding of the moral underpinnings of particular housing ideals, such as the suburban tract home or the frontier homestead, provides a window into the cultural bases of housing injustice.

In this book, I draw on a variety of media to interpret housing's social meaning in the United States, emphasizing material that calls attention to the moral justifications for public policy proposals. Often, these justifications are absent, only implicitly stated, or used for rhetorical purposes rather than to support sound moral arguments. The inquiry into a good's social meaning is an interpretive exercise. Where the justifications for policies and reforms are not apparent, I infer arguments from policy documents, editorials, political pamphlets, and secondary accounts of the context surrounding policy adoption.

I also explore the connections between the social meaning of housing and American society's shared norms and values, paying particular attention to social movements committed to property and housing reform. The fluidity of social meanings implies that several may coexist and simultaneously vie for social recognition. Social movements often interpret social meanings through dissent, calling attention to hidden values not expressed in social institutions. Some movements call for policy changes to bring institutions into conformance with latent social values, while others call for reforms that appeal to new values.

In the pages that follow, I argue that the social meaning of the American home can be understood in relation to America's evolving conception of real property. The home embodies important moral and political values, and property rules define, protect, and reinforce these values. The dialectic tension between America's two dominant political traditions—liberalism and republicanism—provides a metaframework for understanding the historical evolution of the social meaning of home and real property. Liberalism emphasizes the separation between public and private spheres, individual rights, and liberty understood as freedom from government interference, while republicanism emphasizes self-governance, political engagement, civic virtues, and liberty understood as freedom from domination (Dagger 1997; Sandel 1998a; Pettit 1997).[9] While these two traditions share many features, differences in each tradition's political values have contributed to different conceptions of housing's social function and different views of private property's role in defining and protecting that function.

For liberals, the home is a spatial embodiment of the private realm of unfettered freedom from government interference. This idea appears in the writings of eighteenth-century English jurist William Blackstone, who described the right of property as "that sole and despotic dominion which one man claims and exercises over the external things of the world, in total exclusion of the right of any other individual in the universe" (Blackstone 2016 [1765], 1). For John Locke (1980 [1690]), the private sphere is the domain of domestic family life, governed by consensual but paternalistic power relationships, and the public sphere is the realm of government, political authority, and justice. Property rights wrap individuals and families inside a bubble that insulates individual and familial liberty. The government acts as a neutral arbitrator among the competing right claims of households in the public realm. Conflicts within the family, should they arise, are governed by norms of reciprocity and trust (Kelly 2002). Locke's ideas inform the classic liberal understanding of negative liberty, described by Isaiah Berlin as "the area within which the subject—a person or group of persons—is or should be left to do or be what he is able to do or be, without interference by other persons" (Berlin 1971, 121–122).

Republicans emphasize the home's role in cultivating good citizens. Throughout American history, housing, and more specifically the ownership of housing, has been linked to the civic virtues of economic independence, frugality, hard work, and a concern for the common good. Whereas liberals have been more interested in protecting the private sphere from unwanted intrusions from the public realm, republicans have sought to promote the civic virtues cultivated by private home life. Republicans' understanding of housing's connection to civic virtue is associated with a distinctive view of property. Whereas Locke understood the right to own property as a natural right that exists independently of government, republicans understand property as a conventional right created by government to promote stable republican institutions. Housing reform movements throughout American history, from the late nineteenth-century tenement housing reform movement, to Herbert Hoover's homeownership campaign, to the contemporary "new urbanist" civic design movement, have appealed to republican values.

The owned single-family detached home has endured as an ideal American housing type in part because it embodies deeply held liberal and republican values. Single-family homes are separated from one another by rigid property lines that provide privacy and a spatial zone of liberal freedom and autonomy. At the same time, homeownership cultivates a society of republican stakeholders who have an interest in actively engaging in civic affairs to protect the investment value of their homes. The excerpt from Robert Frost's (1917, 12) "Mending Wall," quoted at the beginning of this chapter, paints a picture of this marriage between republican and liberal ideals. In the poem, two neighbors meet periodically to repair a wall separating their adjacent properties. The wall can be interpreted as a metaphor for the civil law that simultaneously separates and unites citizens (O'Neill 2016). For one neighbor in the poem, the constant repair of the wall and the meeting between neighbors upon each repair symbolize the stabilizing force of mutual respect for one another's property rights. The walls that separate homes become the glue that binds them together. Do "good fences make good neighbors," as the one neighbor is fond of saying? Or are fences unnecessary because "apple trees will never get across and eat the cones under his pines," as the other neighbor asserts (Frost 1917, 12)? This book offers one answer: good fences make good neighbors only if all neighbors have fences.

Toward Housing Justice

A theory of housing justice combines certain basic materials—conceptions of value, principles, grounds, and bases—to construct a conception of justice that appeals to the special connection between housing and human lives. The social meanings of home offer additional materials from which to construct just housing arrangements, but social meanings and their underlying moral foundations are often contested. As discussed in the chapters to follow, social reformers throughout American history have appealed to liberal and republican values to justify a range of policies designed to shape the distribution of land and housing. The ideal of the owned single-family detached home has endured even as the arguments justifying this particular housing type have evolved. If we dig deeper to reveal the single-family home's moral underpinnings, we often find that egalitarian ideals conceal exclusionary motives. Chapters 2–5 excavate the justifications for land and housing reforms to unearth the moral foundations supporting the American dream of home.

II Context

2 The Natural Right to a Homestead

> All men have a natural right to a portion of the soil; and that as the use of the soil is indispensable to life, the right of all men to the soil is as sacred as their right to life itself.
> —1852 Free Soil (Free Democratic) Party platform
>   (Cooper and Fenton 1890, 35)

The story of early American housing reform begins and ends with Henry George, author of the international bestseller *Progress and Poverty* (1942 [1879]). Upon accepting the United Labor Party's nomination for candidacy in the 1886 New York City mayoral election, George asked the question, "Why should there be such abject poverty in this city?" He responded that "the vast majority of men and women and children in New York have no legal right to live here at all. Most of us—ninety-nine percent at least—must pay the other one percent by the week or month for the privilege of staying here and working like slaves" (Post and Leubuscher 1961 [1887], 25–26). In contrast to his contemporaries who sought to address housing problems through regulatory means, George fought poverty and housing inequality by attacking the source of the injustice: the unequal distribution of land rent. George's (1999 [1871], 59) claim that "every man born into this world has a natural right to as much land as is necessary for his own uses, and that no man has a right to any more" echoed the rhetoric of generations of American land reformers committed to an egalitarian interpretation of the doctrine of natural rights and a belief in the civic virtues of the American homestead.

This chapter explores the natural rights tradition and its influence on early American land and housing reform movements. The idea of home as a sacred domain deserving of special legal protection is an ancient idea that

American revolutionaries co-opted to justify independence from British rule. The framers of the Constitution appealed to the same idea to justify strong legal protections for private property owners. Some went further, asserting that everyone's natural right to land justifies the disposition of government-owned land, and in some cases the redistribution of large private landholdings, to American workers. This egalitarian interpretation of the natural rights doctrine provided the ideological foundation for a radical nineteenth-century land reform tradition that culminated in the American homestead movement and Henry George's unique "single tax" solution to housing injustice. The nation's first right-based land and housing reform tradition had largely disappeared by the end of the nineteenth century, but the homestead movement's ideological foundations, stripped of their basis in natural rights, later provided rhetorical fuel for the twentieth-century homeownership movement.

The Home as a Castle

The home has always occupied a privileged place in US law. The Second Amendment to the US Constitution protects the right to bear arms for the purpose of defending one's home; the Third Amendment prohibits the quartering of soldiers in homes without the owner's consent; the Fourth Amendment forbids the unlawful search and seizure of property from homes; and the Fifth Amendment guarantees that homes will not be taken from the owner without just compensation and due process.

The idea of home as a sacred realm deserving special legal protection has roots that extend to ancient Rome. In 57 BC, Roman senator and lawyer Marcus Tullius Cicero returned to his home after being banished only to find it demolished and replaced with a shrine to the goddess Liberty by his political adversary, Clodius. In his case, heard before the College of Priests, Cicero pleaded, "What is there more holy, what is there more carefully fenced round with every description of religious respect, than the house of every individual citizen? Here are his altars, here are his hearths, here are his household gods, here all his sacred rites, all his religious ceremonies are preserved. This is the asylum of every one, so holy a spot that it is impious to drag any one from it" (Cicero 1900, 49–50).[1]

The related idea that "a man's home is his castle," also known as the "castle doctrine," was recognized under English common law by the seventeenth century. Sir Edward Coke, attorney general of England, remarked in the 1604 case involving Peter Semayne, who sought to recover posthumous debts owed to him from the living occupant of the house, that "the house of every one is to him as his Castle and Fortress as well for defence against injury and violence, as for his repose" (Sheppard 2003, 137). The castle doctrine later found its way into colonial American jurisprudence (Barros 2006). In *King v. Stewart* (1774), John Adams addressed a jury on behalf of Richard King, whose home and business had been ransacked by an angry mob, arguing (Adams 1965, 137), "An Englishmans dwelling House is his Castle. The Law has erected a Fortification round it—and as every Man is Party to the Law, i.e. the Law is a Covenant of every Member of society with every other Member, therefore every Member of Society has entered into a solemn Covenant with every other that he shall enjoy in his own dwelling House as compleat a security, safety and Peace and Tranquility as if it was surrounded with Walls of Brass, with Ramparts and Palisadoes and defended with a Garrison and Artillery."

By the mid-eighteenth century, the American colonists began to view British extensions of imperial power as intrusions into the privacy and sanctity of the home (Hafetz 2002). William Pitt, the Earl of Chatham, sympathized with the colonists. In a speech before Parliament, he spoke out against the Cider Bill of 1763, a British law authorizing a tax on cider production, invoking the castle doctrine (Cooley 1868, 299): "The poorest man may in his cottage bid defiance to all the forces of the crown. It may be frail; its roof may shake; the wind may blow through it; the storm may enter; the rain may enter; but the King of England cannot enter—all his force dares not cross the threshold of the ruined tenement!"

One source of scorn was the writ of assistance, which gave British officials the right to search for smuggled items within the homes of suspected colonists. In a powerful speech given before the Superior Court of Massachusetts in 1761, James Otis appealed to English common law to condemn writs of assistance:

> Now one of the most essential branches of English liberty is the freedom of one's house. A man's house is his castle; and whilst he is quiet, he is as well guarded as a prince in his castle. This writ, if it should be declared legal, would totally annihilate this privilege. Custom-house officers may enter our houses when they please; we are commanded to permit their entry. Their menial servants may enter, may break locks, bars, and everything in their way; and whether they break through

malice or revenge, no man, no court can inquire. Bare suspicion without oath is sufficient. (Adams 1865, 524)

American revolutionaries drew on these same ideas to oppose British taxation and justify their eventual break from the Crown. John Adams overheard James Otis's 1761 speech and later recounted in a letter to William Tudor that Otis had sparked the American Revolution: "Then and there was the first scene of the first act of opposition to the arbitrary claims of Great Britain. Then and there the child Independence was born" (Adams and Tudor 1819, 246).

The Natural Right to Property and Home

The US Constitution defends the civil rights of individuals within their homes and protects privately owned homes from being taken without just compensation and due process, but what justifies an individual's right to own a home and the land beneath it? This question was on the mind of John Winthrop when he arrived on North American shores with a large group of Puritan settlers in 1630. To reassure settlers that their titles to land would be legally recognized, Winthrop put forth a novel idea that would shape Americans' understanding of property for centuries. In a pamphlet distributed in 1629, Winthrop asserted that "God hath given to the sonnes of men a double right to the earth; theire is a naturall right, & a civill right" (Winthrop 1869 [1629], 311). Hearkening back to the English practice of engrossment,[2] Winthrop claimed that the "inclosinge & peculiar manuerance" (Winthrop 1869 [1629], 311) of land transforms an individual's natural right into a civil right with enforceable legal standing (Linklater 2013).

While the idea that human beings have certain prepolitical natural entitlements reaches as far back as the Stoics, most attribute the modern conception of natural property rights to Dutch lawyer Hugo Grotius. For Grotius (2005 [1625]), the land lies in common prior to appropriation, and each man has a natural right to occupy and use the commons to meet his own needs. To explain the link between the unappropriated commons and the emergence of private property, Grotius appealed to Cicero's public theater allegory. In a public theater, no one owns any particular seat, but once someone occupies a seat, that person has a right to that chosen seat for the duration of the show. Just as a ticketing system may emerge to secure a ticket purchaser's right to a chosen seat, the institution of private property arises to secure landed property claims. According to Grotius, the institution of private property is a human creation that secures preinstitutional natural rights (Mancilla 2016, 32).

John Locke's natural rights conception of property shaped American political thought during the Revolutionary period. In his *Second Treatise of Government* (1980 [1690]), Locke argued that the protection of private property rights was one of government's primary functions. The 1776 Virginia Declaration of Rights, written by George Mason, evokes Lockean language to defend the protection of natural rights to "the enjoyment of life and liberty with the means of acquiring and possessing property, and pursuing and obtaining happiness and safety" (Patrick 1995, 53). When writing the Declaration of Independence, Thomas Jefferson also looked to Locke. The inalienable rights to "life, liberty, and the pursuit of happiness" echo the rights to "life, liberty, and estates" mentioned in Locke's *Second Treatise* (Ely 1998, 29). According to historian Willi Paul Adams (1980, 193), "The acquisition of property and the pursuit of happiness were so closely connected with each other in the minds of the founding generation that naming only one of the two sufficed to evoke both."

Locke derives the right to own property from every man's God-given natural right to own one's body and bodily actions (Locke 1980 [1690], 19): "Though the earth and all inferior creatures be common to all men, yet every man has a property in his own person. This nobody has any right to but himself. The labour of his body and the work of his hands, we may say, are properly his. Whatsoever, then, he removes out of the state that Nature hath provided and left it in, he hath mixed his labour with it, and joined to it something that is his own, and thereby makes it his property."

According to Locke, the earth is held in common prior to the mixing of labor with land. Because those mixing labor with land own their bodies and the fruits of their labor, they also come to own the land that is mixed with labor. Others then have a reciprocal duty to respect the owner's right by not interfering with the land acquired. Locke argues that private property owners will eventually consent to a social contract that outsources the protection of private property rights to a civil government. Given his assertion that individuals do not come to own property until they mix labor with land, Locke is generally acknowledged as the father of the labor theory of property (Becker 1977), an idea that later shaped American land reformers' attitudes about property.

Upon first blush, Locke's theory seems to suggest that everyone enjoys a natural prepolitical right to acquire property for residential use. However, this interpretation raises the question of what forms of labor legitimize land ownership claims. In contrast to Grotius's natural right to appropriate unowned land from the commons, Locke's right to acquire land is derived from the natural right of self-ownership. Since we own our bodies, we also own our body's actions and all things produced by actively modifying unowned natural resources. Locke's mercurial conception of "mixing labor with land" does not establish what kind of labor or how much mixing is required to legitimize one's ownership claims, but Locke would likely have argued that labor mixing entails more than the mere enclosure of or settlement on land, as Winthrop claimed (Waldron 1988).

Locke's theory also justifies significant inequalities in property holdings, particularly if some are physically unable to work or lack the means to establish legitimate property claims. Furthermore, since the more naturally talented and skilled are more productive in the mixing of labor with land, full self-ownership of one's talents and abilities necessarily implies inequality in the distribution of improved property (Cohen 1995). Contemporary liberal egalitarians such as John Rawls (1971) question theories of justice based on the ideal of self-ownership, arguing that no one should be advantaged or disadvantaged by the moral arbitrariness of inherited traits and talents produced by the "natural lottery." Even if everyone has identical talents and abilities, Locke's theory still justifies significant inequalities in residential property holdings, because those first to acquire property will inevitably be in the position to acquire more property than those who later acquire property when land becomes scarce.

John Locke's Provisos and the Distribution of Property

While most interpret Locke's theory of property as a vindication of unequal property arrangements, one feature of his theory opens the door to an alternative interpretation. Locke (1980 [1690], 19) mentions two provisos that constrain the acquisition of property: the spoliation proviso (one must use as much of the property acquired as possible before it spoils) and the sufficiency limitation (one must leave "enough, and as good" unappropriated resources for others to acquire). Underlying these provisos is a fundamental law of nature that requires that everyone first protect themselves and second protect the rest of humanity. As self-owners, individuals have a primary obligation to survive, which gives individuals certain rights to the material means of survival (Waldron 1988). Could any of these provisos justify an equal right to enough land to establish a home?

Those seeking an answer to this question must first distinguish between the property rights acquired through labor mixing and the natural rights secured by the Lockean provisos. Contemporary property theorist Jeremy Waldron (1988), modifying terminology first proposed by H. L. A. Hart (1955), argues that the first of these two rights is a *special right in rem*. It is a *special right* because it is contingent on the occurrence of a specific action taken by the rightholder (mixing labor with land), and it is *in rem* because the right obligates everyone (not just those involved in labor mixing) to respect the rightholder's claim. If the right were *in personam*, only those involved in the labor-mixing transaction would be required to recognize the rightholder's claim. *General rights*, which may be *in rem* or *in personam*, are those that are not contingent on the occurrence of any prior action, event, or transaction. In contrast to Locke's special right to acquire property through labor mixing, a general right to property would support an egalitarian property-based institution, because everyone would enjoy an equal right to property, irrespective of any actions taken to acquire property. If the general right to property is *in rem*, everyone would also have a correlative duty to respect everyone else's property claim. Is it possible to interpret the Lockean provisos preempting property acquisition as general universal rights to the opportunity to acquire minimal property holdings?

Waldron (1988) does not think so. He demonstrates that while Locke's sufficiency limitation resembles something like a general right to the opportunity to acquire property, Locke's nesting of the various provisos and complications that arise from the introduction of money contradict this egalitarian interpretation of Locke's theory. Regardless of whether we can find in Locke a theory of universal minimal property entitlements, some have interpreted his writings in this way, and philosophers since the Middle Ages have discussed the universal duty of charity to those in need and the corollary right of those in need to take matters into their own hands to satisfy their needs when no charity is provided (Mancilla 2016).[3]

Both Thomas Jefferson and Thomas Paine entertained egalitarian views of property along these lines. In *Agrarian Justice* (1995 [1797]), Paine proposed a tax on land inheritances that would be used to create a "national fund" supporting pensions for the elderly, disability assistance, and a stakeholder grant to be distributed equally and unconditionally to all individuals upon reaching adulthood. Since he believed that everyone enjoyed a general right to "natural property, or that which comes to us from the Creator of the universe," Paine viewed the national fund as a form of "compensation in part, for the loss of his or her natural inheritance, by the introduction of the system of landed property" (Kerr 2017, 132). In contrast to Locke, who understood the "enough, and as good" proviso as a constraint on the exercise of one's natural right to acquire property, Paine viewed the national fund as a form of compensation for the establishment of a system of private property that robs some of their natural inheritance (Lamb 2015). *Agrarian Justice* was Paine's attempt to offer a solution to the problem of poverty that was a compromise between the English Poor Laws and the socialism of François-Noël Babeuf. Unlike Babeuf, Paine accepted the legitimacy of the institution of private property. In contrast to English Poor Law advocates, Paine thought that everyone had a right to the means of basic subsistence that was not conditional on inhumane work requirements or other means tests (Kerr 2017).

Thomas Jefferson held that a republican form of government requires a widespread distribution of privately owned land and an agrarian economic base that cultivates the republican virtues of self-reliance, thrift, and economic independence. During a trip to France in the 1780s, Jefferson briefly entertained various redistributive measures designed to reduce the concentration of landownership, but he retracted these ideas when he returned to the United States (Katz 1997). Despite Jefferson's preference for a more egalitarian distribution of landed property, most American founders did not share his views. Paine's *Agrarian Justice* did not appear until after the ratification of the Constitution, and his *Common Sense* appealed to a more traditional Lockean view of property. James Madison, widely regarded as the father of the US Constitution, saw men as inherently unequal in their ability to acquire and improve property and viewed the preservation of those inequalities as one of the government's most important functions (Ely 1998). Moreover, the founders' unwillingness to abolish the institution of slavery belied their egalitarian commitments.

American Liberal Republicanism

According to historian Louis Hartz (1955), America's distinctly liberal political culture is defined by its full-throated embrace of Lockean values: moral individualism, private property rights, economic and social equality, limited government by consent, and toleration of conflicting and controversial ideologies. Hartz (1955) contends that while different political parties have interpreted the content of rights differently and defined consensual government in different ways, no major political party has diverged from the course charted by Locke.

More recently, Hartz's liberal consensus theory has been called into question by Bernard Bailyn (1967), J. G. A. Pocock (2003), Quentin Skinner (1998), Gordon Wood (1998), and other philosophers and historians who argue that the older civic republican tradition played a more important role than the Lockean liberal tradition in shaping Revolutionary political thought. The civic republican tradition has roots that extend to the ancient Roman republic, particularly the writings of Publius, Cato, and Cicero, which were rediscovered during the Italian Renaissance by Machiavelli and Montesquieu and again during the seventeenth century by radical Whig Commonwealthmen. Pocock (2003, 561) contends that while liberalism emphasizes rights "to which one may lay claim (perhaps because it is inherent in one's nature)," republicanism emphasizes the virtues "which one must find in oneself and express in actions undertaken with one's equals." For Philip Pettit (1997), the more important distinction between liberalism and republicanism lies in how each understands freedom. Whereas liberals understand freedom as the absence of external interference, republican freedom consists in the absence of arbitrary domination of the will. The republican emphasis on freedom as nondomination explains republicans' advocacy of self-governance and checks on political opportunism.

James Harrington's *The Commonwealth of Oceana* (1992 [1656]), a seminal republican treatise written after the English Civil Wars, shaped the American founders' views of property and government (Sitaraman 2017). For Harrington, the distribution of property arrangements shapes the distribution of political power, and a roughly equal distribution of property is the most appropriate distribution for a republican form of government. "Equality of estates causeth equality of power," Harrington wrote, "and equality of power is the liberty not only of the commonwealth, but of every man" (Harrington

1992 [1656], 20). To foster an equal distribution of property, Harrington proposed limits on individual property holdings that were inspired by Roman agrarian laws (Sitaraman 2017). In contrast to Locke, who viewed property as a natural prepolitical right justifying consensual government, Harrington believed that property rights are government creations that play an instrumental role in fostering government stability. According to Thomas Gordon and John Trenchard, two eighteenth-century republican English Commonwealthmen writing under the pseudonym Cato, "The first principle of all power is property; and every man will have his share of it in proportion as he enjoys property" (Trenchard 1755, 151).

Despite the revival of scholarly interest in the civic republican tradition, many contemporary scholars now characterize early American political thought in terms of the fusion of liberal and republican ideas.[4] Luigi Bradizza (2013, 24) claims that "the founders supported republican duties—and therefore republican virtues—in addition to liberal rights." According to Thomas West (2017), the founders looked to natural law to derive two complementary roles for government: the liberal protection of individual rights and the republican promotion of the common good. One way of understanding the founders' fusion of liberalism and republicanism is to say that the founders held a Lockean liberal view of rights and a Harringtonian republican theory of government. The fusion of liberalism and republicanism helps to explain the founders' view of property as both a God-given natural right and an instrument for promoting the civic virtues of thrift, economic independence, and civic responsibility.

The founders appealed to republican arguments to defend strong constitutional protections for the liberal institution of private property. According to Jennifer Nedelsky (1990), the founders were anxious about extreme inequalities in property holdings not because inequality per se was problematic but because a propertyless political majority posed a threat to the stability of a republican form of government. James Madison and Alexander Hamilton were in agreement that "nothing like an equality of property existed: that an inequality would exist as long as liberty existed, and that it would unavoidably result from that very liberty itself" (Syrett and Cooke 1962, 218). To protect economic and political stability, Madison proposed various checks and balances on democratic rule, including the separation of powers and other measures designed to reduce the influence of sectional interests. Madison even proposed adding the following Lockean clause to bolster constitutional protections for property rights: "That government is instituted, and ought to be exercised for the benefit of the people; which consists in the enjoyment of life and liberty, with the right of acquiring and using property, and generally of pursuing and obtaining happiness and safety" (Ely 1998, 54).

Civic Republicanism and the Social Meaning of Home

The early American home was the embodiment of republican citizenship. During the colonial period, colonists often evaluated a town's stature, in part, on the quality and consistency of its collective housing stock. In a letter to the first settlers of Plymouth Colony, Robert Cushman wrote that the construction of large homes was a needless waste of the community's resources and should be discouraged (Cohn 1970). When a wealthy group of settlers landed in New Haven in 1636, they were criticized for constructing gaudy and grandiose homes. According to one local observer, the wealthy settlers had "laid out too much of their stocks and estates in building of fair and stately houses, wherein they at first outdid the rest of the country" (Cohn 1970, 10). The colonists denounced pretentious and flamboyant housing styles while simultaneously condemning "huts" and "hovels" as evidence of sloth and idleness (Cohn 1970, 5). A shanty amid a community of stately homes was an insult to the community, while an ample supply of well-kept but modest homes signaled collective success and virtue.

In colonial New England, the political rights of town members, including the right to vote on matters affecting the town, were often restricted to freeholders.[5] The Puritans believed in the Christian duty of charity, but they interpreted this duty as a narrow obligation to assist town members who were physically unable to work. Native Americans were not eligible to receive poor relief, and migrants were screened and cast out if they held unacceptable religious beliefs or were unwilling to work. Before the construction of Boston's first almshouse, community residents viewed to be deserving of aid—mostly the elderly, the disabled, and orphans—were boarded in private houses or were allowed to live on their own at the public's expense, while those unable to find work were often auctioned into indentured servitude (Vale 2000).

Thomas Jefferson fused republican ideas about home and country with his liberal love of private property. He believed that a nation of small-scale property-owning farmers—a yeoman republic—best embodied the republican citizenship ideal. The cultivation of privately owned land fostered good judgment, and those who owned enough land for farming were free from dependence on wage labor or charity. Jefferson's yeoman republican citizen was tethered to the community rather than being constantly on the move, and this attachment gave each citizen a stake in the common good. In *Notes on the State of Virginia* (1954 [1787]), Jefferson gave physical form to this ideal. "A country whose buildings are of wood," he argued, "can never increase in its improvements to any considerable degree" (Jefferson 1954 [1787], 154). He encouraged the use of brick or stone instead because durable homes would more firmly connect citizens to the land and the community, saying, "whereas when buildings are of durable materials, every new edifice is an actual and permanent acquisition to the state, adding to its value as well as to its ornament" (Jefferson 1954 [1787], 154). An appreciation for flexibility and adaptability tempered Jefferson's affinity for republican stability. He recommended that farmers shift to crop rotation to preserve and replenish the soil, thereby stabilizing the nation's agricultural base, and understood that homes often required modification to accommodate evolving household needs. Even though it still stands today in a form that resembles its original design, Monticello is a house that will never be truly finished, much like the Jeffersonian republic (Faherty 2007).

Radical Land Reform and the Homestead Ideal

When Jefferson evoked his ideal of the yeoman republic, he did not anticipate the fundamental economic changes that would reshape America's political economy in the nineteenth century. Although Great Britain was in the midst of an industrial revolution at the time of the American Revolution, the American economy was still primarily driven by agricultural production. Things changed during the nineteenth century with the rise of industrialization and later the rapid growth of cities spurred by rural-to-urban migration and immigration from abroad. By 1860, the United States was producing nearly one-fourth of the world's manufacturing output, second only to the United Kingdom (North 1966).

The nineteenth-century American industrial economy was a boom-or-bust economy that was shaken by economic crises in 1819, 1837, 1857, and 1873. In the wake of each crisis, reformers called for various laws designed to stabilize employment, improve working conditions, and undercut the market power of large monopolies. Trade unionists and labor reformers called for land reforms designed to reduce the concentration of land ownership and promote the economic self-sufficiency of the average worker by opening up the public domain to (white male) workers (Lause 2005).

Calls for land reform began with debates surrounding the disposition of federal land. With the Louisiana Purchase in 1803, the Oregon Compromise with England in 1846, and the cession of lands by treaty after the Mexican War in 1848, the federal government soon came to own the majority of American land. Between 1781 and 2015, the federal government disposed of approximately 1.3 billion acres of the public domain, primarily to private landowners (Vincent et al. 2017). Tensions arose over the often incompatible goals of generating government revenue from public land sales and promoting the settlement of western land by the growing population. Following the Land Ordinance of 1785, the US government sold 640-acre sections of land at $1 per acre, an amount that was well beyond the reach of the average skilled worker. The Land Act of 1796 doubled this price to $2 per acre, but subsequent legislation reduced the minimum acreage for purchase and the down payment requirement. By 1820, land prices were still beyond the means of the average worker (Lause 2005). Most public lands were acquired by land speculators until the passage of the Preemption Act in 1841, which granted squatters' rights to those who resided on and improved public land not officially for sale, at a cost to the squatter of $1.25 per acre (Gates 1941).

With the elimination of property requirements for voting (for white males) in many US states, trade unions began to organize politically in the early 1800s, and land reform was a central platform. Reformers saw land reform as a solution to two related problems. First, granting free land to western settlers would enable those facing poor working conditions in the East to escape wage labor and become self-owners by working their own plot of land. Second, the settlement of western land would provide a "safety valve" to curb the oversupply of labor in eastern US cities. Westward labor migration would eventually boost the wages of those who continued working in eastern cities (Perlman 1923). In Philadelphia and later in New York, reformers commingled land reform with other ideas, including minimum work-hour laws and collective public education schemes inspired by Scottish communitarian reformer Robert Owen.

New York was the site of the creation of the Working Men's Party, a land and labor reform party led by Robert Dale Owen (son of Robert Owen), Thomas Skidmore, Frances Wright, and George Henry Evans. Skidmore and Evans looked to Thomas Paine for inspiration for their cause (Lause 2005). Alexander Ming Jr., whose father was a friend of Thomas Paine, published Skidmore's (1829) *The Rights of Man to Property!* Skidmore was a Jeffersonian, but he objected to Jefferson's use of the phrase "life, liberty, and the pursuit of happiness" in the Declaration of Independence, arguing that "man's natural right to life or liberty, is not more sacred or unalienable, than his right to property" (Skidmore 1829, 59).

Skidmore's understanding of the natural right to property differed from the right conceived by Locke. For Skidmore, neither occupancy, possession, nor labor establishes private property rights. Instead, every person's pre-political natural right to life gives them a right to an equal share of nature's resources. As Skidmore put it, "May not a man expand his lungs and inhale the air; may he not open his eyes, and enjoy the light; may not his body occupy the space which it actually does; without any necessity to suppose the existence of legislation? Most certainly" (Skidmore 1829, 77). Skidmore argued that these natural rights of persons bear no relation to the civil right to own private property, which requires the consent of those excluded from privately owned property.

Skidmore was a primary author of the 1829 Working Men's Party platform, which called for a grant of 160 acres of land to every man and unmarried woman over the age of 21. All land holdings in excess of 160 acres were to be confiscated by the government and redistributed to those without land. Skidmore viewed land redistribution to be the best means of realizing "man's natural right to an equal proportion of property" (Ellis 1992, 832). Robert Dale Owen called for the addition of a communal public education proposal to the Working Men's Party platform. Despite some local electoral success, divisions within the party eventually led to its demise. Skidmore was a primary source of these tensions. His aggressive land redistribution program was not favored by most in the party, and many were turned off by his prickly demeanor (Pessen 1954).

Lewis Masquerier, another New York land reformer and Owenite communitarian with family connections to Thomas Paine, agreed with Skidmore that the natural right to life gave men a natural right to the land, stating that, "As each person's natural wants and producing powers are so nearly equal, they entitle all to an equal share of the soil, appurtenant elements, and the whole product of their labor. . . . The equalness, then, of each one's natural wants for light, warmth, air, water, food, clothing, and shelter, is the true foundation and necessity for an equal share of homestead" (Masquerier 1877, 56). Masquerier merged his land reform ideas with a utopian plan for "rural republican townships" that were six square miles in size and divided into 160-acre farms. In the center of each township was a square mile set aside for parks, public buildings, and lots for those not engaged in agriculture (Masquerier 1877).

George Henry Evans's periodical, the *Workingman's Advocate*, was one of several labor newspapers that disseminated land reform and labor reform ideas between the 1820s and the 1840s. After the demise of the Working Men's Party, Evans continued to advocate for land reforms, drawing inspiration from Paine, Jefferson, Skidmore, and English land reformer Thomas Spence, among others. In 1841, Evans called for the establishment of an organization bound by the agreement "to support or vote for no man for any public office who will not pledge himself to exercise all proper influence of his station to restore to the people, in some equitable manner, the Equal Right to Land" (Lause 2005, 16).

Like other land reformers before him, Evans believed that the right to life grants everyone a natural prepolitical right to land. Although Evans and Skidmore drew inspiration from many of the same sources, Evans did not agree with Skidmore's radical proposal to redistribute existing private property holdings and instead proposed distributing publicly owned land to workers for no charge, an idea that would later be co-opted by the homestead movement. In an 1844 issue of the *Workingman's Advocate*, Evans connected the right to a homestead to the natural right to subsistence (Evans 1844, 2; italics in the original): "If man has a right on the earth, he has a right to land enough to raise a habitation on. If he has a right to *live*, he has a right to land enough to till for his subsistence. Deprive him of any one of these rights, and you place him at the mercy of those who possess them."

Evans and John Windt eventually founded the National Reform Association (NRA), which attracted a large following of land reformers holding a wide variety of ideological views (Lause 2005). One of its famous slogans was the phrase "Vote yourself a farm." Other land reform organizations and publications eventually adopted the phrase. In the Boston labor periodical *True Workingman*, the authors wrote, "If a man have a house and a home of his own, though it be a thousand miles off, he is well received in other people's houses; while the homeless wretch is turned away. The bare right to a farm, though you should never go near it, would save you from many an insult. Therefore, Vote yourself a farm" (Davis 1997). According to economist and labor historian Selig Perlman (1923), of the 2,000 papers published in the United States in 1845, 600 had supported land reform by 1850.

Land reformers managed to push a homestead bill onto the floor of Congress in 1848, but the bill was killed by southern congressmen who viewed the bill as an attack on slavery. If, following the land reformers' Lockean reasoning, property ownership came from mixing land with labor, those enslaved were the only ones with legitimate titles to the land they worked. Southern slaveowners objected to this reasoning and sought to protect the institution of slavery in southern states and newly settled western territories (Arrington 2012).

Although southern slaveowners objected to the implications of homesteading for slaveowning in newly settled western territories, many in the south still acknowledged the appeal of the ideal of home evoked by homestead advocates. Southern legislators adopted various laws designed to protect the sanctity of the home and the institution of the nuclear family by exempting homesteads from debt obligations. The Texas Constitution of 1845 included a homestead exemption, and by the Civil War, 10 of the 11 states that eventually comprised the Confederacy had enacted homestead exemption laws (Hadden and Minter 2013).

The pervasiveness of homestead exemptions in southern states suggests that southern opposition to national homestead legislation was grounded not in opposition to the use of government machinery to protect the homestead ideal but in the implications of a national homestead policy for the preservation and expansion of slavery. Northern opposition to slavery eventually brought abolitionists into the tent of the NRA. Many land reformers who were initially ambivalent about the issue of slavery eventually came to oppose slavery in western territories, not because land reformers necessarily viewed slavery as immoral but because they believed that western slave labor would undercut the wages of white workers migrating to the region (Lause 2005).

In 1849, Evans retreated to his New Jersey farm and the NRA lost steam, but the die had already been cast. The homestead movement gained traction when national political parties adopted the cause and integrated it with the free labor ideology of the antislavery movement. The 1852 Free Democratic (Free Soil) Party platform included a reference to "the right of all men to the soil" (Horne 1990, 226). New York editor and vocal land reformer Horace Greeley insisted that a homestead plan be included as a central component of the Republican Party's national platform in 1860 (Foner 1995).

When homestead bills finally reached the floors of Congress, pro-homestead advocates appealed to republican citizenship ideals to sell their proposals (Zundel 2000). In 1860, eventual US president Andrew Johnson, then a senator from Tennessee, proclaimed (Johnson 1860, 1653), "Let each man have a home, and when your elections come around he is a freeman, he is an independent man; he goes to the ballot-box and votes his own vote, and not the vote of his landlord or his master."

Congress passed the Homestead Act in 1862, in large part because of the secession of southern states following the outbreak of the Civil War. The act allowed any qualifying settler to acquire up to 160 acres of public land. Settlers who paid a small administrative fee, occupied the land within six months, cultivated at least 10 acres, and remained on the property for five consecutive years gained title to the land they occupied (Arrington 2012). Between the Civil War and the New Deal era, Congress also passed several additional homestead acts that expanded opportunities to establish homestead claims in areas not covered by the original act.

Although land reformers initially viewed the 1862 Homestead Act as a success, the program failed to accomplish reformers' larger goals of smoothing labor supply and reunifying laborers with the fruits of their labor. By 1862, most of the remaining federal land was not suitable for farming, and by 1890, the US Census Bureau had announced that the frontier had closed. Many homestead claims were in areas not served by transportation or other community amenities (Lause 2005). Rampant land speculation and fraud also tarnished the program's reputation (Billington 1974; Anderson 2011).

Homestead reformers ultimately missed the mark in their attempts to sell the dream of a Jeffersonian yeoman republic to a rapidly urbanizing society. By the mid-nineteenth century, industrialization was rapidly replacing rural home production, and the practicality of the homestead ideal and its associated safety-value theory of labor was out of step with the role of the home in the new industrial economy. As wage labor physically separated workers from their homes and the means of production, homestead advocates naively clung to dreams of reunifying home and work while ignoring the plight of those who continued working in the urban wage sector.

The homestead also embodied two moral ideals that were in tension with one another: the spatially fixed ideal of republican citizenship and the mobile, dynamic ideal of economic opportunity. For eastern urbanites with no agricultural expertise, the homestead opportunity was a mirage. Most homestead settlements also lacked the sense of community found in older, established eastern cities. As Thomas H. O'Connor observed, in response to a failed effort to encourage Irish workers living in Boston to move to the western territories, the city retained its appeal to "gregarious people devoted to clan, family, and religion, with little experience in large-scale farming and no inclination to see their sons and daughters scattered to the four winds. They preferred to remain in Boston, close to their friends, their relatives, their priests, their sacraments, and their pubs. . . . The small piece of turf they had carved out along the shabby waterfront might be unsightly and unsanitary, but it was theirs, and they did not intend to give it up" (Vale 2000, 103).

By the second half of the nineteenth century, the owned single-family detached home became the new manifestation of the frontier homestead ideal once retrofitted to reflect the new industrial reality of wage sector employment. Although most Americans still lacked the means to purchase a single-family home outright, the ideal became embedded in popular culture. Walt Whitman wrote that a "man is not a whole and complete man unless he *owns* a house and the ground it stands on" (Whitman 1856, 93; italics in the original). Whitman observed that "democracy looks with suspicious, ill-satisfied eye upon the very poor, the ignorant, and on those out of business. She asks for men and women with occupations, well-off, owners of houses and acres, and with cash in the bank" (Whitman 1964 [1892], 384). A contributor to the *American Builder* wrote in 1869, "It is strange how contentedly men can go on year after year, living like Arabs a tent life, paying exhorbitant rents, with no care or concern for a permanent house" (Jackson 1985, 50).

Changes in the nature of work also shaped the families living within American homes. In nuclear families headed by a male wage earner, the daytime physical separation between husbands and wives contributed to a gender-based division of labor within the home. Women became the new stewards of republican civic virtue. Publications such as *Ladies' Home Journal*,

Horace Bushnell's *Christian Nurture*, and Sara Josepha Hale's *Godey's Lady's Book* taught young women the art of homemaking (Jackson 1985). Catherine Beecher's *Treatise on Domestic Economy, For the Use of Young Ladies at Home and at School*, published in 1841 and reprinted dozens of times, became the bible of the new "cult of domesticity" (Jackson 1985, 62). Although the cult of domesticity assigned a new civic role to married female homemakers, women were excluded from active participation in public civic life. Married women also were not compensated for their domestic work and did not enjoy the spatial separation between home and work that male laborers enjoyed (Hayden 1984).

Not everyone accepted the values and ideals attached to the single-family home. A contributor to an 1844 Fourierist journal remarked that the semirural cottage "is wasteful in economy, is untrue to the human heart, and is not the design of God, and therefore it must disappear" (Jackson 1985, 52). First-wave feminists, including Charlotte Perkins Gilman, Melusina Fay Pierce, and Victoria Woodhull, equated the nuclear family and domestic life with the enslavement of women and promoted kitchenless houses and multifamily dwellings as alternative architectural ideals (Jackson 1985). Pierce called for the creation of neighborhood-based domestic labor cooperatives that would enable women to be "paid for what they were already doing" (Hayden 1984, 72).

Henry George and New York Housing Reform

In 1879, Henry George published his international bestseller *Progress and Poverty* (1942 [1879]). Echoing his land reforming predecessors, George blamed poverty and social injustice on the concentration of land ownership. However, George did not call for land redistribution, limitations on landholdings, or the expansion of homesteading. Instead, he proposed that land rent, net of the income earned from improvements to land, be fully taxed and redistributed to the community to support public improvements. His "single tax" proposal appealed to the idea that land's value is a monopoly rent derived from "natural elements which human exertion can neither produce nor increase" (George 1942 [1879], 140). This rent "is due to nothing that the land owners have done." It is a "creation of the whole community" that should be returned to the community through taxation (George 1942 [1879], 306). While the single-tax idea was not new,[6] George attracted a large following, in part because of his unique ability to express concrete policy proposals in the language of populism.

Henry George's engagement with the New York labor movement in the 1880s bears remarkable similarities with George Henry Evans's involvement with labor in the early part of the century. In addition to their similar names and parallel ties to the labor movement, both drew inspiration from John Locke and Thomas Paine, which likely explains why neither reformer comfortably sided with socialists. Apart from these similarities, each offered contrasting reform proposals. Whereas Evans saw homesteading as an urban safety valve that would siphon off excess labor from the city and promote farming on the frontier, George viewed the single tax as a way to help workers live and work in the city. George theorized that by capturing land's speculative value, the single tax would increase the supply of affordable homes and provide a new source of revenue for public improvements.

Urban historians have underappreciated George's contributions to the housing reform movement (Stobo 2008). Most scholarly investigations of the New York housing reform movement begin with the work of private philanthropists and public service advocates leading up to the adoption of New York's tenement housing regulations (see Friedman 1968; Lubove 1962; Radford 1996). George entered the housing reform movement through his work with the labor movement, where he sought to apply his single-tax philosophy to address working tenants' poor housing conditions. To fully appreciate George's contribution to the New York housing reform movement, it is useful to first establish the broader context of land and housing reform in New York.

During the mid-nineteenth century, the New York tenant class was one of the most vocal supporters of measures designed to restructure the rights of housing occupancy to favor tenants. Demands initially came not from New York City renters but from rural tenant farmers living in upstate New York. A remnant of the old Dutch "patroonship" system of feudal landownership existed in upstate New York until the 1800s. Following the death of Stephen Van Rensselaer III in 1839, his sons Stephen IV and William tried to collect overdue rents from the tenant farmers working the Van Rensselaers' land. The farmers refused, and years of tenant agitation ensued. In 1842, the NRA sent Thomas Devyr to assist the tenants in the establishment of an anti-rent association that lobbied for legislative reforms and state assistance to tenant farmers. A proposal to break up large estates upon the death of the owners was defeated, but a new state constitution adopted in 1846 abolished feudal leases and outlawed the selling of tenant property for the nonpayment of rent (Lause 2005).

In New York City, a speculative bubble in the years leading up to the Panic of 1837 caused massive inflation that increased the prices of housing and other commodities. In February 1837, a crowd of between 5,000 and 6,000 gathered in the city to denounce the "landlords, and holders of flour, for the prices of rents and provisions" (Heskin 1983, 16). The depression following the Panic of 1837 temporarily put the brakes on rent increases, but by the mid-1840s, rents began to rise again, particularly following the arrival of large numbers of Irish and German immigrants after 1845 (Blackmar 1989). Irish land reformers established the citywide Tenant League, which called for reforms designed to secure tenants' access to affordable rental housing. In 1848, it called on the municipal government of New York to restrict rents to 7 percent of assessed value, impose a triple tax on unimproved urban land, and sell city lots to homesteaders for a minimal price. It also called for the repeal of regulatory measures thought to increase the cost of housing. During the 1850s, land reform activists joined forces with tenant organizations to call for the distribution of common land to city homesteaders and the construction of working-class housing (Blackmar 1989).[7]

Several factors complicated the New York City tenant movement. Workers were acutely aware of their unsafe and crowded living conditions, and sanitary and social reformers increasingly called attention to these conditions. A newly established board of health conducted home inspections to address the housing issue, but early public health regulations were mostly ineffective. More importantly from the tenants' standpoint, those who complained often faced eviction if inspectors reported their substandard living conditions to the authorities. Labor reformers and tenants often cast the blame for increased rents not on the owners of rental properties but on those who rented several units and subleased the units to individual tenants. Since the owners of rental apartment buildings often collected rents from several sublessors, it was often difficult to determine who should be the object of any organized opposition (Blackmar 1989).

Peculiarities of certain trades, particularly the clothing and cigar-making industries, often shifted the focus of labor's emphasis in the housing arena away from workers' living conditions to the workers' ability to organize effectively. Unlike most workers who lived and worked in separate locations, cigar makers and clothing manufacturers tended to live and work in tenement buildings owned by their employers. These conditions made labor organizing virtually impossible, and organized factory labor soon began to see tenement labor as a threat. As a result, trade unions such as Samuel Gompers's Cigarmakers' International Union called for a boycott of tenement-produced goods and the prohibition of tenement cigar making (Stobo 2008).

Given New York's unique experience with land reform, it is not surprising that labor reformers welcomed Henry George's entry into the housing reform arena. In the 1880s, George moved to New York to put his theory into practice through engagement with the local labor movement. *Progress and Poverty* was widely read and discussed on New York factory floors and in the meeting halls of various leftist organizations. Land reform was also on the agenda of reform-minded Irish American workers, who helped sponsor two of George's European speaking tours (Barker 1955).

In his 1885 testimony before the Senate Committee on Labor and Education, George argued that a single tax could solve New York's housing crisis by creating incentives to construct new housing on underutilized land. In the same meeting, Louis Post of the Central Labor Union argued that George's single tax would ease overcrowding and stimulate housing construction, adding that there was "no remedy for the suffering of the industrial classes short of taking ground-rents for public use" (Stobo 2008, 18). George also attracted followers from the Knights of Labor. Terence Powderly of the Knights stated to the General Assembly in 1884 that land should be taxed at its full value, and the Knights' newspaper, *Journal of United Labor*, helped advertise George's work (Stobo 2008).

In 1886, Henry George was nominated as the Labor candidate for mayor. Upon accepting the nomination, George adopted a platform that applied his single-tax philosophy to the working-class housing crisis. One plank of the platform stated:

> We declare the crowding of so many people into narrow tenements at enormous rents, while half the area of the city is yet unbuilt upon to be a scandalous evil, and to remedy this state of things all taxes on buildings and improvements should be abolished, so that no fine shall be put upon the employment of labor in increasing living accommodations, and that taxes should be levied on land irrespective of improvements, so that those who are now holding land vacant shall be compelled either to build on it themselves, or give up the land to those who will. (Speek 1915, 68)

Both the Democratic Party candidate, Abram Hewitt, and the Republican Party candidate, Theodore Roosevelt, criticized George's single-tax proposal for being overly radical. In the November election, Hewitt received 41 percent of the vote, George received 31 percent, and Roosevelt received 28 percent. Although he did not win, George was the most successful Labor candidate ever to run for mayor of New York City (O'Donnell 2015). George's land reform ideas helped him win the support of the Irish working class, but scholars remain divided over the importance of George's single-tax proposal to his electoral success. Philip Foner (1998, 120), for example, argues that labor and socialists supported George "not on account of his single tax theory, but in spite of it." Others maintain that the single tax was too abstract and not comprehensible to the average voter (Young 1916).

Edward O'Donnell (2015) offers another explanation for George's success. He argues that George's brand of "progressive republicanism" appealed to the laborer's belief in the virtues of work and the perceived injustice of land monopolization without abandoning the American commitment to private property and capitalism. Much as Thomas Paine did a century earlier, George blended liberalism and republicanism into a distinctly American brand of egalitarianism. George appealed to a conception of home and property that was grounded in Jeffersonian ideals, updated for a new urban reality. George's political career and direct engagement with the New York housing reform movement ended with an unsuccessful bid for New York secretary of state but, as discussed in chapter 3, his ideas had a lasting influence on twentieth-century land reform and city planning movements.

The Broader Reach of American Land Reform

The nineteenth-century American land reform movement fostered a reexamination of the institution of property as understood by the founders. At times, American land reformers adopted philosophical positions that sound anachronistic to modern ears. Early American anarchists, unified in their opposition to government reforms, often appealed to strongly communitarian values grounded in religion or secular humanism. Individualist anarchists took the opposite approach. Josiah Warren, initially attracted to Robert Owen's ideas, eventually abandoned communitarianism for a strongly individualist philosophy that resembled American land reformers' radical Lockeanism. Individualist anarchists Ezra Heywood and Joshua Ingalls fought against the problem of land monopoly, arguing that the only legitimate rights of land ownership were the rights of occupancy and use. Ingalls joined the antislavery cause but believed that the abolition of slavery would have little impact on land monopoly, while the end of land monopoly would make slavery untenable (Martin 1957).

After the Civil War, Radical Republicans took up the issue of land reform as part of the Reconstruction effort. The short-lived Freedmen's Bureau, established in 1865, was initially authorized to divide abandoned and confiscated Confederate property into 40-acre plots for rent to former slaves. General William T. Sherman went one step further, issuing Special Field Order No. 15, which promised "forty acres and a mule" to freed slaves, to be acquired from confiscated land along the South Carolina, Florida, and Georgia coasts. Congressional Radical Republicans proposed other similar measures, but Reconstruction ultimately failed to become the land redistribution program that many had envisioned. President Andrew Johnson, an early supporter of land reform, vetoed Sherman's field order, and the Freedman's Bureau was eventually abolished. Reconstruction of the South was further stalled by the rise of Jim Crow laws and hate groups such as the Ku Klux Klan (Foner 1990).

Despite the failure of Reconstruction to remedy the historical injustices associated with slavery, the constitutional amendments adopted by Congress during and after the Civil War extended civil rights to millions of Americans who had previously been denied those rights. Before the Civil War, enslaved Black Americans were considered property, and white male property owners were the only ones who could genuinely claim the full benefits of American citizenship. The Civil Rights Act of 1866 and Thirteenth Amendment extended these benefits to those formerly enslaved, and the Fourteenth Amendment guaranteed full citizenship rights, including the rights of equal protection and due process, to all persons born or naturalized in the United States. During the twentieth century, several social movements fought to expand these and other rights of citizenship previously denied to racial and ethnic minorities, women, persons with disabilities, and the poor.

The Civil Rights Act of 1866 and Civil War–era amendments also opened up new homesteading opportunities for Black Americans on the frontier, including many former slaves who were previously prohibited from owning land. In contrast to many white homesteader settlements, which often struggled to establish self-sustaining community institutions, Black homesteader communities often bonded in solidarity to develop thriving churches, recreational facilities, schools, and other community institutions in places such as Nicodemus, Kansas; Dearfield, Colorado; Empire, Wyoming; DeWitty, Nebraska; and Blackdom, New Mexico. Collective solidarity and thriving community institutions provided security to Black homesteaders seeking to escape the racial violence and oppression they faced in the Jim Crow South (Friefeld, Eckstrom, and Edwards 2019). For these settlers, the right to establish a community was part and parcel of the right to own land.

Perhaps the most enduring legacy of the nineteenth-century land reform movement for US housing policy was its influence on the rhetoric surrounding the burgeoning movement to expand opportunities for homeownership. The building and loan industry, which was still in its infancy during the nineteenth century,[8] promoted homeownership as a way to "remove the youth of the nation from the terrible ever present temptations of the crowded tenement dens" (D. Mason 2004, 27). Articles published in national periodicals such as *Scribner's Magazine* and *North American Review* touted building and loan organizations as a way to "encourage the development of thrift and providence among wage-earners" (D. Mason 2004, 27). Urban reformers appealed to the ideal of the homestead to call for the establishment of mutual aid associations and model homes.

Nowhere was the connection between homesteading, homeownership, and urban reform more apparent than in Boston. Horace B. Sargent wrote in the 1854 pamphlet *Homesteads for City Poor* that single-family homes on the outskirts of town would provide the overcrowded urban poor with "dignity, manhood, moral, and political independence" (Vale 2000, 107). Several homestead clubs and savings and loan organizations were established to promote suburban homeownership (Vale 2000). In 1879, Reverend Edward E. Hale proposed housing cooperatives such as the Boston Cooperative Society and the Pioneer Bank to finance the creation of new towns designed to relieve urban congestion (Kersten 1973). Reverend Hale stressed the need for the "workingmen of our cities" to own homesteads, arguing that civilization required "a separate house, owned by the tenant, with windows on each side, ready ventilation, and a patch of land large enough for the ornament at least of the home" (Vale 2000, 108).

In the end, American land reformers' adherence to natural rights ideology arguably contributed to the demise of the frontier homestead ideal.

By the end of the nineteenth century, the frontier had closed, forcing land reformers to adapt their thinking to the more difficult problem of redistributing privately owned land to those who had less, a task that was not viewed favorably by the US courts. Land and labor reformers also held differing views on the significance of land to the urban housing problem. Those living in the slums often perceived the housing crisis to be the direct result of landlord rent-gouging practices and landlords' reluctance to maintain units at a decent standard of quality. For labor organizations, the problem of poor living conditions was often secondary to the dilemma of organizing those who worked in tenements.

As discussed in chapter 3, turn-of-the-century urban reformers sought to improve the living conditions of the urban poor, but regulations designed to improve housing quality eventually became vehicles for enhancing the value of the owned single-family detached home. The federal government catalyzed the nascent homeownership movement during the 1920s with various public relations campaigns and again during the 1930s with the creation of an expansive federal housing policy infrastructure that bolstered the savings and loan industry. One of the great ironies of the history of American housing reform is that the twentieth-century movement to expand homeownership, which has been vilified for institutionalizing housing inequality, had origins in a radical egalitarian movement to extend rights to housing and land.

3 Housing for the Common Good

>We must go a long way to revise our national viewpoint regarding ownership rights as against community rights in land.
>—Robert D. Kohn, quoted in Carol Aronovici,
>*America Can't Have Housing* (1934, 11)

As historian Richard Hofstadter wrote in *The Age of Reform* (1960, 23), describing late nineteenth-century America on the eve of the progressive revolution, "The United States was born in the country and had moved to the city." Between 1800 and 1900, the percentage of the population living in urban areas swelled from 6 percent to 40 percent (US Bureau of the Census 1949, series B 13–23). In 1800, no American city housed 100,000 people or more, but by 1900, 38 cities of this size existed, with 10 of those added during the previous decade (US Bureau of the Census 1949, series B 145–159). Cities grew in size and density. The island of Manhattan, for example, grew from 2,773 people per square mile in 1800 to 84,091 people per square mile in 1900, with the largest percentage increase in density occurring between 1820 and 1860, when large numbers of Irish and German immigrants settled in the city (Demographia 2001).

The transition from a rural agricultural economy to an advanced urban industrial economy throughout the nineteenth century brought new housing crises that previous generations of reformers were not willing or prepared to address. Migration from rural America and immigration from abroad increased the number, size, and density of American cities, and the private housing market was ill equipped to house the expanding urban workforce. Land prices skyrocketed in employment centers, and to economize on rising land costs, homebuilders reduced the size and quality of homes. Urban property owners subdivided single-family homes into apartments, converted basements to living space, constructed small homes in alleyways, and within the largest cities constructed multifloor tenements to house working families in small, cramped living quarters. With overcrowded living conditions came public health crises, racial and ethnic tensions, and labor unrest.

Social reformers on both sides of the Atlantic responded to urban housing crises in different ways. European reformers were skeptical that the "housing question" could be solved through a capitalist system of housing provision. According to Friedrich Engels, "As long as the capitalist mode of production continues to exist, it is folly to hope for an isolated solution to the housing question or of any other social question affecting the fate of workers. The solution lies in the abolition of the capitalist mode of production and the appropriation of all the means of life and labor for the working class itself" (Engels 1975 [1872], 73–74). Nineteenth-century American land reformers were less critical of capitalism and often turned a blind eye to the plight of the cities, advocating instead for policies designed to depopulate urban areas. For Henry George, the answer to the housing question lay not in urban deconcentration or the abolition of capitalism but in the partial socialization of housing value through the single tax on land.

By the late nineteenth century, a new generation of American reformers had joined the debate, shifting the focus of urban reform from land to housing and reorienting the basis of housing justice from rights to goals and virtues. The late nineteenth- and early twentieth-century generation of American housing reformers sought to address urban housing crises using regulatory means, rejecting both European collectivist housing strategies and American land reformers' natural rights ideology. Some American housing reformers looked to Europe for new ideas, but the solutions imported from abroad were modified with a uniquely American twist, elevating the owned single-family detached home over all other housing types (Hirt 2014). This chapter examines these developments, concluding with an explanation for the shift from the earlier generation's emphasis on right-based reforms toward new utilitarian and progressive strategies.

Natural Rights and Laissez-Faire Constitutionalism

To fully comprehend the ideological underpinnings of the late nineteenth-century American housing reform movement, it is first important to understand the evolving legal framework within early postbellum America. The US courts had historically defined private property rights in Lockean terms, upholding the right to acquire and transfer property but denying the existence of a general right to property as such. In *Vanhorne's Lessee v. Dorrance* (1795, 2), Justice William Patterson asserted that "the right of acquiring and possessing property, and having it protected, is one of the natural, inherent and unalienable rights of man." James Kent wrote in *Commentaries on American Law* that "the right to acquire and enjoy property" is among the "absolute rights of individuals" (Kent 1826, 1). In 1848, Daniel Webster questioned the government's power of eminent domain, writing that if "the legislature or their agents are to be the sole judges of what is to be taken, and to what public use it is to be appropriated, the most levelling ultraisms of Anti-rentism or agrarianism or Abolitionism may be successfully advanced" (Ely 1998, 78).

Three crucial developments marked the period extending from the Civil War through the New Deal era. First, the courts recognized corporate entities as having many of the same rights as persons under the US Constitution.[1] Second, state and local governments expanded their authority under the police power doctrine (Gerstle 2015).[2] These two developments combined to shape the strategies adopted by state and local governments to address housing problems. Although the courts recognized municipal governments as right-bearing corporate entities, the courts also distinguished between public corporations or municipalities and private corporations or firms. A fuzzy boundary separated municipalities' public and private activities (Frug 1980). In his influential *Treatise on the Law of Municipal Corporations* (1872), John Dillon argued that most municipal functions should be understood as public activities, and state governments enjoyed wide discretion to define the scope of these public functions. Several states subsequently adopted "Dillon's Rule" laws that limited the scope of municipal governments' police powers, complicating the realization of the Jeffersonian ideal of a decentralized self-governing republic (Frug 1980; Wiebe 1967).

After the Civil War, a third development, combined with the first development mentioned, strengthened and extended the Lockean understanding of private property rights. The doctrine of "laissez-faire constitutionalism," best exemplified in the *Lochner v. New York* (1905) Supreme Court decision invalidating a minimum work hour law, united the liberty of contract doctrine with the substantive due process concept to insulate businesses from government attempts to constrain corporate rights of property and contract (Lindsay 2010).[3] Those appealing to the liberty of contract doctrine understood the Fourteenth Amendment as placing significant limits on the government's ability to interfere with voluntary contracts between individuals and corporations. The Supreme Court relied on the liberty of contract doctrine in *Allgeyer v. Louisiana* (1897) to invalidate a state law that prohibited out-of-state insurance companies from conducting business in Louisiana. In *Lawton v. Steele* (1894), the court relied on similar reasoning to rule that the "legislature may not, under the guise of protecting the public interests, arbitrarily interfere with private business, or impose unusual and unnecessary restrictions upon lawful occupations" (Ely 1998, 90).

The second component of laissez-faire constitutionalism was a substantive interpretation of the due process clauses of the Fifth and Fourteenth Amendments. In contrast to procedural due process, which addresses the question of whether the government follows fair rules when infringing on life, liberty, or property, substantive due process asks whether the infringement is justified by a legitimate public purpose and whether it relies on legitimate means to achieve the public purpose. In a dissent to the majority opinion in the *Slaughterhouse Cases* (1873), Justice Joseph Bradley foreshadowed this doctrine with his argument that "a law which prohibits a large class of citizens from adopting a lawful employment, or from following a lawful employment previously adopted, does deprive them of liberty as well as property, without due process of law" (Wallace 1873, 122). In *Mugler v. Kansas* (1887), Justice John Marshall Harlan declared that the courts could "look at the substance of things" in cases involving the exercise of police powers, adding that there were "limits beyond which legislation cannot rightfully go" (Ely 1998, 89).

In *Jacobs* (1885), the New York State Court of Appeals invoked substantive due process to invalidate a law prohibiting cigar manufacturing in tenements, finding no rational relationship between cigar manufacturing in tenements and the health of cigar makers or the public. Theodore Roosevelt, the sponsor of the bill to enact the law, recalled later in his autobiography that "conditions rendered it impossible for the families of tenement-house workers to live so that the children might grow up fitted for the exacting duties of American citizenship," linking housing conditions to republican citizenship ideals (Roosevelt 1924, 80). While some may have viewed this case as a blow to efforts to regulate housing conditions in tenement buildings, the courts in *Jacobs* based their decision on the tenement's role as a workplace, leaving open the question of the legality of regulations designed to improve residential living conditions (Garb 2003).

The American housing reform movement was born within this legal context. Laissez-faire constitutionalism and Dillon's Rule limited the range of solutions that housing reformers could pursue to address slum housing conditions. At the same time, the courts upheld legitimate uses of the police power to enhance public health, safety, and welfare. Two overlapping approaches to housing reform emerged within this legal environment: (1) a utilitarian approach that rejected natural rights ideology but otherwise held on to the liberal Lockean conception of property, and (2) a progressive approach that offered a new interpretation of property that was more firmly grounded in a concern for the common good. The first approach shaped tenement housing regulations, whereas the second provided an ideological basis for land-use zoning ordinances.

The Utilitarian Origins of American Housing Reform

The American housing reform movement has intellectual origins in the English sanitary reform movement, particularly in the work of British social reformer Edwin Chadwick. Chadwick was a student and secretary for Jeremy Bentham, founder of the utilitarian approach to government reform. According to Bentham, just actions are those that produce the greatest happiness for the greatest number of people, where happiness is defined in terms of the presence of pleasure and the absence of pain. Bentham held that no actions are intrinsically good or bad. Actions are instrumentally good to the extent that they produce pleasure and instrumentally bad to the extent that they cause pain.[4]

Bentham's instrumental view of morality signaled a significant departure from the natural rights tradition. Famously referring to natural rights as "nonsense upon stilts" (Waldron 1987, 53), Bentham only acknowledged those rights recognized and enforced by positive law and saw the promotion of aggregate utility as both the goal of legislation and the means of evaluating social progress. Natural rights theorists such as Locke acknowledged a role for government in the promotion of the common good but believed that preinstitutional natural rights constrain government actions, even if the government action increases aggregate social welfare. Although Bentham welcomed restrictions on property rights that enhanced social welfare, his utilitarian understanding of rights was not a significant departure from the moral individualism of the Lockean liberal tradition. Since utilitarian social welfare is merely the sum of individual pleasures minus pains, in Bentham's view there exists no separate "common good" that is distinct from the sum of the individual utilities that compose it.

Utilitarians' understanding of equality was also a departure from the natural rights tradition. For natural rights theorists, equality means equal respect for individual rights, and the extent of equality turns on the definition of what those rights are. For utilitarians, equality means equal consideration for each person's utility in the utilitarian calculus (Kymlicka 2002). Bentham argued that to evaluate the morality of a given action, one needed only to examine the intensity, duration, certainty, proximity, fecundity, and purity of an action's consequences (Crimmins 2017). The utilitarian principle of diminishing marginal utility implies that more equal distributions will tend to produce more utility, but equality per se has no independent value.

Edwin Chadwick's social reform work put Bentham's ideas into action. As a member of the 1832 Royal Commission into the Operation of the Poor Laws, Chadwick worked to transform poor relief in accordance with utilitarian principles. The Poor Law Amendment Act of 1834 incorporated many of his ideas, particularly those designed to improve the efficiency of the poor relief system by transferring the administration of relief to formal institutions. The act also limited relief to those deemed "deserving" of aid, curtailing public assistance for the able-bodied poor. Through a policy known as "less eligibility," the act intentionally stigmatized relief so that the poor would be discouraged from seeking it (Slack 1995).

Chadwick also pioneered the use of sanitary surveys to document and propose Benthamite solutions to public health problems. His 1842 *Report on the Sanitary Condition of the Labouring Population of Great Britain* proposed various engineering and administrative reforms designed to improve sanitary conditions in urban residential areas. The report also concluded that the overcrowded and low-quality housing conditions of the poor harmed the inhabitants' moral state.

Similar sanitary surveys conducted in mid-nineteenth-century New York provided ammunition for an organized attack on the American slum. Following outbreaks of cholera in Lower Manhattan that claimed over 5,000 lives, in 1843 a group of wealthy Protestant businessmen established the Association for Improving the Condition of the Poor (AICP) to address the problem of the slum. The AICP warned that unless conditions in the slums improved, the poor would "overrun the city as thieves and beggars—endanger public peace and the security of property and life—tax the community for their support, and entail upon it an inheritance of vice and pauperism" (Lubove 1962, 7). The AICP proposed reforms that ranged from utilitarian administrative and engineering reforms to "model tenements," which Roy Lubove (1962, 8) describes as tenements "built by the individual capitalist or company which voluntarily limited profits in favor of higher structural and sanitary standards than those found in the ordinary speculative tenement. Model tenements, sound investments rather than speculative adventures, might reap diminished profits, but investors would be rewarded by the pleasure of having served the poor."

John Griscom, a devout Quaker and medical doctor for the city's poor, who worked with the AICP, was inspired by Chadwick's report to lead a similar effort in New York. In *The Sanitary Conditions of the Laboring Population of New York* (1845), Griscom argued that the slum's filth, polluted air, and overcrowding harmed the moral fiber of the urban poor. Despite Griscom's equation of poor housing conditions with the "subjection of the tenantry to the merciless inflictions and extortions of the sub-landlord" (Foglesong 1986, 64), his proposed solutions did not address landlord exploitation. Instead, he recommended the appointment of a city health inspector and other administrative reforms, very much in line with Chadwick's earlier report.

Other US cities soon conducted similar sanitary surveys and reached comparable conclusions about the social costs of the slums. In Chicago, Oscar Coleman De Wolf led a tenement housing inspection campaign during the 1880s that called attention to the poor living conditions of slum dwellers, making a clear distinction between the tenement slum and the neighborhoods inhabited by owners of single-family detached homes. Health inspectors entered tenement dwellings without court orders, but they inspected single-family homes only at the request of physicians, occupants, or owners. Although De Wolf acknowledged that low wages and seasonal employment left workers unable to afford adequate housing, he did not support labor's demands for higher wages or shorter working hours, advocating instead for the construction of model tenements to alleviate workers' poor housing conditions (Garb 2003). In Boston, reformers characterized the slum as "a perfect hive of human beings . . . in many cases, huddled together like brutes, without regard to sex, or age, or sense of decency" (Vale 2000, 60). As in Chicago, Boston's reformers proposed model tenements to alleviate slum housing conditions. In 1871, Henry Bowditch established the Boston Co-operative Building Company, which sponsored the construction of small single-family homes for "applicants of good character, and of habits of neatness" (Vale 2000, 64).

Back in New York, the recommendations of the Council on Hygiene led to the creation of the Metropolitan Sanitary District and Board of Health of New York and, in 1867, the adoption of the nation's first tenement housing law (Foglesong 1986). The 1867 law and a revised 1879 version were largely viewed as ineffective because they permitted the construction of "dumbbell" tenements with poor external lighting and central air shafts that collected garbage and waste. The New York State Tenement House Act of 1901 perfected New York's regulatory apparatus, adding requirements that new tenements include sufficient lighting and ventilation, an open courtyard, indoor toilets, and adequate fire protection systems. Lawrence Veiller, secretary of the New York State Tenement House Commission (which he helped create) and previous secretary and director of the Tenement House Committee of the Charity Organization Society, played a key role in drafting and lobbying for the adoption of New York tenement housing regulations. The Tenement House Act of 1901 soon became a model for national housing reform. Veiller produced a model ordinance based on the New York law, and most state and local housing laws passed between 1901 and 1920 were based on the model ordinance (Lubove 1961).

While Veiller was more a pragmatist than a philosophically consistent utilitarian, the New York tenement house laws were a landmark achievement of utilitarian housing reform. Extensive empirical analysis and evaluation of the efficiency of alternative solutions supported the design and redesign of each tenement housing law. According to Veiller (1914, 77), "The question which every housing reformer must face is, what method will give the largest results with the least expenditure of energy and effort? It is largely a question of emphasis. The method which will return 90 per cent of results and not 10 per cent is obviously the method to follow." Housing reformers viewed tenement housing regulations as a way to maximize social benefits while minimizing social costs, where social costs included both the internal costs incurred by tenement housing dwellers and the external costs inflicted on society at large (Marcuse 1980; Friedman 1968).

American housing reformers appealed to "associationism" to provide a moral and psychological foundation for their utilitarian reforms. According to the doctrine of associationism, exposure to the external world of experience leaves a mental imprint that can elevate or degrade one's mental faculties and moral sensibilities (von Hoffman 1998a). Associationism provided the groundwork for a paternalistic and environmentally deterministic brand of utilitarianism that reaffirmed the republican belief in the home's civic function. Statistical surveys of overcrowded tenement housing conditions in large cities like New York, given life by muckraking journalists such as Jacob Riis, painted an image of slum housing that was in sharp contrast to the republican ideal of the single-family home. In *How the Other Half Lives*, Riis (1890, 2; italics in the original) attributes the majority of crimes against property and persons to slum inhabitants who "have either lost connection with home life, or never had any, or whose *homes had ceased to be sufficiently separate, decent, and desirable to afford what are regarded as ordinary wholesome influences of home and family.*" In contrast to the image of home as a refuge of privacy and a platform for the cultivation of civic virtue, American housing reformers saw the urban slum as a parasitic force, degrading the tenement dweller's moral fiber and infecting middle-class urban society (Friedman 1968).

The synergy between utilitarianism and republicanism helps to explain why early housing reformers rejected housing reform ideas that were filtering in from abroad. Members of the National Housing Association, founded by Lawrence Veiller with support from the Russell Sage Foundation, traveled abroad to learn about European collectivist housing strategies but returned unconvinced that such ideas would work in America. According to Veiller,

> In housing reform we need especially to beware of importations from across the sea, not because they are from across the sea—I hope no such provincial view of life controls us—but because the conditions which exist in the old-world countries are so totally different from those which prevail in America. . . . The methods which have been successful in Europe have been so because they have been suited to the conditions which exist there. To be successful here we should have

to engraft upon our civilization the governmental bureaucracy which we find in Europe. For these reasons the label "made in Germany" when attached to plans for housing reform should be viewed with caution. (Veiller 1914, 77)

Early American housing reformers interpreted American housing problems through the evolving American social meaning of housing. The owned single-family home on a detached lot was the physical manifestation of republican virtue, and the slum threatened the American ideals of individualism, economic independence, and self-reliance. According to Veiller,

> There is probably no country in the world where the individual detached house occupied by a single family, containing most of the comforts and conveniences of living, exists to the extent that it does in America. This is the normal type of home of the American wage-earner. The conditions which are found in the foreign colonies and slums of our large cities are exceptional and abnormal, symptoms of disease, not of health; conditions which of course must be dealt with. But we should not let their existence overshadow or cloud our vision with regard to the real conditions which exist. (Veiller 1914, 72)

Although Veiller saw the owned single-family detached home as an ideal housing type, he did not believe, as many in the nascent building and loan industry did, that homeownership provided the best solution to the tenement housing crisis. He saw the tenement housing problem as a more "serious social menace which threatens to overwhelm American institutions" and believed that "any effort toward considering more interesting and attractive forms of housing had to wait" until tenement housing conditions were improved (D. Mason 2004, 42). Veiller also objected to the promotion of low-income homeownership on utilitarian grounds. He observed that in cities where the working class owns their own homes, "sanitary authorities have the greatest difficulty meeting health needs, securing adequate appropriations, and enforcing higher standards" (D. Mason 2004, 42).

Progressivism and Zoning

Land-use zoning was the second significant regulatory approach to American housing reform to appear around the turn of the twentieth century. Many urban scholars tend to characterize zoning as an extension of earlier tenement housing reforms. To some extent, this is accurate. For example, Lawrence Veiller, the father of tenement housing regulations, was also an ardent advocate of zoning. The "balancing test," developed by progressive jurists Oliver Wendell Holmes and Louis Brandeis and later applied in *Pennsylvania Coal Co. v. Mahon* (1922) to evaluate the constitutionality of a regulatory restriction on subsurface mining, is a clear-cut application of utilitarian ethics. Despite these similarities, zoning emerged later, during a time when progressivism overshadowed utilitarianism as the intellectual foundation for urban reform. Progressives were more receptive to ideas from abroad, particularly from Germany, and their justifications for reform appealed to a new view of property and a collectivist conception of the common good.

By the early twentieth century, social and economic conditions were considerably different from the conditions prevailing during the initial years of the tenement housing reform movement. Although the plight of the unemployed worker during the late nineteenth century was dire, prices declined steadily from 1865 through 1896, increasing real wages for those able to find and secure work. Things changed during the early twentieth century, when the United States entered a period of economic prosperity but rising inflation. Between 1900 and 1914, real hourly wages remained stagnant as increases in the prices of goods and services offset nominal increases in wages (Hofstadter 1960).

According to Hofstadter (1960), the progressive movement arose to meet the urban consumer's demands for new forms of organization. As Walter Lippmann observed in 1914, "We hear a great deal about the class-consciousness of labor; my own observation is that in America to-day consumers'-consciousness is growing very much faster" (Lippmann 1914, 73). One object of middle-class scorn was the monopolist. Industrial monopolists enjoyed market power and exacerbated consumer status inequality through what Thorstein Veblen described as "conspicuous consumption," where "members of each stratum accept as their ideal of decency the scheme of life in vogue in the next higher stratum, and bend their energies to live up to that ideal" (Veblen 1912 [1899], 84). At the same time, middle-class consumers criticized labor unions for fomenting urban unrest and political corruption. Urban consumers were stuck in the middle, searching for new voices who could address their concerns.

Progressives answered the call, appealing to the common good to justify reforms on behalf of urban consumers. By the early 1900s, the target of urban reformers' scorn had evolved from the slum to the problem of urban congestion more broadly. According to Florence Kelley, organizer of the

New York Committee on Congestion of Population (CCP), "When people are crowded, poverty, tuberculosis and crime arise among them" (Kelley 1906, 81). Progressive urban reformers such as Kelley viewed spatial congestion as the by-product of the concentration of land ownership, just as progressive economists blamed economic inequality on the concentration of financial capital. Kelley went so far as to criticize other housing reformers who ignored the "land problem" (Marsh 1953, 30).

Within this context, American land-use zoning was born. In contrast to the first generation of housing reformers, who appealed to American exceptionalism to justify property-use restrictions, progressive zoning reformers welcomed ideas from abroad, particularly those from the late nineteenth-century German intellectual tradition that appealed to historical contingency; an organic view of society; scientific experimentation; a strong role for the state; and a positive, instrumental, and social conception of rights. Late nineteenth-century German intellectuals welcomed British utilitarians' rejection of natural rights but criticized the British liberal affinity for laissez-faire economics. For American progressives trained in the German tradition, the institutional economists from the German historical school (Adolph Wagner, Gustav Schmoller, Karl Knies, and Johannes Conrad) and the jurists from the German historical school of jurisprudence (Gustav von Hugo and Friedrich Carl von Savigny) were particularly influential. Many American economists who would later become leaders in the progressive movement, including John Commons, Richard T. Ely, Edwin R. A. Seligman, and Simon Patten, traveled abroad to receive their training from these and other German professors teaching at the universities of Halle, Berlin, and Heidelberg (Rodgers 1998; Schafer 2000; Leonard 2005).

In 1885, Ely and Seligman founded the American Economic Association (AEA). In private correspondence, Ely stated that "the idea of the AEA is to accomplish in America what the Verein für Socialpolitik has done in Germany" (Rodgers 1998, 102). The founders of the AEA saw the new profession of economics as providing service to a muscular reformist state. As stated in the opening line of the AEA Constitution, "We regard the state as an agency whose positive assistance is one of the indispensable conditions of human progress" (Ely 1886, 35). Ely also wanted to include a statement that "the doctrine of laissez-faire is unsafe in politics and unsound in morals," but not all founding members of the AEA shared his views (Rodgers 1998, 102).

Several leaders in the American zoning reform movement had either been educated in German universities or been influenced by German historicist thinking. Benjamin Marsh, the first executive secretary of the New York CCP, studied with Simon Patten at the University of Pennsylvania. Patten had earlier convinced Richard T. Ely to enroll in Johannes Conrad's economics course at the University of Halle, an experience that convinced Ely to switch from philosophy to economics (Rodgers 1998). Rexford Tugwell, planner and head of the Resettlement Administration during the New Deal, was also a student of Patten. Edwin R. A. Seligman, a German-trained economist and professor at Columbia University, was a member of the CCP's executive committee. For Seligman, "unrestricted individualism" and the "unaided and unregulated sway of private competition" were to blame for urban congestion, and German-style planning offered the best solution to the congestion problem (Peterson 2009, 126). Ernst Freund, author of the classic text *The Police Power* (1904), which zoning advocates widely cited to defend the constitutionality of zoning, was educated in the German historical school of jurisprudence at the universities of Berlin and Heidelberg (Schafer 2000). The attendance roll for the first National Conference on City Planning and Congestion was a who's who list of American progressives with degrees from German universities (Kantor 1974).

Two important ideas borrowed from the German tradition established the intellectual foundation on which American zoning was built: (1) the idea that property rights are not natural or prepolitical but are socially and historically contingent "bundles" of rights created and defined by the state, and (2) the idea that the concept of and justification for private property cannot be understood without reference to the common good.

The Unbundling of Property
German institutional economists viewed rights not as eternal gifts from God but as historical creations that evolved in response to social contingencies. Richard T. Ely (1914, 165) held that "private property is established and maintained for social purposes." He explicitly rejected Locke's assertion that individuals' rights to own private property could be derived from their natural rights of self-ownership, "so we cannot trace an absolute right of private property to the absolute right over one's person, because on the one hand we may have to give our life for the general welfare, and on the other hand we must not take it" (Ely 1914, 176). According to John Dewey,

who received his PhD from Johns Hopkins University under the tutelage of German-trained Hegelian philosopher George Sylvester Morris, natural rights theory "blinded the eyes of liberals to the fact that their own special interpretation of liberty, individuality and intelligence were themselves historically conditioned, and were relevant only to their own time. They put forward their ideas as immutable truths good at all times and places; they had no idea of historic relativity" (Pestritto and Atto 2008, 5). Progressive reformers and legal realists argued that legal principles do not embody static ideals but are dynamic, contextual, and responsive to the needs of society. In *Muller v. Oregon* (1908), Louis Brandeis applied this reasoning to defend a state-imposed limit on the working hours of women factory workers. He argued that the unique health needs of women justified their disparate treatment under the law (Ely 1998).

The view that property rights are social creations opened the door for a more significant role for the government in defining, protecting, and even limiting private property rights. Freund (1904, iii) defined the state's police power as "the power of promoting the public welfare by restraining and regulating the use of liberty and property." In true German historicist fashion, Freund agreed with Veiller that laws appropriate for Germany might not be suitable for the unique circumstances found in America. Freund argued that the police power should be understood "not as a fixed quantity, but as the expression of social, economic and political conditions. As long as these conditions vary, the police power must continue to be elastic, i.e. capable of development" (Freund 1904, 3). Given that laissez-faire constitutionalism defined the early twentieth-century American legal context, Freund concluded that "government powers ought not to run very far ahead of that conservative sentiment which is represented by the courts" (Schafer 2000, 135). New York attorney Edward M. Bassett and political scientist Robert H. Whitten took the same approach as they crafted the legal arguments supporting New York's landmark 1916 comprehensive zoning law. Bassett and Whitten's careful attention to the constitutional constraints on state regulatory power "made it easier for judges to accept their innovations by providing the jurisprudential analogies necessary to make zoning seem like a familiar, legitimate regulatory activity" (Revell 1999, 56).

Other progressives offered a more expansive interpretation of the government's power to not only restrain property use but also define the meaning of property. Progressives argued that an owner's property rights are best understood as "bundles" of rights. The state's role was to define those bundles, adding or subtracting elements from the bundle to ensure that the institution of property served the common good. As progressive economist John R. Commons wrote, property is "not a single absolute right, but a bundle of rights. The different rights which compose it may be distributed among individuals and society" (Commons 1893, 92).[5] Wesley Hohfeld (1919) contributed to this project by developing a structural system of legal relations tying claims of right to their corollary duties. He argued that all legal incidents could be defined in terms of privileges, claim rights, powers, immunities, or some combination of these four, with many rights having a complex internal structure.

According to Eric Claeys (2004), zoning marked a transition from an exclusion-based regime of land-use regulation typical of the tenement housing regulation era to a governance-based regime. Henry Smith (2004, 973) defines an exclusion property regime as one that "grants owners a gatekeeper right that protects the owners' interest in a wide and indefinite class of uses without the need ever to delineate—perhaps even to identify—those uses at all." Tenement housing regulations prohibited property owners from taking actions that compromised the health and safety of occupants. Still, owners had wide latitude over property use decisions within the constraints established by minimum property standards. Progressive zoning, on the other hand, delineated "a list of use rights holding between all potential pairwise combinations of persons with respect to any (at least heretofore) conceivable activity that has any impact on anyone" (Smith 2004, 972–973). Zoning transferred the individual property owner's previously unencumbered rights over property use to local political bodies and zoning commissions, who used their powers to define broad categories of uses that would be prohibited from certain zones and in some cases from the community at large.

The bundle-of-rights conception of property deconstructed property rights, and the new governance conception of property defined how the various sticks in the bundle were to be reassembled to enhance community welfare. By creating a command-and-control form of land-use regulation that empowered local administrative and political bodies to dictate community land-use goals, zoning marked a transition toward a more substantial collective role in property use (Claeys 2004). As described in the next section, this transfer of power often had negative consequences for low-income renters and people of color.

Property and the Common Good

Progressives and utilitarians both believed that property rights should promote the common good, but progressives' definition of the common good appealed to an image of society that was a stark contrast with the utilitarians' collection of atomistic individuals. Institutional economists trained in the German tradition understood society as an organism whose purpose is growth and survival. Herbert Croly described American society as an "enlarged individual." John Commons believed that individuals were organs "bound up in the social organism," which was "a living thing, actuated, like all the higher creatures, by the instinct for self-preservation." Walter Rauschenbusch argued that the aim of economic reform was not a matter of saving individuals "but of saving the social organism" (Leonard 2016, 101). Early American city planners appealed to these same organic metaphors. Frederick Law Olmstead Jr. described city planning as "a growing appreciation of a city's organic unity, of the interdependence of its diverse elements" (Akimoto 2009, 458). Frederic Howe (1913, 186) described the planning profession as one that "treats the city as a unit, as an organic whole."

A Darwinian view of social progress informed progressives' embrace of the society-as-organism metaphor. Both defenders and detractors of laissez-faire economics looked to Charles Darwin to support their views. Whereas laissez-faire apologists such as Herbert Spencer and William Graham Sumner interpreted Darwin as implying that economic agents deserved the profits they earned because they were the fittest to survive in the marketplace, progressives looked to Darwin to defend "artificial," rather than natural, selection. Social biologist Lester Frank Ward appealed to the selective breeding of plants and animals to argue that the administrative state should guide social change by manipulating the process of human evolution. Herbert Croly believed that the state had a responsibility to "interfere on behalf of the really fittest." The purpose of legislation was to improve "the methods whereby men and women are bred" (Leonard 2016, 104).

Nowhere was the society-as-organism metaphor stronger than among University of Chicago sociologists, who developed the human ecology approach to sociology during the 1920s. For Robert Park, two different social processes operated at different scales to give order to urban life. Neighborhood life was organized according to symbolic and cooperative ties, while, at the city level, separate communities interacted through competition and differentiation. Park's student Roderick McKenzie developed these ideas further, arguing that spatial economic competition resulted in the most successful groups occupying the most favored locations within the city. Based on these ideas, Ernest Burgess developed a model of urban growth that explained urban agglomeration and differentiation in terms of competition over the most desirable spaces within the city, producing "concentric zones" of differentiated land uses within cities. University of Chicago economist Homer Hoyt developed a "sector model" of urban growth that modified and extended Ernest Burgess's model to account for outward urban expansion (Gottdiener, Hutchison, and Ryan 2014).[6]

Progressives' organic conception of society had implications for their understanding of individual liberty and its relation to the common good. Most progressives rejected the negative conception of liberty advanced by Lockean liberals, arguing instead that individuals could be free from government interference but still lack the resources to live purposeful lives.[7] Most progressives argued that the appropriate role for the state was not simply to step aside but rather to create the conditions that fostered the cultivation of positive liberty.

For American progressives who were influenced by Thomas Hill Green, Leonard T. Hobhouse, John A. Hobson, and others from the British "new liberal" tradition, positive liberty meant individual self-development through the pursuit of the common good (Freeden 1978). For Green, the common good was a relational concept, and free actions were those taken by individuals acting to develop their individual goods in concert with others. Green understood rights as instrumental means of promoting the general welfare and rejected the idea that rights had preemptive authority over state actions. For Green, the common good was not reducible to the sum of individual goods, because the common good was a shared ideal that justified individual rights (Weinstein 2007).

The German institutionalists also appealed to a positive conception of liberty, but their view of society as having a will and telos that were independent of and prior to the individual pointed to a potential conflict between individual and collective freedom. Freund, for example, saw the police power as a collective power that conflicted with individuals' rights of due process. In the face of conflicts between individual and collective positive freedom, many German institutionalists argued that individuals should renounce their individual desires and beliefs and submit to the will of the collective. Freund, while influenced by this tradition, was reluctant to go this far, advocating instead for a more conservative interpretation of the police power. Freund was concerned not with motivating individuals to submit to the collective will but with narrowly tailoring the scope of police powers to promote collective health, safety, and welfare (Schafer 2000).

Even though progressives appealed to the common good to justify reform proposals, they rarely defined the common good in terms of the good for all humanity. Woodrow Wilson and Herbert Croly appealed to a nationalistic conception of the common good, while Howe, Ely, and Albert Shaw advanced a localized conception of the common good. Within cities, progressive planners also often prioritized the collective interests of those who owned residential property and those from certain socioeconomic groups. When progressives defined the common good narrowly in this way, proposals for reform had an exclusionary character.

Land-use zoning fostered exclusion by elevating the ideal of the owned single-family detached home, enhancing the collective value of owned homes, and insulating homeowners from invasion by people and property uses deemed inferior. New York City's 1916 comprehensive zoning law, for example, was designed in part to "enhance the value of the land of the city and conserve the value of the buildings" (Foglesong 1986, 220). In *Village of Euclid v. Ambler Realty Company* (1926), the Supreme Court decision that established the constitutionality of zoning, Justice George Sutherland supported the division of property into districts in part because property division enhanced the collective value of residential property (Ely 1998). According to Garrett Power (1989, 7), "Zoning, when viewed as a technique for suppressing nuisances, turned utilitarianism inside out; it sought the greatest good for the fewest and richest in number." For these reasons, it should come as no surprise that some of the strongest advocates for zoning, such as Lawrence Veiller and Richard T. Ely, later played important roles in the debates leading to the adoption of federal homeownership legislation (Weiss 1989).

Progressives also relied on zoning to exclude certain socioeconomic groups from neighborhoods and entire communities. Before 1917, when the practice was ruled unconstitutional in *Buchanan v. Warley*, progressive planners relied on zoning and other land-use restrictions to promote the segregation of cities by race and ethnicity. In the late nineteenth century, several California cities adopted regulations designed to contain the spread of laundries owned by Chinese immigrants. In 1910, Baltimore mayor J. Barry Mahool, an advocate of various progressive reforms, enacted the nation's first citywide racial zoning ordinance (Power 1983).[8] The southern cities of Richmond, Atlanta, Greenville, Winston-Salem, Birmingham, and Louisville soon followed the exclusionary path established by Baltimore (Silver 1997). Even after explicit racial zoning was ruled unconstitutional, cities continued to use zoning and other land-use restrictions to perpetuate racial segregation and exclusion, often through indirect means that obscured the racist motivations underlying racially neutral policies (Silver 1997; Rothstein 2017).

Progressives often defended racist and xenophobic policies by appealing to the scientific method's cover of objectivity. For social Darwinists drawn to the idea of artificial selection, the state's role was to promote human development through the selection of and support for those with the most desirable racial and ethnic characteristics, with native-born whites placed atop the social hierarchy. Several progressive economists drawn to this idea called for race-based immigration restrictions to forestall "race suicide." Edward Ross, a founding member of the AEA, feared a time when "the higher race quietly and unmurmuringly eliminates itself rather than endure individually the bitter competition it has failed to ward off by collective action" (Leonard 2005, 209).

Progressives also developed scientific classification methods to inform the design of exclusionary urban policies. Richard T. Ely (1917, 27) observed that urban land "needs extensive classification in order to frame wise urban land policies." Harland Bartholomew developed scientific land classification and allocation methods that he applied to the design of land-use zoning ordinances in communities across the nation (Akimoto 2009). According to Bartholomew, a goal of the 1919 St. Louis zoning ordinance was to prevent movement into "finer residential districts . . . by colored people." He observed that without a zoning law, neighborhoods would fall into decline, and homes would either become "vacant or occupied by colored people" (Rothstein 2017, 1919). As discussed in chapter 4, Homer Hoyt developed a method that the Federal Housing Administration employed to reinforce racial and ethnic housing market inequalities by institutionalizing whites' reluctance to purchase homes in minority-majority neighborhoods (Light 2011). W. E. B. Du Bois was one of the rare progressives to call for reforms that were designed to reduce the racial inequalities that he documented in his social science investigations. On the first page of his landmark study *The Philadelphia Negro* (2007 [1899]), Du Bois attributes the plight of Black Philadelphians to the same patterns of racial segregation that other progressives sought to reinforce.

Land-use zoning combined all these elements—a bundle-of-rights conception of private property, an organic conception of the social division of labor, the spatial separation of social groups and economic functions deemed incompatible, and the empirical classification of urban land into different functional types—to carve urban space into zones that maximized the perceived organic unity of land utilization. The Frankfurt Zoning Act of 1891 was the first modern application of these ideas, and American planners trained in Germany or who had visited Germany on international excursions were particularly taken by the Frankfurt approach (Hirt 2013). When zoning appeared in the United States, it was transformed with a distinctly American twist. Unlike most European ordinances, US zoning laws separated residential districts according to exclusive use categories and within those districts designated space solely for the single-family detached home (Hirt 2013). Thus, just as tenement housing reformers fused utilitarianism with republicanism to elevate tenement homes to a level of quality deemed compatible with civilized American life, appealing to the ideal of the single-family home as a model of how that life should be lived, American zoning reformers fused progressivism and German institutionalism with republicanism to create organically unified single-family districts that were spatially isolated from threats to American ways of living.

The Death and Resurrection of Henry George

Following Henry George's failed mayoral bid, he largely disappeared from the housing reform movement, but his ideas were later resurrected as old wine in new bottles, stripped of their natural rights foundations and repackaged under the auspices of progressivism. The story of the evolution of George's ideas provides additional insights into the ideological basis of early twentieth-century housing and land-use reforms.

On the eve of the twentieth century, Henry George's single-tax idea was uniquely positioned to update land reformers' natural rights ideology for a new urban era, but a series of events stood in the way of efforts to implement the single tax. Labor's initial support for the single-tax idea as a solution to the housing crisis was more strongly tied to the personality of Henry George than to the idea itself, and organized labor's advocacy on behalf of the single tax waned after George's death. Lawrence Veiller saw tax reform as part of the "postgraduate" phase of housing reform, to be pursued only after the adoption and implementation of regulations governing building quality (Veiller 1914). Veiller's close alliance with real estate interests, who were adamantly opposed to any form of property taxation, also shaped his views of the single tax (Foglesong 1986).

Another source of conflict came from the courts. In 1892, a single tax enacted in Hyattsville, Maryland, was overturned by the Maryland Court of Appeals in *Wells v. Commissioners of Hyattsville* (1893). Representative James Maguire of California proposed a national land tax, but the US Congress rejected the measure (Young 1916). In *Pollock v. Farmers' Loan & Trust Co.* (1895), the Supreme Court invalidated an income tax designed to offset lost tariff revenue, ruling it to be a direct tax that the Constitution required be apportioned among the states according to their populations (Ely 1998). In addition to temporarily halting any discussion of the income tax until the adoption of the Sixteenth Amendment, *Pollock* also likely put the brakes on any further discussion of anything resembling a national land tax.

Several early twentieth-century New York progressives proposed reforms similar to the single tax but never managed to successfully implement their ideas. As mentioned, by the early 1900s, the concern with the slum had morphed into a concern for urban congestion more broadly. Florence Kelley, who earlier had worked to address women's working conditions in the factories of Lower Manhattan, assembled a group of reformers to establish the CCP. In 1907, Benjamin Marsh became the committee's executive secretary. Marsh had earlier been captivated by Simon Patten's progressive economics and Henry George's single tax and sought to apply Georgist solutions to the problem of urban congestion.

Others in the New York housing movement were less receptive to George's ideas. Robert De Forest, who was instrumental in the adoption of New York's tenement housing laws, warned Marsh, "If you touch the land problem in New York, you probably won't last here two years" (Marsh 1953, 35). Marsh did not drop his obsession with the single tax. Later, as a member of a city commission established to address the congestion issue, Marsh pushed for a land tax. Fellow progressive Frederic Howe initially supported Marsh, stating that "the housing question is the land question" and that "an ounce of land taxation will do more than a pound of regulation" (Kantor 1974, 425). While the commission's report did not go so far as to propose a single tax, it recommended similar measures, and this alone was enough to scare off those closely aligned with real estate interests. Leaders of the nascent city planning profession were also critical, including Charles Mulford Robinson, who criticized Marsh's push for a "radical change in methods of taxation" (Kantor 1974, 426). Despite writing an early text on city planning and helping to establish the first National Conference on City Planning and Congestion, Marsh soon became marginalized from the American city planning movement. After the first National Conference on City Planning and Congestion, Veiller and De Forest formed a separate National Housing Association, and the word "congestion" (and with it the emphasis on the single tax as a solution to congestion) disappeared from the subsequent National Conference on City Planning. The city planning profession soon placed more emphasis on technical analysis and professionalization, dropping their attention to social problems related to housing until the 1960s. With this new emphasis, zoning, rather than the single tax, became the solution of choice for city planners (Kantor 1974).

Professional economists, including many progressive founders of the AEA, such as Francis A. Walker, Edwin R. A. Seligman, Richard T. Ely, and John Commons, were also resistant to George's ideas. Some were critical of the natural rights foundation of George's ideas, while others expressed reservations about his single-tax proposal. Seligman devoted an entire chapter of his book on taxation to refuting the single tax. John Bates Clark, one of the founders of the marginalist revolution in neoclassical economics, went so far as to deny that land was a distinctive factor of production that deserved any special emphasis in economic analysis (Gaffney and Harrison 1994).

George's ideas eventually filtered into the American municipal reform movement. As mayor of Cleveland from 1901 to 1909, Tom Johnson championed George's single-tax proposal and transformed it into a broad progressive reform platform that included municipal ownership of streetcars and electric power, acquisition of lakefront property for public spaces, and a successful campaign to secure "home rule" (the antithesis of Dillon's Rule) for Ohio's cities (Miller 2010). Single-tax advocates were active throughout Washington, Oregon, and Colorado. Several Pennsylvania cities adopted a variation on the single tax known as "split-rate" taxation, taxing land at a higher rate than buildings, and single-tax communities appeared in Arden, Delaware, and Fairhope, Alabama (Young 1916).[9]

George's ideas were influential abroad and later returned to the United States in a slightly modified form. In the 1880s, through sponsorships from

New York's Irish working class, George took several trips to Great Britain and Ireland. Irish nationalists appealed to George's ideas to attack landlords and advocate for stronger Irish representation in Parliament. George also found a receptive audience among members of the socialist Fabian Society, particularly Edwin Pease, Sidney Webb, and George Bernard Shaw. Thomas Hill Green and Leonard T. Hobhouse fused Fabianism and liberalism to create British new liberalism. Chancellor of the Exchequer David Lloyd George incorporated Henry George's ideas into his 1909 "people's budget," which relied on a land tax to fund social welfare programs (Lough 2013).

Several single-tax communities appeared in Europe, Australia, and Asia. In Germany, Adolf Damaschke established the Union of German Land Reformers, which advocated for a variation on the single tax. Frankfurt applied an "increment tax" to the unearned incremental increase in land values between sales. Hundreds of other German cities and counties soon followed suit with the adoption of similar tax policies, and in 1911 the German Reich briefly introduced an increment tax as a replacement for certain state taxes (Bryson 2011; Ladd 1990). Henry George inspired Ebeneezer Howard's plans for English garden cities, and the transnational garden city movement influenced several American New Deal initiatives (Rodgers 1998). Later in the twentieth century, George's ideas morphed again into the community land trust movement.

Although the American radical land reform tradition died with Henry George, the idea that the community should recapture socially created value was consistent with progressive zoning advocates' desire to organize land uses to promote the common good. Zoning was less objectionable to real estate interests and lacked the populist political baggage attached to the single tax. The courts also looked more favorably on zoning and tenement housing regulations because they were justifiable under the police power doctrine and not seen as purely redistributive measures.

Explaining the Demise of Right-Based Housing Reform

American progressive reformers set out to redefine private property and reform property-based institutions to promote the common good. In practice, most reformers pursued a conservative regulatory approach to reform, using the state's police powers to transfer particular sticks in the property rights bundle to government bodies, thereby collectivizing the right to exclude. Early American housing reformers studied European collectivist housing strategies but rarely strayed from the path of American exceptionalism.

With the rise in collective authority over land-use decisions came the demise of the previous generation's right-based approach to social reform. Around the turn of the century, the most vocal supporters of expanded rights for the urban poor were women activists and settlement house workers. Sophonisba Breckinridge, a professor at the Chicago School of Civics and Philanthropy, argued that to fulfill the "critical right" of citizenship, the Black American must be able to "claim a decent home for his family in a respectable neighborhood and at a reasonable rental" (Argersinger 2010, 795). This tradition of "progressive maternalism" ultimately did not have the same level of influence on housing and land-use reform, partly because progressive maternalists were less interested in deferring to the demands of property owners (Argersinger 2010). Although male reformers ostensibly sought to improve the housing conditions of the poor and working class, their reforms failed to expand access to decent, low-cost housing. Instead, they prioritized the minimization of social costs, the containment of communities of color, and the enhancement of urban property values (Marcuse 1980).

Why did a reform movement that was so critical of laissez-faire capitalism ultimately leave existing institutions of property intact without seeking to expand tenants' rights to property and decent housing? One answer is that American progressive reformers were, in the end, pragmatists and not ideologues, so they adopted tools from home and abroad that were best suited to addressing American housing problems. Reformers such as Veiller and Freund did not seek to abandon private property but instead sought to retool private property institutions to address new urban social problems. While this may be an accurate description of some reformers, others, such as Frederick Howe and Frederick Law Olmsted, appealed to a utopian image of the good city to justify their reforms.

Richard Foglesong (1986) argues that America's conservative regulatory approach to housing reform satisfied capitalists' political and ideological interests in social control without fundamentally disrupting the property-based institutions that enabled capital accumulation. According to Foglesong (1986), American housing reformers did not challenge the prevailing laissez-faire, free-market ideology of the times but instead sought reforms that were legally justifiable within that framework. While this is true of reformers such as Ernst Freund and Lawrence Veiller, who worked within the framework of the prevailing interpretation of the US Constitution, others, such as Richard T. Ely and Frederic Howe, sought to upend laissez-faire individualism and fundamentally reform the institutions of private property to promote the common good. Ultimately, Foglesong's explanation overplays the role of capitalists in shaping the character of reform without adequately accounting for the role played by the urban reformers themselves.

Most accounts of the early American housing reform movement also fail to adequately explain labor's limited role in it. Ira Katznelson (1981) argues that most American labor organizations prioritized concerns for working and workplace conditions over housing issues. As the discussion in chapter 2 illustrates, this argument ignores nineteenth-century labor organizations' support for expanded tenants' rights and land reform. A more likely explanation for labor's limited influence on the late nineteenth-century housing movement is that labor was highly fragmented and lacked the support of an organized socialist movement. In contrast to Europe, where capitalists sought to reproduce labor power by responding to workers' demands for collective forms of consumption (Castells 1979), the flow of immigrants to the United States during the late nineteenth century reduced the pressure on capitalists to bend to the demands of the working class. Things changed during the early twentieth century, as immigration dropped off considerably and labor became more organized. Still, even during this period, the relationship between labor and housing movements was often more contentious than conciliatory.

Even if we accept some role for labor, the early American housing reform movement was never really a working-class movement. Hofstadter (1960) convincingly argues that the constituency for urban reform was not the disenfranchised worker but rather the middle-class American native who had recently migrated to the city for professional employment. For these new urban professionals, who still held firmly to rural American republican values, the slums were a concern because they threatened deeply held American cultural values. Furthermore, urban reformers often viewed organized labor as more of a threat than an ally. The violence associated with the Haymarket riot, Homestead strike, and Pullman strike caused middle-class professionals to fear, not bond in solidarity with, the urban working class. Progressive reformers were also more interested in breaking up the political patronage systems that benefited urban immigrant workers than in organizing on their behalf (Hofstadter 1960).[10]

Sonia Hirt (2014) provides a cultural explanation that accounts for the power of the ideal of the owned single-family detached home. She argues that "zoning ultimately gained legitimacy because its advocates presented it as a mechanism that was deeply embedded in the noble American traditions of political, economic, and spatial individualism" (Hirt 2014, 134). Her argument is consistent with Walzer's (1983) proposition that societal conceptions of distributive justice reflect the social meaning of the good being distributed. Housing reform strategies that were out of step with the prevailing social meaning of housing were difficult to sell to the different constituencies competing in the space of ideas.

An understanding of the evolving social meaning of American housing casts the early housing reform movement in a different light. Both tenement housing and zoning reformers appealed to an ideal American housing type—the owned single-family detached home—to justify a variety of reforms that protected the ideal while demonizing housing types deemed inferior, such as the multistory rental tenement building. As a symbol, the owned single-family detached home flexibly accommodated the values embedded in America's liberal and republican political traditions. It embodied America's liberal love of privacy while at the same time providing a connection to republican civic virtues.

By the late nineteenth century, the ideal of the owned single-family detached home had evolved considerably from the frontier home revered by American land reformers. With the rise of wage labor and the separation of home from work, the home evolved from a site of production into a site of consumption. Whereas land reformers sought to address the alienation of the urban worker by returning the worker to home-based production and restoring Lockean self-ownership, tenement housing reformers sought to improve the quality of life of the working poor in the places where they lived. Veiller was especially critical of efforts to address urban problems by depopulating the city: "In a city where the children of the poor were dying from typhoid because of impure milk, I think we should feel that it was trifling with a serious problem if it were urged that nothing could be done through legislation but that the only way to insure a better milk supply was to encourage the people to move to the country where they could have their own cows and thus insure the right kind of supply for their children" (Veiller 1914, 76).

The American home, which had earlier been viewed as a private sphere to be protected from government intrusion, had become a public concern by the late nineteenth century, thanks in large part to the work of muckraking journalists such as Jacob Riis. During the same period, Samuel Warren and Louis Brandeis (1890) made the case for a right to privacy, but they understood this right as a personal right, ignoring the home's role in securing the right to privacy (Igo 2018). As E. L. Godkin observed, privacy is "a distinctly modern product, one of the luxuries of civilization, which is not only unsought for but unknown in primitive or barbarous societies" (Godkin 1890, 12). The courts expanded legal protections for personal and familial privacy over the course of the twentieth century but failed to recognize a public duty to provide private spaces for the exercise of privacy rights.

As the legal concern for privacy shifted from the home to the person, the privacy provided by the home came to be viewed as a virtue to be promoted through the establishment of minimum property standards. Tenement housing reformers' primary concern with the slum was that it caused overcrowding and robbed people of the virtues cultivated by privacy. The shift away from the earlier generation's emphasis on rights shaped the solutions that tenement housing reformers considered. Rather than view the lack of privacy in the slums as a right to be more equally protected or more widely distributed, tenement housing reformers looked to restrictions on private property to guarantee that homes provided enough privacy to cultivate civic virtue.

These three changes in the social meaning of home—the spatial separation of work and home, the increased attention to housing's consumption value, and the publicity of housing—limited the rhetorical value of natural rights language while at the same time increasing the utility of republican appeals to civic virtue. Once the reality of wage labor was accepted, Lockean appeals to self-ownership and the unification of land and labor appeared anachronistic. With the abandonment of the ideal of home as a site of production, the home became a thing to be consumed, and private consumption took on a public dimension. Homeowners engaged in conspicuous consumption to signal their relative social status, and reformers sought to cultivate civic virtue by securing a minimum level of privacy in working-class homes.

The republican conception of home complemented utilitarian and progressive ideologies. Republicans and utilitarians both viewed property rules as instrumental means of achieving collective ends. For republicans, the ends were self-governance and republican liberty, while for utilitarians the ends were defined in terms of aggregate utility. Progressivism was also consistent with the republican tradition, once republicanism was stripped of its natural rights foundations. Echoing James Harrington, progressives argued that property rights embodied social conventions about the use of land that were legitimized and enforced by the state. Both Veiller and Freund contextualized their justifications for reforms by appealing to a historicist understanding of private property's role in American society.

The idea of the common good also played an important role for both progressives and republicans, even though each interpreted the obligation to promote the common good in different ways. The American founders sought to promote the common good through checks and balances on the exercise of government power and strong protections for individual rights. Nineteenth-century liberal-republican land reformers appealed to the civic virtues of home to promote an egalitarian distribution of owner-occupied housing. For progressives, the common good was an organic thing in and of itself, defined through citizens' collective engagement with each other, and the home was central to this engagement. As the social meaning of the American home evolved, republicanism survived, but liberalism and the natural rights tradition fell by the wayside, carving a path for utilitarian and progressive approaches to housing reform.

4 Modern Housing and the Homeownership Republic

> Modern housing means complete new communities planned entirely from the point of view of fullest *usefulness* and long time amenity—instead of chaotic subdivision and the erection of dwellings designed only to bring quick speculative profits. It means that rentals must be geared to the capacity to pay and not to the "market." It means that a decent dwelling is not a reward withheld for the successful, but a fundamental right to which every citizen is entitled, the provision of which becomes a responsibility of government.
>
> —Catherine Bauer, quoted in Carol Aronovici,
>   *America Can't Have Housing* (1934, 21; italics in the original)

In the 1930s, a new coalition of housing advocates influenced by the previous generation's progressive ideals called for the creation of a new federal government housing program, but this coalition faced opposition from conservative politicians and real estate interests who opposed adding homebuilding to the federal government's portfolio of responsibilities. An expansive new "two-tier" federal housing policy apparatus emerged from the ideological and political compromises among these constituencies.[1] To assist low-income renters, the federal government established new programs to support the construction and management of public housing, and for middle- and high-income homeowners, the federal government created a new safety net to insure mortgages and provide liquidity to the savings and loan industry. These new housing programs were part of President Franklin D. Roosevelt's larger New Deal program, which blended right-based liberalism with progressives' pragmatism and consumerism. Roosevelt proposed a vision of the welfare state that transformed housing into one of the basic entitlements of American citizenship, but the federal housing policy apparatus that he created failed to realize its full potential. By the 1950s, New Deal–era housing programs had established the foundation of a new homeownership republic that expanded suburban housing opportunities while simultaneously denying those opportunities to people of color.

The New Deal–era two-tier federal housing policy apparatus expanded during the 1960s, but by this time many had become disillusioned by the federal government's failure to act on its 1949 goal of housing every American family (42 U.S.C. § 1441). New federal programs designed to decentralize control over community development activities paradoxically spurred new grassroots right-based housing movements that opposed strong federal oversight of housing construction in low-income areas and communities of color. This chapter examines these developments, tracing the arc of housing justice from the New Deal era through the end of the 1960s.

The New Deal–Era Federal Housing Policy Apparatus

Except for two federally funded commissions appointed to investigate slum conditions in large US cities, the federal government played virtually no role in housing provision until World War I, when Congress addressed wartime housing shortages by chartering two corporations—the US Housing Corporation and the Emergency Fleet Corporation—to construct housing for wartime workers. Following the war, a new generation of advocates began to call for a more permanent government role in housing provision, with labor advocates proposing Georgist solutions and local officials calling for the extension of wartime-era emergency rent controls (McDonnell 1957). Edith Elmer Wood, an economist and influential advocate for a stronger federal government role in housing provision, criticized these solutions. She characterized the single tax as "contrary to our habits" (Wood 1931, 153) and rent controls as "the most radical interference with the rights of private property of any housing measure adopted outside of Soviet Russia" (Wood 1931, 95). She also criticized regulatory housing solutions, claiming that a restrictive regulation "may forbid the bad house, but it does not provide the good one" (Radford 1996, 31), and viewed model tenements as untenable on a large scale because "the combined requirements of sanitation and cheapness leave so small a margin of profit that capital is not attracted to such a proposition on a business basis" (Radford 1996, 36). On this latter point, Wood was correct. From 1895 until 1914, the cost of residential construction increased by 50 percent, compared to a 20 percent increase in consumer prices, because of rising labor and material costs and restrictive regulation (Radford 1996). Given the undesirability of the alternatives, Wood was among the first to call for a more substantial federal government role in the provision of housing.

During the decade following World War I, federal officials largely abandoned the idea of large-scale government-supported housing provision, instead devoting energy to various public relations campaigns designed to promote homeownership. In 1919, the US Department of Labor joined forces with the National Association of Real Estate Boards' (NAREB) Own Your Own Home campaign. The campaign distributed promotional pamphlets, newspaper ads, buttons, banners, and posters that extolled the republican virtues of homeownership and celebrated homeowners as patriots in the battle against Bolshevism (Vale 2007). Herbert Hoover, who served as secretary of commerce from 1921 to 1928 before becoming president, picked up the homeownership mantle and elevated it to a cabinet-level policy priority. At the request of Marie Meloney, editor of the women's interest periodical *The Delineator*, Hoover presided over the Better Homes in America campaign, which promoted homeownership through an extensive network of more than 7,000 local Better Homes committees around the country that sponsored home improvement contests, demonstrations of remodeling and construction techniques, and lectures on the home's role in promoting civic virtue and good character (Wright 1981). Hoover also established the Commerce Department's Division of Building and Housing to modernize the homebuilding industry through education and the distribution of model housing and zoning codes (Vale 2007).

The Great Depression fundamentally altered the political dynamics of the housing debate. From a record high of 937,000 urban housing starts in 1925, housing construction plummeted to 330,000 new units in 1930 and 93,000 in 1933 (Barrows 1983). Although the drop in housing construction was a national policy concern, that was not because it was contributing to a housing shortage. With reduced national birth rates and lower rates of rural-to-urban migration, the ratio of new units to new urban population increased during the 1930s and 1940s (Barrows 1983). Overcrowding was also on the decline, in part because of the housing reforms adopted earlier in the century.[2] The real crisis was the inability of Americans to afford housing and remain in their homes as wages fell. Although the cost of living dropped during the Great Depression, real wages fell by a much larger percentage.[3] With the decline in wages, many homeowners were unable to stay current on their mortgages, particularly given that most loans matured within a short time, often with large balloon payments due at maturity. The foreclosure rate increased from 3.6 per 1,000 mortgages in 1926 to a high of 13.3 per 1,000 mortgages in 1933, with approximately 1,000 home mortgages foreclosing every day by 1933 (Wheelock 2008).

As president, Herbert Hoover viewed the Great Depression as an externally induced crisis caused by European economic and political turmoil. Hoover saw homeownership as part and parcel of America's exceptionalism, and solving America's economic crisis required bolstering this distinctive American institution (Rodgers 1998). In 1931, as the economic crisis deepened, Hoover convened the President's Conference on Home Building and Home Ownership in Washington, DC, and tasked Richard T. Ely's Institute for Research in Land Economics and Public Utilities with providing research support and policy guidance (Weiss 1989). Lawrence Veiller served on the conference planning committee, and Harland Bartholomew chaired a committee on subdivision design. The conference revealed a consensus around some form of new limited-government public-private partnership that would support, but not alter, existing housing market institutions. The savings and loan industry favored any proposal that would consolidate their industry's position by excluding other types of lenders from mortgage markets (Quinn 2010).

Congress passed two housing bills near the end of Hoover's term. The Emergency Relief and Construction Act empowered the Reconstruction Finance Corporation to make loans to private firms engaged in low-income housing provision and slum clearance. The Federal Home Loan Bank Act established 12 regional Federal Home Loan Banks, capitalized by member-purchased stock and deposits from member institutions, to provide a stable source of mortgage funds to local savings and loan banks (Schwartz 2015).

During Franklin D. Roosevelt's presidency, progressive ideas that had been circulating for decades finally found a more receptive audience (Rodgers 1998). One of the earliest actions taken by Roosevelt in the housing policy arena came with the adoption of the Home Owners Loan Corporation Act of 1933, which created the Home Owners' Loan Corporation (HOLC) to purchase and refinance distressed mortgages, extending loan terms on refinanced mortgages to 15 years, thereby reducing monthly mortgage payments. The HOLC issued over one million loans in just under three years and established a precedent for the long-term, fixed-rate, self-amortizing, low–down-payment mortgage that was institutionalized in more comprehensive legislation adopted one year later.

With the National Housing Act of 1934, Congress expanded the supply of mortgage credit to middle-class homebuyers. In contrast to the Federal Home Loan Bank Act, which provided liquidity to member banking institutions, and the HOLC, which refinanced mortgages in default, the National Housing Act of 1934 created the Federal Housing Administration (FHA) to insure lenders against long-term mortgage risk. FHA insurance increased the terms of allowable mortgages to 25 to 30 years and increased the loan-to-value ratio on mortgages issued from one-half to two-thirds of the appraised value up to 93 percent, lowering down-payment requirements considerably. Reducing the risks associated with private mortgage lending caused mortgage interest rates to drop. By 1939, FHA-insured mortgages had risen to one-quarter of all mortgages issued, and the additional capital for mortgage financing played an important role in reinvigorating the housing industry, with housing starts increasing by 86 percent between 1937 and 1941 (Wheelock 2008; Schwartz 2015; Quinn 2010).

In addition to establishing a new institutional structure for private mortgage lending, HOLC and FHA underwriting practices had long-lasting impacts on the types of homes constructed and who would be eligible to gain access to those homes. The HOLC relied on detailed socioeconomic information and housing quality data to construct "residential security maps" that categorized neighborhoods into ordinal lending risk categories. The HOLC's methodology downgraded communities of color and neighborhoods experiencing racial or ethnic change, institutionalizing the discriminatory lending practice known as "redlining" (Jackson 1980). Neighborhood racial and ethnic characteristics were also incorporated into the FHA's *Underwriting Manual*, authored in the 1930s by Frederick Babcock, who had written a real estate appraisal text in 1924 as part of Richard T. Ely's Land Economics Series (Nightingale 2012). Until ruled illegal by the US Supreme Court in *Shelley v. Kraemer* (1948), private restrictive covenants prohibiting home sales to people of color were a powerful means of enforcing the *Underwriting Manual*'s preference for "retaining stability" by ensuring that "properties shall continue to be occupied by the same social and racial classes" (Jackson 1980, 436). The *Underwriting Manual* also incentivized suburbanization, favoring single-family structures over multifamily ones as well as new structures over rehabilitated existing ones (Jackson 1980). Once new home sales rebounded after World War II, the FHA's underwriting standards fostered the proliferation of racially and ethnically segregated neighborhoods.

The FHA turned to economist Homer Hoyt, who had been trained at the University of Chicago, to create and implement a methodology to streamline the mortgage underwriting process. Hoyt proposed replacing expensive onsite field studies with an automated cartographic method similar to the one employed by the HOLC. He instructed the FHA's insurance officers to designate the locations of different land uses and housing types on a city map and then outline blocks with "a considerable number" of populations thought to be associated with low real estate values, including "Italians or Jews in the lower income group," as well as those with 10 percent or more "negroes or race other than white" (Light 2011, 499). While Hoyt believed that race was a social construction, he also believed that if prejudice played a role in shaping one's willingness to pay for a house, scientific analysis should record this fact. Even though Hoyt viewed his method as neutral and objective, it only reinforced existing patterns of prejudice by institutionalizing bias into the standards that loan officers adopted to assess mortgage risk (Light 2011).

As Roosevelt was laying the foundations for the mortgage finance tier of the federal housing policy apparatus, a new generation of housing advocates—including Mary Simkhovitch, Edith Elmer Wood, Ira Robbins, and Louis Pink—established the National Public Housing Conference (NPHC) to push for the creation of a new public housing program that would house the working class (McDonnell 1957). The NPHC's first legislative success came in 1933, when Simkhovitch convinced Senator Robert Wagner to include a provision in the National Industrial Recovery Act empowering the new Public Works Administration to construct low-cost housing (Hunt 2005). Although housing advocates viewed this as a step forward, most acknowledged that it was only a temporary pump-priming economic stimulus measure (McDonnell 1957). Advocates sought a more permanent federal government housing construction and slum clearance program, organized along the lines of European limited-dividend and cooperative housing programs, but the courts saw things differently. In *United States v. Certain Lands in the City of Louisville* (1935), a circuit court of appeals ruled that the federal government could not exercise the power of eminent domain for slum clearance and low-cost housing construction. In *New York City Housing Authority v. Muller* (1936), the New York Court of Appeals ruled that local housing authorities could use eminent domain for this purpose, thus signaling that any slum-clearance program going forward would have to be carried out by state and local authorities (Fish 1979).

Labor organizations also shaped the public housing debate. The Labor Housing Conference, established in 1934, hired as executive director one of the rising stars in the housing movement, Catherine Bauer,[4] whose book *Modern Housing* (1934) introduced European housing strategies to the American public. Through her experiences in Europe and work with the Regional Planning Association of America, Bauer came to view the housing issue through the broader lens of modernism, regionalism, and new town planning. She was less interested in slum clearance than in the creation of a "modern housing" program that would house a broad cross section of the working class in new suburban towns, modeled after Ebeneezer Howard's garden city concept (Oberlander and Newbrun 1999).

The political battles among these and other constituencies illustrate the complexity of the social meaning of housing among New Deal–era housing reformers. While housing advocates were unified in their support for some form of government-led effort to create housing for low-income workers, Simkhovitch and the NPHC saw slum clearance as central to this effort. In contrast, Bauer saw the problem as "not nearly so much the existing slums as it is the incapacity of private enterprise to meet the great need for new housing in the near future" (Hunt 2005, 200). Housing reformers also faced opposition from the Roosevelt administration, from Roosevelt himself, who was reluctant to lend his full support to earlier versions of the public housing bill, and from the FHA. According to urban historian Bradford Hunt (2005, 202), "Bauer resented the FHA's insistence on single-family housing, disliked its homeownership rhetoric, and distrusted its leadership, largely taken from the real estate industry."

The 1937 Housing Act established a federal public housing program, but various political compromises produced a program that bore little resemblance to Bauer's modern housing vision. The act included amendments that capped allowable construction costs, imposed income restrictions, limited participation by nonprofit housing societies, and required the "equivalent elimination" of one slum housing unit for each new public housing unit constructed (Hunt 2005). These amendments ran counter to Bauer's goal of establishing a comprehensive government housing program that would house a broad cross section of the working class in areas outside existing slums, with widespread participation from nonprofit housing organizations (Hunt 2005; Schwartz 2015). Even though she initially came out in opposition to many of the act's amendments, Bauer wrote in the *New Republic* in 1937 that the Housing Act was "a radical piece of legislation—perhaps the most clear-cut and uncompromising adopted under the New Deal" (Hunt 2005, 210).

Roosevelt did not live to see the fruits of the federal public housing program that he helped create. Anti–New Deal politicians elected in 1938 and 1942 embargoed funding for the program. During World War II, Congress funded housing for defense purposes but banned its use for low-income households (von Hoffman 2000). In the meantime, Roosevelt began to publicly express a new vision for a more expansive welfare state that secured positive rights to minimal consumer welfare. In his 1941 State of the Union address, Roosevelt outlined a list of "four freedoms" that every human being should enjoy. The third freedom on the list—freedom from want—was the basis for rights that guaranteed access to the means of material subsistence. In his 1944 State of the Union address, Roosevelt declared, "We have come to a clear realization of the fact that true individual freedom cannot exist without economic security and independence. Necessitous men are not free men" (Sunstein 2004, 12). With this statement, Roosevelt was not making a virtue-based argument, nor was he saying that necessitous men do not deserve to govern. Instead, he aimed to instill a much broader understanding of the rights guaranteed to all Americans. His "Second Bill of Rights" was based on the idea that a "new basis of security and prosperity can be established for all—regardless of station, race, or creed." The fifth right on this list was "the right of every family to a decent home" (Sunstein 2004, 13).

Roosevelt's Second Bill of Rights was never formally enacted into law, but his successor, Harry Truman, embraced it. Following Roosevelt's death in 1945, Truman requested that Congress pass a list of domestic reforms that included housing reform (von Hoffman 2000). While there was public support for measures designed to alleviate the nation's pent-up demand for housing, particularly for workers returning from World War II, conservative opponents of the New Deal in Congress and real estate interests played a more significant role than in earlier debates and set an agenda that prioritized slum clearance and redevelopment over public housing. Not wanting to be left out of the growing movement to reform housing and urban development policy, public housing advocates eventually threw their support behind a new law that would combine urban redevelopment with public housing provision. It would take several years for the fragile alliance between public housing advocates and real estate interests to coalesce, but by the end of the decade, Congress had passed the Housing Act of 1949. It established, for the first time, the national goal of providing "a decent home and a suitable living environment for every American family" (Housing Act of 1949, 42 U.S.C. § 1441). Title I of the act authorized $1 billion in loans to help cities acquire blighted properties for redevelopment, and Title III authorized federal loans and grants to build 810,000 public housing units over the next six years.

For the first time since the homestead acts, the federal government assumed a significant role in the acquisition and disposition of land for human habitation, this time in urban areas rather than on the frontier. The 1954 and 1956 revisions to the Housing Act expanded this provision of the law, adding the term "urban renewal" and expanding the scope of the act beyond mere land clearance, providing funds for the rehabilitation and conservation of existing structures, enforcement of building codes, relocation of displaced inhabitants, and citizen participation in urban renewal planning (Schwartz 2015). The 1954 and 1956 revisions reflected the growing influence of a constituency that was inspired by the success of the 1945 Baltimore Plan, which emphasized aggressive code enforcement, quasijudicial enforcement mechanisms, and property rehabilitation over the mere clearance of slum properties. The political alliances supporting the Baltimore approach to redevelopment mirrored those established in turn-of-the-century New York, with landlords objecting to restrictive regulations and real estate developers and investors favoring comprehensive code enforcement as a way to stabilize urban property values in the face of change (von Hoffman 2008).

In the end, the ideological underpinnings of the New Deal–era federal housing policy apparatus reflected a marriage of convenience between right-based liberalism and progressivism. Whereas classic liberals such as John Locke looked to government to protect the rights of property-owning producers, the intellectual leaders of the New Deal–era housing movement saw government as the guardian of rights that secured positive freedoms to minimal consumer welfare. According to Catherine Bauer (Aronovici 1934, 21), "A decent dwelling is not a reward withheld for the successful, but a fundamental right to which every citizen is entitled, the provision of which becomes a responsibility of government." Echoes of this same idea resurfaced in Roosevelt's "right of every family to a decent home" (Sunstein 2004, 13) and the 1949 Housing Act's goal of providing "a decent home and a suitable living environment for every American family" (Housing Act of 1949, 42 U.S.C. § 1441).

When asked about the intellectual origins of his New Deal, Roosevelt hearkened back to the British new liberalism of David Lloyd George: "Lloyd George a quarter of a century ago put through in two years a greater body of radical reforms than the New Deal has attempted in five." It is for this reason that Roosevelt preferred to describe his New Deal initiatives using the term "liberal" rather than "progressive" (Rodgers 1998, 423–424). Roosevelt resurrected right-based liberalism using the language of progressivism while appealing to middle-class consumers as individual bearers of rights rather than members of a collective class (Donohue 2003). As discussed in the next section, the New Deal–era federal housing policy apparatus ultimately failed to secure rights to housing, and the contradictions between expanded housing opportunities for some and the denial of these same opportunities to others defined the postwar American housing debate.

The Postwar Homeownership Republic

By the 1950s, America had established the foundations of a new "homeownership republic," characterized by homeownership, suburbanization, homogeneous housing styles, and socioeconomically segregated neighborhoods. The FHA partially enabled the homeownership republic through expanded access to financial capital and restrictions on who could access that capital and where. Local zoning ordinances reinforced the homogeneity of housing styles, the separation of residential and commercial areas, and the exclusion of low-income rental housing from neighborhoods dominated by the owned single-family detached home. Frank Lloyd Wright's Broadacre City, with its similarly sized single-family homes on one-acre lots stitched together by a vast network of roads, elevated the homeownership republic into a utopian ideal. While Wright celebrated the homeownership republic as a spatial manifestation of America's legacy of moral individualism and freedom, cultural critics William H. White and David Riesman equated the homeownership republic with conformity and the loss of freedom (Fishman 1987).

The homeownership republic was also made possible by changes in homebuilding. By the 1950s, the American homebuilding industry had evolved beyond its early origins in small-scale craft production. Landowners constructed early American homes directly, with assistance from local friends and relatives or local craft builders. During the late nineteenth and early twentieth centuries, prospective homebuyers purchased land and paid for home construction using the proceeds from construction loans financed by local building and loan associations.[5] This process began to change in the 1920s, when large-scale community builders emerged to purchase large plots of suburban land and construct homes in advance of home purchase agreements. By the 1950s, mass-produced tract-home subdivisions had proliferated throughout America (Harris 2009).

The rise of community builders transformed the prospective homebuyer into an anonymous consumer, whose tastes and preferences had to be anticipated in advance rather than communicated through a personal face-to-face dialogue between the builder and homebuyer (Harris 2009). With this transformation, community builders, rather than housing consumers or social reformers, began to play a more important role in shaping the American social meaning of housing. Not everyone preferred to live in homogeneous suburbs, of course, and some large community builders responded to the latent demand for neighborhood diversity by offering developments characterized by a variety of housing styles, price ranges, and types. For example, during the 1960s, Maryland developer James Rouse, a leading figure in the implementation of the Baltimore Plan, built the large master-planned suburban mixed-use community of Columbia, Maryland, touting its diversity of housing options as a selling point. Regardless of whether community builders provided homogenous suburbs or mixed-use communities, they were the ones shaping the social meaning of housing.

The anonymization of the housing consumer and the proliferation of suburban master-planned communities also transformed the connection between housing and citizenship. The homeownership republic required a new type of citizen—the "consumer-voter"—whose most important democratic act was voting with their feet to satisfy individual preferences for housing and local public goods and services. Charles Tiebout's (1956) classic article provided an economic justification for decentralized public good provision and, by implication, suburbanization, because the proliferation of local governments on the urban periphery enabled those with unique preferences for local public goods to live among others who shared their preferences. Bruce Hamilton (1976) demonstrated that when local governments rely on property taxes to finance local public goods, they face strong incentives to "zone out" inexpensive homes that do not generate enough property tax revenue to cover the home's share of the cost of providing local public goods and services. The insights of Tiebout (1956) and Hamilton (1976) suggest that in the homeownership republic, homeowners face incentives to become more civically engaged, not because they are more virtuous or more attuned to the common good but because they have an economic interest in propping up the collective value of owned homes (Fischel 2005).

Although the mortgage finance tier of the two-tier federal housing policy apparatus remained intact during the 1950s, several forces converged to threaten the long-term viability of New Deal–era antipoverty initiatives. Economic prosperity during the postwar era led many to conclude that the United States had solved the problem of poverty. In reality, the nation had only isolated and hidden the problem from the tract homes of the suburban homeownership republic. The sterility and security of suburban life lulled Americans into believing that New Deal–era antipoverty initiatives were no longer needed. By the mid-1950s, most of those receiving direct aid from the federal government were served by the Aid to Dependent Children (ADC) program, and an increase in the share of single Black women receiving ADC payments fueled racially motivated attacks on the program. Many states and localities added fuel to the fire, restricting ADC eligibility through residency rules and intrusive "man-in-the-house" policies. The fates of New Deal–era antipoverty programs were also shaped by Cold War politics. Senator Joseph McCarthy and the House Un-American Activities Committee launched a full-scale attack on individuals, organizations, and ideas that smacked of communism, and many conservative members of Congress leveled the same attacks on the New Deal–era public housing program (Katz 1996).

By the late 1950s, many began to question the truth of the prevailing narrative of an increasingly prosperous and affluent American society. John Kenneth Galbraith, a post-Keynesian economist who coined the term "affluent society" in his 1958 book of the same name, questioned whether the rising economic tide would lift all boats (Galbraith 1958). Social critics such as Michael Harrington (1962) argued that the affluent society masked a growing population of "invisible poor" who were concentrated, isolated, and segregated within urban neighborhoods and rural Appalachia. A decline in the demand for unskilled labor combined with an increase in migration to cities fueled a rise in urban poverty. Foreign aid programs awakened Americans to the plight of the poor in developing nations, and the persistence of US poverty gave the Soviet Union rhetorical ammunition for its Cold War propaganda machine (Immerwahr 2015). John F. Kennedy responded to these trends and made poverty alleviation a central component of his presidential platform. One of the signature efforts of his administration was the 1962 Public Welfare Amendments to the Social Security Act, which greatly expanded federal support to states for local casework, job training, job placement, and other social services. As Kennedy focused attention on the problem of poverty, the civil rights movement shone a bright light on urban poverty and the institutional racism that perpetuated it.

The Return of Right-Based Housing Reforms

By the 1960s, many had become disillusioned by the federal government's failure to act on its 1949 goal to provide "a decent home and suitable living environment for every American family" (Housing Act of 1949, 42 U.S.C. § 1441). Although the Housing Act of 1949 committed the nation to constructing 810,000 units of public housing within six years, that goal was not met until 1968 (von Hoffman 2000). Efforts led by the federal government to decentralize control over housing and community development activities paradoxically spurred new grassroots housing movements that were opposed to strong federal oversight of housing provision in low-income areas and communities of color. These movements spoke a new language of rights, translated from the liberal and natural rights traditions into a more inclusive tongue, to underscore the moral urgency of their demands for reform.

The Civil Right to Fair Housing
Throughout the twentieth century, America's civil rights warriors fought to dismantle the discriminatory housing market barriers that excluded people of color from the homeownership republic, but the moral language of American housing reform offered few words to express warriors' rallying

cries. Under the classic liberal interpretation of property and contracts, individual property owners enjoyed the right to sell or lease property to whoever they wished. While some republicans called for the redistribution of landed property to people of color, others appealed to republican values to deny access to housing and property. The debates surrounding the terms of labor contracts during the Progressive Era rarely extended into the realm of housing contracts, and progressive reforms such as zoning more often restricted rather than expanded access to housing for people of color.

Despite liberalism's poor track record, many civil rights advocates still understood the right to fair housing as a liberal right that had been constitutionally guaranteed but not yet extended to all Americans. In *Buchanan v. Warley* (1917), Boston attorney and National Association for the Advancement of Colored People (NAACP) member Moorfield Storey led the fight against a Louisville, Kentucky, racial zoning ordinance that prohibited people of color from seeking housing on blocks where whites were in the majority. Classic liberalism provided the ammunition needed to strike down the ordinance. The Supreme Court concluded that the Louisville law deprived people of color of their right to alienate property without due process, a testament to the power of the liberal interpretation of property rights when those rights are taken seriously (Ely 1998).

After racial zoning ordinances were ruled unconstitutional, whites turned to racially restrictive covenants—private deed restrictions that prohibited the sale of homes to people of color—to maintain racial segregation patterns. The legal battle against racially restrictive covenants proved to be more of a challenge because, unlike racial zoning ordinances, deed restrictions were enforced through voluntary private contracts, not state actions. Several restrictive covenants were successfully challenged on technical grounds, but it was not until 1948, in *Shelley v. Kraemer*, that racially restrictive covenants were ruled unconstitutional.

Shelley marked a shift in legal tactics from *Buchanan*. In *Muller v. Oregon* (1908), Louis Brandeis had established a precedent for the application of statistical data and consequentialist reasoning to cases questioning the legitimacy of government regulations. At a 1945 NAACP meeting in Chicago, Charles Houston, dean of the Howard University Law School, recommended that the same strategy be applied to racially restrictive covenant cases. In *Shelley*, attorney George L. Vaughn presented social science evidence to demonstrate that restrictive covenants were antithetical to sound public policy because they forced Black persons to live in segregated conditions, and segregation was detrimental to Black quality of life (Ware 1989).[6] Thurgood Marshall later relied on the same strategy to argue the landmark civil rights case *Brown v. Board of Education* (1954).

Shelley and *Brown* sent a clear message to those in the fair housing movement that the courts were more likely to dismantle discriminatory housing market barriers that produced harmful segregation patterns. Armed with new social science evidence linking racial segregation with social disorder and "institutionalized pathology" (Clark 1965), civil rights activists and activist-scholars began to call more forcefully for the elimination of de facto segregation patterns that perpetuated racial concentrations of urban poverty. The Commission on Race and Housing, an independent citizens group that included several prominent social scientists among its members, released a report in 1958 recommending that "authorities in charge of low-rent public housing should vigorously combat the tendency for public housing projects to become low-income and racial 'ghettos'" (Commission on Race and Housing 1958, 66). In 1965, the National Committee against Discrimination in Housing (NCADH) held a national conference on "How to Break Up the Racial Ghetto" (von Hoffman 1998b).

In 1968, two presidentially appointed commissions also called attention to the harms of segregation. The National Advisory Commission on Civil Disorders, also known as the Kerner Commission, linked segregation to racial inequality and urban poverty, claiming that America was moving toward "two societies, one black, one white—separate and unequal" (National Advisory Commission on Civil Disorders 1968, 1). The Kerner Commission presented two options for addressing the social ills caused by residential segregation: "enrichment" strategies designed to improve living conditions in majority-Black central city neighborhoods and "integration" strategies designed to open up majority-white suburbs. Of these two options, the Kerner Commission expressed a clear preference for the second option but conceded that some mixture of the two was likely needed (Farley 2008). The National Commission on Urban Problems, also known as the Douglas Commission, released a report titled *Building the American City* that echoed the Kerner Commission's concerns with segregation but placed more emphasis on state and local housing plans and the elimination of local regulatory barriers to affordable housing (National Commission on Urban Problems 1968).

Against this backdrop, the US Congress considered the adoption of fair housing legislation.[7] Initial attempts to pass a fair housing law failed, in part because of opposition from the real estate community and the lack of support among moderate Republicans and southern Democrats. The assassination of Rev. Dr. Martin Luther King Jr. and subsequent demonstrations in Washington, DC, and other large American cities spurred a call to action that forced congressional opponents of fair housing legislation to reconsider their positions. Following an emergency session of Congress called amid the turmoil surrounding demonstrations in DC, Title VIII of the 1968 Civil Rights Act—the Fair Housing Act (FaHA)—was enacted into law.

Although the harms caused by residential segregation were in full view by 1968, the words "segregation" or "integration" did not appear in the final version of the FaHA. The bill's sponsors, Massachusetts Republican senator Edward Brooke and Minnesota Democratic senator Walter Mondale, tended to view the elimination of private-sector housing market discrimination as sufficient to create more racially integrated residential patterns (Yinger 1995). One HUD general counsel later agreed, saying, "Congress anticipated that the abolition of racially discriminatory housing practices would ultimately result in residential integration" (Polikoff 1986, 48). While those in Congress held different views of what was required to achieve integration, the FaHA's sponsors viewed integration as a legitimate government interest that was later acknowledged by the courts in *Linmark Associates, Inc. v. Willingboro* (1977) (Yinger 1995).

Although the version of the FaHA signed into law by President Lyndon B. Johnson never addressed residential segregation directly, one provision of the FaHA has since been interpreted as a desegregation mandate. Section 808 of the FaHA requires the federal government (HUD) to administer programs and activities "in a manner affirmatively to further the purposes of" fair housing, a directive that fair housing advocates have dubbed the "affirmatively furthering fair housing" (AFFH) mandate (Fair Housing Act 1968, § 808). The scope of the AFFH mandate—and the question of how to affirmatively foster integrated housing patterns without compromising other housing policy goals—eventually drove a wedge between integrationists and advocates committed to the goal of housing people of color in the places where they already lived.

The Right to Community

In contrast to the civil right to fair housing, understood by most as an individual right not to be denied housing opportunities on the basis of race or ethnicity, and for some the right to live in an integrated neighborhood, the "right to community," as I define it, has been understood as a collective right held in common by the members of a minority racial or ethnic group inhabiting a place.[8] For right to community advocates, the civil right to housing embodies more than nondiscrimination. It recognizes a person of color's racial or ethnic identity, acknowledges a racial or ethnic group's shared historical experience of discrimination and oppression, protects a community's right to foster a distinctive place-based sense of collective identity, and secures the political right to collective self-determination and self-governance.

There are many similarities between the idea of a right to community and the republican ideal of self-governance. Jefferson's yeoman republic and Lewis Masquerier's rural republican townships were each based on visions of a nation of stakeholders bound to the earth and to each other by networks of decentralized self-governing communities. Municipal governments had the potential to play an important role in the realization of these republican ideals, but the proliferation of Dillon's Rule laws during the late nineteenth century constrained cities' ability to effectively govern themselves until twentieth-century progressive reformers such as Cleveland Mayor Tom Johnson successfully secured home rule for some municipalities (Frug 1980).

Throughout America's history, Black and Indigenous people of color have appealed to the right to community only to have their pleas ignored. During the Jacksonian years of territorial expansion, George Henry Evans was among the few who called attention to the injustice of America's forced displacement of native tribes, appealing to Native Americans' rights to community throughout his career. Evans attacked the Indian Removal Act of 1830, claiming that the states had "no more right to jurisdiction over the territory of the Cherokees than we have to be King of France" (Buhle and Dawley 1985, 17). The success of postbellum Black homesteader colonies and freedmen's towns hinged crucially on collective solidarity and strong local institutions, but this sense of community emerged in the absence of, not because of, America's formal recognition of Black Americans' collective rights to land as restitution for the evils of slavery (Friefeld et al. 2019).

The contemporary right to community movement began as a way to open up housing opportunities for people of color, a goal that was originally broadly consistent with the integrationist aims of the fair housing movement. In 1942, the Metropolitan Life Insurance Company began planning for Stuyvesant Town, a large development designed to house returning war veterans. From the beginning, the project was designed to be an exclusively white enclave. The chairman of Metropolitan Life told a reporter that "Negroes and whites don't mix. Perhaps they will in a hundred years but not now" (von Hoffman 1998b, 19). Low-income families were displaced, and the rental policy for Stuyvesant Town homes banned people of color. A protracted legal battle ensued, led by the NAACP, the American Civil Liberties Union, and the American Jewish Congress. In *Dorsey v. Stuyvesant Town Corp.* (1949), housing and civil rights advocate Charles Abrams argued the case, claiming that government-subsidized property constituted a "state interest" and that the "right to lease and occupy a home is a civil right" protected by the equal protection clause of the Fourteenth Amendment (Gold 2014, 48). The appeals court ultimately rejected this argument. Refusing to give up the fight for minority tenants' rights, the coalition of advocates who argued the *Dorsey* case formed the New York Committee on Discrimination in Housing, which eventually grew into the NCADH (von Hoffman 1998b).

During the 1950s and 1960s, the right-to-community movement faced a new foe: the federal urban renewal program. Although urban renewal projects enjoyed broad support among many central city mayors, critics argued that urban renewal projects took too long to complete, subsidized high-value real estate projects rather than low-income housing construction, displaced the poor and people of color, and destroyed the social fabric of many thriving communities of color (Wilson 1966). Although fair housing and right to community advocates presented a unified front in the fight for open housing within suburban areas, the urban renewal battles exposed new conflicts between integrationists and right to community advocates (Goetz 2018). Urban renewal plans often appealed to the integrationist aims of "stabilizing" urban neighborhoods and stemming white flight, goals that right to community advocates interpreted as coded language for gentrification and displacement. For example, in one 1959 description of the Hyde Park-Kenwood Urban Renewal Plan, University of Chicago anthropologist Sol Tax (1959, 22) painted a picture of a neighborhood that, prior to urban renewal, was "being engulfed by a tidal wave of population from the segregated, long-contained black belt at the borders of our neighborhood." He applauded the Hyde Park-Kenwood Urban Renewal Plan, characterizing it as "the first case of an urban neighborhood's being saved from becoming a slum" by "breaking the pattern of racial residential segregation which has characterized cities in the North."

In addition to mobilizing in opposition to top-down government programs that threatened to destroy communities, right to community advocates have fought to catalyze the bottom-up development of local economic, political, and social institutions required for effective self-governance. In the early 1950s, residents of the Back-of-the-Yards district in Chicago[9] tried to secure resources to upgrade the neighborhood's housing stock, but the district had been redlined, and banks were unwilling to lend to residents. The Back-of-the-Yards Council, created in the late 1930s by community organizer Saul Alinsky, leveraged its organizational power to secure services from city hall and convince local banks to lend to district residents (Jacobs 1961).[10] By the late 1950s, community advocates in partnership with large philanthropies mobilized to spur grassroots community uplift campaigns in other American cities. The Mobilization for Youth program in Manhattan and the Ford Foundation's Gray Areas initiative attracted the attention of US senator Robert Kennedy and later served as a national model for community development.

As part of his Great Society domestic policy initiative, President Johnson marshaled the power of the federal government to lend support to grassroots community development efforts. Soon after being sworn into office, President Johnson launched a full-scale "war on poverty." A centerpiece of Johnson's war on poverty was the 1964 Economic Opportunity Act, which funneled federal money through the Office of Economic Opportunity (OEO) to local nongovernmental community action agencies (CAAs) that were designed to be the fiscal agents for a variety of antipoverty initiatives. CAAs were designed to enable the "maximum feasible participation" of local community residents in the design and implementation of community development strategies (Halpern 1995). The CAAs embodied the ideals of republican self-governance, as reflected in one early OEO bulletin, which stated: "Above all, an acceptable antipoverty plan must be a program in which projects are carried out not *for* the community, but rather *by* the community—with external financial assistance—to attack community problems" (Katz 1996, 267; italics in the original).

Although Johnson's community action program created a large number of local institutions supporting community uplift and self-governance, many of which still exist today, the program was not without its critics. Community representatives on CAA boards often represented the narrow interests of friends and families rather than the broad interests of the most disenfranchised members of the community. As Daniel Patrick Moynihan observed, "Patronage, which was the source of stability in the original ethnic neighborhood political organization, became a source of instability in the contrived organizations created to fill the gap left by the destruction of the real thing" (Moynihan 1969, 138).

Johnson failed to fully appreciate the inherent contradictions embedded within his top-down approach to community development. Many community organizations relied on OEO funds to contest formal local governance institutions and support militant forms of community action. In Syracuse, for example, an organization led by Saul Alinsky relied on federal community action funds to organize tenants' unions, bail protesters out of jail, and run a voter-registration drive to defeat the incumbent mayor (Immerwahr 2015).

The use of community action funds to support radical forms of community activism should not have come as a surprise. If discriminatory federal policies were responsible for creating conditions of concentrated poverty and racial segregation, it was only natural that once gaining power, disenfranchised communities would seek to alter the structures of inequality that produced the problems they faced. As Saul Alinsky wrote in the first chapter of his influential book *Rules for Radicals* (1971, 3), "The Prince was written by Machiavelli for the Haves on how to hold power. Rules for Radicals is written for the Have-Nots on how to take it away." In their calls for reform, some community advocates began to see the nation-state as an increasingly irrelevant actor. In 1970, Huey Newton called on the global "dispersed collection of communities" to "seize the means of production and distribute the wealth" within "a small unit with a comprehensive collection of institutions that exist to serve a small group of people" (Immerwahr 2015, 159).

In the end, the philosophical contradictions embedded within the community action program and the political backlash facing Democrats in the years leading up to the 1968 presidential election eventually contributed to the demise of the OEO. In 1967, Congress required that state or local governments supervise the activities of all CAAs. These changes, along with an eventual reduction in funding for the program, led to the departure of those within the OEO who supported the ideals of maximum feasible participation. Moynihan recommended dismantling the OEO entirely, and during the Nixon administration, the administration of the OEO was placed into the hands of Donald Rumsfeld and Dick Cheney, neither particularly sympathetic to the idea of community action. Nixon tried to dismantle the OEO, but it remained intact until the Reagan administration (Immerwahr 2015).

The perceived failures of the community action program led to changes in the federal government's approach to community development within low-income communities. Under the 1966 Model Cities program, citizen participation in community development was encouraged, but federal funding flowed to municipal governments rather than directly to community organizations. In 1968, as part of an amendment to the Economic Opportunity Act, the Special Impact Program was created to fund the establishment of local community development corporations (CDCs)—private nonprofit corporations that received funding from a variety of sources, often working in collaboration with government and industry to promote neighborhood revitalization, housing, job training, and social service coordination (von Hoffman 2012b). The CDCs' collaborative public-private partnership organization model was a stark contrast to the radical anticapitalist approach favored by many CAAs.

The transformation of The Woodlawn Organization (TWO), an Alinsky-supported civil rights organization in Chicago, illustrates how CDCs charted a path toward community development that was markedly different from the path favored by advocacy-oriented CAAs. When it was initially created in 1961, TWO favored confrontational tactics, such as rent strikes and protests. Organizers drove groups of 40 to 50 tenants to the suburbs to picket the homes of slumlords. When TWO became a CDC, it reoriented its mission toward community development projects funded by private foundations and government agencies (Fisher 1994). Robert Fisher (1994, 144) describes TWO's evolution from an activist neighborhood organization to a professional mission-oriented organization as a transition from "confrontation to coexistence."

Tenants' Rights and Welfare Rights

As the homestead movement grew throughout the nineteenth century, a quiet revolution simmered beneath the surface as tenants mobilized to secure new rights to remain on rented land without being evicted during times of economic hardship. The New York anti-rent movement scored an early victory in the mid-nineteenth century with changes to the New York State Constitution that outlawed feudal tenure arrangements. In response to rising rents on New York's Lower East Side during the early twentieth century, tenants staged a series of rent strikes that resulted in landlord concessions (Lawson 1984).

The tenants' rights movement has been more sporadic and disorganized than other right-based housing movements. Tenant organizing has always been difficult, because rent increases often displace potential tenant organizers. Furthermore, tenant groups tend to disband after securing landlord concessions. In New York, alliances between tenants' rights groups and socialist organizations scared away mainstream social reformers, particularly during periods when US anticommunist sentiment ran high. Labor's support for tenant causes has been episodic, and in some cases labor organizations have actively opposed tenant organizations (Drier 1984).

One of the tenant movement's most significant policy victories came with the adoption of rent controls in large US cities such as New York and Washington, DC. During World War I, the US Housing Corporation established vacancy registration bureaus and "fair rent" committees in several US cities to handle complaints about unjustified rent increases during the war-induced housing shortage (Radford 1996). Several local jurisdictions followed up with emergency rent controls. In *Block v. Hirsch* (1921), the Supreme Court upheld the constitutionality of the District of Columbia's emergency rent controls. Justice Oliver Wendell Holmes argued that there was a public interest in the temporary regulation that was analogous to the public interest in utilities (Ely 1998). Three years later, in *Chastleton Corp. v. Sinclair* (1924), the courts concluded that the housing emergency had passed, and the rent control law was struck down. In New York, a similar emergency rent control ordinance was revoked in 1929 by preemptive state action. Rent controls returned to New York during World War II, when the federal government froze rents in several cities to curb inflation. Although the federal government no longer plays a role, rent control has remained in New York City since then. Rent controls eventually returned to other US cities in the 1960s, but states often responded by enacting laws that preempted the further adoption of local rent controls (Keating, Teitz, and Skaburskis 1998).

During the 1960s, the tenant movement aligned with the civil rights movement to pursue new avenues for reform on behalf of renters of color. The rent strike was a common method of protest. In 1963, Black and Puerto Rican tenants organized a rent strike in Harlem to protest their dilapidated living conditions. The strike eventually grew from 16 to 500 buildings, according to some estimates (Fox Piven and Cloward 1967). The Northern Student Movement, Mobilization for Youth, East Harlem Tenants' Council, the Congress of Racial Equality (CORE), and the Metropolitan Council on Housing joined the tenants' cause. Tenants won an early legal victory when the courts recognized tenants' right to refuse to make rent payments when facing hazardous living conditions. The city responded with a vermin remediation and rental housing renovation campaign, but the tenant coalition lacked the strength to endure drawn-out legal battles, and the rent strike came to an end in 1964 (Fox Piven and Cloward 1967). Other similar rent strikes later broke out in the District of Columbia, Brooklyn, Cleveland, and Detroit. In Pittsburgh, Citizens against Slum Housing was initially formed to promote neighborhood upgrading and other self-help strategies, but the group soon turned its attention to tenants' rights issues, winning a series of legislative and administrative reforms, including a strengthened rent withholding law, a housing court, and a new city relocation agency (Indritz 1971).

Apart from the NAACP legal defense fund, there were few resources available to assist those seeking to test the plaintiff's arguments in *Dorsey v. Stuyvesant Town Corp.* that the "right to lease and occupy a home is a civil right." That changed in the 1960s, as funds became available under the Economic Opportunity Act to support local legal aid and advocacy organizations. The expanded legal advocacy network supported activism and legal action on behalf of tenants' rights. In 1969 alone, tenant advocacy organizations acted on 67 occasions to support tenants' rights. In that same year, the Chicago Tenants' Union, the Chicago Urban League, and American Friends Service Committee formed the National Tenants' Organization (NTO) to unite tenants nationally around the cause of tenants' rights (Indritz 1971). With the help of organizers sent by Rev. Dr. Martin Luther King Jr., tenants' unions were established in Chicago to act as collective bargaining agents on behalf of tenants. Civil rights attorney Gilbert Cornfield described the East Garfield Park Tenants Union as follows:

We had been picketing, there had been a lot of excitement on the West Side, and finally, here we were: they were willing to talk to us. But after all of that action, publicity and excitement, you couldn't go in and say you wanted some toilets repaired after they asked you what you wanted. We decided that what we wanted was a contract, like a collective bargaining contract, a piece of paper that guaranteed certain rights to the tenants that they hadn't had before, and that set forth some responsibilities of management to the tenant instead of always the other way around. Once you have a collective bargaining agreement, you had to have somebody to sign it on behalf of the tenants. That's how the East Garfield Park Tenants Union was born. (Indritz 1971, 18)

The expansion of legal advocacy in the 1960s also provided ammunition for the welfare rights movement, which fought to establish legal rights to welfare payments and other forms of government assistance. In 1966, Richard Cloward and Francis Fox Piven wrote an influential article in *The Nation* titled "The Weight of the Poor: A Strategy to End Poverty," which called for a mass information campaign to end poverty. The authors sought to instigate a political crisis by recruiting large numbers of the poor to enroll for the welfare benefits to which they were entitled. The authors hoped that such a crisis would lead to legislation authorizing a guaranteed minimum income. Leaders in the civil rights movement, such as George Wiley, former associate director of CORE, joined the welfare rights movement and worked to establish a coalition of civil rights and antipoverty advocates under the umbrella of the National Welfare Rights Organization (NWRO) (Fox Piven and Cloward 1971).

Legal advocates advanced new legal arguments on behalf of the right to welfare. Charles Reich (1964) argued that federal assistance to the poor should be interpreted as a new form of property and protected with the same guarantees as any other privately owned asset. If, as progressives argued, property rights were created by positive law, why should this same reasoning not be applied to rights to welfare and other forms of public assistance created by law? In *Goldberg v. Kelly* (1970), the Supreme Court declared that welfare recipients could not be removed from the welfare rolls without a fair hearing. Although the court did not say that the government had to provide welfare benefits, it did rule that the termination of welfare benefits had to respect constitutional due process rights (Sunstein 2004).

Reich's (1964) argument had the potential to revolutionize thinking about public housing and other forms of housing assistance. Echoing Roosevelt's 1944 State of the Union address, legal philosopher Frank Michelman (1970,

207) argued that welfare rights could be understood as the minimum material conditions required for equal citizenship, and the "right to be housed" could be understood as "a claim upon organized society, on behalf of each individual or household unit, to be assured of access to minimally adequate housing." In *Shapiro v. Thompson* (1969), a case that questioned the legality of a waiting period for the receipt of California welfare benefits, the court relied on this reasoning to heavily scrutinize efforts to eliminate "food, shelter, and other necessities of life" (Sunstein 2004, 163). Other legal advocates encouraged public agencies to withhold welfare payments to landlords operating substandard rental properties. In Illinois, for example, the Cook County Department of Public Aid established a no-payment program that resulted in an injunction ordering landlords to bring buildings up to code (Indritz 1971).

Although the Supreme Court became more critical of the welfare rights argument during the 1970s, the expansion of tenant advocacy spurred the adoption of several modifications to state landlord-tenant laws, including laws recognizing an implied obligation to maintain decent living conditions for tenants (the "implied warranty of habitability") and protections against evictions in retaliation for complaints or tenant organizing. Other reforms addressed security deposits, the right to withhold rents, utility shutoffs, and the seizure of tenants' possessions (Drier 1984). These reforms marginally expanded tenants' rights vis-à-vis landlords but still fell short of guaranteeing full legal rights to be housed regardless of tenure. Jesse Gray, a leader of the 1963 Harlem rent strike, had proposed merging the NTO and the NWRO to create a "real people's movement." According to Gray, "We both are dealing with the same people. . . . People on welfare are tenants too" (New York Times 1971). Despite Gray's enthusiasm, both the NTO and NWRO eventually disbanded.

The Human Right to Housing

In 1943, Norman Rockwell unveiled a series of paintings titled the *Four Freedoms*, memorializing Franklin D. Roosevelt's 1941 State of the Union address. The third painting in the series, *Freedom from Want*, depicted a family free from want, gleefully anticipating a holiday feast. The *Saturday Evening Post*'s reproduction of the painting was accompanied by an essay by Carlos Bulosan, a farmer, labor activist, and author who migrated to the United States from the Philippines during World War II. Reflecting on his journey to America, Bulosan observed that, "Our march to freedom is not complete unless want is annihilated" (Bulosan 1943).

The international human rights movement was born from the dream of extending to the world the four freedoms outlined in Roosevelt's 1941 State of the Union address. Following the Anglo-American Atlantic Conference of 1941, the United States and the United Kingdom released the jointly authored Atlantic Charter, which called for a postwar world order that would "afford assurance that all the men in all the lands may live out their lives in freedom from fear and want" (Borgwardt 2005, 4). The two allied nations expressed a desire "to bring about the fullest collaboration between all nations in the economic field with the object of securing, for all, improved labor standards, economic advancement and social security" (Anderson 2008, 81).

In June 1945, delegates from 50 nations gathered in San Francisco, two months after Franklin D. Roosevelt's death, to sign the United Nations (UN) Charter. After the end of military conflict in September 1945, one of the first items of business for the UN was the establishment of an international declaration that would put an end to the atrocities committed by all sides during World War II. The UN Commission on Human Rights was charged with drafting the declaration, and former first lady and US delegate to the UN Eleanor Roosevelt served as the founding chair of the commission (Glendon 2002).

As the commission began its work to develop a declaration of human rights, philosophical tensions among the delegates rose to the surface. Representatives of liberal democracies appealed to the values of individualism, negative liberty, and equality, while representatives from Soviet Bloc countries argued that these same values only perpetuated the oppression of the working class. Yugoslavian delegate Vladislav Ribnikar argued that true liberty consists in "perfect harmony between the individual and the community," evoking a positive conception of freedom that echoed the German institutionalists and their American progressive pupils (Glendon 2002, 39). Lebanese delegate and eventual chair of the commission Charles Malik countered with a liberal view of human rights that hearkened back to the natural rights tradition, saying, "The 'human person' [comes before] any group to which he may belong, whether it be class, race, or nation; his 'mind and conscience' were the 'most sacred and inviolable things about him'; the group can be wrong, just as the individual can be" (Eshet 2010, 150).

A statement prepared in 1947 by the American Anthropological Association questioned the universality of human rights, warning that a declaration of human rights should not be "a statement of rights conceived only in terms of the values prevalent in the countries of Western Europe and America" (Glendon 2002, 222).[11] Advocating for a conception of rights that incorporated the right to community, the association challenged the delegates "to formulate a statement of human rights that will do more than just phrase respect for the individual as an individual. It must also take into full account the individual as a member of the social group of which he is a part, whose sanctioned modes of life shape his behavior, and with whose fate his own is thus inextricably bound" (Glendon 2002, 222). Despite some delegates' sympathy for collective right claims, most delegates held that one of the primary purposes of a human rights declaration was to protect individual persons from state-sanctioned atrocities such as those committed by Nazi Germany. Canadian delegate John Humphrey, the author of the "Humphrey Draft" of the declaration, stated that "one purpose of both drafts was to protect individuals from their governments. If the protection of human rights did not mean that, it did not mean much" (Eshet 2010, 160).

These debates revealed three different, and often conflicting, conceptions of human rights: "first-generation rights," the Enlightenment Era political and civil rights found in most liberal democratic constitutions; "second-generation rights," which guaranteed rights to minimal social and economic guarantees; and "third-generation" collective rights, which protected the right of self-determination for peoples. The Soviets charged that communist nations were doing much more than most Western nations to guarantee second-generation rights, and despite Franklin D. Roosevelt's prior endorsement of rights to the means of economic subsistence, many in the United States were reluctant to commit the nation to supporting second-generation rights (Eshet 2010; Glendon 2002).

Another sticking point was the issue of civil rights. The broad and inclusive language of the Atlantic Charter initially gave hope to American civil rights leaders who saw the emerging global human rights conversation as a potential forum for advancing the cause of racial justice in the United States and abroad. For many in the civil rights movement, racial justice meant securing "freedom from want" for everyone, regardless of the color of their skin. According to NAACP board member William Hastie, former dean of Howard University's law school, "Starvation has no bill of rights nor slavery a Magna Carta" (Anderson 2008, 82–83). Following the war, the NAACP outlined a list of "basic civil rights" that included the right to "unsegregated and unrestricted housing" (Anderson 2008, 83).

W. E. B. Du Bois lobbied the US State Department to have the NAACP recognized as an official consultant to the United States' UN delegation, but the NAACP's presence attracted the ire of southern Democrats such as Texas senator Tom Connally, who stubbornly opposed any measure that challenged southern Jim Crow laws and practices. In discussions surrounding the establishment of the UN Charter, the phrase "nothing in the Charter shall authorize . . . intervention in matters which are essentially within the domestic jurisdiction of the State concerned" was added by future secretary of state John Foster Dulles to appease Connally and other southern Democrats (Anderson 2008, 85–86). The Soviets, recognizing the inherent contradictions between the United States' advocacy for human rights and its legacy of racial oppression, urged the creation of the Sub-commission on Prevention of Discrimination and Protection of Minorities (MINDIS). The US State Department shrewdly shaped the agenda of the subcommission in ways that would not draw attention to the United States by redefining minorities in a way that excluded Black Americans, referring only to "national minorities," such as the Kurds, Armenians, and Basques (Anderson 2008).

These and other actions taken to downplay the United States' unflattering historical record on civil rights issues brought protests from American civil rights leaders. In 1947, W. E. B. Du Bois authored a petition on behalf of the NAACP titled *An Appeal to the World: A Statement of Denial of Human Rights to Minorities in the Case of Citizens of Negro Descent in the United States of America and an Appeal to the United Nations for Redress*. The petition called attention to the hypocrisy of a nation founded on the ideals of equality and democracy that still "finds itself continuously making common cause with race-hate, prejudiced exploitation and oppression of the common man" (Du Bois 1947, 2). Walter White of the NAACP asked Eleanor Roosevelt to be present when *An Appeal to the World* was to be submitted to John Humphrey, but she declined. While her official reason for declining was her belief that the commission should not receive petitions from anyone but member states, she was also conscious of the sensitive position of the United States on the issue of civil rights. She knew that the Soviets would use *An Appeal to the World* for their anti-American propaganda and was reluctant to support a measure that opposed the government she represented (Eshet 2010). *An Appeal to the World*, along with an earlier petition submitted by the National Negro Congress, was eventually discussed within MINDIS but was never heard by the full UN delegation (Anderson 1996).

Sensing the potential for opposition to a human rights treaty in Congress, particularly among southern Democrats, Eleanor Roosevelt proposed unrolling the document in stages, first in a nonbinding declaration, then a treaty, and then a binding enforcement mechanism. On December 10, 1948, the United Nations General Assembly voted to adopt the Universal Declaration of Human Rights (UDHR). The UDHR defines a right to housing in Article 25(1), which states that, "Everyone has the right to a standard of living adequate for the health and well-being of himself and of his family, including food, clothing, housing and medical care and necessary social services, and the right to security in the event of unemployment, sickness, disability, widowhood, old age or other lack of livelihood in circumstances beyond his control" (Hohmann 2014, 16). Although no countries voted against the UDHR, five Soviet Bloc countries abstained in opposition to the overemphasis on "eighteenth-century rights" and underemphasis on economic, social, and cultural rights (Eshet 2010, 178). Yugoslavia, Saudi Arabia, and South Africa also abstained.

Implementation of the UDHR through the establishment of treaties and enforcement mechanisms was stalled by Cold War politics, but human rights language soon became incorporated into the constitutions of several new nations. Debates surrounding the UDHR then turned to the establishment of a binding treaty implementing the UDHR. To get the treaty through the southern-dominated Senate, the Truman administration proposed breaking the treaties, or "covenants," into two parts, one that dealt with civil and political rights and another that dealt with social and economic rights. The International Covenant on Civil and Political Rights and the International Covenant on Economic, Social, and Cultural Rights (ICESCR) were not officially adopted until 1966 and were not enforced until 1976. The ICESCR enumerates the right to housing in Article 11(1) as "the right of everyone to an adequate standard of living for himself and his family, including adequate food, clothing and housing, and to the continuous improvement of living conditions" (Hohmann 2014, 17). Importantly, although President Jimmy Carter signed the ICESCR in 1977, it has remained dormant in the

Senate Foreign Relations Committee since 1979 and has never been ratified with the advice and consent of the Senate, which implies that the United States is not bound by the ICESCR to protect the human right to housing (Lewis 2008).

UN delegates held different views of what the right to housing entailed. In the deliberations leading up to the adoption of Article 11 of the ICESCR, delegates were divided over the question of whether the right to housing should be singled out or be included as a component of a more general right to an adequate standard of living. Some argued that the right to an adequate standard of living could theoretically encompass all the rights listed in the ICESCR, not merely those enumerated in Article 11. Others objected that the concept of an adequate standard of living varied among countries and over time. Delegates from the Soviet Union proposed that the right to housing be defined as a right to living accommodations, but the proposal was rejected because some felt that the language proposed by the Soviets placed undue emphasis on state-supported housing provision. The final language of the ICESCR reflected the majority opinion of the delegates that adequate housing be understood as a component of the more general right to an adequate standard of living (Craven 1995).

The marginalization of American civil rights organizations from the human rights debate ultimately shaped the tactics pursued by civil rights leaders. The NAACP's strategy of highlighting America's embarrassing record on civil rights alienated the organization from the US human rights delegation, and by broadly defining civil rights as emphasizing interracial economic equality and second-generation rights, the NAACP was labeled a communist sympathizer. Caught between a rock and a hard place, the NAACP leadership eventually left the global human rights movement, relabeled itself as an "American organization," and reoriented its civil rights advocacy work toward the fight for interracial political equality (Anderson 2003). Civil rights advocates reinvigorated calls for interracial economic equality in the late 1960s, but the movement hit a brick wall in 1968. Rev. Dr. Martin Luther King Jr. was assassinated not long after the launch of his Poor People's Campaign, and the American public shifted its attention to the Vietnam War following the disastrous Tet Offensive. The lily-white faces in Norman Rockwell's *Freedom from Want* painting were a reminder that in the United States, people of color continued to be excluded from the rights guaranteed to all humanity.

From the Common Good to Social Citizenship

Roosevelt's two-tier federal housing policy apparatus was both the apotheosis of the progressive movement's consumer consciousness and a return to the right-based rhetoric of the liberal tradition. In his Second Bill of Rights, Roosevelt gave voice to Catherine Bauer's vision of housing as a "fundamental right to which every citizen is entitled, the provision of which becomes a responsibility of government" (Aronovici 1934, 21). Unfortunately, progressivism's exclusionary legacy tainted the egalitarian aims of New Deal–era housing policy. Rather than extend housing rights to all American citizens, the housing policies adopted during the Roosevelt and Truman years gave birth to a postwar homeownership republic that denied housing opportunities to people of color and destroyed vibrant communities.

The postwar welfare state evolved to grapple with these contradictions, and several social movements proposed new conceptions of rights that redefined the obligations of the state, the rights of citizens, and the meaning of citizenship itself. Welfare rights advocates fought for the formal recognition of second-generation rights. On the international stage, UN delegates called for the formal recognition of third-generation collective rights for national ethnic minorities, and, in the United States, right to community advocates appealed to a similar conception of rights to empower disenfranchised communities, at times evoking the same civic republican ideals of self-governance espoused by the American founders.[12]

Thomas Humphrey (T. H.) Marshall, a British social theorist and student of Leonard T. Hobhouse, proposed the concept of "social citizenship" in 1950 to capture the new right-based understanding of citizenship introduced by the twentieth-century welfare state. According to Marshall,

> Citizenship is a status bestowed on those who are full members of a community. All who possess the status are equal with respect to the rights and duties with which the status is endowed. There is no universal principle that determines what those rights and duties shall be, but societies in which citizenship is a developing institution create an image of an ideal citizenship against which achievement can be measured and towards which aspiration can be directed. The urge forward along the path thus plotted is an urge towards a fuller measure of equality, an enrichment of the stuff of which the status is made and an increase in the number of those on whom the status is bestowed. . . . Citizenship requires a bond of a different kind, a direct sense of community membership based on loyalty to a civilization which is a common possession. It is a loyalty of free men endowed

with rights and protected by a common law. Its growth is stimulated both by the struggle to win those rights and by their enjoyment when won. (Marshall 1950, 28–29, 40–41)

Echoing Franklin D. Roosevelt's 1944 State of the Union address, Marshall argued that *social rights* include "the whole range from the right to a modicum of economic welfare and security to the right to share to the full in the social heritage and to live the life of a civilized being according to the standards prevailing in the society" (Marshall 1950, 11). While Marshall does not appear to have shaped the thinking of those in the American civil rights movement, his understanding of citizenship captures the ideals expressed by civil rights leaders, who fought to extend full citizenship—through equal civil, political, and social rights—to American citizens who had historically been denied those rights. Civil rights leaders such as Rev. Dr. Martin Luther King Jr. would likely have agreed with Marshall that the ideal of full social citizenship, if realized, could have a powerful "integrating effect" by instilling in all citizens a feeling of equal social worth (Marshall 1950, 40).

Although Marshall was not directly involved in the international human rights dialogue, he shared the American Anthropological Association's skepticism of appeals to universal moral principles. His experience leading the Social Sciences Department of the United Nations Educational, Scientific and Cultural Organization (UNESCO) between 1956 and 1960 further solidified his view that universal human rights would be difficult to realize in a world with diverse sociopolitical cultures (Moses 2019). For Marshall, citizenship embodies a common understanding of what it means to be a full member of a political community. This understanding, in turn, establishes the moral foundation of rights and duties. Since the definition of citizenship varies among nations, the grounds of rights and duties also vary.

Marshall's conception of social citizenship offers a different interpretation of the common good than the one favored by republicans and progressives. For Marshall, the common good is not a goal that a chosen few strive for but rather a justification for society's obligations to its members. A society's institutions are bound by a duty to protect civil, political, and social rights so that all citizens are full members of society, regardless of their virtues. As discussed in later chapters, the right to a decent home, the civil right to fair housing, and the right to reside securely in one's chosen community can all be interpreted as extensions of the rights of social citizenship.

5 Homes without Foundations

> The basis on which the structure rests seems to me to be chalk. . . . . .
> —Edgar Allan Poe, "The Light-House," in *Poetry and Tales* (1984 [1849], 925)

In 1980, UK prime minister Margaret Thatcher appeared on British television to promote the 1980 Housing Act. One of its key features was the "right to buy" government-subsidized council housing. According to Thatcher, "If you have been a council tenant for at least three years, you will have the right, by law, to buy your house" (Beckett 2015). The years that followed saw the largest divestiture of council housing since the program's creation in the nineteenth century. Thatcher's right-based rhetoric, which elevated private property rights over the social rights of citizenship, embodied the ideology of *neoliberalism*. From its gestation in a 1938 conference designed to chart a "third way" between socialism and laissez-faire capitalism to its violent birth in the 1973 Chilean coup d'état that brought Augusto Pinochet to power, neoliberalism emerged during the 1970s as a counterrevolutionary response to left-wing social movements of the 1960s. In the United States, President Richard Nixon set the stage for the rise of neoliberal housing policy with the appointment of four conservative Supreme Court justices, the devolution of the federal government's responsibility to house low-income renters, and the reorientation of federal rental housing policy away from housing production subsidies to tenant-based rental vouchers. Ronald Reagan put the final pieces of the neoliberal puzzle together by slashing HUD's budget and deregulating mortgage finance. Since the Reagan years, neither Republican nor Democratic administrations have veered substantially from the neoliberal path, even after the housing market crashed under its own weight in 2007.

The contemporary American neoliberal housing landscape is a far cry from Catherine Bauer's modern housing utopia. Today's postmodern housing reality is defined by the absence of the federal government and a housing market that is fragmented, decentralized, and segmented, exhibiting inequalities in housing price, quality, type, tenure, and location. Residential property rights that were unbundled during the Progressive Era have been reassembled during the neoliberal era into a variety of new housing options, including prefabricated homes, tiny homes, cohousing, shared-equity ownership arrangements, and flexible live-work spaces.

Contemporary American housing justice movements share a common foe in neoliberalism, but these movements are also fragmented, appealing to different moral frameworks to justify housing policy approaches that are often inconsistent with one another. The alliance between tenants' rights advocates and right to community advocates has recently clashed with a new generation of renter advocates over the question of gentrification, and the fair housing movement has come to be defined by its contentious relationship between integrationists and right to community advocates. A new housing justice movement that combines a cosmopolitan human right to housing with the collective right to the city has the potential to unify housing advocates. Still, it remains to be seen whether this new alliance can transcend the historical divisions within and between the human rights and civil rights movements.

The Neoliberal Turn

In contemporary academic and advocacy discourse, the terms "neoliberalism" and "capitalism" are often used interchangeably to describe the underlying logic of virtually any market-based economic system. Unfortunately, neoliberalism's ubiquity has obscured its meaning. Critics of capitalism often apply the neoliberal label to a straw man caricature of the current economic order rather than pin down what is "new" or "liberal" about contemporary economic processes. The first new liberals—Green, Hobhouse, Hobson, and members of the Liberal Party who shaped British domestic policy in the early twentieth century—were staunch critics of the laissez-faire economies that today's neoliberals endorse.

David Harvey (2005, 2) describes neoliberalism as "a theory of political economic practices that proposes that human well-being can best be advanced by liberating individual entrepreneurial freedoms and skills within an institutional framework characterized by strong private property rights, free markets, and free trade." Contemporary neoliberalism more closely resembles the classic liberalism of John Locke and Adam Smith and the legal doctrine of laissez-faire constitutionalism that prevailed in late nineteenth- and early twentieth-century America. Contemporary neoliberalism has roots in the free-market ideology of Austrian economists Friedrich von Hayek and Ludwig von Mises and American neoclassical economists Milton Friedman, James Buchanan, and Gary Becker.

Neoliberalism first emerged not from conservative nostalgia but from a progressive attempt to define a "third way" between socialism and laissez-faire capitalism. In 1938, a group of scholars convened in Paris at the Walter Lippmann Colloquium to discuss Lippmann's new book, *An Inquiry into the Principles of the Good Society* (1938). The discussions revolved around the topic of how liberalism could be rescued from what most at the conference saw as the failings of both laissez-faire capitalism and state-led collectivism. Although the term "neoliberalism" was coined by Alexander Rüstow to describe the third way, it has come to be associated with the views of Hayek and Mises, two attendees of the colloquium who were more optimistic about the possibilities of unchained laissez-faire capitalism than the third way (Mirowski and Plehwe 2009).

As critical geographers have observed, contemporary neoliberalism has a distinctly spatial manifestation. The erosion of the welfare state has been associated with a simultaneous rise in local and global processes that Erik Swyngedouw (1997) describes as "glocalization." At the international level, the erosion of trade barriers (at least until the recent rekindling of trade wars between the United States and its trade partners) and deregulation of financial markets have sent capital on a global search for tax havens and a "spatial fix" (Harvey 1989). At the same time, as nation-states have devolved elements of the welfare state to state and local governments, municipalities have evolved into "growth machines" to attract the financial and physical capital needed to provide jobs and services to residents (Hackworth 2007). As discussed later in this chapter, housing justice movements during the neoliberal era have also "jumped scale," linking local advocacy efforts with the global human rights movement (Hackworth 2007).

Although scholars have defined neoliberalism in different ways, I will stick with its common understanding as an ideology characterized by a limited role for the nation-state in the management of economic and social policy outside the protection of private property rights. In the housing policy arena, neoliberalism is often associated with Thatcherite public housing privatization initiatives, but since government-owned housing constitutes such a small share of the US housing stock, American-style neoliberal housing policy has come to be defined by the outsourcing of the federal government's obligation to house the poor to private and nonprofit entities, the devolution of federal housing policy to state and local governments, a shift from housing production subsidies to tenant-based vouchers, and an overall decline in government low-income housing expenditures across all levels of government (Goetz 2013). Other US neoliberal housing strategies include the deregulation of home finance and various initiatives designed to stimulate private-sector affordable housing production. Although the Republican Party has embraced elements of the neoliberal agenda since the New Deal era, neoliberalism did not significantly shape federal housing policy until the 1970s, and since then both Democrats and Republicans have embraced elements of the neoliberal agenda.

Richard Nixon set the stage for neoliberal housing policy by fulfilling his campaign promise to appoint strict constructionists to the Supreme Court. The appointment of Chief Justice Warren Burger and Justices Harry Blackmun, Lewis Powell, and William Rehnquist tilted the balance of the court against those who supported the recognition of social rights. In *Lindsey v. Normet* (1972), a group of tenants refused to pay rent unless the landlord agreed to make the repairs needed to bring the renters' dwelling units into compliance with local housing codes. The lawyers representing the tenants argued that the "need for decent shelter" and the "right to retain peaceful possession of one's home" should be protected as "fundamental interests which are particularly important to the poor and which may be trenched upon only after the State demonstrates some superior interest" (Lehrer 1973, 310). The Burger court rejected this argument and found that there is no "constitutional guarantee of access to dwellings of a particular quality" and that "the Constitution does not provide judicial remedies for every social and economic ill" (Lehrer 1973, 317).[1]

In *San Antonio School District v. Rodriguez* (1973), the Supreme Court rejected the plaintiff's argument that the state's public school system discriminated against poor people because expenditures per pupil were higher in wealthy areas that generated more local property tax revenues. The court went on to deny any fundamental right to education, asking, "How, for instance, is education to be distinguished from the significant personal interest in the basics of decent food and shelter? Empirical examination might well buttress an assumption that the ill-fed, ill-clothed, and ill-housed are among the most ineffective participants in the political process" (Sunstein 2004, 167). Since the Burger court had already denied that decent shelter was a fundamental right, it was clearly not going to concede that public education rose to that standard. With these and other similar cases, the Burger court resurrected the doctrine of laissez-faire constitutionalism to derail further attempts to recognize social rights to redistribution.

The Devolution and Outsourcing of Federal Housing and Community Development Policy

The trajectory of federal housing policy during the early years of Nixon's presidency did not veer much from the path charted by President Johnson. Aside from the establishment of a short-lived new town program, the 1970 Housing and Urban Development Act retained most programs of the Great Society era. Things changed in 1973, when Nixon issued an 18-month moratorium on HUD funding in response to widely publicized scandals in the Section 235 and 236 programs and the perceived failings of the public housing program. That same year, Nixon tried to abolish the OEO, but the courts intervened because he had failed to gain congressional approval for Howard J. Phillips's appointment as acting director (and lead dismantler) of the OEO (Fish 1979; Welfeld 1992).

In 1972, Nixon launched his "new federalist" approach to devolving and decentralizing the administration of domestic policy.[2] New federalism was implemented through two channels: (1) a general revenue sharing program that redistributed federal income tax revenues directly to state and local governments and (2) the consolidation and simplification of existing categorical intergovernmental grant programs into new "block" grants that provided state and local governments more discretion over spending priorities. The 1974 Housing and Community Development Act embodied the new federalism, consolidating several categorical community development grant programs into the single Community Development Block Grant (CDBG) that was allocated to states and local governments on a formula basis for use on a wide range of community development activities.

The outsourcing of community development activities to private nonprofit organizations and CDCs that began during the Johnson administration continued apace during the Nixon years. A large national network of private philanthropic organizations emerged to provide financial support and technical assistance to local CDCs. NeighborWorks America was created from a partnership between HUD and members of the Federal Home Loan Bank Board, drawing on the lessons learned from a successful grassroots effort to attract private funding for community development activities in Pittsburgh. The Local Initiatives Support Corporation was created from a joint effort between the Ford Foundation and six major corporations to provide loans, grants, and technical assistance to CDCs. Real estate developer James Rouse founded the Enterprise Foundation (now named Enterprise Community Partners) to issue grants and loans to support low-income housing and community development activities. Initially established to support six organizations operating in six locations, Enterprise had expanded to assist 54 organizations in 27 locations within six years (von Hoffman 2012b).

The Deconstruction of the Federal Housing Policy Apparatus

During President Ronald Reagan's administration, the two-tier federal housing policy apparatus began to unravel, first with cuts to HUD's budget authority and second with the deregulation (and eventual collapse) of the savings and loan industry.

The Low-Income Rental Housing Tier

Whereas neoliberalism under Nixon meant devolution of the federal government's role in the administration of housing and community development programs, Reagan wanted the federal government out of the housing and social policy business altogether. During the Reagan administration, the federal government dramatically decreased funding for its federal housing programs and reduced HUD's budget authority. According to Reagan's director of the Office of Management and Budget, David Stockman, "The idea that has been established over the last ten years, that almost every service that anyone might need in life ought to be provided and financed by the government as a matter of right, is wrong. We reject that notion" (Blau 1992, 49).

Reagan's policies attacked the social rights movement at its very core. Reagan began by slashing funding for Aid to Families with Dependent Children (formerly Aid to Dependent Children), Social Security, food stamps, and unemployment insurance. He also abolished several community development programs that had been established during President Carter's administration, along with the OEO, which had been on the Republican chopping block since the end of the Great Society era. The signature neoliberal achievement of the Reagan administration was a 70 percent reduction in HUD's budget authority. HUD's budget authority had been around 8 percent of the total federal budget in the late 1970s. With the Reagan cuts, it fell to around 1–2 percent, where it has remained since then (Schwartz 2015).

In many ways, Reagan sought to administer the welfare state according to the same principles that had guided the English Poor Law amendments of 1834, differentiating between those deserving and those undeserving of public assistance, while making public relief so undesirable that no one would prefer it over wage work. During his presidential campaigns in 1976 and 1980, Reagan regularly distinguished between those deserving and those undeserving of public assistance, evoking the racialized and feminized trope of the "welfare queen" to characterize welfare recipients as lazy, corrupt, and undeserving scam artists. The stigmatization of the poor also explains why programs targeted to the needs of the "deserving" poor, such as the elderly and disabled, received more political support. In 1959, Congress created the Section 202 program, which provided targeted housing assistance to the elderly and disabled, and in 1990 it created Section 811 to serve the housing needs of nonelderly persons with disabilities (Dawkins and Miller 2017).

Reagan also ushered in a new approach to financing affordable housing construction. Prior to the 1980s, subsidies for affordable housing production came in one of two flavors. The public housing program subsidized the construction of units that were owned and managed by local public housing agencies, and a variety of mortgage subsidy programs enacted during the 1960s incentivized private-sector developers to construct and operate affordable housing units. Most mortgage subsidy programs had been terminated by the early 1980s, and Reagan's plan to eliminate accelerated depreciation and other multifamily housing tax benefits as part of tax reform brought protests from affordable housing advocates and the homebuilding industry. In response to an aggressive lobbying campaign by these constituencies, the

Low Income Housing Tax Credit (LIHTC) was added to the Tax Reform Act of 1986 as a new incentive to stimulate the private construction of affordable housing (Case 1991). The LIHTC is currently the nation's largest federal subsidy for affordable housing production.

The Homeownership Tier

By the 1980s, the long-term viability of the savings and loan, or "thrift," industry was threatened by short-term interest rate volatility, competition from new household savings vehicles, home price deflation, and Regulation Q, which limited interest payable to savings account holders (Schwartz 2015). President Reagan offered a predictably neoliberal solution to the impending savings and loan crisis: deregulation. Reforms such as the elimination of Regulation Q, the removal of restrictions on high-risk real estate investments, reductions in capital reserve requirements, and the elimination of geographic banking restrictions only exacerbated the problems facing the savings and loan industry, encouraging thrifts to pursue failed speculative real estate ventures.[3] In 1989, Congress passed the Financial Institutions Reform, Recovery, and Enforcement Act (FIRREA) to bail out the thrift industry through the newly established Resolution Trust Corporation (RTC). Under the new Office of Thrift Supervision, established to replace the Federal Home Loan Bank Board, thrifts faced new restrictions that were designed to shore up capital reserves and reduce speculative investments, but the damage had already been done. Because of failures of preexisting thrifts along with new restrictions on lending, thrifts' market share declined from 56 percent of mortgages originated in 1975 to less than 1 percent by 2009. Between 1986 and 1995, more than one thousand thrifts collapsed, costing American taxpayers $124 billion (Schwartz 2015).

During the post-thrift era, the American mortgage finance industry evolved from a regional enterprise into a global juggernaut, because of several changes in the mortgage industry that were spurred in part by federal policy, including an increase in the secondary mortgage market activity of government-sponsored enterprises (GSEs),[4] the rise in private-label mortgage-backed securities, the vertical disintegration of the mortgage industry, innovations in the pricing of credit risk, and the rise of subprime lending (Acharya et al. 2011; Immergluck 2009).

The success of the mortgage industry in the post-thrift era hinged crucially on two interrelated factors: the globalization of finance and rising American home prices. Investors in rich but slow-growing countries sought new global investment vehicles, and mortgage-backed securities created from US home loans were very appealing, particularly with home prices on an upward trajectory. Ultimately, the housing finance tier of the federal housing policy apparatus, which during the neoliberal era had evolved into a vehicle for the global financialization of housing, was too weak to support the weight of overspeculation and lax lending practices. Home prices had risen well above historical averages, and when home prices eventually began to decline in 2006, the US mortgage market unraveled and sent shock waves across the globe. While it is tempting to blame the mortgage crisis on GSEs' increased role in low- and moderate-income homeownership, the evidence belies this claim. While GSEs did invest heavily in subprime mortgages to meet new affordable housing goals enacted during President Bill Clinton's administration, GSE purchases of subprime securities declined during the period when the subprime market rose most rapidly (Schwartz 2015; Immergluck 2009).

Reconstructing Federal Low-Income Housing Policy for a Neoliberal Era

The election of President Bill Clinton was welcomed by many housing policy advocates, who had high hopes that after more than a decade of Republican leadership, a new Democratic administration would return HUD to its prior glory. Clinton expressed a desire to do so, but in practice he sold his housing policy platform by co-opting elements of the neoliberal agenda under the guise of welfare reform. There were two important elements of Clinton's housing policy strategy: public housing reform, which was initially set in motion under President George H. W. Bush, and the expansion and reform of tenant-based housing assistance. A third element—supply-side housing policy reform—reflected a continuation of trends that had been in motion throughout the twentieth century.

The End of Public Housing as We Knew It

Originally conceived by Catherine Bauer as a way to house two-thirds of the working class, public housing eventually came to be viewed as a low-quality, last-resort housing option for welfare recipients and the very poor. In many ways, the politics surrounding the 1937 and 1949 Housing Acts foreshadowed this outcome. In response to the desire of real estate industry lobbyists to limit competition between private and public housing, public housing units were constructed in areas that were physically isolated from the surrounding community, and income eligibility was set below what was necessary to secure housing in the private market. Limitations on allowable construction costs meant that public housing units were often constructed according to low standards of quality, and congressional public housing appropriations were often driven by political priorities rather than actual facility needs. With declines in the average incomes of tenants over time, most local public housing agencies lacked the resources to cover rising building maintenance costs. The devolution of program administration contributed to a spatial distribution of public housing that reinforced existing patterns of residential segregation by race and income. Many suburban public housing agencies simply refused to participate in the program, and those that did participate faced vocal opposition from majority-white neighborhoods. Often, communities of color that had been abandoned by the private market were the only ones to welcome public housing investment (Schwartz 2015; Goetz 2013).

By the 1970s, critics blamed the public housing program for contributing to the same slum housing conditions that public housing was meant to replace. Apart from occasional adjustments to operating subsidies, Congress did not take any major steps to reform the public housing program until 1989, when it created the National Commission on Severely Distressed Public Housing to evaluate the condition of the nation's public housing stock. The commission concluded that about 6 percent of the nation's 1.3 million public housing units were "severely distressed," with severely poor residents living in deteriorated structures located in high-crime neighborhoods (Popkin et al. 2004). In 1992, Congress launched the HOPE VI demonstration program to replace severely distressed public housing with mixed-income housing. HOPE VI also included funding for the physical renovation of properties, various management reforms, and supportive services for residents. Consistent with the neoliberal emphasis on an active private-sector role in social policy implementation, HOPE VI was structured as a public-private partnership.

HOPE VI embodied the new urbanist design philosophy that swept urban planning circles during the 1990s. New urbanism resurrected the ideals of civic republicanism, emphasizing the civic value of front porches, small lots, diverse housing arrangements, streetscape improvements, and other amenities thought to cultivate "social capital," particularly among households earning different incomes. In contrast to the US homeownership movement, which seeks to instill a concern for the common good through the creation of a nation of stakeholders, new urbanists aim to create community from above, through design-based solutions, just as early American settlers shaped the design and configuration of colonial homes to signal collective virtue and tenement housing reformers regulated the urban environment to combat moral decay. President Clinton's HUD secretary, Henry Cisneros, was a firm believer in the value of the new urbanism and sought to incorporate the same design principles into the HOPE VI program.

HOPE VI and the larger new urbanism movement itself have been criticized for failing to achieve economic inclusivity and community through design. Critics claim that HOPE VI perpetuates social segregation, only at a smaller geographic scale, through the physical separation of subsidized housing and high-priced ownership units, the displacement of former public housing residents, and the establishment of separate governing associations for homeowners and subsidized housing residents (Goetz 2013; Chapple and Goetz 2011). While the HOPE VI program has produced many successful mixed-income developments in communities around the nation, it ultimately reduced the total number of subsidized affordable housing units, often without the provision of any other subsidized alternative (Popkin et al. 2004).

Tenant-Based Housing Assistance
The US Chamber of Commerce and National Association of Real Estate Boards (NAREB) first proposed the idea of providing in-kind rent subsidies directly to households in the debates leading up to the 1937 Housing Act, but progressive housing reformers feared that such a policy would simply reward slumlords. By the 1960s, the battle lines had switched. Robert Weaver, the first HUD secretary, strongly favored rent subsidies, while the US Chamber of Commerce and NAREB opposed the idea. Others saw rent subsidies as a form of social engineering designed to foster the socioeconomic integration of neighborhoods. New York congressman Paul A. Fino called rent subsidies "a social planner's dream" that gave "the Housing Administrator a blank check to federalize American residential patterns and subsidized forced economic integration" (von Hoffman 2009, 19). President Johnson found an ally for rent subsidies in the National Association of Homebuilders, and

in part because of their support, the Rent Supplements program found its way into the Housing and Urban Development Act of 1965. Despite being enacted into law, the Rent Supplements program received little funding in subsequent appropriations bills (von Hoffman 2009).

In 1968, the President's Committee on Urban Housing (the Kaiser Commission) released a report that recommended the establishment of an experimental housing allowance program (von Hoffman 2012a). The report was released just as Richard Nixon was being sworn into office, and some in the Nixon administration saw rent subsidies as a more efficient way to provide low-income housing assistance. Despite opposition from some at HUD who feared that rent subsidies would distract attention from the guaranteed income program being developed by Daniel Patrick Moynihan, the 1970 Housing and Urban Development Act established the Federal Experimental Housing Allowance Program (EHAP), which provided tenant-based vouchers on an experimental basis to residents in select counties within the states of Arizona, Pennsylvania, Wisconsin, and Indiana. An early empirical evaluation of EHAP offered encouraging evidence to supporters of tenant-based subsidies, but the study was barely under way when Nixon called for a moratorium on HUD funding (Hays 2012). Before the findings from EHAP were released, Nixon stated in a message to the Congressional Committee on Banking and Currency that "of the policy alternatives available, the most promising way to achieve decent housing for all of our families at an acceptable cost appears to be direct cash assistance" (von Hoffman 2012a, 48). In a separate report to the Council on Environmental Quality, President Nixon objected to the "old approach" of publicly subsidizing the construction of affordable homes, claiming it was based on the erroneous "underlying assumption that the basic problem of the poor is a lack of housing rather than a lack of income" (von Hoffman 2012a, 48).

With the Watergate crisis looming, Nixon faced pressure to rescind the HUD moratorium, and a tenant-based subsidy program found its way into the Housing and Community Development Act of 1974 (Hays 2012). Section 8 of the act created the Existing Housing Program, which provided rental certificates to households earning 80 percent of the area median income, covering the difference between 25 percent (later 30 percent) of a family's adjusted income and the fair market rent (FMR), which was initially defined in terms of the median rent charged for recently leased apartments, adjusted for family size. In 1983, under the Freestanding Voucher Program, local public housing agencies designated "payment standards" that served as the basis for maximum allowable rents. Like the Existing Housing Program, the Freestanding Voucher Program covered the difference between 30 percent of income and the payment standard, but households could choose to live in housing that cost more (or less) than the payment standard if the household covered (or kept) the additional rent. The Quality Housing and Work Responsibility Act of 1998 merged these two rental subsidy programs into the single Housing Choice Voucher (HCV) program that exists today. Under the current program, local housing agencies set payment standards between 90 and 110 percent of the FMR (up to 120 percent in some circumstances), and HUD covers the difference between the payment standard and 30 percent of a household's income. Households can spend no more than 40 percent of their income on rent and can take the voucher anywhere in the United States. Between 1976 and 2009, the number of households receiving tenant-based rental subsidies grew from 100,000 to 2.2 million (Schwartz 2015).

Initially proposed as a more flexible alternative to supply-side production subsidies, tenant-based rental vouchers eventually became an important tool in the fight against racial segregation and the concentration of poverty. In 1966, Dorothy Gautreaux and three other Black tenants of the Chicago Housing Authority (CHA) filed a class-action lawsuit charging the CHA and HUD with discrimination in the location of federally assisted housing. The suit charged that CHA-managed public housing units were exclusively located in majority-Black residential areas and that there were few options for Black tenants seeking to live in majority-white communities. In *Hills v. Gautreaux* (1976), the Supreme Court paved the way for the CHA's implementation of a metropolitan-wide desegregation plan that relied on tenant-based vouchers to achieve racial integration. Public housing residents and those on the waiting list for assisted housing were awarded tenant-based vouchers restricted to locations in either majority-white suburban areas or minority-majority areas located within the city of Chicago. Because tenants were randomly assigned to urban and suburban locations, the *Gautreaux* program created a unique social experiment that allowed researchers to observe the social and economic impacts of racial desegregation. Researchers found that suburban movers were more likely to be employed than those moving to urban locations, and the children of adult suburban movers reported higher levels of educational attainment upon reaching adulthood (Rubinowitz and

Rosenbaum 2000). These findings were complemented by research by William Julius Wilson (1990) and John Kain (1992), who found that the spatial isolation of central city Black workers exacerbated the problem of Black unemployment.

The *Gautreaux* evidence was of interest to policymakers at HUD who saw mixed-income housing strategies as important components of the HOPE VI program and HUD housing policy more broadly. Despite the encouraging findings from *Gautreaux*, policymakers still had limited evidence to support the claim that residential integration by income, rather than race, would produce the same benefits. In 1992, Congress responded by creating the Moving to Opportunity (MTO) demonstration program to evaluate the social and economic impacts of residential mobility out of high-poverty areas. The MTO program randomly assigned tenant-based vouchers to public housing residents for use in low-poverty neighborhoods located within the metropolitan areas of Baltimore, Boston, Chicago, Los Angeles, and New York. The findings from early studies examining the impact of residential mobility to low-poverty MTO neighborhoods were not as encouraging as the results from *Gautreaux*. Although those moving to low-poverty neighborhoods reported improvements in health conditions, MTO had little to no effect on the economic self-sufficiency of movers. More recent research examining the long-term impacts of MTO has found that the children who grew up in low-poverty MTO neighborhoods earned higher wages and were more likely to attend college upon reaching adulthood (Chetty, Hendren, and Katz 2016).

Supply-Side Housing Policy Reform
Neoliberal housing policy requires a robust private housing sector, and the federal government has taken a variety of steps to promote the diffusion of cost-saving mass-production technologies and removal of regulatory impediments to housing production. In contrast to the New Deal–era supply-side subsidy approach, neoliberal supply-side housing policy emphasizes a lean regulatory environment, an innovative housing sector, and limited subsidies. As early as 1919, Le Corbusier called on the homebuilding industry to "occupy itself with building and establish the elements of the house on a mass-production basis" (Wallis 1991, 97). For architect Walter Gropius, the standardization of building components through mass production enabled consumers to assemble individual components into a variety

of housing configurations, thereby enhancing consumer choice (Schneider and Till 2007).

Unlike the auto industry, which was transformed by Henry Ford's assembly-line production methods, the homebuilding industry has been slow to adopt mass-production techniques. Most homebuilders are small, operate on thin margins, and lack the capital to invest in research and development. Things began to change in the early twentieth century, with the introduction of "kit homes" that could be ordered by catalog from companies such as Sears, Roebuck, and Company and Aladdin and assembled on-site. During the 1920s, several companies began to produce "travel trailers" that could be transported behind an automobile. Initially viewed solely as recreational housing options, travel trailers eventually morphed into more permanent mobile homes. By the 1950s, mobile home parks appeared in retirement communities and rural areas (Wallis 1991). In response to the shortage of housing following World War II, President Harry Truman appointed Wilson W. Wyatt as the federal government's special housing expediter. One of Wyatt's pet projects was prefabricated housing. He convinced the Reconstruction Finance Corporation to loan $90 million to prefabricated housing companies, but the program was eventually shelved (Wheildon 1946).

In 1966, the Demonstration Cities and Metropolitan Development Act authorized HUD to conduct research and promote the adoption of industrialized housing construction methods. Through the In-Cities Experimental Housing Project, HUD produced a report that examined how local regulations, labor rules, and other policies constrained the rapid adoption of cost-saving housing innovations. During President Nixon's administration, HUD Secretary George Romney established the Operation Breakthrough demonstration program, which produced nine factory-built housing prototypes and nearly 3,000 units before the program was terminated (US Department of Housing and Urban Development 2016). Romney also established the Open Communities program, a fair housing initiative that threatened the withdrawal of HUD funding from communities that had adopted exclusionary land-use regulations. President Nixon ultimately pulled the plug on the Open Communities initiative because of vocal opposition from suburban communities.

By the 1970s, the manufactured housing industry faced two challenges. First, housing consumers viewed mobile homes as recreational vehicles or low-quality housing options that were only viable in rural areas where mobile home parks were permitted. Second, producers of manufactured housing faced a regulatory maze of building codes that varied from state to state and land-use regulations that varied from city to city. This complex regulatory environment made it difficult for them to achieve economies of scale through high-volume production. In 1976, HUD responded by adopting the Manufactured Home Construction and Safety Standards, also known as the "HUD Code," which created a single national construction standard for all manufactured homes (Fish 1979). The HUD Code standardized building codes for manufactured homes but did nothing to address the regulatory barriers created by local zoning and land-use regulations.

In 1998, during the Clinton administration, HUD established the Partnership for Advancing Technology in Housing (PATH) as a public-private partnership to encourage the diffusion of new homebuilding technologies, emphasizing innovations designed to promote energy efficiency in housing. One of the major initiatives to come out of the PATH program before its demise was an effort to reform local land-use and building regulations to encourage production of affordable housing. In contrast to Romney's Open Communities program, the PATH "regulatory barriers" initiative was designed as a carrot rather than a stick, which would encourage local regulatory reform through research and the promotion of best practices. The regulatory barriers initiative produced several research reports and advanced knowledge about the extent of local regulatory barriers (US Department of Housing and Urban Development 2016), but it still failed to produce widespread local regulatory reform, primarily because many communities viewed local zoning and land-use regulations as sacred cows.[5]

HUD's regulatory barriers initiatives and other similar efforts appealed to the theory that all forms of housing production ultimately benefit low-income households even if the new homes constructed are not immediately affordable. Through the "filtering" process, aging homes will eventually decline in value and be sold by higher-income households seeking to move up in the housing market, making older homes available to low-income populations at affordable prices (Ratcliff 1949). Since the New Deal era, housing advocates have cautioned against relying exclusively on the filtering process to provide affordable housing. Edith Elmer Wood (1931), for example, worried that sole reliance on the filtering process would simply relegate low-income households to inadequate homes. Filtering also does nothing to address the short-term shortage of affordable housing.

Neoliberalism and the Postmodern American Housing Landscape

During the contemporary neoliberal era, the focus of federal low-income housing policy has shifted from public housing and urban renewal to tenant-based vouchers and affordable housing production tax credits. Catherine Bauer's dream of modern housing and Franklin D. Roosevelt's aspiration to extend social rights to housing have gone unrealized. The new postmodern neoliberal housing landscape is one that emphasizes homeownership over renting, housing choice over housing stability, and private- versus public-sector housing production. Two features of this landscape are particularly noteworthy: its overall inequality and its geographic segregation.

According to David Albouy and Mike Zabek (2016), inequality in housing values and rents declined between 1930 and 1970, roughly corresponding to the period when the New Deal–era two-tier housing policy apparatus was still firmly in place. Since 1970, inequality in housing rents and values has increased. In 2012, those owning homes valued in the top 20 percent of the home value distribution held 50 percent of all home value, a level of housing inequality that was almost identical to the level of housing inequality observed in 1930. Matthew Rognlie (2015) finds that rising housing wealth inequality accounts for much of the recent rise in global wealth inequality reported by Thomas Piketty (2014).

The US housing market is also geographically segregated by socioeconomic class. Most metropolitan areas are more integrated by race than they were in 1970, but the average white household still lives in a neighborhood with few people of color (Logan and Stults 2011). US households are also increasingly sorting into communities that are homogeneous by income, education level, political affiliation, and lifestyle preference (Bischoff and Reardon 2014; Bishop 2009). Residential sorting on the basis of preferences for local amenities has transformed overall housing inequality into geographic divides within metropolitan areas (Albouy and Zabek 2016). Residential sorting is not only creating a geographic dimension to the housing divide but also reinforcing that divide. Since 1980, the residential sorting of wealthy people into wealthy places has amplified interregional income disparities (Manduca 2019).

By enabling an increasingly unequal and segregated housing market substructure, neoliberalism has eroded previously shared social meanings of American housing. The traditional owned single-family detached home, a cultural ideal that inspired generations of housing and land reformers, no longer has the same appeal, particularly for those who watched the value of their single-family home plummet during the 2007–2010 foreclosure crisis. Perhaps this is a good thing. The American housing market now provides a wider range of choices in home styles than has ever existed before. Tiny homes tailored to the needs of young homebuyers coexist with homes that are modifiable as families grow and shrink over time. Prefabricated modular housing components now enable homebuyers to plan and assemble homes into an infinite combination of housing styles. Housing consumers can also now choose which bundle of rights to attach to the home. Shared-equity homeownership options and community land trusts enable homeowners who seek housing security but not profit to forgo the right to earn home equity in exchange for a more affordable home. The challenge for housing reformers is to find a way to retain neoliberalism's benefits for housing diversity, flexibility, and choice while mitigating its tendency to reproduce segregation and inequality.

Fragmented Responses to Neoliberalism

Just as laissez-faire constitutionalism shaped the battle lines of the progressive attack on private property during the early years of the twentieth century, the Burger court and rise of neoliberal housing policies set the stage for a new generation's demands for housing justice. Although echoes of the Progressive Era attack on private property still linger, neoliberal-era housing advocacy differs in important ways from the progressive attack on laissez-faire constitutionalism, and advocates resisting neoliberalism have pursued divergent paths to reform, with most contemporary housing advocates embracing rather than rejecting right-based approaches.

During the late nineteenth and early twentieth centuries, laissez-faire constitutionalism flourished, in part because the federal government had emerged from the Civil War as a strong protector of individual rights. Progressives generally supported a strong role for government but understood that role as that of a steward of collective welfare and the common good, even if certain individual rights, such as the rights to use and earn income from property, were constrained. Many progressives viewed the language of rights as impoverished, atomistic, and antithetical to the pursuit of the common good. By the 1960s, the quandary facing housing advocates was that many Progressive Era reforms defined the common good in ways that excluded the poor and people of color. Progressive zoning had produced segregated neighborhoods, urban renewal had destroyed communities of color, and public housing had reinforced the spatial concentration of poverty. Right-based reforms regained their appeal during the 1960s because claims of right directly challenged the majoritarian institutions that had infringed on the social rights of people of color and those living in poverty. Furthermore, the reinterpretation of rights as collective moral claims allowed community-based advocates to avoid the critique that rights were grounded in an overly individualistic morality.

During the neoliberal era, housing advocates abandoned their 1960s era antipathy for top-down federal housing programs and challenged the state's inaction rather than its overextension, fighting against the rising tide of neoliberalism while simultaneously demanding new federal subsidy programs geared toward specific categories of housing need and the recognition of minimal entitlements for those marginalized by neoliberal institutions. At the same time, the contemporary housing justice movement's nearly unanimous opposition to neoliberalism has fostered an antipathy toward liberal housing policy solutions, both of the "neo" and "welfare state" varieties.

As the federal government largely withdrew from the low-income housing policy arena during the 1980s, community-based organizations and CDCs picked up the slack. The expansion of the philanthropic sector and large national networks such as the National Low Income Housing Coalition and the Coalition for the Homeless provided a new institutional structure to support community-based housing movements, and nonprofit foundations such as the Enterprise Foundation provided financial support. International nongovernmental organizations charged with monitoring compliance with human rights treaties provided a new global platform for discourse on housing justice issues. The new global infrastructure supporting community organizations did not flatten the place-based orientation of the housing justice movement. Instead, the emphasis on place only became stronger with the global attention drawn to gentrification and forced displacement, fostering new alliances while simultaneously exposing inherent contradictions within the housing justice movement. The remainder of this section explores how the social movements examined in chapter 4 coevolved during the neoliberal era, at times producing new movements on behalf of those facing housing insecurity.

Enough Housing Is Good Enough

Individuals and families have gone without homes throughout America's history, but curiously homelessness never became a major focus of federal housing policy until the 1980s. Assistance to those without homes has historically been viewed as the responsibility of state and local governments and charity organizations. Single room occupancy apartments and hotels provided inexpensive temporary housing until the postwar era, when many were demolished as part of larger downtown redevelopment and urban renewal initiatives (Feldman 2004). By the 1970s, the homelessness problem had attracted national attention, and housing advocacy organizations began to mobilize on behalf of the homeless. In 1979, Robert Hayes, founder of the Coalition for the Homeless, brought a class-action lawsuit against the city and state of New York in *Callahan v. Carey* (1979). The suit charged that both had violated the New York State Constitution, which states that "the aid, care and support of the needy are public concerns and shall be provided by the state and by such of its subdivisions" (N.Y. Const. art. XVII § 1). As part of a consent decree, the city agreed to provide shelter that met basic health and safety standards to all homeless men who were on welfare or were homeless because of disability, effectively creating a right to shelter in New York. *Eldredge v. Koch* (1983) extended the same right to homeless women. A handful of other municipalities soon followed suit by enacting local right-to-shelter ordinances (Foscarinis 2004).

Advocates for the homeless also called for the establishment of a federal program designed to address the homelessness problem. One of the most visible mobilization efforts was the Association of Community Organizations for Reform Now (ACORN) squatter campaign. ACORN was created in 1970 by Wade Rathke, who had been approached by welfare rights advocate George Wiley to form an antipoverty organization comprised of working-class and poor people (Mandell 2012). In 1979, ACORN organized a squatter campaign designed to push city officials to make vacant city-owned properties available for those in need of housing. This effort expanded in the 1980s to 13 cities and in June 1982 led to the creation of a squatters' "Tent City" in Washington, DC. ACORN's advocacy work had impact. ACORN criticized HUD's urban homesteading program for ignoring city-owned properties and failing to prioritize housing to those most in need.[6] Congress listened and incorporated most of ACORN's suggestions into the Housing and Urban-Rural Recovery Act of 1983 (Rohe 1991).

The National Union for the Homeless and the Community for Creative Non-Violence (CCNV) joined ACORN to draw attention to the growing problem of homelessness. Their tent cities were often described as "Reaganvilles," a jab hearkening back to Depression-era "Hoovervilles." Mitch Snyder of the CCNV held a hunger strike that led to negotiations with the White House and congressional action on the homelessness issue (Mink and O'Connor 2004). Legal advocates also joined the antihomelessness cause, drafting model legislation that was eventually incorporated into federal law (Foscarinis 2004). This broad coalition's signature achievement was the 1987 Stewart B. McKinney Homeless Assistance Act, named in honor of its Republican sponsor and advocate, who died soon after the bill's adoption. The McKinney Act (later named the McKinney-Vento Act to acknowledge Representative Bruce Vento's ongoing support) established the Interagency Council on Homelessness and federal funding to support a variety of homeless assistance initiatives.

Antihomelessness advocacy since 1987 has focused primarily on extending the limited funding provided through the McKinney-Vento Act and improving its effectiveness. In 2009, President Obama signed the Helping Families Save Their Homes Act, which reauthorized the McKinney-Vento Act and modified it to emphasize the new "housing first" philosophy of providing rapid rehousing before the provision of social services. The act also consolidated several existing programs into a single Continuum of Care program and expanded the definition of homelessness to include people at imminent risk of homelessness.

In addition to their work lobbying for the passage of federal antihomelessness legislation, legal advocates have mobilized in opposition to local and state laws that criminalize homelessness. In contrast to the strategy of advocating on behalf of government funding for shelter provision, this strategy accepts the reality of homelessness while working to protect a homeless person's ability to access the guaranteed rights of citizenship. During the welfare reform years of the 1980s and 1990s, many local governments in the United States either eliminated their right-to-shelter laws or imposed work requirements and other limits on shelter stays. Other cities imposed criminal sanctions on those sleeping in public. In response to these trends, the National Coalition for the Homeless called for the adoption of "Homeless Bills of Rights," and several states and localities have passed laws that recognize special legal protections for those without shelter (Rankin 2015).

Legal advocates have also put forth new legal arguments to strike down laws that criminalize homelessness. In *Pottinger v. City of Miami* (1989), for example, the court found that because of the scarcity of shelter beds in Miami, the homeless had no alternative to sleeping in public and that criminal punishments for life-sustaining conduct were cruel and unusual and in violation of the Eighth Amendment (Foscarinis 2004).

Regardless of whether antihomelessness advocates have pushed for homeless assistance funding, legal rights to shelter, or legal protections for those without homes, antihomelessness advocacy has emphasized the distributive goal of *sufficiency* over *equality*. Harry Frankfurt describes the "doctrine of sufficiency" as follows: "With respect to the distribution of economic assets, what is important from the point of view of morality is not that everyone should have the same but that each should have enough. If everyone had enough, it would be of no moral consequence whether some had more than others. I shall refer to this alternative to egalitarianism—namely, that what is morally important with respect to money is for everyone to have enough—as 'the doctrine of sufficiency'" (Frankfurt 1987, 21–22).

Samuel Moyn (2018, 3; italics in the original) argues that "sufficiency concerns how far an individual is *from having nothing* and how well she is doing *in relation to some minimum of provision* of the good things in life. Equality concerns how far individuals are *from one another* in the portion of those good things they get." What matters, from the antihomelessness advocate's standpoint, is that some lack housing, not that some live in homes that are more lavish than others. While an emphasis on sufficiency has helped advocates secure several legal and legislative victories on behalf of the homeless, advocates have largely ignored the role that neoliberal property markets play in excluding the propertyless from privately owned spaces. Instead, many of the strategies pursued by antihomelessness advocates actually *require* neoliberal property markets to generate enough income and wealth to fund redistributive programs adequately. By focusing attention on the state's role as a redistributor of propertied income rather than its role as the architect of property-based institutions, antihomelessness advocates have left the institution of private property intact.

Tenants' Rights and Renter Advocacy
In contrast to the antihomelessness movement's deference to neoliberal institutions, tenants' rights advocates have demanded that property-based

institutions be restructured to favor renters. The contemporary tenants' rights movement has joined forces with the right to community movement to advance a conception of housing justice that appeals to collective rights. Alongside the tenants' rights movement, a new generation of renter advocates, identified by their embrace of the YIMBY (yes in my backyard) acronym, is calling for reforms that protect private developers' rights to produce rental housing. The question of gentrification has driven a wedge between these two movements.

Much as the labor movement has challenged employers' rights to define the terms of wage contracts, tenants' rights advocates have sought to restructure laws governing lease contracts to prioritize tenants' occupancy rights over landlords' rights to earn income from, manage, and control the use of privately owned residential property. During the 1970s, tenant advocates achieved several state and local legislative victories. For example, advocacy by the New Jersey Tenants Organization led to one of the nation's strongest state landlord-tenant laws and rent controls in 120 New Jersey municipalities (Ceraso 1999). In 1972, the National Conference of Commissioners on Uniform State Laws published the Uniform Residential Landlord and Tenant Act (URLTA), and several states adopted state landlord-tenant laws that were based on the URLTA or the American Law Institute's Model Landlord Tenant Act, on which the URLTA was based (Glendon 1982).

There have been a few sporadic attempts to organize tenants nationally. The NTO, described in chapter 4, had affiliates in most large and medium-sized cities within a few years, but the organization's membership declined in the 1970s (Drier 1984). In 1980, tenant organizations around the country held the first convention for a newly created National Tenants Union, but the organization eventually lost steam because of the twin difficulties of attracting funding and organizing tenants (Ceraso 1999).

The historical alliance between tenants' rights advocates and right to community advocates has shaped the character of tenants' rights claims, with tenant organizations often appealing to a collective conception of tenants' rights. In theory, the expansion of tenants' rights vis-à-vis landlords does not require viewing tenants as members of a collective group. Tenants' rights could be defined in terms of tenants' individual claims of right, taken severally, not to be deprived of their means of material subsistence, but the Burger court questioned the constitutional basis of such claims. Ironically, by denying the extension of social rights to individual renters, the courts provided ammunition for the tenant movement's appeal to collective rights. During the neoliberal era, tenants' rights advocates have expanded the idea of housing security to encompass collective rights to live securely in a place and sustain the community where tenants live, particularly in cities facing gentrification. The new antigentrification alliance emphasizes the "right to stay put" amid housing price inflation (Hartman 2002; Imbroscio 2004). Just as Native Americans asserted their rights to community during the nineteenth century in response to the US government's confiscation of native lands, the new antigentrification alliance condemns gentrification as a form of neocolonialism, which, according to Neil Smith (2010, 117), "justifies monstrous incivility in the heart of the city."

The case of Washington, DC, illustrates how the politics of race and place often intersect around tenants' collective rights claims, particularly in cities facing gentrification. In 1973, the District of Columbia gained the home rule right to govern itself at the same time that market forces were threatening to displace the city's majority-Black population. The conflux of these two events meant that tenants' collective rights not to be displaced from DC were part and parcel of their collective rights of self-governance. The District of Columbia subsequently passed several laws designed to shift the balance of residential property rights from landlords and property developers to renters. The Citywide Housing Coalition lobbied for the successful adoption of a rent control ordinance in 1975. The Condominium Conversion Act of 1976 required mayoral and tenant approval of condominium conversions. In 1978, DC imposed an antispeculation excise tax on those who held property for a short period in order to discourage speculation and the flipping of residential property. In a novel twist on Thatcher's "right to buy," tenant advocates successfully pushed for the adoption of the Tenant Opportunity to Purchase Act (TOPA) in 1980. In contrast to Thatcher's policy adopted that same year, TOPA granted tenants the right of first refusal to purchase their occupied rental buildings before the building was offered for sale on the private market. The city also provided financing to assist with a home purchase. Under TOPA, tenants could accept a payment to vacate their occupied rental unit, negotiate to stay for a negotiated or reduced rent, purchase their home, or assign their rights to a third-party negotiator (Huron 2018; Gallaher 2016).

California's coastal cities have also been at the center of debates surrounding gentrification and rental housing affordability. Like DC, California has a long history of tenant advocacy. Proposition 13, which reduced local property taxes by an average of 57 percent, was primarily intended to benefit homeowners, but it was also sold as a form of tax relief that would be passed on to renters (Capek and Gilderbloom 1992). When renters were greeted with notifications of pending rent increases shortly after the adoption of Proposition 13 in 1978, tenants' rights organizations erupted in protest (Heskin 1983; Capek and Gilderbloom 1992). In the following months, Los Angeles, Beverly Hills, Berkeley, and Davis froze and rolled back rents. Voters in Santa Cruz approved an antispeculation tax similar to what was enacted in Washington, DC. In 1979, voters in Santa Monica approved rent control legislation (Leepson 1979; Capek and Gilderbloom 1992). The real estate industry, represented by the California Housing Council, was alarmed by the backlash from renters and over the next decade and a half lobbied to pass a statewide law that preempted local rent control laws. They were successful in 1995 when Democratic state senator Jim Costa and Republican assemblyman Phil Hawkins jointly sponsored the 1995 Costa-Hawkins Rental Housing Act, which limited cities' ability to enact rent regulation and extend existing rent control laws. Since then, tenants' rights organizations have been united in their opposition to the Costa-Hawkins Act. Bills to repeal the act have been defeated due to pressure from real estate organizations and lobbyists representing landlords.

For the new California YIMBY coalition, the solution to rising rental housing prices is not rent control or tenant protections but instead the removal of regulatory barriers to affordable housing production, a solution that hearkens back to the neoliberal supply-side approach that has been advanced by HUD for decades. While YIMBY advocates support private developers' rights to produce rental housing, California's tenants' rights advocates and their allies oppose market-oriented solutions to the housing crisis, advocating instead for tenant protections combined with an expansion of government subsidies for public housing construction. Led in California by the Los Angeles Democratic Socialists of America, so-called PHIMBY (public housing in my backyard) advocates initially aligned with the YIMBYs but were turned off by the YIMBY pro-market ideology. For the PHIMBYs, a large-scale social housing program on the scale of that found in many European countries offers the most effective solution to the contemporary housing crisis (Keeling 2018). Tracy Jeanne Rosenthal, cofounder of the Los Angeles Tenants Union, calls for a resurrection of Catherine Bauer's modern housing vision, echoing Bauer's belief that "the private market cannot provide adequate housing for poor and working people" (Keeling 2018).

The YIMBYs have also encountered opposition from the right to community wing of the civil rights movement. YIMBY activists want to make it easier to construct housing at any price range, but tenant advocates and right to community advocates object to market-rate housing development when it results in displacement and gentrification. Although for decades housing advocates have objected to NIMBY opposition to affordable housing construction, the California YIMBY movement is a relative newcomer to the housing advocacy movement. Tenants' rights advocates and anti-gentrification groups have characterized California YIMBYs as being out of touch with the housing advocacy movement's roots in civil rights and community organizing, a charge also levied against ACORN in its early years (Mandell 2012). The conflict between tenant advocates and the YIMBYs was on public display in 2018, when YIMBY activists disrupted a rally to oppose SB 827, the controversial statewide zoning reform bill mentioned in the introduction (Axel-Lute 2019).

The state of Oregon has managed to overcome these divisions to pass sweeping reforms of local land-use and rent control laws. In 2019, Oregon legislators passed Senate Bill 608, which restricts yearly rent increases to 7 percent and provides just-cause protections against evictions, two measures that tenant advocates have sought for decades. Later that year, Oregon passed House Bill 2001, which requires cities with a population of 10,000 or more to allow duplexes in single-family zones. Since Oregon's housing advocacy movement has not been characterized by the same divisions that have shaped the California housing debate, Oregon has managed to address the rental housing affordability crisis from multiple angles (Axel-Lute 2019).

There is a growing national constituency for the local land-use policy reforms favored by YIMBY advocates. Several states are now considering the adoption of Oregon-style laws, and in September 2019, Democratic US House representative Denny Heck and Republican representative Trey Hollingsworth introduced the "Yes in My Backyard" Act (YIMBY Act, US House of Representatives 2020) for consideration by the US Congress. The act requires CDBG recipients to report periodically on progress removing local regulatory barriers to affordable housing production. As of this writing, the YIMBY Act has been passed by the House and is awaiting consideration by the Senate.

The tenants' rights movement has assumed a different character in cold housing markets facing disinvestment and decline. In these markets, the challenge has been to find ways of enabling low-income tenants to remain in their homes when faced with job loss and the outmigration of friends and family. During the 1970s and 1980s, the tenants' rights movement pursued various self-help strategies to gain access to homes that had recently been acquired through tax delinquency or foreclosure proceedings. In response to a series of rent strikes in New York City, the state of New York adopted the Article 7-A Amendment, which allowed residents of deteriorated rental buildings to deposit rents with the local judge, who then appointed an administrator to allocate the collected rents to needed repairs. When a recession hit New York City during the 1970s, many landlords simply walked away from their properties, and tenants relied on Article 7-A to collectively acquire and manage the buildings themselves (Gold 2014). Thus, advocacy on behalf of tenants' rights to live in habitable buildings was expanded into a collective right to acquire and manage residential buildings.

In other communities facing disinvestment and decline, community-based organizations have turned to collective land acquisition strategies to catalyze successful grassroots community development campaigns. The Boston-area Dudley Street Neighborhood Initiative (DSNI) has received national acclaim for its efforts to reverse decades of disinvestment. Through a novel arrangement that granted the Dudley Neighbors Incorporation powers of eminent domain, DSNI catalyzed the construction of deed-restricted affordable housing that was then sold to low-income buyers and rented to low-income households (Meehan 2014).[7] The DSNI and other similar community land trust initiatives are the latest manifestation of Henry George's strategy of recouping land value to promote community investments.

Despite some successes, both the old and new generations of the tenants' rights movement face many of the same challenges. Expanded tenants' rights benefit those who are already tenants but do not guarantee a rental unit to those who are currently homeless. Strong antieviction laws may actually have the opposite effect of reducing the turnover of rental units to the next prospective renter. Furthermore, stringent rent controls may restrict the supply of new rental housing and discourage landlords from making property improvements. Tenant advocates have devoted most of their energy to tenure-specific solutions while ignoring broader inequalities in housing wealth and housing security between those who rent and own homes and those with and without housing. Just-cause eviction laws and rent control ordinances improve rental lease terms for those who already have a lease, but these measures do nothing to alter housing inequalities that span the tenure spectrum.

Divergent Paths to Fair Housing
Just as tenants' rights advocates have fought to alter the institutions of private property to favor renters, civil rights advocates have fought for legal reforms designed to open up housing opportunities to people of color. It was widely recognized by many in the fair housing movement that the compromises needed to pass the 1968 FaHA limited its effectiveness, and much of the advocacy work in the post-FaHA era has been oriented toward improving the fair housing enforcement apparatus through the adoption of various laws that complemented the FaHA, including the 1974 Equal Credit Opportunity Act, the 1975 Home Mortgage Disclosure Act, and the 1977 Community Reinvestment Act. In 1988, Congress also amended the FaHA to strengthen its enforcement mechanisms (Yinger 1995).

Despite relative agreement on the FaHA's overall objective of eliminating housing market discrimination on the basis of race and ethnicity, philosophical disagreements among advocates over the issue of residential segregation have splintered the fair housing movement. In the early 1970s, HUD interpreted the FaHA's AFFH clause as a mandate to integrate the suburbs through regionalist housing policy strategies. The short-lived Open Communities program described earlier conditioned the receipt of HUD funding on the removal of regulatory barriers to affordable housing, and the Regional Housing Mobility program provided incentives to expand regional affordable housing opportunities (Goetz 2003; Goering 1986). Central city mayors, civil rights organizations, affordable housing advocates, and even some HUD officials criticized these and other regionalist initiatives for "allowing housing only where it's not wanted and not putting it where the people are in dire need," in the words of then HUD undersecretary Victor Marrero (Goering 1986, 201).

Tensions also arose over HUD's subsidized housing siting guidelines. In response to *Shannon v. HUD* (1969), which found that the construction of subsidized housing in a majority-Black Philadelphia neighborhood violated the FaHA's AFFH mandate, HUD developed new guidelines that steered

HUD-subsidized housing away from minority-majority neighborhoods. Black politicians criticized HUD's siting guidelines because they limited housing options for Black residents who needed housing assistance but preferred to live in majority-Black neighborhoods (von Hoffman 1998b). Congress held hearings on the HUD siting guidelines in 1979. Representative Cardiss Collins of Illinois objected that residents in minority-majority neighborhoods were in a "Catch 22 situation" that prevented "those who wish to remain in their present neighborhoods from enjoying better housing" in those neighborhoods (Goetz 2018, 107).

The HOPE VI and MTO programs have been criticized on similar grounds. Critics of HOPE VI argue that the program caused massive displacement, catalyzed the gentrification of low-income communities, and failed to foster meaningful social connections between low-income and high-income residents (Goetz 2003; Chapple and Goetz 2011). Critics of MTO argue that the program overemphasized residential choice through mobility while ignoring the needs of communities left behind by movers (Imbroscio 2012). Some also cite the early evaluations of the MTO program, which failed to find conclusive evidence of positive economic impacts for those moving to low-poverty neighborhoods, to argue that the benefits from moving to opportunity were overstated (Goetz and Chapple 2010). Those responding to these critiques point out that MTO and HOPE VI addressed poverty deconcentration but not necessarily racial desegregation, unlike the earlier *Gautreaux* program, on which MTO was based, so the evidence from these studies should not be interpreted as an indictment against initiatives designed to promote racial integration (Goering and Feins 2003).

Two recent developments have rekindled tensions between the integrationist and right to community wings of the fair housing movement. The 2015 *Texas Department of Housing and Community Affairs v. The Inclusive Communities Project, Inc.* Supreme Court case found that the Texas Department of Housing and Community Affairs' (TDHCA) policy of disproportionately allocating LIHTCs to low-income communities of color constituted a disparate impact violation of the FaHA. A disparate impact is said to have occurred whenever public or private entities rely on policies or practices that adversely impact members of a protected class without having any other legitimate purpose, even if the policy does not explicitly reference the protected class being discriminated against (Yinger 1995). Recognition of the constitutionality of the disparate impact doctrine in fair housing cases is significant because, unlike individual instances of discrimination, the disparate impact doctrine has a uniquely spatial interpretation, given that disparate impacts are often explicitly defined in terms of segregated residential patterns (Dawkins 2018).[8]

The second source of recent tension can be traced to President Barack Obama's decision to implement the FaHA's AFFH mandate more aggressively. Under previous presidential administrations, local recipients of HUD funding were required to submit an Analysis of Impediments to Fair Housing Choice (AI) plan to demonstrate compliance with the FaHA. A report by the US Government Accountability Office (2010) reviewed 441 AI reports and found widespread problems, including AIs that were outdated, incomplete, and lacked clear implementation guidelines. HUD had previously proposed a regulation in 1998 to clarify and improve the AI process, but the rule was rescinded because of opposition from US mayors.

In 2015, HUD promulgated new rules requiring that all recipients of HUD funds adopt and submit to HUD an Assessment of Fair Housing (AFH) that identified fair housing issues in the local jurisdiction, identified the factors contributing to those issues, and established goals and strategies for responding to those issues. The AFH differed from the previous AI in important ways. First, the AFH was a more standardized process that gave HUD more oversight over the local fair housing planning process. Second, HUD provided online geospatial data to assist in the completion of the AFH. Third, and perhaps most importantly, AFFH objectives were more explicitly tied to residential integration (overcoming historic patterns of segregation and fostering inclusive communities) and geographic access to opportunity goals (US Department of Housing and Urban Development 2015, § 5.152).

Just as HUD seemed poised to tackle residential segregation head-on, President Donald Trump's administration reversed the pro-integrative housing policy path charted by his predecessor. After initially exploring a new AFFH rule that would have downplayed the emphasis on residential integration objectives, the Trump administration officially dismantled the 2015 AFFH rule in July 2020. The Trump administration also significantly revised an Obama-era HUD disparate impact rule to remove references to segregation and make it more difficult to prove disparate impact claims. It remains to be seen whether these reforms will survive beyond the Trump presidency, but President Joe Biden's vocal support for Obama's policy agenda points to a return to pro-integrative housing policy. As of this writing, the future direction of fair housing policy remains uncertain.

The Human Rights Umbrella

On the international stage, the human rights debate around housing issues did not begin in earnest until the 1990s. The content of the right implied by the UDHR and the ICESCR was clarified in December 1991, when the Committee on Economic, Social and Cultural Rights (CESCR) adopted General Comment Number 4, which for the first time outlined the specific entitlements that comprised the right to adequate housing. These include the legal security of tenure; the availability of services, materials, facilities, and infrastructure; affordability; habitability; accessibility; location; and cultural adequacy (Committee on Economic, Social and Cultural Rights 1991). General Comment Number 7 outlined additional protections against forced evictions (Committee on Economic, Social and Cultural Rights 1997). In 2000, the Commission on Human Rights appointed a special rapporteur on adequate housing, whose mandate has been to focus on adequate housing as a component of the right to an adequate standard of living as recognized under international human rights law.

In the United States, several housing advocacy organizations built on the momentum from the 1996 UN Habitat II conference in Istanbul to initiate a national dialogue on the human right to housing. Initial advocacy efforts following the conference addressed homelessness as a human rights violation. The National Law Center on Homelessness & Poverty (NLCHP) produced several reports identifying litigation strategies and advocacy approaches. In 2003, the NLCHP organized a national forum on the human right to housing, and in 2004 it released a report detailing the homelessness problem in the United States and its human rights implications. Several other organizations followed suit with similar efforts, including the American Civil Liberties Union and the Ford Foundation (Foscarinis 2006).

In 2008, Catherine Powell wrote an influential report titled *Human Rights at Home: A Domestic Policy Blueprint for the New Administration* (Powell 2008). The paper launched a new coalition committed to applying the human rights framework to a variety of federal, state, and local policy reforms. The NLCHP, an important partner in the aptly named "Human Rights at Home Campaign," published *Human Rights to Human Reality: A 10 Step Guide to Strategic*

Human Rights Advocacy to assist those seeking to employ the language of human rights to advocate on behalf of rights for the homeless. According to the guide (National Law Center on Homelessness and Poverty 2014, 7), "We have understood that if we are to achieve our mission of ending and preventing homelessness in America, we must gain recognition—by the government, and by the public at large—of housing as a human right to which all are entitled. For close to two decades, we have learned much, through trial, error, and dogged persistence, about how we could use the tools of human rights to strategically aid in our domestic advocacy on behalf of poor and homeless people across the country."

Human rights advocates have also joined forces with a new generation of advocates in the fight against urban gentrification. Some have interpreted the CESCR's language on forced evictions to obligate public and private actors to refrain from actions that threaten the legal security of tenure (Ponder 2016). The new human rights campaign against gentrification draws on Henri Lefebvre's (1968) concept of the "right to the city," which integrates the right to contribute to the production of urban space with the right to access, occupy, and use urban space (Purcell 2002). Both UN Habitat and UNESCO have supported efforts to incorporate a right to the city into the broader human rights agenda (Purcell 2013).

In the United States, the Right to the City Alliance draws on the human rights framework to incorporate a right to a decent and sustainable home into a broader conception of inhabitants' right to inhabit and participate in the creation of their community (Knafo 2015). The Right to the City Alliance, an umbrella organization that includes 45 organizational members, combines a place-based orientation with an emphasis on housing justice, economic justice, racial justice, environmental justice, and immigrant justice to oppose neoliberal urban policies directly. The Alliance's "Homes for All" campaign supports a Renter Rights Committee, comprised of 12 community organizations seeking to pass renters' rights ordinances, and Renter Nation assemblies that advocate on behalf of tenants' rights and antigentrification causes (Right to the City Alliance 2015).

The new US human rights and right to the city coalition has been shaped by its interactions with the global human rights movement. The Chicago Anti-Eviction Campaign, an urban homesteading and antigentrification organization, was instrumental in organizing a 2009 visit to the United States by the UN special rapporteur on adequate housing, Raquel Rolnik. Ashraf

Cassiem, a leader of the Western Cape Anti-Eviction Campaign in South Africa, visited leaders of the Chicago Anti-Eviction Campaign to provide tactical advice on how to mobilize the poor to oppose displacement and eviction (Roy 2017). Cassiem saw his visit to Chicago as a way to get to the heart of the global urban crises created by neoliberalism. According to Cassiem,

> The problem, you see, is not in South Africa. It's in America. I wanted to go to the root of it, to the root of neoliberal capitalism, to the University of Chicago where the policy was born. It was created in Chicago and so it was there that it had to be dismantled. Evictions were not really the point. It was about the monetization that had made us separate individuals. And so it was in Chicago that I wanted to show up. It was there that we had to kill neoliberalism, rescind it, burn it. That's where we had to shut down the Milton Friedman project. I thought that if we won in Chicago, we would automatically win in South Africa, we would win all over the world. This is why winning in Chicago mattered for us. (Roy 2017, A6)

So far, the new alliance between human rights advocates and right to the city advocates has yet to have a major impact on federal housing policy. Advocacy on behalf of the human right to housing has been complicated by the United States' reluctance to ratify the ICESCR. Proposals to enact the right to housing in US law through a constitutional amendment and legislation were introduced but never adopted (Foscarinis 2006). The Obama administration expressed support for, but failed to act on, a United Nations Human Rights Council recommendation that the United States "continue its efforts in the domain of access to housing, vital for the realization of several other rights, in order to meet the needs for adequate housing at an affordable price for all segments of the American society" (Byrne and Culhane 2011, 386).

As legal historian Samuel Moyn documents in *Not Enough: Human Rights in an Unequal World* (2018), the human rights movement was born from the aspiration to extend the egalitarian welfare state to the world, but human rights advocates abandoned their concern for global egalitarianism just as neoliberalism was on the rise. As neoliberalism exacerbated the gap between the global rich and the global poor, human rights advocates refocused their efforts to assist those hurt most by global capitalism. Something similar happened to US housing advocates during the neoliberal era. Except for those aligned with the PHIMBY movement, most housing advocates no longer call for a large-scale, state-sponsored "modern housing" program, as Catherine Bauer proposed decades ago. Instead, advocates have become hyperfocused on protecting the basic housing entitlements that are most threatened by the neoliberal tide, while paddling against the political rhetoric surrounding welfare dependency and the stigmatization of those without homes. Antihomelessness advocates have fought to provide minimally adequate housing to the homeless during times of urgent need, and tenants' rights advocates have aligned with right to community advocates to protect low-income renters from imminent eviction and the loss of community. Meanwhile, the overall rise in housing inequality during the neoliberal era has been ignored.

The American Home's Chalk Foundations

The passage by Edgar Allan Poe cited at the beginning of this chapter is from Poe's last written work, "The Light-House," in which Poe describes a structure that had become a place in which to be "thoroughly *alone*" (Poe 1984 [1849], 924; italics in the original). By the end of the passage, the narrator's quest to find peace and quiet within the cylindrical walls of the lighthouse has been derailed by the discovery of structural flaws in the building's foundation. "It seems to me that the hollow interior at the bottom should have been filled in with solid masonry" (Poe 1984 [1849], 925). Poe, the presumed narrator, tries to find comfort in the fact that "a structure such as this is safe enough under any circumstances," but he eventually accepts the precarity of his living situation: "The basis on which the structure rests seems to me to be chalk" (Poe 1984 [1849], 925).

The American home and the policies that govern its distribution rest on a similarly chalky foundation. The contemporary neoliberal postmodern housing landscape is defined by the ascendency of private property rights, the deregulation of the institutions of housing finance, the absence of minimal entitlements to basic housing, and a housing market that is characterized by its inequality, fragmentation, and segregation. While the US housing market now provides a wider range of choices in styles and tenure arrangements than has ever existed before (for those with the means and willingness to vote with their feet), neoliberalism has eroded previously shared social meanings of housing.

American housing advocacy has evolved beyond its origins in nineteenth-century social and land reform movements. Nineteenth-century land reformers attacked land and housing inequality directly, through right-based reforms designed to reduce the number of propertyless citizens. Progressive and utilitarian reformers criticized liberal rights and their natural law foundations, shifting the basis of housing justice from rights to collective goals and civic virtues. Franklin D. Roosevelt presented a vision of the welfare state that included housing among the social rights guaranteed to all citizens, but his vision was never realized. During the 1960s, a variety of social movements resurrected and redefined rights to save communities from the exclusionary consequences of previous generations' reforms. The housing advocacy movement splintered during the neoliberal era, primarily around the issues of segregation and gentrification, and has largely ignored broader housing inequalities, focusing instead on securing minimal housing entitlements for those hurt most by the retrenchment of the welfare state. The contemporary human rights umbrella provides home to a mosaic of new housing justice causes. Still, it remains to be seen whether the prevailing conception of housing justice, grounded in the human right to the city, provides a coherent and actionable basis for American housing reform. The next several chapters provide reasons to be skeptical.

III Structure

6 The Architecture of Housing Justice

> Our vision is rooted in the belief that housing is a human right, not a commodity to maximize profit. We believe it is possible to create a just housing system in which everyone has affordable and dignified housing.
> —"Homes for All" campaign of the Right to the City Alliance
> (Baiocchi 2018, 8)

Despite lingering tensions among US housing advocates over the issues of gentrification and residential segregation, a radical coalition has formed beneath the human rights umbrella. Advocates of the human right to the city appeal to a conception of justice that is based on the perceived incompatibility between the right to housing and the right to own private property and the perceived complementarities among the right to housing, human rights, and the collective right to the city. The remaining chapters of this book deconstruct this consensus view and reconstruct a conception of housing justice that draws on the lessons from the previous chapters.

In this chapter, I assemble the materials of justice into an evaluative framework that provides the tools to analyze housing institutions and policies. I begin with an exploration of several themes from part II of the book that provide insights into the link between housing's social meaning and housing justice. I then examine the grounds of housing justice. I argue that the idea of human dignity implicit in the ground of human status is best understood within the context of what a dignified life means in a given society. The ground of citizenship avoids many of the limitations of the human status ground while providing a more persuasive justification for measures designed to reduce housing inequality. I express the ground of citizenship through the ideal of civic equality, which weaves T. H. Marshall's

(1950) idea of social citizenship with elements of the liberal and republican traditions. I conclude the chapter with a discussion of the basis of housing justice, emphasizing how the rights of citizenship structure housing policy design.

Lessons from the History of US Housing Reform

American housing reformers have understood housing's social meaning in a variety of ways and have drawn different conclusions about the distributive implications of housing's social meaning, but several unifying themes span reformers' diverse views. Three themes provide points of departure for the conception of housing justice developed in the remaining chapters of this book: the enduring quality of the single-family housing ideal, the tilted balance between housing's public and private functions, and the consensus around housing's special connection to American social and cultural life.

The owned single-family detached home has endured as an idealized housing type, despite changes in the underlying values that have justified the ideal. From the founding period through the late nineteenth century, reformers appealed to republican virtues and natural law to call for the expansion of liberal rights to landed property. Progressive and utilitarian reformers offered new moral frameworks that updated republican virtues for an urban era while retooling the liberal institution of private property to elevate the single-family home above other housing types. The New Deal–era federal housing policy apparatus established new institutions that transformed the American housing landscape into a homeownership republic dominated by single-family housing. Some have rejected the single-family ideal. Social critics have questioned the single-family home's contribution to domesticity, social isolation, and cultural conformity. As I argue later in this chapter, a conception of housing justice can appeal to the most morally compelling values without fetishizing the physical embodiment of these values or committing to an idealized conception of how life should be lived. The American home can accommodate a diversity of American dreams.

Housing has valuable public and private functions, yet reformers have tended to downplay the moral significance of the privacy that homes deliver. Housing reformers have linked privacy with civic virtue but have rarely appealed to privacy's value to defend the extension of rights to a private realm. Progressive legal theorists recognized a personal right to privacy but ignored the material conditions necessary for the enjoyment of this right. From the 1960s onward, social reformers have redefined housing's public function in terms of its collective importance to those who have been historically denied access to housing. During the neoliberal era, advocates and scholars have continued to elevate housing's contribution to community life while simultaneously attacking the privatization of space and the value of privacy itself. David Harvey (34, 2007), for example, equates neoliberal capital "accumulation by dispossession" with the conversion of common and collective property into exclusively private property. In the pages that follow, I maintain that housing's role in securing privacy is an essential function that should not be ignored by housing justice theorists and practitioners. Housing has valuable public functions, but a house ceases to be a home if it does not provide a minimum of privacy and separation from the external world. This observation has implications for the link between housing and human lives, the grounds of housing justice, and the right to housing.

One public function of housing acknowledged by all of America's housing and land reform movements that plays an important role in the conception of housing justice developed in this book is housing's special connection to American social and cultural life. American life is organized around social practices that originate in, and take place in relation to, the home. Access to a home is a precondition for participation in civilized ways of living. The idea of home also pervades shared ambitions of how Americans aspire to live. Importantly, housing's connection to American social and cultural life is a vital *public* function that is defined in terms of access to the *private* space that housing secures. The homeless are ostracized, not praised, for their public exposure. These connections explain why the unequal provision of private residential space is such a moral concern.

Adam Smith provides an analogy that helps convey the moral significance of housing's connection to social and cultural life. He makes a distinction between goods that are luxuries and those that are necessaries, defining the latter as those that are "indispensably necessary for the support of life" and "whatever the custom of the country renders it indecent for creditable people, even of the lowest order, to be without." He observes that in the greater part of Europe during his time, a linen shirt was a necessary because a "credible day-laborer would be ashamed to appear in public without a linen shirt" (Smith 1827 [1776], 368). Anne Phillips makes a similar point when she says that "in a society where access to common culture has come to depend on watching the same programmes on TV, having a television set becomes a necessity rather than a luxury. In a society where car ownership has become widespread, it can be hard for those without cars to get access to basic amenities: shopping centers are often located in areas difficult to reach by public transport; indeed public transport may collapse when richer members of the community no longer use it" (Phillips 1999, 62–63).

Throughout American history, housing has been a marker of social status, an essential ingredient of "common culture," and a vehicle for distributing the rights and benefits owed to all citizens. Housing is bundled with important local public goods, such as public education and public safety, and a home's location in space affects the inhabitant's ability to access social and economic opportunities. Importantly, those without homes are often socially stigmatized, labeled as homeless, and dismissed by other members of society.

Does housing's link with common culture imply that housing should be more widely distributed, or does the link imply that goods bundled with housing, such as public education, should be decoupled from housing and allocated according to separate distributive principles? Returning to Phillips's (1999) example, the automobile's link to common culture may imply either that everyone should have access to an automobile or that transportation systems should be designed so that those without cars can easily access basic amenities. I argue in chapter 7 that the loss of housing entails such significant injustices that housing should be distributed to everyone. In chapter 8, I offer a housing policy reform proposal that can be understood as a way to decouple the distribution of local public goods from the distribution of housing. In the next two sections, I argue that, regardless of the distributive implications of housing's social meaning, housing's link to common culture has fundamental consequences for the grounds of housing justice.

The Grounds of Housing Justice

American housing reformers have historically appealed to one of two grounds of justice: *human status* and *citizenship*. The natural rights and human rights traditions are each grounded in a nonrelational conception of human status that appeals to human beings' intrinsic value. Human

The Architecture of Housing Justice

qualities or conditions that contribute to this value, or without which human life would have no value, provide the grounds for principles of justice. For John Locke, human beings are intrinsically valuable because they are created in God's image, and this idea grounds the natural right to property. Thomas Paine and most of the nineteenth-century land reformers that he influenced held a similar view of the natural right to property grounded in a secular conception of humanity's intrinsic value.

Despite sharing a similar ground, the human rights tradition departs from the natural rights tradition in two important ways. First, human rights such as those expressed in the UDHR are not typically understood as the products of God's law, pure reason, or some universal morality that governs human actions in a prepolitical state of nature but are instead interpreted as a set of overlapping moral concerns shared by all legitimate political systems that describe the "features of an acceptable [global] institutional environment" (Bietz 2009, 55). Human rights provide a justification for preempting national laws when citizens' human rights have been violated or are otherwise not protected by a nation's laws and institutions. According to Hannah Arendt (1968, 298), "This new situation in which 'humanity' has in effect assumed the role formerly ascribed to nature or history would mean in this context that the right to have rights or the right of every individual to belong to humanity should be guaranteed by humanity itself."

Second, many of the rights listed in the UDHR are more expansive than natural rights, which were often understood by Enlightenment-era philosophers as negative protections against government interference. According to Charles Malik, one of the framers of the UDHR, the second-generation social rights outlined in the UDHR are "rights of the individual as a member of society" rather than rights "of the individual as such" (Bietz 2009, 57). According to Charles Bietz (2009, 57), second-generation rights "represent a more ambitious assumption of responsibility for the public sphere than was required by the motivating concerns of classical natural rights theories." The UDHR also identifies several third-generation collective rights that protect the right of self-determination for peoples.

Progressives, homeownership advocates, and most civil rights reformers have appealed to the ground of citizenship to derive rights, obligations, and principles of justice from the relational obligations among citizens and between citizens and the nation-state. As Karl Marx observed, political rights are rights "which can only be exercised if one is a member of a community. Their content is *participation* in the *community* life, in the *political* life of the community, the life of the state" (Tucker 1978, 41; italics in the original). The ground of citizenship implies an elevated role for the moral value of equality, understood as the requirement to treat each member of society as an equal participant in a social order and abide by the rules that set fair terms of social cooperation (Miller 1999). Whereas the ground of human status supports a conception of equality defined by the equal protection of certain minimal entitlements, the ground of citizenship requires that any social and economic inequalities produced by institutional arrangements be justified relationally to all who are coerced by those arrangements.

An interesting question is whether there are additional grounds of housing justice that are defined by a scope that is smaller than the nation-state. It is important to separate purely local grounds of justice from local demands that appeal to a broader population and contextual considerations that justify stronger obligations among members of local communities. Most claims of housing justice made by communities are best understood as demands made to other citizens or the nation-state to respect the special rights of community members. If the audience for community demands is an external population, the scope of justice extends beyond the community's borders. Alternatively, members of local communities may have special obligations to their members that do not hold for a broader population. For example, spatial differences in housing costs often arise from local market conditions that are in turn shaped by local public policy decisions. While this implies that there may be special obligations of justice that arise from these local contextual factors, it does not necessarily mean that local grounds of justice exist independently of those defined for a larger population. Most local obligations are best understood as nested within a broader scope of justice. They must be consistent with the principles of justice defined for a larger population, or the community must be recognized as having special rights that possibly conflict with the rights held by a broader population of individuals. In chapter 8, I explore an example of nested local obligations that arise from the capitalization of local public goods into housing prices and critique the view that housing justice requires the recognition of collective subnational rights.

Human Status as a Ground of Housing Justice

The ground of human status is often expressed in terms of the idea of *human dignity*, which gives the reasons that human beings are bearers of intrinsic value. Philosophers have understood human dignity in a variety of different ways. Immanuel Kant's (2012 [1785]) view of morality is based on the idea that human beings are worthy of being treated as ends rather than as means for some other end. While most conceptions of justice accept this fundamental premise, this idea alone does not explain why human beings should be treated as ends. For Kant, morality is the law of reason, and human beings' unique capacity for moral agency is the source of human beings' intrinsic value. For Karl Marx (1978 [1843]), a critic of natural human rights, human dignity resides in one's consciousness of the social nature of the human condition and authentically acting in accordance with one's true nature as a social being. For Ronald Dworkin (2008), human dignity is an idea that expresses the intrinsic value of humanity and the fact that each person has a special responsibility for how their life goes. Jeremy Waldron (2009) defines dignity in terms of social status and rank, with equal dignity implying that all human beings are elevated to a similarly high rank. Martha Nussbaum's (2000) understanding of dignity combines the idea of an equally elevated rank with the Kantian conception of dignity.

The first challenge facing those appealing to human status to ground principles of housing justice is that human dignity, however it is understood, is an overly abstract concept that says little about the content of human rights. What constitutes a dignified life, and what role does housing play in delivering such a life? At a minimum, a life must be lived, which implies that human rights should minimally secure the basic conditions required to sustain human life. Unlike other material resources, housing is not consumed and converted to energy to maintain bodily functions. Housing produces bodily health indirectly through the provision of comfort. Still, it is hard to argue that everyone has a right to a climate-controlled home kept to a temperature of 72 degrees Fahrenheit. Housing delivers *security* by offering a private protective realm that insulates human beings from external threats to bodily integrity. If housing is mold infested, decorated with toxic lead-based paint, or permits the penetration of noxious chemicals, it has failed to perform its most basic function of securing the human body from harmful environmental threats.

Housing also provides a platform for the development and exercise of *normative agency*, which refers to the capacity to offer and respond to reasons (*reason-responsiveness*) and the capacity to chart out one's own course in life (*autonomy*). Moral agents must possess the capacity to recognize and acknowledge their own intrinsic worth while simultaneously acknowledging others' intrinsic worth. Moral agents must also be able to formulate, evaluate, and act on a conception of what the good life entails. Housing supports normative agency by providing a private realm for reflection and deliberation, which in turn enables individuals to form a conception of the good life and freely pursue valued projects, unimpeded by the threat of environmental harm or the social obligation to obtain permission from others for actions performed within the home. According to Waldron (1988, 310–311), "If a man's subsistence depends on the management of resources over which he has exclusive control and for which he has sole responsibility, then habits of foresight and prudential calculation will develop, as he learns what he does today may affect his life chances tomorrow." To fully exercise normative agency, human beings must have a reasonable expectation that the home they occupy will be available for an extended period. Those continually facing the threat of eviction may be unable to fully develop their autonomous capacities, because they lack long-term control over private space. Housing also enables normative agency indirectly through the security that it provides. Human beings are unable to exercise their full moral capacities if all their time and energy is spent fending off environmental threats.

Even if we reduce human dignity to more concrete concepts such as security and normative agency, any universal conception of dignity faces a second challenge: it risks appealing to a controversial conception of human nature that not everyone would endorse. Some object to Kant's conception of human dignity, for example, because morality is not exhausted by universal obligations. Human beings have obligations that arise from particularistic social commitments and relationships that are not always consistent with universal moral law. Likewise, some object to Dworkin's (2008) elevation of responsibility as a component of human dignity, because it provides a convenient excuse for relinquishing the obligation to assist those who are in a state of deprivation because of choices for which they should be held morally responsible (Anderson 1999). Others object to conceptions of human dignity that appeal to an atomistic, asocial conception of human nature (Sandel 1998b).

A third challenge is that the moral significance of the connection between housing and human dignity is mediated by contingent facts such as environmental conditions, legal institutions, and local market conditions. Housing minimizes exposure to extreme environmental conditions (e.g., rain, extreme cold, extreme heat, or natural hazards), but in most places on the earth that human beings inhabit, this need can be satisfied by a temporary shelter. The bodily need to be secure varies temporally and spatially. Inhabitants of temperate climates can live in comfort with minimal shelter. In contrast, those living on the Siberian tundra during the coldest winter months would quickly die from exposure without secure access to a climate-controlled shelter. Although the need to be protected from external weather conditions may be a universal need, the risk to human life from not having that need satisfied varies across space and time, and human beings' sensitivity to environmental conditions varies from person to person. A house is a sufficient but not a necessary condition for being secure.

Social contingencies also mediate the exercise of normative agency. Although normative agency may be a universal human capacity, the exercise of that capacity requires the existence of socially and historically contingent practices. According to Joseph Raz (1986, 205), "If having an autonomous life is an ultimate value, then having a sufficient range of acceptable options is of intrinsic value, for it is constitutive of an autonomous life that it is lived in circumstances where acceptable alternatives are present." Raz goes on to argue that the range of acceptable options for living an autonomous life is in turn determined by the social forms and practices prevailing in a given society. "One cannot have an option to be a barrister, a surgeon, or a psychiatrist in a society where those professions, and the institutions their existence presupposes, do not exist" (Raz 1986, 205). Similarly, one's ability to pursue a conception of the good life that includes a way of living in a home of a particular type is conditioned by the availability of that housing type.

So far, we have examined how environmental and social contingencies mediate the realization of human dignity. A related objection is that the concept of human dignity is inherently social in nature and cannot be understood without reference to what a dignified life means within a given society. Adam Smith's example of the linen shirt, discussed at the beginning of this chapter, illustrates this point. If housing provides access to common culture, those who are unhoused experience a form of social deprivation. Smith's analogy demonstrates that if dignity is understood as an equally elevated human status, the threshold level at which a life is considered dignified—and the necessary conditions for living that life—cannot be determined without appealing to the social bases of human dignity within the context of a given culture. While the concept of human dignity may ground a universal right to live a dignified life in whatever society a person happens to live, the content of that right is determined by prevailing social norms and the social meaning of housing. Pairing Smith's observations with Raz's (1986) argument about the importance of social practices to the exercise of autonomy, one can also conclude that in pluralistic societies such as the United States, where many different conceptions of the good life are allowed to flourish, the diversity of housing options is constitutive of housing's contribution to human dignity. Housing policies that promote a single housing style, such as the owned single-family detached home, may thwart many other lifestyles worth pursuing.

James Griffin (2008) attempts to circumvent the problems that arise from the contingent nature of human dignity by claiming that "practicalities" provide separate grounds for human rights that determine the content of rights and duties, but it is not clear that they provide adequate grounds of justice. While practicalities may be understood as external constraints that affect the feasibility of actions taken to satisfy human needs, they play no direct role in grounding the obligation to satisfy needs in the first place. In the United States, the most significant barrier to adequate shelter is its cost, which in turn derives from the fact that shelter is allocated according to exchange values and transactions legitimized by private property law. *Pace* Griffin, it would be odd to argue that the institution of private property creates the need to be protected from the cold and thus provides a ground for alleviating that need. It seems more appropriate to say that biological needs arise independently of markets, but markets may make it more difficult to satisfy needs.

Nussbaum (2000) offers one way of addressing the challenges discussed so far. Her conception of human dignity is derived not from a controversial conception of human nature but from a political conception that is the outcome of a cross-cultural dialogue among peoples designed to achieve an overlapping consensus on the basic capabilities required to lead a dignified life in all cultures. Nussbaum argues that a cross-cultural dialogue would arrive at a list of 10 central human capabilities that should be protected as basic human rights. She does not include "housing" or "shelter" as distinct capabilities, but she mentions shelter as a component of the central capability of "bodily health," which she defines as "being able to have good health, including reproductive health; to be adequately nourished; to have adequate shelter" (Nussbaum 2000, 78).[1] Although Nussbaum (2000) does not elaborate on this possibility, housing also enables the realization of several other central capabilities on her list, including bodily integrity (through the provision of privacy), affiliation, play, and material control over one's environment (which she explicitly defines in terms of access to property).

While an improvement over other conceptions that ground human rights in transcendental ideals that have no connection to social practices, Nussbaum's capabilities approach also has several limitations as a ground for the human right to housing. Nussbaum understands housing's value instrumentally, with housing serving as a means to the realization of bodily health (and possibly other capabilities). According to Eric Nelson,

> Shelter, for example, is not a "functioning," and so "being able to have shelter" is not a "capability" as Nussbaum defines it. Simply employing a participle does not remove the difficulty. If shelter is to have any place on this list, it must serve as a condition for the acquisition of various capabilities. Nussbaum might have said, for instance, that one cannot learn effectively without shelter and that, as a result, an entitlement to shelter follows from the entitlement to learning. But this would be to treat shelter as a wholly instrumental good, rather than as a central human "functioning," and would therefore contradict one of the organizing principles of the list. (Nelson 2008, 96)

Thus, as formulated, shelter either is not a central capability at all or only has instrumental value as a means of achieving higher-order functionings. A purely instrumental understanding of housing ignores housing's constitutive value as a component of the good life itself. As argued in chapter 1, individuals often desire homes styled in a particular manner not because housing so configured would more effectively enhance personal well-being but rather because individuals often define the good itself in terms of a concrete ideal of how they aspire to live (Dawkins 2017a). The home and its sociospatial context also shape the identity of the inhabitant. Housing's constitutive value is simultaneously private and relational—private because housing's most important function derives from the sheltered zone of spatial autonomy that housing provides, and relational because the home provides a platform for voluntarily engaging in associations and activities outside the home. If housing is constitutive of one's conception of the good life, it is more than merely an instrumental catalyst to human functioning.

Another limitation of Nussbaum's approach, and most other conceptions of human rights, is that the obligation to secure minimum capabilities grounds sufficientarian, rather than egalitarian, distributive arrangements. According to Nussbaum, "an adequate house or other shelter seems to be inherent in the idea of human dignity," but "it is not at all clear that an equal house is required by the very idea of human dignity or even of equal human dignity; for indeed a mansion may not be better than a modest house. House size, above a certain threshold, does not seem intrinsically related to equal dignity" (Nussbaum 2006, 293). As I discuss later in this chapter, there are reasons to be concerned about housing inequality, even if everyone is adequately housed.

Not only does Nussbaum's approach ground a sufficientarian conception of housing justice, but the threshold level of housing considered adequate across all societies is also likely much lower than the sufficientarian threshold that would be recognized within societies that assign significant meanings to housing or rely on housing to distribute access to other goods. For example, a global sufficientarian conception of housing justice may fail to account for housing's distinctive role in distributing access to local public education if most nations do not finance public education from residential property taxes. Given that nations define and distribute housing in a variety of ways, an overlapping consensus among nations is likely to yield a very thin, watered-down view of minimal housing entitlements that ignores housing's distinctive contribution to each nation's common culture.

Two Concepts of Citizenship

Unlike the ground of human status, which appeals to the intrinsically valuable features of human life, the ground of citizenship derives its force from individuals' participation in the shared social practices that define what it means to be a citizen. Before examining the ground of citizenship, I compare and contrast the two conceptions of citizenship implied by America's two dominant political traditions—liberalism and republicanism. The discussion draws on Corey Brettschneider's (2007) distinction between citizens' democratic roles as authors and addressees of the law. Liberalism and republicanism offer two different ways of understanding these roles.

Liberals such as John Locke and John Rawls emphasize citizens' roles as addressees of the law and are concerned with establishing the conditions under which the exercise of government coercion would be considered legitimate from the perspectives of those coerced. Citizenship is a legal status that defines the terms of social cooperation among free and equal persons (Rawls 1971). In most liberal theories, citizens' roles as authors of the law are limited to their passive roles as voters and occasional holders of public office. In the liberal conception of citizenship, political participation has no intrinsic value, although it may have instrumental value as a way of legitimizing the state's use of force. Liberalism is often tied to a democratic conception of political life not because democracy has intrinsic value but rather because the terms of social cooperation are defined by the laws and institutions that citizens endorse.

The liberal conception of American citizenship has evolved since the nation's founding. In the classic liberal understanding of citizenship, citizens' roles as authors of the law are limited to their consent to or dissent from the terms of a social contract. Beginning in the Progressive Era, citizens' roles as economic consumers became intertwined with their roles as citizens. Zoning and other land-use regulations gave citizens an economic reason to engage in local politics to protect the value of their homes. With the rise of the homeownership republic, residential mobility was elevated to the status of a political act, as consumer-voters revealed their political preferences by voting with their feet. With the globalization of capital and the retrenchment of the welfare state during the neoliberal era, local governments responded to the mobility of labor and capital by retooling the machinery of local government to minimize tax burdens while simultaneously providing amenities desired by employers and their workers. These trends have strengthened the link between liberal citizenship and housing consumption. With the devolution of public goods and other rights and benefits of citizenship to local governments, those without homes have been denied an important means of exercising democratic citizenship.

The distinction between the public and private realms is central to the liberal conception of citizenship. The public-private distinction does not necessarily refer to a strict separation between the private lives of individuals and their social or political lives, but it does assume that private home life has intrinsic value worth protecting. The public-private distinction also implies a division of labor between the types of reasons that can be offered in defense of public actions versus private actions.[2] Within private realms, a diversity of conceptions of the good life is allowed to flourish, with individuals choosing from among a variety of conceptions of the good. Within the public realm, individuals must reach agreement on the laws and institutions that will govern public and private behavior. A justificatory separation between the public and the private realms ensures that certain privately held views will be excluded from arguments supporting public laws. Locke's view of religious toleration is an expression of this ideal. As he puts it, "All the power of civil government relates only to men's civil interests, is confined to the care of the things of this world, and hath nothing to do with the world to come" (Locke 1895 [1689], 150). By granting households the sovereignty to determine who may enter their private homes, the institution of private property introduces a spatial dimension to the liberal conceptual distinction between public and private reasoning. According to Thad Williamson,

> The basic concept of private personal space embodied in privately owned domiciles today retains an appeal not only to traditional nuclear families but to many other groups as well. Consider, for instance, gay couples who rely on the privacy of the home to sustain their lifestyle, fundamentalist Christians who homeschool their children in an effort to counter the dominant strains of mass culture, or any number of private projects (some of which have public relevance) that are made possible by private ownership of homes and the assumed sanctity of private home space. Given the close connection between the practice of political liberalism and the historical institution of the private home, liberals can plausibly view private control of domestic space not merely as a cultural practice to be tolerated but as a positive good that appears to be an indispensable institution within existing liberal societies. (Williamson 2010, 152)

In contrast to the liberal tradition, the republican tradition emphasizes citizens' roles as authors of the law. Republican citizenship is an active status defined by one's engagement in public political life and does not assume a strict separation between the public and private realms. The republican citizen's public role is a virtue to be extolled and perfected, and many republicans argue that private life should play some role in the cultivation of these excellences. Whereas liberals assume that private home life has intrinsic value to individuals, republicans emphasize the instrumental value of home life for the cultivation of civic virtue. The ideal of home thought to cultivate civic virtue has evolved over time. During the nineteenth century, liberal-republican land reformers appealed to the civic virtues of the frontier homestead. By the end of the nineteenth century, the owned single-family detached home had replaced the homestead as the archetype of civic life in an industrialized society. The homeownership republic suburbanized this ideal, and the new urbanists' nostalgia for compact living questioned the civic value of the suburban home.

Although republicans value an active citizenry, they have not always supported egalitarian conceptions of democracy. Alexander Hamilton and James Madison were more concerned with establishing the appropriate checks and balances on democracy to control the tyranny of the majority than with promoting widespread participation in governance. John Adams relied on republican reasoning to argue that voting privileges should be restricted to freeholders (Williamson 2019). Progressives appealed to similar arguments to justify exclusionary zoning policies.

Certain elements of the liberal and republican traditions are worth incorporating into a conception of citizenship that grounds housing justice, while other features are worth abandoning. I make three arguments that inform the conception of citizenship that I defend in the next section. First, I argue that housing justice should acknowledge the moral significance of the link between housing and citizenship, but justice does not require viewing housing as a means of promoting or cultivating civic virtue. Second, there are compelling reasons to acknowledge the intrinsic value of the private sphere and distinguish between public and private reasoning even if the home's value derives in part from its social and civic functions. Third, the republican conception of freedom offers a valuable way of understanding the moral significance of the privacy that homes secure.

Empirical evidence does not support the claim that homeowners are "better citizens" (McCabe 2016). If anything, homeownership encourages civic engagement for the self-serving purpose of elevating the value of one's home and isolating homeowners from other social or economic groups (Fischel 2005). It is also questionable whether the type of housing the United States promotes through homeownership policy—the owned single-family detached home—supports the cultivation of the social capital required to instill a concern for the common good (Glaeser 2011). Aside from the empirical question of whether homeownership or any other tenure arrangement promotes civic virtues, the aim of promoting virtue or human excellence is morally questionable because it is premised on a controversial conception of the good life not shared by everyone. Virtue-based justifications for housing policy also license objectionable paternalistic government actions that violate personal autonomy. There are more examples throughout history of virtue-based arguments being used to deny rights to those not deemed virtuous rather than to support the egalitarian aim of extending rights that secure the conditions required to cultivate virtue.

The liberal distinction between the public and private realms recognizes the home's intrinsic value to inhabitants while preserving a division of labor between public and private reasoning. Although the home's value and meaning are created, in part, from the home's social functions, the home would cease to be a home if it failed to offer a minimum level of privacy and protection from external threats. This is true even for homes that shelter communal ways of living. At the same time, the home can never be fully isolated from public life, nor should it be. The privacy of the home does not provide immunity against the laws of society, and privacy itself is protected by the publicly recognized institutions of private property and civil law. Without the protection provided by a local police force, housing occupants would be unable to enforce their right to exclude unwanted trespassers. As Rawls puts it, "If the private sphere is alleged to be a space exempt from justice, then there is no such thing," because "the equal rights of women and the basic rights of their children are inalienable and protect them wherever they are" (Rawls 1997, 791).

The liberal distinction between the public and private realms is best understood as a moral division of labor that preserves privacy and freedom of association while providing a platform for engaging in public life. The private realm "acts as an enabling device whereby rival and possibly incommensurable conceptions of the good may be implemented and realized without any recourse to any collective decision-making procedure" (Gray 1993, 314). Within the public realm, citizens come together to engage in social life and agree on the laws that govern public and private lives. The public-private distinction protects individuals' freedom to voluntarily enter into and exit from each of these realms. According to Rawls (1975, 550), "The basic liberties are not intended to keep persons in isolation from one another, or to persuade them to lead private lives, even though some no doubt will, but to secure the right of free movement between associations and smaller communities."

Some feminist philosophers have criticized the liberal public-private distinction for ignoring, or in some cases contributing to, the marginalization and oppression of women within the home. Carole Pateman (1988) argues that the liberal distinction between private domestic life and the public affairs of civil society and the state denies any significant role for women in political life. Within the home, women often work for no compensation while being confined to gendered roles that do not afford the same spatial separation between home and work life that male heads of household enjoy (Hayden 1984). The home's isolation from the public sphere also subjects women to the threat of domestic violence. As Jessie Hohmann (2014) observes, women who live in abusive relationships are "essentially homeless" because of their inability to escape an oppressive living environment.

Most strains of Western philosophy, including both liberal and nonliberal traditions, are unfortunately guilty of perpetuating a gendered understanding of the public and private spheres (Okin 1979), so one should be careful not to equate a patriarchal understanding of the public-private distinction with the liberal tradition. The ancient Greeks, for example, assumed a "sharp distinction between the domestic household and the public realm which condemned women to public invisibility" (Kymlicka 2002, 390). The oppression of women within the public and private spheres arises not from the public-private distinction itself but instead from the failure of many liberals to take the public-private distinction seriously as a separation that protects the rights of individuals within the home. Since Locke equates the protection of familial rights with the protection of individual rights, his theory does not have the conceptual tools to handle instances where conflicts of rights arise within the home (Kelly 2002). Still, this problem only reflects a weakness of Locke's understanding of the public-private distinction rather than an inherent weakness of the distinction itself. The American ideal of home and the Supreme Court's interpretation of that ideal have contributed to the confusion by simultaneously insulating heterosexual nuclear families from government intrusion while ignoring the rights of women within the home. This explains why many feminists have only reluctantly supported the Supreme Court's findings in *Griswold v. Connecticut* (1965). While this case established the constitutionality of the right to privacy, invalidating a law that denied access to contraception for married women, the right to privacy secured by *Griswold* has since been interpreted by the courts as a right that protects the rights of family units, not women within families. As Catherine MacKinnon (1987, 101) observes, "The legal concept of privacy can and has shielded the place of battery, marital rape, and women's exploited labor."

According to Will Kymlicka (2002, 396; italics in the original), the family-based conception of privacy fails in two ways: "On the one hand, it has failed to protect women's desire for privacy when threatened by abusive husbands or fathers. On the other hand, it has condoned the *involuntary* privacy of women—i.e. it has condoned the unwanted isolation, seclusion, or forced modesty of mothers and daughters who desired to escape from the confinement of domestic roles to participate in public life."

Anita Allen (1988, 180–181) describes this "privacy problem" as the "problem of getting rid of unwanted forms of privacy" and "acquiring the privacy they do not have." This problem can only be solved by decentering the right to privacy from household units to individuals within the household. If the right to privacy is an individual right supported by the right to housing, both the right to housing and the right to privacy protect the rights of women to exit oppressive relationships without having to compromise their right to a secure private realm. This interpretation of the right to privacy also justifies supporting a woman's right to enjoy the same spatial separation between home and work enjoyed by male heads of household who labor outside the home. As Virginia Woolf observes, "A woman must have money and a room of her own if she is to write fiction" (Woolf 1929, 4).

Although I have so far defended a liberal conception of citizenship that is grounded in a distinction between the public and private realms, I also argue that the republican conception of freedom provides a more useful way of understanding the value of privacy and the home's contribution to that value. According to Philip Pettit (1997), republican (which I henceforth refer to as "civic") freedom is distinct from liberal freedom in its emphasis on nondomination, or independence from the arbitrary will of others. Pettit gives the example of a slave who is free from interference but whose will is still dominated by a master. This slave enjoys liberal freedom but does not enjoy civic freedom because the master has dominion over the actions taken by the slave. The value of privacy, in the civic conception of freedom, lies in the ability to pursue projects and life plans without the constant need to gain external approval for projects pursued. As Arendt observes, "What is necessary for freedom is not wealth. What is necessary is security and a place of one's own shielded from the claims of the public. What is necessary for the public realm is that it be shielded from the private interests which have intruded upon it in the most brutal and aggressive form" (Arendt 2018, 512). As discussed in chapter 7, the idea of civic freedom provides a useful way of understanding the injustice of tenure insecurity.

The Normative Foundations of Equal Citizenship

The previous section made the case for a liberal-republican conception of citizenship that is not virtue based, recognizes a moral division of labor between public and private reasoning, and appeals to the value of civic freedom. In this section, I expand on this conception by incorporating T. H. Marshall's (1950) idea of social citizenship. The Supreme Court's opinion in *Goldberg v. Kelly* (1970) paints a picture of the conception of social citizenship that I have in mind:

> From its founding the Nation's basic commitment has been to foster the dignity and well-being of all persons within its borders. We have come to recognize that forces not within the control of the poor contribute to their poverty.... Welfare, by meeting the basic demands of subsistence, can help bring within the reach of the poor the same opportunities that are available to others to participate meaningfully in the life of the community. [Public] assistance, then, is not mere charity, but a means to promote the "general Welfare, and secure the Blessings of Liberty to ourselves and our Posterity." (Sunstein 2004, 161–162)

Whereas human status is a ground of justice that derives its moral force from the intrinsically valuable aspects of the human experience, citizenship is a relational ground that appeals to a shared understanding of what citizens owe one another and what the government owes its citizens. Civil institutions such as private property laws, the judicial system, and government tax-and-spend policies are expressions of social citizenship. These institutions are based on, and in turn define, what it means to live a dignified life in a society governed by those institutions. According to Marshall (1950, 29), "Societies in which citizenship is a developing institution create an image of an ideal citizenship against which achievement can be measured and towards which aspiration can be directed. The urge forward along the path thus plotted is an urge towards a fuller measure of equality, an enrichment of the stuff of which the status is made and an increase in the number of those on whom the status is bestowed."

To deny housing to an American citizen is to deny that person one of the materials required to live a civilized life. Not only is housing a prerequisite for a civilized life, but it is also unfair to ask those who are unhoused to make sacrifices for the public good when their basic housing needs have not been met. Although unhoused Americans may be recognized as citizens in the legal sense, they are not citizens in the sense of enjoying the full rights of citizenship that legitimize the obligations of citizenship. According to Arendt (2018, 510), "To ask sacrifices of individuals who are not yet citizens is to ask them for an idealism which they do not and cannot have due to the urgency of the life process. Before we ask the poor for idealism, we must first make them citizens; and this involves so changing the circumstances of their private lives that they become capable of enjoying public life."

I propose the concept of *civic equality*, understood as an ideal where every citizen is treated as an equal in accordance with a shared understanding of what citizens owe one another and what the government owes its citizens, as an expression of social citizenship. Civic equality includes two dimensions: *moral equality* and *relational equality*.[3]

Moral equality is a concept best expressed by T. M. Scanlon (2018, 4) as "the idea that everyone counts morally, regardless of differences such as their race, their gender, and where they live." According to David Rondel (2018), liberal egalitarian philosophers often appeal to moral equality to express the ideal vertical relationship between citizens and the state. Ronald Dworkin (1978, 272), for example, understands this ideal in terms of the state's duty to "treat those whom it governs with concern, that is, as human beings who are capable of suffering and frustration, and with respect, that is, as human beings who are capable of forming and acting on intelligent conceptions of how their lives should be lived."

Egalitarian conceptions of justice often appeal to two separate dimensions of moral equality: *equal concern* and *equal respect.* Equal concern refers to the equal provision of goods that are owed equally to all citizens and a corollary requirement to offer an acceptable justification for the unequal provision of such goods. According to Scanlon (2018, 7), objections to inequality "apply when an institution or agent owes some benefit to every member of a certain group but provides this benefit only to some, or more fully to some than others." Showing equal concern to citizens implies that when goods or benefits are provided unequally, the agent distributing the good provides a sound reason for doing so that is acceptable to those who receive less. In the case of housing, the equal concern requirement may apply to housing or goods distributed through housing, such as local public education. If positions in society are awarded according to meritocratic criteria that reward educational attainment, it can be argued that all individuals have an equal claim to the benefits provided by public education. Given the comparative and competitive nature of the advantages conveyed by public education, it is not enough that some students simply receive a minimally adequate education, because a child's ability to succeed in life depends in part on the child's relative education level compared to others (Brighouse and Swift 2006; Dawkins 2017b). Distributing local public education according to the ability to pay for housing violates the principle of equal concern by unfairly providing higher-quality educational opportunities to some and not others.

Equal respect implies treating citizens as moral agents capable of formulating and pursuing a conception of the good as they define it within the context of the opportunities provided by society. According to Charles Larmore (2003, 56), to show equal respect for a person is to "view him as capable of elaborating beliefs that we would respect." The obligation to show equal respect is met by equally recognizing everyone's capacity to work out a coherent view of the world (Larmore 2003). Stated differently, equal respect can be understood as a moral standard that expresses the state's obligation to respect citizens' capacity for normative agency.

Both dimensions of moral equality provide guides for evaluating the public justifications for policies that alter the distribution of housing. Recall from chapter 1 that a public justification is based on the idea that "the application of power should be accompanied with reasons that all reasonable people should be able to accept" (Macedo 1990, 41). Following the requirement to show equal concern for all citizens, a public justification must demonstrate that those disadvantaged by the exercise of coercive political authority would accept (or not reject) the exercise of that authority. For example, an institution of private property rights that denies property to some must be justifiable to those who are denied property. Furthermore, the use of taxation to provide public goods must be justifiable to those who are taxed and those denied public goods.

Whereas equal concern identifies what needs to be publicly justified (deviations from equality) and to whom (those with less), equal respect provides a justification for public justification itself along with a path to justification. The norm of equal respect provides a reason to keep the conversation going in the face of reasonable disagreement. As Larmore puts it,

> Whatever we do that affects another is something with which he must deal with from within his own perspective. When he demands that we justify our action to him, he is recognizing that we, too, have a perspective on the world in which presumably our action makes sense, and indicating his willingness to discuss it rationally with us. . . . The *obligation* of equal respect consists in our being obligated to treat another as he is treating us—to use his having a perspective on the world as a reason for discussing the merits of our action rationally with him. (Larmore 2003, 56–57; italics in the original)

Given the plurality of conceptions of the good life to which parties engaged in a rational conversation may appeal, equal respect implies that justifications for actions will, to the extent possible, bracket and set aside justifications based on controversial beliefs that reasonable people may reject. If equal respect is a requirement that binds government actions, public justification implies a corollary commitment to *state neutrality*, which means that government agents should not justify their actions by appealing to controversial conceptions of the good life that are subject to reasonable disagreement (Rawls 1993). In this way, public justification is distinguished from private justification by the types of reasons offered in support of actions (Gaus 2011).

Relational equality is an ideal achieved when all citizens view one another as equal participants in the social order and equally respect one another's civic freedom. According to Elizabeth Anderson (1999, 331), an egalitarian social order is one "in which persons stand in relations of equality. They seek to live together in a democratic community, as opposed to a hierarchical one." Citizens should not fall into a state of absolute social deprivation such that they are not viewed as full members of civil society. Likewise, citizens should not experience relative social deprivation because of the unequal distribution of social, political, and economic power. Relational equality is an expression of the *antisubordination* theory of equal protection, which "looks to the shared effects of an action in order to address persistent group disparities in a social system in which some are systematically disadvantaged" (Steil 2018, 2).

In contrast to moral equality, which is a vertical conception of equality that obtains when the state treats everyone with equal respect and equal concern, relational equality is a horizontal egalitarian ideal that refers to the relationships among people in society (Rondel 2018). Given that state actions often shape the horizontal distribution of civic freedom, I argue that the state has an obligation both to respect citizens' relational equality vis-à-vis one another and to take actions to alleviate unjust relational inequalities, because the laws and institutions of the state play an important role in determining who counts as a citizen and how citizens are treated by one another. For example, antidiscrimination laws such as the FaHA have symbolic meaning beyond their direct purpose because they undermine "the racist social meanings built into contemporary American society" (Lessig 1995, 1013). The disparate impact doctrine discussed in chapter 5 signals to local governments that exclusionary land-use policies having an adverse impact on protected classes will not be tolerated, even if the adverse impact is unintentional.

While the moral equality requirement constrains the state from engaging in overly paternalistic or intrusive measures to shape private lives, relational equality implies a more proactive role for the state to ensure that citizens actively respect one another as equals. This proactive stance runs the risk of violating moral equality if the state appeals to a *perfectionist* morality to justify its actions. According to Steven Wall (1998), a perfectionist political morality is one that is committed to the promotion of one or more sound ideals of human flourishing, even if those ideals are controversial or subject to reasonable disagreement.

To promote relational equality in a manner that simultaneously respects moral equality, I argue that government agents should, to the extent possible, avoid perfectionist policy justifications. For example, US homeownership policies are often justified by appealing to the idea that homeowners are better citizens or that suburban lifestyles are superior. These perfectionist justifications clearly violate moral equality because they appeal to a controversial standard of human excellence or a contested ideal of human flourishing. A neutral justification for homeownership might begin by asking whether an owned home is one of the basic material goods that society is obligated to provide to all citizens. If the answer is yes, this provides a justification for securing everyone's social right to own a home and a corresponding duty on the part of society to support the fulfillment of such a right.

Deconstructing Civic Equality

In this section, I elaborate on the relationships among the moral dimensions of civic equality by exploring the tension between autonomy and state neutrality, investigating the distributive implications of civic equality, and examining the implications of civic equality for those who are not legally recognized as citizens.

Autonomy and State Neutrality

I have argued that the moral significance of home can be traced, in part, to the home's contribution to the development and exercise of personal autonomy. Autonomy is an aspect of normative agency and provides one reason to treat citizens as moral agents capable of formulating and pursuing a conception of the good as they define it. One potential problem with this view is that autonomy-based justifications for housing provision risk violating the principle of state neutrality if autonomy is interpreted as an elevated ideal of human flourishing or an aspect of the good life.[4]

The ground of citizenship provides a useful way around this dilemma. The ideal of civic equality is derived from a shared understanding of the material ingredients of a civilized life in a given society. A home that fails to provide secure and durable privacy, or one that is disconnected from the social and economic opportunities required to live a flourishing life, falls below the threshold of adequacy in American society. Autonomy, while not necessarily a component of the good life within all societies, is an important ingredient of a flourishing American life, and to deny some the resources required to cultivate autonomy would fail to show equal respect and equal concern to all citizens. The ideal of autonomy that emerges from this shared understanding of the material ingredients of a civilized life should not be confused with a conception of the good. As Ben Colburn (2010) suggests, conceptions of the good refer to first-order valuations of states of affairs. In contrast, autonomy is a second-order value that tracks the specification of nested first-order values. Stated differently, autonomy is among the second-order conditions that make it possible to formulate and pursue a conception of the good in the first place.

It is also important to emphasize that the principle of state neutrality is a prohibition on justifications for government action that appeal to *controversial* conceptions of the good (Larmore 1987). The discussion of the

American home's social meaning in part II and the beginning of this chapter revealed that certain aspects of the home's social meaning have been contested throughout history, whereas others have been shared widely. My argument is tied not to a controversial claim about housing's connection to the good life, such as the idea that homeowners are more virtuous or that certain lifestyles are superior, but to the more modest claim that adequate shelter is a necessary ingredient of a flourishing American life that enables citizens to reflect on, formulate, pursue, and possibly revise their conception of the good. This is a mildly perfectionist view, to the extent that autonomy is constitutive of the second-order conditions required to live a successful American life. Still, nothing I have said implies that autonomy is the *only* ingredient of a flourishing American life. Furthermore, the state's obligation to promote autonomy through the provision of housing does not prohibit citizens from living nonautonomous lives or pursuing communal ways of living. The balance between state neutrality and autonomy that I defend is consistent with John Stuart Mill's antipaternalist "harm principle," which states that "the only purpose for which power can be rightfully exercised over any member of a civilized community, against his will, is to prevent harm to others" (Mill 1978 [1859], 9).[5]

The Distributive Implications of Civic Equality

What are the implications of civic equality for the distribution of housing, and how do the distributive principles implied by civic equality relate to the distributive principles implied by the ground of human status? I argue that civic equality is consistent with a two-part distributive ideal that combines a sufficientarian threshold, where everyone has access to shelter that would be recognized by society as providing a minimum level of security and comfort, with an egalitarian distribution above the floor of sufficiency defined by the absence of extreme housing inequalities. This ideal is achieved if everyone is adequately housed, there are no stark disparities in housing consumption and wealth, and the spatial distribution of housing does not foster extreme inequalities in access to local public goods and amenities.

The sufficientarian threshold implied by civic equality may be more or less demanding than the threshold implied by the ground of human status. In communal societies where autonomy is not constitutive of a dignified life, access to a spatial zone of privacy may not be important, for example. Similarly, in nations where local public goods are not distributed in a decentralized fashion through housing, the spatial geography of housing may be less of a concern. In nations such as the United States, where housing is constitutive of the good life and distributes access to other important local public goods, civic equality justifies a threshold level of housing services for everyone that is likely higher than the threshold that would be justified by appealing to the ground of human status alone.

As discussed previously, the ground of human status says little about the distribution of housing above the threshold of sufficiency. The world currently lacks a global government whose exercise of coercive authority must be justified, so it is difficult to extend the public justification requirement beyond national borders to justify a global egalitarian distribution of housing. Although some may argue that the actions of certain global institutions—such as the United Nations, the World Trade Organization, and the International Monetary Fund—are pervasive in human lives and must be publicly justified to all global citizens (see, for example, Pogge 2002), these institutions do not directly influence the distribution of American housing. Furthermore, realizing global housing equality in a world where housing is distributed through national and subnational institutions and markets is simply not feasible. Housing inequality *within* nations is arguably at least as concerning, if not more, from the standpoint of housing justice.

Within the United States, civic equality provides reasons for being concerned about extreme levels of housing inequality, even if everyone is adequately housed. From the perspective of moral equality, an equal distribution of housing has prima facie legitimacy as a way to show equal concern to all citizens, with all deviations from equality being subject to a public justification requirement. Typical justifications for deviations from equality include utilitarian considerations (an unequal distribution may maximize total utility)[6] or choice (those who have freely chosen to have less deserve no compensation, and those who have freely chosen to have more without harming others should not be penalized).[7] Given that housing distributes access to important local public goods and amenities, housing inequality is objectionable from the standpoint of moral equality if it produces extreme inequalities in the distribution of bundled public goods guaranteed to all citizens, such as public education and public safety. Ignoring inequalities in public goods bundled with housing, inequalities in housing consumption above the sufficientarian threshold may or may not violate moral equality, depending on the public justification offered for the policies that influence the distribution of housing. Requiring everyone to be equally housed may be self-defeating from the standpoint of moral equality because absolute equality may fail to respect the diverse ways of living that appeal to diverse conceptions of the good. Similarly, if government housing policies are justified by appealing to the superiority of particular housing types, styles, or tenure arrangements, these policies may fail to equally respect individuals' capacities to choose their own paths in life.

From the standpoint of relational equality, extreme inequalities in housing consumption and wealth are a concern if they are associated with unjust social relations. As discussed in previous chapters, American housing has historically been denied to the members of certain racial and ethnic groups. The housing choice constraints resulting from discrimination are both a direct concern of housing justice, because certain groups are unjustly denied housing options made available to others, and an indirect concern, because the constraints were justified on the basis of prejudiced beliefs. Extreme housing inequalities produced by conspicuous consumption are also a concern from the standpoint of relational equality. If housing consumption is a marker of social status, all members of society face strong incentives to overconsume housing to acquire power and prestige. The hierarchical social structure produced by the pressure to signal social status through housing consumption undermines the ideal of relational equality.

When local public goods and amenities are bundled with housing, housing inequalities may also be associated with unacceptable relational inequalities in access to local political and economic power. Majority-white suburban communities often act collectively to protect their accumulated housing wealth and exclusive local public goods through private gated communities, restrictive covenants, and exclusionary zoning ordinances (Goetz, Damiano, and Williams 2019). For example, in the suburbs of Atlanta, Georgia, unincorporated majority-white neighborhoods have consolidated local political power by seceding from their surrounding majority-Black counties and incorporating into new municipalities (Rosen 2017). This "opportunity hoarding" (Tilly 1999; Reeves 2017) violates relational equality and the principle of equal concern if certain groups are excluded from the enjoyment of public goods owed equally to all citizens.

Unjust relational inequalities may or may not require that housing be distributed equally. If housing inequality places some in a state of absolute material or social deprivation, relational equality calls for the elimination of this injustice through the provision of adequate housing to everyone. The contribution of conspicuous consumption to *relative* social deprivation may also justify additional measures that reduce extreme levels of housing inequality, even if everyone is adequately housed. If housing inequality is caused by the social domination of one group over another, it may be more appropriate to address this relational inequality directly rather than being concerned about its effects on housing distributions. If, on the other hand, housing inequality causes or exacerbates relational inequality, reducing housing inequality may be the only way to eliminate this injustice. The injustice associated with opportunity hoarding, for example, persists as long as majority-white communities enjoy exclusive access to certain local public goods.

These arguments imply that even if everyone is adequately housed, civic equality has additional procedural and substantive implications for the distribution of housing above the sufficientarian threshold. Procedurally, civic equality requires that housing be distributed in a manner that respects the variety of ways that individuals value and assign meaning to housing. Civic equality is consistent with policies that promote a variety of housing styles and living arrangements and is inconsistent with policies justified on the basis of the moral superiority of particular ways of living. Civic equality is also consistent with the procedural aim of ensuring that public policies and private housing market agents do not unfairly discriminate against particular racial or ethnic groups. Substantively, civic equality calls for measures that reduce extreme inequalities in housing consumption and wealth, even if everyone's basic housing needs are adequately met, to reduce social status inequality and eliminate unjust concentrations of local political and economic power.

The tension between state neutrality and the promotion of autonomy, and the conflict between the sufficientarian and egalitarian aims of civic equality, implies that housing justice practitioners will often face difficult choices among incommensurable moral principles. These tensions are exacerbated by resource scarcity. If public funding for housing provision is prioritized to those who are homeless, there may be no additional funds to improve the housing conditions of those who are currently housed but live in unsafe conditions. In the face of resource scarcity, there are compelling reasons to support a lexical ordering of distributive principles, prioritizing the sufficientarian aim of minimally adequate housing provision over the realization of other distributive goals.

Despite these tensions, there are areas of complementarity between the sufficientarian and egalitarian aims of civic equality. In general, a tendency toward distributional equality will increase the number of those who are adequately housed. Strategies that reduce housing inequality while expanding the diversity of housing options, and antidiscrimination measures that expand housing choices for people of color, simultaneously promote moral equality and relational equality. "Win-win" distributive outcomes such as these offer useful avenues for prioritizing the allocation of scarce resources.

Civic Equality and Legal Citizenship
Although the argument so far has emphasized the appeal of the citizenship ground of housing justice over the ground of human status, particularly as a justification for egalitarian distributive aims, the two grounds considered together provide insights into the obligation to house those who are not legally recognized as citizens. Rather than view human status and citizenship as competing grounds of justice, it is more useful to consider each as nested grounds, with human status grounding obligations binding on all humanity and citizenship grounding special relational obligations among members of a political community.

Even though the United States has not ratified the ICESCR, it is a nation that recognizes and protects human rights, including the right of asylum, and to be a US citizen is to be a member of a society that protects human rights. If the United States takes this charge seriously, it should not uphold conditions that place any human being in a state of deprivation so severe that their humanity is compromised, nor should it deny the benefits of citizenship to those who have been forced from nations that do not recognize and protect human rights. As Nancy Kwak (2015) documents, the US government promulgated foreign aid policies during the Cold War era that were explicitly designed to promote the global proliferation of America's distinctive homeownership institutions. This fact provides an additional reason to mitigate the harms associated with these particular institutions wherever they arise, whether in the United States or abroad.

Global justice theorists argue that the geographic location of one's birth is a morally arbitrary circumstance that should not influence one's prospects in life. According to Alvaro de Vita (2007, 109), "It is nowadays difficult to find such a morally arbitrary factor that weighs as heavily on a person's life chances as the place of the world where one happens to be born. As a matter of moral argument, it is difficult to make sense of the idea that a person being born a few miles to the north or a few miles to the south of the Mexican–American border should make such a huge difference in her opportunities to have a good life." This argument suggests that those who were not born in the United States should not be excluded from the benefits of US citizenship simply because they were born elsewhere.

Citizenship entails voluntary acceptance of the obligations of citizenship and a willingness to respect the equal rights of other citizens. Those who move to the United States to establish citizenship and refugees who are fleeing oppressive political regimes register their tacit acceptance of the obligations of US citizenship by voting with their feet. Thus, the ground of citizenship, as I understand it, implies a more expansive and inclusive conception of citizenship than what is implied by the formal legal definition of US citizenship. All who permanently reside within US borders—both legally recognized citizens and those who have tacitly accepted the obligations of citizenship by moving to the United States to establish permanent residence—deserve to be treated in accordance with the ideal of civic equality.

Rights and the Structure of Moral Reasoning

As discussed in chapter 1, most theories of justice have either goals, rights, duties, or virtues as their basis. As revealed by the discussion in part II of this book, American housing reformers have frequently appealed to rights to underscore the moral urgency of their demands for reform. Before the Civil War, an egalitarian interpretation of the natural right to private property fueled radical land reform movements. Right-based reforms did not sit well with progressives, who rejected natural rights and the preemptive authority of individual rights, or utilitarians, who justified policies on the basis of their aggregate consequences. Franklin D. Roosevelt's welfare state was based on a conception of social rights that secured positive freedoms to minimal consumer welfare, but his federal housing policy apparatus ultimately failed to extend the basic entitlements of social citizenship to everyone. Human rights and civil rights reformers appealed to more inclusive conceptions of second- and third-generation rights. By the neoliberal era, housing justice advocates were calling for an expansion of human rights to housing and collective rights to the city while rejecting liberal individual rights, particularly the right to own private property. This chapter has provided reasons to interpret the right to housing as a civil right that is grounded in a conception of social citizenship, but this still leaves open the question of whether rights offer a morally compelling basis for housing justice.

One way of understanding the appeal of a right-based approach is to consider it in relation to the alternatives. A well-known criticism of goal-based policy justifications is that appeals to aggregate consequences or the common good may license morally objectionable trade-offs between individual and collective aims. For example, utilitarianism justifies the sacrifice of an individual's life if the sacrifice would save several other lives. Policies justified on the basis of their aggregate consequences or collective good also fail to respect the separateness of persons. As Robert Nozick (1974, 33; italics in the original) observes, "To use a person [for another's benefit] ... does not sufficiently respect and take account of the fact that he is a separate person, that his is the only life he has. *He* does not get some overbalancing good from his sacrifice."

Virtue-based and duty-based theories also face limitations. While virtues may be worthwhile individual aims, it does not follow from this that I am obligated to behave virtuously or that others have a right to insist that I exercise my duty to be virtuous. As discussed, the perfectionist quality of virtue-based theories also violates the state neutrality requirement to respect the reasonable plurality of conceptions of the good. Duty-based conceptions of justice tend to get the relationship between rights and duties backward. Since rights are generally understood as interests sufficient to ground duties (Raz 1986), it seems odd to justify an obligation to act in some way to promote someone else's benefit without first acknowledging whether or how that person benefits from a duty. The conception of housing justice presented in this book appeals to the duties of social citizenship to derive principles of justice, but these duties are secondary to the fact that individuals have fundamental rights to be treated as moral equals. The duties of social citizenship are empty without some prior acknowledgment of one's moral entitlement to equal citizenship.

To more fully understand the benefits of a right-based approach, it is useful to say more about the role that rights play in moral reasoning.[8] According to Gerald Gaus (2011, 373), rights can be understood as "spheres of moral authority in which the rightholder's judgement about what is to be done provides others with reasons to act." Rights partition social space by decentralizing normative control over certain actions to the individual rightholder (Mack 2000). In the cases of the rights to housing and property, the partitioning implies a further partitioning of geographic space. John Gray (1993, 314) illustrates how private property rights function in this way: "The importance of several [i.e., private] property for civil society is that it acts as an enabling device whereby rival and possibly incommensurable conceptions of the good may be implemented and realized without any recourse to any collective decision-making procedure. . . . One may even say of civil society that it is a device for securing peace by reducing to a minimum the decisions on which recourse to collective choice—the political or public choice that is binding on us all—is unavoidable."

This "jurisdictional" view of rights provides an account of a common structural feature of rights within moral theories. According to Ronald Dworkin (1978), rights "trump" other moral considerations, including the obligations that one has to others and collective aims to promote the common good or aggregate utility. By partitioning social space so that some have legal powers over defined spheres of social activity, rightholders can demand justifications from those violating their social space. According to David Lyons (1982, 111), "If I have a right to do something, this provides an argumentative threshold against objections to my doing it, as well as a presumption against others' interference." This preemptive feature of rights does not necessarily imply that rights are absolute but rather that the burden of proof rests on violators of rights to demonstrate that violations of rights are justified by stronger moral considerations. Rights also structure democratic decision-making so that majoritarian aims do not subject minority rightholders to morally objectionable harms.

According to Jeremy Bentham (1843), rights also shape expectations and the incentives of individual actors acting in a decentralized fashion. Take the right to own property, for example. If property owners enjoy all rights to use, modify, earn income from, and exchange the property owned, the authority of the owner over the object's use limits what others can expect to gain from any attempt to use or modify the object. Homeowners can appeal to the state's police power to enforce their rights to evict squatters, for example. Similarly, constitutional restrictions on government takings of private property without due compensation provide assurances to owners that their plans and projects that make use of property will not be frustrated by government interference. A different property rights regime that acknowledged the right to own, use, and modify an object but limited the right to earn income from the object would create a different set of incentives and expectations for owners and nonowners.

By structuring the incentives of economic actors prior to exchange, a right-based housing policy approach is distinct from traditional redistributive policies that rely exclusively on taxes and subsidies to reallocate economic resources. Right-based approaches rely on "predistribution,"[9] rather than redistribution, to reassign rights and alter economic incentives without necessarily having to correct inequalities after the fact. For example, just-cause eviction laws and rent control ordinances expand tenants' rights while simultaneously reducing landlords' rights to evict tenants arbitrarily or earn rent above a predefined ceiling.

A right-based housing policy approach also gives official recognition to a nation's "constitutive commitment" to housing its citizens. According to Cass Sunstein (2004, 62), a nation's constitutive commitments "have a special place in the sense that they are widely accepted and cannot be eliminated without a fundamental change in social understanding. These rights are genuinely constitutive in the sense that they help create, or constitute, a society's basic values. They are also commitments in the sense that they are expected to have a degree of stability over time. A violation would amount to a kind of breach—a violation of trust."

By establishing a constitutive commitment to housing provision, a right-based approach prioritizes housing in public deliberations that involve the allocation of scarce resources. Canada's right-based National Housing Strategy provides an example of how a nation's constitutive commitments can structure public decisions. In 2017, Canada rolled out an ambitious Can$40 billion plan to reduce chronic homelessness and meet the housing needs of its most vulnerable citizens. Canadian officials tied the National Housing Strategy to specific targets that embody Canada's commitment to progressively realizing the human right to housing. The federal government is required to report regularly to Parliament on progress toward the achievement of these targets. By establishing a constitutive commitment to realizing the right to housing, Canada elevated the satisfaction of housing needs to a special place of importance within public policy deliberations (Government of Canada 2017).

Not all arguments for a right to housing are right based, and not all right-based arguments appeal to a conception of the right to housing. As an example of the former, many contemporary tenants' rights advocates justify stronger tenant right protections by appealing to the beneficial consequences of having tenants' rights secured. As an example of the latter, welfare rights advocates often called for the recognition of rights to public assistance without including housing assistance on the list of rights to be recognized. Arguably, US housing policy is already right based to the extent that private property rights shape the allocation of housing. Owners enjoy the right to occupy owned residential property, while renters' rights are limited to the terms of a lease agreement. This observation implies that the relevant question for policymakers is not whether rights are the appropriate basis of justice but rather whether the rights of those who occupy dwellings should preempt owners' rights to evict occupants. I return to this question in chapter 7.

Placing the American Home on a Solid Foundation

This chapter assembled the materials of housing justice. I began by exploring the significance of housing's social meanings for a conception of housing justice. I also explored different grounds of housing justice and argued that citizenship provides the most defensible ground for it. I proposed the ideal of civic equality and argued that its two dimensions—moral equality and relational equality—offer distinctive reasons for being concerned about housing inequality. These reasons justify different distributive principles that are in tension with one another, yet complementarities among the principles suggest ways to prioritize the allocation of scarce resources. I also argued that all US inhabitants, regardless of legal status, deserve to be treated in accordance with the ideal of civic equality. I concluded with an exploration of the basis of housing justice and a defense of a right-based approach to housing justice. Chapter 7 examines the content of the right to housing in more detail.

7 Private Property and the Injustice of Tenure Insecurity

> Freedom for the wolves has often meant death to the sheep.
> —Isaiah Berlin, *Four Essays on Liberty* (1971, xlv)

Chapter 1 examined the multiple sources of housing's value to inhabitants. This chapter examines this issue from the perspective of those who lack secure access to housing. This nonideal theoretic approach reorients the investigation of housing justice to the concrete reality of injustice and provides an application of civic equality to the public justification for private property. I argue that tenure insecurity, if taken seriously, presents a serious challenge to any public justification for private property, because if private property affords legal protections and rights to property owners, it simultaneously denies the same to those without property. I compare and contrast different approaches to publicly justifying private property by appealing to the interests of the propertyless and defend a version of Christopher Essert's (2016) argument that private property is justified not in spite of property's contribution to tenure insecurity but because it uniquely solves the problem of tenure insecurity. I extend Essert's argument by examining the features of a "secure tenure" property regime. I argue that a secure tenure property regime is one that is structured to guarantee the general right to secure tenure, permits the separate incidents of private property to be flexibly assembled into new bundles that protect the right to secure tenure, and creates economic incentives that are compatible with the aim of extending secure tenure to all. The right to housing, understood as a right to secure tenure, is constitutive of, and provides a justification for, the institution of private property. This understanding of the right to housing differs from other conceptions that are based on assumed conflicts between liberal private property rights and the right to housing (see, for example, Madden and Marcuse 2016).

The Injustice of Tenure Insecurity

According to the CESCR's General Comment Number 4, the first entitlement of the human right to housing is the legal security of tenure. The term "tenure insecurity" is often discussed in terms of land tenure, so it is useful to say a bit more about the use of this term as a way to characterize insecure housing arrangements. A person's residential tenure is insecure if they lack access to a safe, private dwelling space for a duration of time that they define. Tenure insecurity is not a binary condition but varies in degree from sleeping outdoors to homeownership tenures threatened by foreclosure. Between these extremes, there exist various insecure temporary tenure arrangements, including homeless shelter occupancy and stays on a friend's couch. The insecurity of these arrangements arises not from the temporary nature of occupancy spells or the absence of a roof and four walls but from inhabitants' lack of control over their living situation. Jet-setting millionaires vacationing in luxury hotel suites, college professors hiking the Appalachian Trail while on sabbatical, and retirees living out their golden years in recreational vehicles can choose at any moment to transition from temporary to more permanent living arrangements. Precarious tenure arrangements are associated with several distinct forms of injustice, including insecurity, heteronomy, alienation, indignity, marginalization, and domination.

Insecurity refers to the condition of being exposed to external environmental conditions that threaten bodily integrity and human life. Durable, insulated homes are essential for those living in harsh environments with extreme weather conditions. During global pandemics, proximity to other human beings poses risks to human life, regardless of prevailing environmental conditions, and private spaces protect households from exposure. In high-crime neighborhoods, private spaces reduce the threat of personal violence.

What is surprising about the injustice of insecurity is how weakly it alone supports a universal right to housing. As discussed in chapter 6, a house is a sufficient but not a necessary condition for being secure. In temperate climates, a lean-to or a tent may provide adequate protection from

Private Property and the Injustice of Tenure Insecurity 195

occasional environmental threats. Although climate change may increase the frequency, severity, and duration of extreme weather events, there is nothing about the severity of those events that requires one to be sheltered in a structure that we recognize as a home. Global pandemics and the threat of violence create a need for social isolation, but the extent of this need depends on the risk of encountering others in public spaces.

Heteronomy, the antonym of autonomy, refers to the inability to chart out and pursue one's chosen course in life. As discussed in chapters 1 and 6, human beings who lack secure access to a private space are unable to engage in self-reflection and experiment with different ways of living away from the wandering eyes and judgment of others. As Waldron writes,

> It would seem to follow that there must be a realm of private freedom somewhere for each individual—an area where he can make decisions about what to do and how to do it, justifying these decisions if at all only to himself. Again, to the extent that all action involves a material element, it seems to follow that such a realm of private decision would require an individual to have control of a certain material environment (a home, for example) from the use of which the interests and concerns of others and of society generally could be taken to be excluded. (Waldron 1988, 295)

A house does not guarantee full autonomy, but those who lack a home or whose tenure is insecure are unable to effectively exercise their capacity for autonomy or pursue autonomously chosen paths in life.[1]

The injustice of heteronomy further elucidates the moral significance of insecurity. Consider Alejandra Mancilla's (2016) distinction between a lone hiker caught in a snowstorm and a homeless person who seeks protection from the cold throughout the winter months. Whereas the lone hiker may be comforted by the knowledge that once the storm passes, their episodic need will no longer exist, the homeless person must engage in long-term planning to ensure that shelter is available for several consecutive nights. Thus, a homeless person's chronic insecurity is not only a harm in and of itself but also the constant need to attend to one's biological needs reduces the time that individuals have to devote to the formulation and pursuit of larger life plans.

Alienation refers to the condition of being separated from one's identity or personhood. According to Radin (1993), an individual's sense of personhood is often bound up with the home they inhabit, and the strength of this relationship can be measured by the pain that is occasioned by the loss of home. Those who have formed a strong emotional and psychological connection to a place suffer an intensely personal loss when forced to move, even if they are not rendered homeless by the eviction. Mindy Fullilove (2004, 11) refers to this loss as "root shock," which she describes as "the traumatic stress reaction to the destruction of all or part of one's emotional ecosystem. It has important parallels to the physiological shock experienced by a person who, as a result of injury, suddenly loses massive amounts of fluids. . . . Just as a burn victim requires immediate replacement of fluids, so, too, the victim of root shock requires the support and direction of emergency workers who can erect shelter, provide food, and ensure safety until the victim has stabilized and can begin to take over these functions again."

Madden and Marcuse (2016, 56) also refer to alienation, but they equate it with the elevation of housing's exchange value relative to its use value. The authors appeal to Karl Marx to argue that just as the selling of labor to a capitalist in exchange for money separates the laborer from their species-being, the commodification of housing alienates inhabitants from their home. I understand alienation slightly differently. The commodification of housing and conversion of inhabited space into a tradable market good may or may not foster alienation as I define it. Indeed, the opposite may be true if individuals freely acquire homes that embody their autonomously chosen life paths. What matters is whether an inhabitant's identity-based attachment to home is secured or severed by the exchange of money for property (Dawkins 2020b).

Indignity, the antonym of dignity, refers to the loss of the social bases of self-respect and the respect of others. Someone without a private place to defecate, urinate, bathe, and engage in intimate activities invites the scorn of bourgeois society (Waldron 1991). Those recognized as homeless also invite others' feelings of pity or in some cases contempt. As discussed in chapter 6, dignity is a socially constructed concept that embodies a society's conception of what constitutes a dignified life. If access to a home is an important part of that conception, those who lack homes are unable to participate in society's common culture and are stigmatized as a result (Phillips 1999). The social meaning of home defines a home's contribution to human dignity.

In the United States, for example, the indignity of homelessness is a direct juxtaposition of the elevated social rank that homeowners enjoy.

Marginalization refers to the loss of the rights, privileges, and benefits of social citizenship. Whereas indignity refers to social stigmatization, marginalization refers to the loss of the formal legal entitlements and public goods owed to all citizens. The bundling of housing with the rights of citizenship provides a justification for viewing the right to housing as a "basic right" because without housing one is unable to fully enjoy many of the other rights of citizenship (Shue 1996). Those who are homeless are unable to fully exercise their right to privacy. Laws that punish those who sleep in public violate a homeless person's right to be free from cruel and unusual punishment. Until recently, the right to vote was often tied to residency requirements, and even if no proof of residency is required to vote, homeless persons often lack access to information about voting alternatives and public meetings. A variety of local public services, such as libraries and educational institutions, are only made available to those who are residents of a local jurisdiction.

Domination refers to the state of being subject to the arbitrary will of others, or the state of lacking civic (republican) freedom. A homeless person who sleeps on property owned by someone else faces legally sanctioned eviction and possible punishment, and many local governments in the United States sanction the same sorts of punishment for those who sleep in public spaces. Those who are homeless and those who lack secure tenure have no private space where they can engage in activities without being subject to the arbitrary will of others (Waldron 1991). According to Arendt (1958, 29–30), "What prevented the polis from violating the private lives of its citizens and made it hold sacred the boundaries surrounding each property was not respect for private property as we understand it, but the fact that without owning a house a man could not participate in the affairs of the world, because he had no location in it which was properly his own." One implication of the connection between homelessness and domination is that some forms of collective housing provision may simply replace one form of unfreedom with another. If the government provided all housing, citizens would be subject to the arbitrary will of a government agent rather than the decentralized wills of private property owners (Essert 2016).

Tenure Insecurity and the Public Justification for Private Property

If tenure insecurity is unjust, then the institution of private property is complicit in this injustice. While private property protects the security, autonomy, identity, dignity, citizenship status, and civic freedom of those with secure tenure, it simultaneously fails to safeguard the same conditions for those who lack rights to private residential property.[2] In a city where all land is carved into privately owned lots, the propertyless must either receive the permission from a property owner to shelter, compromising their civic freedom, or face legal punishment (Waldron 1991). In this section, I explore the implications of tenure insecurity for the public justification of private property and compare and contrast different approaches to integrating the concerns of the propertyless into a public justification for private property.[3]

Any public justification for private property must satisfy certain minimum conditions. First, the justification offered must be truly "public," in the sense of satisfying a condition of acceptability for everyone (Gaus 1996). Publicity is a particularly important dimension of the justification for private property because not everyone owns property. Since property rights are in rem rights, a justification for private property must also consider reasonable objections that may arise from noncitizens. For this reason, the public justification for private property faces a stronger justificatory burden than justifications for other laws and institutions that only apply to citizens.

What constitutes an acceptable public justification? It is unreasonable to base a public justification on the actual consent of all members of the public because this would be practically impossible, particularly if the relevant public includes those who are not citizens. Nor does acceptability necessarily require that public reasons arise from a democratic procedure, as majoritarian processes often fail to account for the interests of minority groups. Jürgen Habermas (1996) proposes a procedural interpretation of acceptability that stipulates that public deliberation processes satisfy certain ideal speech requirements. This, too, is often impractical, because public deliberation rarely corresponds to ideal speech conditions. I follow Scanlon (1998) in defining acceptability as the absence of any reasonable objection to the justification offered. Acceptability as Scanlonian reasonable rejectability is strengthened by, but does not require, deliberative processes that reveal all relevant reasons. I also follow Rawls's (1993) suggestion that only reasonable and uncontroversial objections not based on a conception of

Private Property and the Injustice of Tenure Insecurity

the good qualify as candidates for rebutting a public justification. A useful way of interpreting the condition of acceptability is to ask what justifications would be reasonably rejected by Adam Smith's (2000 [1759]) impartial spectator, who is from a different society but is still capable of offering an impartial judgment on reasons for actions (Sen 2009).

The challenge facing property theorists is to find a justification for the exclusionary institution of private property that would not be reasonably rejected by those who are excluded from that same institution. I will examine five ways in which property theorists have responded to this challenge.

Preemptory Rights to Necessity

Some appeal to the human right to life to argue that this right is so important that it preempts private property rights when one is in a state of severe material deprivation. Many have argued that the need to preserve human life grounds a duty of charity to the needy, but Hugo Grotius was the first to propose that human beings have a natural right to necessity that preempts private property rights during times of need. Grotius also argued that individuals have a right to take what is needed from those who own property during times of need, under certain conditions (Mancilla 2016). In times of dire need, the "ancient Right of using Things, as if they still remained common, must revive, and be in full Force: For in all Laws of human Institution, and consequently, in that of Property too, such Cases seem to be excepted" (Grotius 2005 [1625], 434). Mancilla (2016) and Pogge (2002) offer contemporary understandings of the human right to necessity.

This justificatory argument is distinguished by its ground (human status) and preemptory force. In most accounts of property, the right to own property is grounded in an appeal to citizenship and can be overridden by civil laws that constrain property rights. The right to necessity, on the other hand, is a basic human right that grounds other rights, including the right to own property. In contrast to other justificatory strategies examined here that appeal to positive rights to the provision of public assistance, the right to necessity can be interpreted as a purely negative right that prevents others from interfering with a needy person's use of the resources required to sustain human life.

One limitation of this approach is that it fails to address all injustices associated with tenure insecurity. The right to necessity, at most, grounds a right to inhabit a shelter owned by others during episodic environmental threats. It does not ground a homeless person's right to remain in that shelter after the threat has been lifted, nor does it ground a homeless person's positive right to shelter provision. Grotius placed conditions on the exercise of the right to necessity. He argued that a needy person must first ask the magistrate for aid before appealing to a private property owner for shelter, and only if the property owner refuses shelter does the right to necessity have preemptive force. Furthermore, the owner must be compensated for any inconveniences caused by the trespass (Horne 1990).

Another limitation of the right to necessity is that current human rights law decentralizes the responsibility for progressively realizing human rights to individual nations. As discussed in chapter 5, the United States has not ratified the ICESCR, which secures the human right to housing. While the right to necessity explains why the United States *should* ratify the ICESCR, the human right to necessity does not currently have preemptory force under US law.

A final limitation of the preemptory right to necessity is that it does not justify the institution of private property itself. Instead, it provides a reason for rejecting the institution of private property. If the right to necessity is fully recognized by a nation that also recognizes private property rights, the institution of private property must be justified on separate grounds that possibly conflict with the human right to necessity.

The Right to Redistribution

Another justificatory strategy emphasizes not the justification for private property but the justification for the right to a share of the resources generated from private property ownership. Legal advocates appealed to this type of argument during the 1960s to argue on behalf of welfare rights to public assistance. This approach is consistent with, but differs slightly from, Rawls's (1971) proposal to distribute economic resources so that the least advantaged are as well off as possible. Chester Hartman (1998) presents the case for a right to housing along these lines.

Unlike the preemptory right to necessity, the right to redistribution assumes the prior existence of an institution of private property that generates enough wealth and income to be redistributed to those who have less. According to Rawls's (1971) "difference principle," if the distribution of economic resources maximizes advantages for those who are least advantaged, those without private property have no complaint. One familiar objection to this argument is the sufficientarian's claim that redistribution of government-collected largesse may fail to raise everyone to an acceptable threshold level of economic sufficiency. Although the disadvantaged may be better off than under any other possible distributive arrangement, the disadvantaged may still lack the resources required to live a dignified life.

Another problem is that a needy person's rights to redistribution do not strictly assign a space of freedom within which the needy person is permitted to act with a corresponding duty on the part of others to respect the needy person's freedom. In other words, the right to redistribution cannot be interpreted as a claim right, according to Hohfeld's (1919) typology, because those who generate income are not obligated to earn enough money to satisfy the needs of others. Whereas the right to necessity can be understood as a claim right to occupy private property owned by others during times of urgent need, the right to redistribution does not correlate to a similar obligation, because the right only pertains to a share of the income generated from private property, not a right to the use of property itself.

Conditional Justifications for Private Property

This justificatory strategy specifies the conditions under which private property itself is justified. Since the acquisition of private property entails a loss of others' opportunity to acquire the same property, this justification appeals to the argument that those without property should be compensated for the reduction in property acquisition opportunities created by an owner's appropriation. If the redistribution of government-collected largesse is interpreted as a form of compensation owed to those who are disadvantaged by a private property regime, this justification is comparable to the right to redistribution argument. Unlike the right to necessity argument, the conditional justification for private property derives from the original justification for property rather than from the human right to life. The similarities between this approach and the two examined previously suggest that the conditional justification approach faces many of the same problems already discussed.

Compensation may be a necessary or a sufficient justification for an owner's appropriation. Locke (1980 [1690]) offers a classic version of the sufficient justificatory approach. According to Locke, the property rights held by those mixing labor with land are justified when enough property is left for others to acquire, property is not allowed to spoil, and human life is preserved. Locke viewed seventeenth-century America as an example of a place on earth with enough property for others to acquire; however, one might question whether he would view contemporary America in the same light (Waldron 1988). Michael Otsuka (2003) interprets the Lockean proviso to leave "enough, and as good" for others as a sufficient condition for legitimate property acquisition as long as property owners leave enough unappropriated property to guarantee equal access to the opportunities from property acquisition. For Thomas Paine, the emergence of private property entails a loss of one's "natural inheritance," or the natural right to unowned property in a state of nature. He argues that if land inheritances are taxed and redistributed in support of a universal social insurance system, private property is conditionally justified (Lamb 2015). Corey Brettschneider (2012) offers a contemporary version of the necessary justificatory approach. He argues that private property institutions must be publicly justifiable to those who are excluded from property. Still, he offers several possible forms of legitimate compensation and stops short of claiming that any one provides a sufficient justification for private property.

A problem with any conditional justification for private property is that the condition may not cohere with the original justification for private property and may lack force if the form of compensation is not necessary and sufficient to justify private property. Under Paine's proposal, for example, pensions for the elderly, disability assistance, and a stakeholder grant would be funded from a 10 percent tax on land inheritances. Still, there is no guarantee that this amount or these forms of social insurance adequately offset each person's loss of natural inheritance. Even if we accept that the revenues from an inheritance tax are sufficient to compensate everyone for their loss of the natural right to property, the mere presence of the compensation scheme itself calls into question the original justification for property. If private property creates the need for a compensation scheme to offset its negative effects, then why institute private property in the first place?

Justifications for Limited Private Property Rights
Others interpret the objections of the propertyless to imply that the separate incidents of property require different justifications, where the incidents of ownership include the right to possess, use, modify, manage, exclude non-owners, earn income from, and alienate owned property for a term determined

by the owner (Honoré 1961). As discussed in chapter 2, nineteenth-century anarchists such as Ezra Heywood and Joshua Ingalls argued that only the right to occupancy and use of property could be justified.

John Christman (1991; 1994) contends that A. M. Honoré's (1961) classic conception of "full liberal ownership" includes two distinct types of rights—*control rights* (rights to use, possession, management, modification, and alienation) and *income rights* (rights to the increased benefit from relinquishing ownership temporarily or permanently)—each requiring separate justifications. According to Christman (1991, 30), "If control rights are to be justified at all, essential reference must be made to individualist interests such as liberty, autonomy, and self-determination." He further argues that whereas the justification for control rights stands on its own without reference to the distribution of those rights, the justification for income rights is connected to their distribution. Individuals do not necessarily have a claim to all profits earned from the sale or rent of property because property-based income depends on several factors that are beyond the control of the property owner. Prices are determined by market conditions, which are in turn determined by the structure of property rights and other rules of the game that influence the distribution of profits. Using Rawls's (1971) terminology, prices are determined by the "basic structure of society," which shapes the distribution of advantages and disadvantages.

Given that control rights secure the primary interests that justify property ownership, a distributive arrangement of income rights that enables a more widespread distribution of control rights is more defensible than one that distributes control rights narrowly. Henry George (1942) appeals to a version of this idea to argue that landowners have no claim to the full economic rent from landownership because land rent is produced by natural resources and the collective efforts of society. George's arguments resemble those of Thomas Paine, who writes in *Agrarian Justice* (Paine 1995 [1797], 428; italics in the original) that "personal property is the *effect of Society*; and it is as impossible for an individual to acquire personal property without the aid of Society, as it is for him to make land originally. . . . All accumulation, therefore, of personal property, beyond what a man's own hands produce, is derived to him living in society; and he owes, on every principle of justice, of gratitude, and of civilization, a part of that accumulation back again to society from whence the whole came."

Gaus (2012) identifies one problem with this argument. If the justification for private property derives in part from property's contribution to autonomy and the freedom to pursue autonomously chosen projects, this justifies the most expansive conception of property possible so that owners have the flexibility to autonomously alter the incidents of ownership, including the right to alienate certain incidents, to meet their individual needs. This critique is not very persuasive. One does not require full income rights to use property freely and autonomously, particularly if others have a similar right to property use.

General Rights to Private Property
In the view of nineteenth-century land reformers such as Thomas Skidmore, everyone enjoys a natural right to enough landed property to establish a homestead, and government distribution of free land combined with limitations on the right to accumulate property are justified ways of distributing private property as widely as possible. In contrast to Henry George, who endorsed the partial attenuation of income rights, Skidmore sought to extend full liberal ownership rights to all workers, subject to the condition that everyone owned some property. The advantage of this approach is that the original justification for private property is connected to a justification for its widespread distribution.

G. W. F. Hegel's *The Philosophy of Right* (1967 [1821]) offers an argument for private property along these lines. For Hegel, property is constitutive of freedom itself because property represents the externalization of an individual's will in material objects. Individuals need some property to transform their purely subjective conception of themselves into one that is concretely realized in and recognized by the external world. Thus, property is something that everyone needs and is only justified if everyone has access to some property. For this reason, Waldron (1988) argues that Hegel's argument, if taken seriously, is an argument for a *general* right to property (see chapter 2).

It is important to emphasize that a general right to property is not a general right to the *opportunity* to acquire property, nor is it a right to *compensation* for being excluded from property that is owned by others. A general right to property is only satisfied if everyone has something recognizable as property (Waldron 1988). Katy Wells (2016) argues that citizens' interests in privacy justify the inclusion of a right to rent or occupy housing (but not necessarily full liberal ownership rights to housing) among the basic liberties guaranteed to all citizens under Rawls's (1971) first principle of justice as fairness. According to Wells (2016, 374), "This is because citizens' interest in having privacy, which, I have suggested, has clear connections to the protection of self-respect, personal independence and to guaranteeing the supporting basic liberties, requires the protection of something very close to this set of rights. The right in question is a right to actually have these rental rights, rather than simply a right to be eligible to have them, because privacy is secured by actually having these rights over some living space, not by having the ability to have such rights."

Christopher Essert (2016) offers a similar argument without appealing to Rawls's (1971) conception of justice. In Essert's account, homelessness and tenure insecurity are not conditions that weaken the case for private property, but they are the very reason that private property is instituted in the first place. According to Essert (2016, 281), "The moral problem of homelessness calls for the creation of an institution of property, and any such institution can be justified only insofar as and to the extent that it solves this problem." Essert argues that private property is uniquely positioned to secure republican (civic) freedom. To reach this seemingly paradoxical conclusion, Essert observes that in a state of nature where private property is not recognized, no one has the moral or legal authority to exclude anyone else from an inhabited space. Those who occupy space must continually receive permission from everyone else and are therefore in a state of perpetual unfreedom because all actions are subject to the arbitrary will of others. Collective housing provision is also insufficient because it merely replaces one form of unfreedom with another. Private property provides a unique solution to this problem by decentralizing normative control over geographic space to an individual designated as the owner.

In contrast to Christman's (1991; 1994) justificatory strategy, Essert does not offer a separate justification for each incident of private property but appeals to the aim of extending to everyone the tenure security enjoyed by private property owners. Essert rejects justifications for limited private property rights. Still, he allows for the possibility that the structure of private property rights may be modified to eliminate homelessness. For example, a landlord's reversion interest and power to terminate a lease puts the renter at a disadvantage if the landlord has the power to evict a tenant without notice. Laws specifying minimum lease durations or those that require the landlord to show just cause for a failure to renew a lease restructure property rights to favor those with less secure tenure.

By appealing to private property's role in alleviating homelessness, Essert's (2016) justification is tied to a defense of private property's widespread distribution. This has a corollary disadvantage: private property, as currently defined, fails to live up to its justification because it fails to alleviate homelessness and tenure insecurity. In the United States, private property is allocated according to ability and willingness to pay, which precludes those with limited economic resources from obtaining secure tenure. Allocating private property in accordance with willingness to pay is also arguably procedurally unfair because the allocation mechanism distributes property in a way that is inconsistent with the rationale for private property's existence (Scanlon 2018). The justificatory strategy proposed by Essert (2016) ultimately fails unless the institution of private property has some inherent feature guaranteeing that property will be distributed first to those with no means to acquire it.

The Secure Tenure Property Regime

The failure of Essert's (2016) justificatory strategy stems in part from the object of justification: the bundle of full liberal ownership rights. He is unable to justify all elements of the bundle because income rights (rights to earn income from the rent or sale of property) enable the exclusion of those unable to afford rent. In this section, I address this challenge and extend Essert's argument in two ways. First, I demonstrate that Essert's homelessness alleviation argument provides an instrumental justification for (limited) income rights. Second, I extend Essert's approach by applying it more broadly to the justification for a "secure tenure" property regime that includes the right to housing as a constitutive element.

Property theorists often justify income rights by appealing to the idea that property owners deserve rental income as appropriate compensation for investing in a socially beneficial activity (Dewilde and Ronald 2017). This desert-based meritocratic argument has been criticized by political economists and philosophers. Henry George (1942) maintains that property owners only deserve to collect earned income. Monopoly rents are unearned because they arise from the monopolist's market power, and land rents are unearned because they are produced from nature, which no one deserves to own, or from the collective efforts of society, in which everyone has an equal ownership stake. Rawls (1971) goes one step further to argue that because natural talents and endowments result from the natural lottery, no one deserves the unequal advantages that arise from the exercise of talents. Most desert-based justifications for income rights ultimately fail because it is difficult to establish a reason for someone's deservingness that justifies a reward equal to the full rental value of property. The most an owner deserves is a profit sufficient to induce the owner to invest in the first place. If, as suggested in chapter 1, the justification for property holdings derives from property's special connection to leisure, not labor, those who lack space for leisure arguably have a stronger claim to improved space than those who use property only to extract economic value.

Property theorists have also appealed to utilitarianism to justify income rights. According to Bentham (1843), private property maximizes utility by encouraging the efficient use of resources. If property owners enjoy the right to keep all profits from the sale or rent of property, they face strong incentives to improve property using the least costly methods. The utilitarian justification for income rights is a combination of two separate arguments: (1) the instrumentalist argument (income rights create incentives to use property in ways that produce the best outcomes) and (2) the maximum utility argument (the best outcomes are those that maximize aggregate utility). The instrumentalist argument does not entail the maximum utility argument. For example, private property can be instrumentally justified on egalitarian grounds if income rights are structured to equalize, rather than maximize, the utility from property use.

The instrumentalist argument provides a way to incorporate (limited) income rights into Essert's homelessness alleviation justification for private property. According to Christman (1991; 1994), the most important sticks in the property rights bundle are control rights to property use, possession, management, modification, and alienation. Those who enjoy secure control rights to residential space avoid the injustices of tenure insecurity mentioned previously. If control rights deliver the tenure security that justifies residential property ownership, income rights are then instrumentally justified to the extent that property-based income encourages property owners to invest in the production of residential space for those experiencing tenure insecurity. The strength of this argument is tied to the nature of the incentives facing residential property owners.

Given that a variety of property-based institutions shape the incentives to invest in the production of housing, the appropriate object of justification is not merely the bundle of rights held by property owners but the entire private property "regime," which includes the rights held by property owners, inhabitants, and investors; the public regulations that constrain certain incidents; and the tax and subsidy policies that redistribute the income earned from property. If the incentives created by the entire regime have the combined effect of encouraging the provision of housing first to those who are unsheltered, the regime is justified according to Essert's argument, even if the bundle of private property rights or individual sticks in the bundle fail to reward actions that alleviate homelessness. For example, if individual property owners enjoy unrestricted income rights but face a progressive tax schedule that redistributes a portion of rental income to those unable to afford residential space, the combination of these two incentives may work together to address the problem of tenure insecurity.

I define a "secure tenure" property regime as one that recognizes the right to housing, understood as a general right to secure tenure, as the most important stick in the property rights bundle. Other sticks in the bundle, including income rights, would be structured to extend the right to secure tenure to everyone. While it is beyond the scope of this book to fully examine the complex issues associated with the design of a secure tenure property regime, I argue that such a regime is one that minimally satisfies three requirements. First, a secure tenure regime delivers *tenure security* by guaranteeing everyone's general right to occupy and use a private dwelling space. Second, a secure tenure regime fosters *bundle flexibility* by allowing the incidents of ownership to be easily modified to enhance tenure security. Third, a secure tenure regime exhibits *incentive compatibility* when the regime's various economic incentives work together to encourage the provision of housing to those experiencing tenure insecurity. I will explore each of these requirements.

Tenure security A secure tenure property regime is one that first and foremost guarantees security of tenure for all. The general right to secure tenure can be understood as a partitioning of property rules that reassigns the rights over certain incidents—such as the right to possess, use, manage, and possibly modify residential space—to those who inhabit or seek to inhabit a dwelling. If residential property owners enjoy full liberal ownership rights, an owner's right to own property will necessarily conflict with a nonowner's right to establish secure tenure on that same property. Still, if ownership arrangements leave open the possibility that inhabitants hold rights to occupancy that prohibit owners of the same property from interfering with the inhabitant's residential use, the right to housing is constitutive of, rather than in conflict with, ownership rights.

To better understand the right to secure tenure's role in housing justice, it is useful to examine how those who own homes free and clear avoid the injustices described previously. Those who own well-constructed homes enjoy security from external environmental threats. Within the home, owner-occupants can freely engage in autonomous pursuits and pursue a conception of the good life. Homeownership provides a place-based frame of reference that shapes the homeowner's personal identity. Homeowners enjoy an elevated social status and receive all the place-based benefits of citizenship. Homeownership secures a private realm where civic freedom can be enjoyed. Although some homeowners enjoy these benefits more extensively than others do, all homeowners enjoy a minimum level of tenure security that provides protection from the most severe forms of housing injustice. Importantly, homeowners do not require full liberal ownership rights to avoid these housing injustices.

The most important stick in the homeowner's property bundle is the control right to occupy and use a private residential space for a duration of time determined by the homeowner. The tenure security requirement extends this stick in the property bundle to everyone, while possibly modifying other sticks in the bundle to guarantee equal access to secure housing arrangements. The expansion of control rights to secure tenure may require the contraction of rights to labor income (if resources financed by income taxes are used to finance affordable housing subsidies) or property income (if rent stabilization measures are adopted to enhance tenure security). Still, if tenure security justifies the private property regime, income rights are secondary to the right to secure tenure.

The principle of state neutrality discussed in chapter 6 suggests that actions taken to expand tenure security should not favor any particular housing type or tenure arrangement. Given that most homeowners already enjoy secure control rights,[4] state neutrality is consistent with measures designed to enhance the level of housing security that alternative tenure arrangements deliver. State neutrality justifies granting renters a "vested interest" in the occupancy of their property for a term of occupancy determined by the renter, effectively transforming renters' occupancy rights into rights that are comparable to those enjoyed by owner-occupants (Indritz 1971). Limited-equity cooperative (LEC) tenure arrangements that convert renters to shareholders,[5] just-cause eviction laws, and rent stabilization ordinances are a few examples of reforms that enhance the tenure security of rental tenure arrangements. State neutrality also justifies local land-use policy reforms that create regulatory parity among different housing types and styles. If taken seriously, state neutrality justifies radical changes in local land-use practices, including the repeal of single-family-only zoning regulations and the elimination of prohibitions on nontraditional housing types.

For those who are homeless, the right to secure tenure can only be satisfied by providing a home directly, providing the resources to enable those who are homeless to secure a home for themselves, or allowing the homeless to occupy property that is currently owned by someone else. If the right to secure tenure is to be understood as a claim right, the solution to homelessness should address what homeless persons can claim for themselves, not what others are obligated to do (Mancilla 2016). The right to secure tenure should do more than merely justify homeless persons' right to complain; it should provide them with an expectation of what they may claim as a right. A homeless person's claim right can only be satisfied by allowing them to occupy property currently owned by someone else during times of urgent need.

Does the homeless person's right to secure tenure trump the rights of those who currently occupy residential property? Margaret Radin's (1993) personhood justification for property implies that the rights of current occupants may trump the rights of the homeless because current occupants more strongly identify with the property that they occupy. Because the homeless, by definition, lack any personal attachment to a residence, existing occupants have a stronger claim to their occupied dwelling. This argument suggests that although the homeless may not have special claims to inhabit property currently occupied by others, the homeless have a right to inhabit vacant residential structures or public parks if shelter space is otherwise unavailable. An interesting implication of this argument is that the potential threat of unwelcome squatting provides the very reason that property owners should support the public provision of homeless shelter space under a private property regime where the right to secure tenure is recognized. A legal regime that recognizes and protects the right to secure tenure delivers tenure security to current and prospective inhabitants of residential property.

Bundle flexibility The bundles of private property rights recognized under a secure tenure property regime should be flexible enough to permit a variety of ways of realizing secure tenure. In one sense, this requirement seems to only further promote the "disintegration of property" (Grey 1980, 69) that first began during the Progressive Era, but this is not necessarily true. The goal of bundle flexibility is not to arbitrarily disassemble the property rights bundle or reassign use and occupancy rights to collective agents but rather to deconstruct and reassemble the bundle in ways that promote a widespread distribution of individual rights to secure tenure.

In some cases, it may be appropriate to reassign control over certain incidents to collective agents to facilitate the expansion of individual rights to secure tenure. This does not mean that the right to housing is a collective right, because the right to secure tenure is still a privately held individual right guaranteed to everyone (see chapter 8). Still, if some lack rights to secure tenure, establishing collective control over certain property incidents, particularly the right to earn income from property, may facilitate the expansion of individual rights to secure tenure. Washington, DC's, TOPA law, for example, grants tenants the collective right of first refusal, thereby enhancing the tenure security of individual tenants. Similarly, rent stabilization laws expand tenure security for individual renters by reassigning the right to earn rental income from individual rental property owners to the community at large. Collective rights to land use, such as those established under land-use zoning, may conflict with the goal of expanding tenure security if collectivized land-use rights exclude affordable housing.

Incentive compatibility The inner workings of the private property regime, as evidenced by the incentives facing owners and occupants of property, should encourage the provision of secure housing tenure to those who lack it. Under the current US property regime, private owners of residential property capture all returns from increases in land value attributable to collective community improvements. Furthermore, owners have significant control over the terms of rental contracts. While these rights have been attenuated somewhat by fair housing laws, and in some states implied warranties of habitability and rent control statutes, landlords still offer rental contracts as take-it-or-leave-it options subject to contract durations defined by the landlord.

Housing producers also have few incentives to invest in cost-saving innovations that lower the price of housing. Rather than earn profits by reducing production costs, many housing producers maximize profits by taking advantage of housing market segmentation and product differentiation. The segmentation of housing markets by location and type increases the market power of housing producers within submarkets. Facing few competitors for differentiated products, housing producers can set the price and/or quantity of housing offered to consumers that exhibit unique housing preferences (Leishman 2001). In highly segmented markets, the profits gained by catering to distinctive tastes may outweigh any benefits from high-volume production. Land-use regulations contribute to housing market segmentation by differentiating neighborhoods into submarkets defined by housing type, use, size, and density.

Although a secure tenure property regime will likely attenuate the right to earn monopoly profits within segmented housing markets, extraction of all profits from the residential sector through the full decommodification of housing would eliminate the economic incentives to invest in housing production. The challenge facing policymakers is to create market incentives that stimulate the production of low-cost housing in underserved markets. One approach is to eliminate regulations that stifle innovative low-cost housing solutions such as manufactured housing, tiny homes, and accessory dwelling units. Another is to devote public funding to housing research and development.

Toward Secure Tenure for All

Many contemporary housing advocates view the right to housing as a right that conflicts with the right to own private property. Reform proposals based on the decommodification of housing through the socialization of housing provision ignore the possibility that private property provides a unique solution to the very problem it creates. Private property both creates and solves the problem of tenure insecurity. This chapter presented an argument for a right to housing, understood as a right to secure tenure, that is constitutive of, and justifies, the institution of private property. I argued that a secure tenure property regime is one that is structured to guarantee the general right to secure tenure, allows the incidents of property to be flexibly assembled to extend the right to secure tenure to everyone, and creates economic incentives that are compatible with the aim of extending tenure security to all. Chapter 8 expands this argument by demonstrating how the objective of extending tenure security to all can be achieved while simultaneously promoting housing equality.

8 Taking Housing Justice Seriously

> There can be no fairness or justice in a society in which some live in homelessness, or in the shadow of that risk, while others cannot even imagine it.
> —Jordan Flaherty, *Floodlines* (2010, 184)

The right to secure tenure grounds a sufficientarian conception of housing justice, but the ideal of civic equality provides reasons to be concerned about housing inequality, even if everyone is adequately housed. This chapter completes the circle by demonstrating how to extend the right to secure tenure in a way that is consistent with civic equality and social justice more broadly. I argue that the ideal of civic equality provides an answer to the question of who should bear the cost of extending tenure security, and after all tenure security needs have been met, civic equality provides a justification for additional measures designed to reduce inequality in housing consumption and wealth. My proposal for extending tenure security through the promotion of housing equality is based on the idea of a negative income tax, applied to housing consumption and increases in housing wealth. The proposed "negative housing tax" can be implemented through the federal income tax code by treating income spent on owner occupancy and rental occupancy equivalently. The proceeds from the tax would fund a guaranteed monthly housing allowance and a supplemental block grant allocation designed to reduce spatial inequality in housing costs. After describing the negative housing tax, I discuss complications that arise from the spatial geography of housing affordability and explore the connections among housing justice, racial justice, and the right to the city.

Civic Equality and Housing Finance Reform

Chapters 6 and 7 provided justifications for housing policy reforms that (1) guarantee that everyone has access to a minimally adequate home, (2) reduce overall levels of housing inequality, and (3) are tenure neutral. In this section, I examine the elements of a proposed federal housing policy reform that appeals to the ideal of civic equality and the public justification for private property to achieve these three goals. The proposal includes four elements: (1) a guaranteed monthly housing allowance that offsets a portion of housing costs for those experiencing the most severe housing needs, (2) a housing consumption tax, (3) a housing wealth increment tax, and (4) a supplemental block grant designed to reduce spatial inequalities in housing costs. This section examines the first three elements, which together constitute the negative housing tax, and the following section examines the fourth.

Guaranteed Housing Allowance

One straightforward way of meeting the basic housing needs of everyone in the United States is to convert the tenant-based HCV into a guaranteed monthly housing allowance. Ideally, from the standpoint of civic equality, the allowance would be universally provided to everyone regardless of the income they receive from other sources. If housing is a basic right of social citizenship, it should arguably be made available to all citizens regardless of whether or the extent to which one chooses to work to earn income. Tying the guaranteed monthly housing allowance to a work requirement may also stigmatize the poor rather than treating everyone as equal citizens who equally deserve to be housed in dignified ways. While there are sound moral reasons to prefer a universal guaranteed housing allowance, the reality of resource scarcity implies that policymakers must make certain trade-offs to prioritize housing assistance to those most in need.

A universal guaranteed monthly housing allowance potentially conflicts with the sufficientarian aim of extending the right to secure tenure to those whose tenure is most insecure if resources that could be spent alleviating homelessness are distributed first to those who earn enough income to afford decent housing. One way to prioritize housing subsidies to those experiencing tenure insecurity is to restrict the guaranteed monthly housing allowance to very low-income households who are struggling to cover housing expenses. The question of whether the subsidy should be targeted more narrowly to those earning extremely low incomes or more broadly to those earning low or moderate incomes—and the question of whether subsidies should be targeted to those with high housing cost burdens or only on the basis of income—are questions of resource availability. If resources are scarce, then arguably housing subsidies should be targeted to households with very low incomes who experience "worst-case" housing needs. These households include those who earn incomes no more than 50 percent of the median income earned by those living in the surrounding metropolitan area and who pay more than half their income in rent, live in severely inadequate conditions, or both (Watson et al. 2020).

One potential downside of an income-based qualification test is that it may discourage work, even without an explicit work requirement, because workers may be reluctant to accept wage employment if additional income triggers the loss of a guaranteed housing allowance. Wage employment may also create other familial hardships, particularly if an affordable childcare center is not easily accessible in the neighborhood at home or work. The concern here is not that some who are currently employed will forgo higher-paying jobs but that those who currently work low-wage jobs or are unemployed may choose unemployment over wage employment rather than risk the loss of a guaranteed monthly housing allowance. To avoid these "cliff effects," any income qualification should be high enough that those who choose to accept low-wage jobs will not risk losing their housing allowance. Alternatively, the subsidy level could simply decline proportionately with income. The goal of minimizing the disincentive to work conflicts with the aim of targeting assistance to those facing the highest housing needs, but presumably there is some optimal balance between these two priorities.

How should the guaranteed housing allowance payment level be determined? Most federal housing subsidies offset the difference between some percentage of the metropolitan FMR and 30 percent of a household's income. The question of how to define affordable housing for the purpose of calculating housing subsidies has generated a substantial amount of research, much of which criticizes the use of an arbitrary 30 percent threshold as a basis for determining housing subsidy levels (see, for example, Bieri and Dawkins 2016). I do not wish to engage with that debate here, but from the standpoint of civic equality, the 30 percent threshold risks limiting households' freedom to choose an optimal mix of housing and nonhousing consumption. Providing the allowance as an in-kind subsidy that must be spent on housing expenses has a similar effect. For these reasons, the monthly housing allowance would ideally be distributed in the form of cash or a refundable tax credit. Although some will likely spend a portion of the allowance on the consumption of other goods, this is not necessarily a concern from the standpoint of civic equality, as long as households had the option of freely choosing to spend the additional income on an affordable home. The monthly housing allowance should also be made available to prospective owners of housing to guarantee tenure neutrality and more widespread access to housing options. A cash subsidy preserves this flexibility.

Determining the level of the guaranteed monthly housing allowance is more complicated if we abandon the 30 percent affordability threshold. One idea is to tie the subsidy to the median gross rent, which includes the contract rent plus payments for utilities and home fuel. In 2017, the US median gross rent was $1,012, according to one-year American Community Survey estimates. Interestingly, this is roughly equivalent to the monthly payment on a $200,000 mortgage at 4.5 percent interest. According to Joseph Gyourko (2009), $200,000 would cover the cost of providing the physical structure for a standardized, modest-quality, single-family home with 2,000 square feet of living space almost anywhere in the country, excluding land costs. If we assume that a $1,000 monthly housing allowance is provided to all homeless persons in the United States (567,715 in 2018; see Henry et al. 2020) and all renters with very low incomes who experience worst-case housing needs (approximately 7.7 million renters in 2017; see Watson et al. 2020), this would cost roughly $99 billion per year, which would make the monthly housing allowance payment second only to overall military spending in terms of the dollar value of discretionary spending. This seems substantial, but it is still smaller than the income tax benefits that homeowners currently receive. The Office of Management and Budget (OMB) estimated that in the 2020 tax year, the mortgage interest deduction, state and local property tax deduction, capital gains tax exclusion, and exclusion of imputed rental income would be approximately $209 billion (Office of Management and Budget 2019b).[1] The cost of the monthly housing allowance could be fully funded by eliminating the exclusion for homeowners' imputed rental income. This change alone would generate an additional $126 billion in income tax revenue or about

60 percent of the estimated homeownership-related income tax expenditures in 2020 (Office of Management and Budget 2019b). By comparison, HUD requested only $44 billion in gross discretionary funding in FY2020 to support its low-income housing and community development programs (Office of Management and Budget 2019a).

Housing Consumption Tax

Who should bear the burden of funding the guaranteed monthly housing allowance? The incidence of redistributive policies is often evaluated by comparing the degree of horizontal and vertical equity associated with some tax proposal against a baseline of market outcomes in a world without taxation. As Liam Murphy and Thomas Nagel (2002) point out, this "everyday libertarianism" approach leaves open the question of which public goods and services will be provided in the first place, treating taxation as though taxes were simply dumped into the ocean after they have been collected.

The ideal of civic equality and the public justification for private property provide a different way of determining who should bear the burden of funding the guaranteed monthly housing allowance. If private property is justified to the extent that it provides security of tenure, the solution to housing insecurity should inhere in the residential property regime itself. Under the current American housing policy framework, all payers of income tax share in the cost of subsidizing low-income housing. Still, the burden falls more heavily on renters, who do not receive tax relief from the income spent on housing costs and face higher cost burdens as housing prices rise. Homeowners deduct a portion of the income spent on housing costs while simultaneously capturing all the gains from individual and collective investments that increase the value of their homes. Since the current owners of residential property are complicit in the creation of tenure insecurity by supporting and benefiting from the conditions that give rise to tenure insecurity, homeowners and residential property owners should bear a larger share of the burden of alleviating tenure insecurities caused by high housing prices.

A direct tax on housing consumption provides a way of funding a guaranteed monthly housing allowance that shifts the burden of the tax to residential property owners. The guaranteed monthly housing allowance combined with a housing consumption tax can be viewed as a form of negative housing consumption tax. To see this, we can draw on Philippe Van Parijs and Yannick Vanderborght's (2017) observation that the negative income tax is equivalent to a universal basic income with a linear income tax under the assumption that with a negative income tax, income above a threshold is taxed and redistributed as a subsidy to those below the threshold.[2] Assume that the housing consumption tax is linear and equal to 25 percent of housing consumption. Also, ignore any income cap on the monthly housing allowance and assume that everyone receives a housing allowance as a refundable tax credit equal to $1,000 per month. Under this scenario, $1,500 in monthly housing consumption would be associated with an incremental housing allowance of $625 (because $1,500 in consumption is taxed at a rate of 25%, and this amount is subtracted from the monthly housing allowance). The breakeven level of housing consumption (the point at which the monthly housing allowance net of consumption taxes is equal to zero) is equal to $4,000 per month. Someone spending this amount on housing consumption receives no subsidy because their housing consumption tax exactly offsets their monthly housing allowance. More generally, for levels of monthly housing consumption above $4,000, individuals would be taxed on their housing consumption and receive no guaranteed monthly housing allowance.

Economists often favor consumption taxes for positional goods such as housing, to reduce both socially wasteful forms of conspicuous consumption and the tax penalty on savings (Frank 2007). Civic equality provides a similar reason to support a housing consumption tax, because the tax curbs the incentive to exacerbate social status inequality through the overconsumption of housing. Civic equality also provides reasons to tie the housing consumption tax to a guaranteed housing allowance. A housing consumption tax that funds a guaranteed housing allowance reduces housing insecurity while tying redistribution directly to the source of the injustice that gives rise to the need for redistribution as well as targeting subsidies to those who consume less housing. The negative housing consumption tax helps to ensure that a market-based system of housing allocation is more acceptable to those disadvantaged by the system while also alleviating the need to rely exclusively on an income qualification test to target scarce resources to those most in need.

One concern with a negative housing consumption tax is the possibility of "downward filtering" resulting from higher-income households moving into lower-cost housing to maximize their incremental housing allowance. An income requirement on the monthly housing allowance would mitigate this effect to some degree. However, even if high-income households receive no housing allowance, these households would still have an incentive to reduce housing consumption to lower their tax burden. One could argue that downward filtering is simply evidence that the negative housing tax is working if households earning higher incomes respond to the tax by reducing their levels of conspicuous consumption. The problem from the standpoint of civic equality is not that some high-income households choose to consume less housing than they could otherwise afford; the problem is that if the supply of housing is inelastic in the short run, purging housing consumption of conspicuous consumption will create a scarcity of homes available for rent or purchase at lower prices. This objection can be flipped on its head and serve as a justification for policies that expand the supply of affordable homes, an issue to which I will return.

Housing Wealth Increment Tax
The ideal of civic equality justifies supplementing the housing consumption tax with an additional tax on accumulated housing wealth. Following John Stuart Mill (1965 [1848]), who proposed a similar tax on unearned wealth gains, I refer to the tax on accumulated housing wealth as the "housing wealth increment tax."[3]

An important issue from the standpoint of civic equality is that housing wealth gains often arise from unearned increases in home equity created by collective investments in local public goods. By creating an additional source of revenue to fund the guaranteed monthly housing allowance, a housing wealth increment tax helps to expand access to the local public goods bundled with housing that are owed equally to all citizens. A housing wealth increment tax also potentially reduces homeowners' incentives to support exclusionary policies that have the sole purpose of elevating the collective value of existing homes. From the standpoint of moral equality, a combined housing consumption and housing wealth increment tax provides a way of satisfying the state neutrality principle by treating renters and owners equivalently for comparable levels of housing consumption.

Implementation of a negative housing tax that consists of both a housing consumption tax and a housing wealth increment tax may seem to be administratively burdensome, but this is not necessarily true. Most features of the tax can be implemented through the existing income tax system by simply eliminating the favored tax treatment of homeownership. Wage income spent on rental housing consumption is already taxed like a consumption tax because renters pay tax on the income spent on rent and utilities (Hall 1997). Consumption taxes for owner-occupied homes could be levied by adding the imputed rental income for owner-occupied homes directly to the tax base and eliminating the deduction for mortgage interest payments and property taxes. There are several ways to calculate imputed rental income, but all face the challenge that an owner's imputed rental income is not observed. A simple approach is to set imputed rental income equal to some fraction of the housing value estimated by local property tax assessors (Brueckner 2014). The housing wealth increment tax can be implemented by simply removing the current income tax exclusion on housing capital gains up to $250,000 and replacing it with a progressive capital gains tax schedule to reduce the tax burden on low-income homeowners.[4] To alleviate the tax burden facing first-time homebuyers, the tax value of the initial down payment spent on a first home purchase could be ignored and taxed when the home is sold.

One question is whether to differentiate between the housing capital gains that are reapplied to another home purchase and capital gains that are saved or applied to nonhousing consumption. Proponents of a pure consumption tax would favor taxing proceeds that are recycled into another home purchase or other goods consumption while exempting proceeds that are saved. From the standpoint of civic equality, there is a strong justification for fully taxing all housing equity gains, regardless of how the proceeds are spent. If the proceeds spent on the purchase of a second home are not taxed, this potentially encourages overconsumption of housing relative to other goods or savings.

Another question is whether to exclude capital gains on home improvements from the housing wealth increment tax base. Henry George (1942) would likely favor this approach to encourage residential property investment. One problem with this strategy is that it may create incentives to flip older properties and convert small, affordable dwellings into large luxury homes. Henry George's single tax also requires a complex assessment process that separates the value of land from the value of improvements. A second-best way to approximate a Georgist tax while minimizing property-flipping incentives is to allow deductions for home improvement expenditures but tax the profits earned on those expenditures.

If housing capital gains taxes are added to the tax base, capital gains tax relief provides a useful way to incentivize the creation of long-term affordability options. Residential property owners who sell or rent their homes at deed-restricted affordable prices could receive a refund on their capital gains tax liabilities. The refund would ideally be provided in the form of a refundable credit so that the value of the incentive does not vary with marginal tax rates. Structured in this way, the supply of residential capital gains tax credits would be unrestricted, similar to the 4 percent credit currently available under the LIHTC program. Just as the negative housing tax may reduce the incentive to engage in collective action to increase residential property values, a capital gains tax credit may incentivize the expansion of affordable rental housing options and shared-equity homeownership opportunities.

This use of capital gains tax relief provides a response to critics who argue that the negative housing tax may thwart efforts to promote low-income homeownership. While the negative housing tax may discourage traditional fee-simple homeownership, the negative housing tax combined with capital gains tax relief provides a way of expanding nontraditional homeownership opportunities, because those who sell their homes at deed-restricted prices to prospective low-income buyers would receive a capital gains tax credit for expanding the number of shared-equity homeownership opportunities. Although deed-restricted homeownership does not provide the same opportunities for housing wealth accumulation, it does expand access to one of the most important features of homeownership: tenure security.[5]

Taken together, the three features of the negative housing tax—the guaranteed housing allowance, the housing consumption tax, and the housing wealth increment tax—complement the property reforms discussed in chapter 7 by targeting resources directly to those facing the most severe forms of housing insecurity. The negative housing tax supplemented by a property system that secures the right to secure tenure can also be viewed as a way to implement the two-part distributive ideal discussed in chapter 6. The sufficientarian portion of the distributive ideal is satisfied by a property and tax system that guarantees everyone's right to secure tenure. The negative housing tax goes one step further to reduce housing inequality above the sufficientarian threshold. By restructuring the property regime to guarantee secure tenure while reducing the incentives to accumulate housing wealth and engage in conspicuous consumption, it is possible to realize housing justice without abandoning a market-based system of housing provision.

The Geography of Housing Justice

Homes are attached to the earth, and each home's geographic location distributes access to a wide variety of natural amenities, local public goods, social networks, and employment opportunities. Not only is housing bundled with these other spatially fixed goods, but the demand for housing is also often correlated with these goods. Those planning to raise a family, for example, often seek homes in high-performing school districts. Furthermore, because of the time and monetary costs of commuting to employment centers, most do not view homes in one labor market as substitutes for homes located in other labor markets. These features of housing imply that the price of housing exhibits considerable geographic variability.

The geographic variability in housing prices is a concern for housing justice because those unable to afford housing in high-cost areas will be excluded by the price mechanism from the enjoyment of local public goods and amenities provided in those areas. While justice does not necessarily require that everyone have access to a beachfront vista or a mountain view, certain local public goods, such as public education and public safety, are essential ingredients of social citizenship. The principle of equal concern requires that goods owed equally to all members of society be equally distributed unless there is a morally compelling reason to support unequal provision.

Under a tenant-based subsidy program, such as the HCV, that allows subsidies to vary with metropolitan-area rents, households receive higher subsidies to live in more expensive metropolitan areas. One limitation of this approach is that it induces inefficient residential mobility to expensive high-amenity locations. If a household is indifferent between living in a high-amenity area and a low-amenity area because spatial differences in housing costs offset spatial differences in amenities, a location-varying tenant-based subsidy tied to a fixed percentage of household income disrupts this equilibrium. With the subsidy, the household can choose to live in a high-amenity area and consume housing that costs the same percentage of income as a home located in a low-amenity area (Bieri and Dawkins 2016). In addition to inducing inefficient residential mobility, spatially varying tenant-based subsidies also potentially violate state neutrality by implicitly favoring housing located in particular areas.

A spatially varying tenant-based subsidy funded by a national income tax also fails to equitably apportion the benefits and burdens of the subsidy. Although all US citizens have an obligation to share equally in the burden of providing a minimally adequate home on an average-priced lot, those living in Baltimore arguably have no additional obligation to share in the cost of placing that minimally adequate home in San Francisco, where land costs are higher. If San Francisco residents vote to approve higher local public expenditure levels and these expenditures inflate the cost of housing, why should Baltimoreans be held accountable for the local democratic decisions of San Franciscans? San Franciscans support the conditions that inflate local housing costs and should arguably face a higher burden to alleviate those costs. Moreover, residential property owners *within* San Francisco, who gain financially from the capitalized value of local public investments, should arguably redistribute a portion of this capitalized value to San Francisco renters, who enjoy the same public investments but do not benefit from the capitalized value of those investments.

The current US housing policy mixture of spatially varying tenant-based subsidies and supply-side LIHTCs also poorly targets housing subsidies to the conditions that give rise to spatial differences in housing cost burdens. Housing policymakers should arguably target tenant-based subsidies to soft markets and housing production subsidies to tight markets, but these two subsidies are not fungible (McClure 2019). The LIHTC also ignores land costs in the calculation of subsidy amounts. Even if it makes sense from a housing policy perspective to subsidize the construction of affordable homes in San Francisco to alleviate the shortage of affordable housing there, the current intergovernmental housing policy apparatus encourages low-income households to move to San Francisco, where tenant-based subsidy payments are higher, while at the same time making it more difficult to develop affordable housing in San Francisco because of the Bay Area's restrictive land-use regulations.

Spencer Banzhaf and Kyle Mangum (2019) provide a useful way of thinking about the geographic determinants of housing costs. They draw on the analogy of a two-part tariff to decompose housing prices into a "ticket" price that reflects the capitalized value of local public goods and amenities and a "slope" price that is spatially invariant and increases with the level of housing services. The negative housing tax described in the previous section provides a subsidy that offsets a portion of the slope price of housing, ignoring land costs. The question that remains is how to account for the ticket price of housing, which reflects spatial variation in the implicit price of local public goods and amenities bundled with housing.

A national Georgist single tax provides one way to account for spatial variation in housing costs. Returning to Banzhaf and Mangum's (2019) two-part tariff analogy, a national single tax would be equivalent to a "ticket tax" that recoups the portion of housing cost differences attributable to spatial differences in the capitalized value of amenities. Within the United States, implementation of a national single tax is likely to be administratively difficult and possibly unconstitutional, which points to the need to identify an alternative approach. If local public expenditures are endogenously chosen by local governments, the choice of an alternative approach becomes more complicated because local public officials can influence the geographic determinants of housing prices by altering local property tax rates and expenditures on local public goods.

The negative housing tax is similar in spirit to the single tax, with the exception that land value is taxed at less than 100 percent and a portion of the housing structure's value is taxed. With endogenously chosen local public expenditures, the revenue raised by the "ticket tax" portion of the negative housing tax—the tax on the portion of housing value attributable to the capitalized value of local public goods and amenities—could either compensate households with high housing cost burdens in more expensive areas or be redistributed to subsidize local public good provision in jurisdictions with low property tax bases, thereby equalizing the capitalized value of local public goods across space. I refer to the first of these two strategies as the *compensation* approach and the second as the *equalization* approach. The compensation approach is similar to the policies favored by "fair share" regional housing policy advocates, who seek to equalize affordable housing opportunities across jurisdictions. In contrast, the equalization approach is similar to the policies favored by "new regionalist" proponents of regional tax-base sharing and regional public service coordination.

Walzer (1983) provides a useful way of understanding the differences between the compensation and equalization approaches. According to Walzer's ideal of "complex equality," the distribution of goods should be determined by criteria internal to the goods being distributed, and the sphere of distribution for one good should not dominate the sphere of distribution for another good.[6] Geographic variability in housing prices that produces an unequal distribution of social and economic opportunities is objectionable according to the principle of complex equality not because an unequal distribution of social and economic opportunities is inherently unjust but because the distributive sphere of housing dominates other distributive spheres.[7] The two different ways of responding to spatial differences in housing prices—compensation for geographic differences in housing costs that arise from local public expenditure capitalization and equalization of the capitalized value of local public expenditures—are two different ways of achieving complex equality by decoupling the distribution of housing from the distribution of local public goods. The compensation approach takes the distribution of local public goods as given and subsidizes housing for a given level of local public expenditures. In contrast, the equalization approach levels the geographic determinants of housing prices, making the distribution of housing costs dependent only on housing's geographically invariant features. Whereas the first approach accepts differences in the capitalized value of local public expenditures, the second approach is predicated on everyone having the same level of local public goods, thereby removing local public goods from the residential choice set.

An effective decoupling strategy likely involves some combination of equalization and compensation approaches. Full equalization of the capitalized value of local public goods is likely impossible because certain amenities are naturally occurring while others result from the natural tendency of human activities to cluster in space. Goods produced through collective political decisions are more amenable to equalization, and civic equality calls for the equalization of local public goods that are owed equally to all citizens. However, households should still be compensated for any remaining unjust inequalities.

To decouple the distribution of housing from the distribution of local public goods in a way that targets resources to areas with the highest affordable housing needs, I propose that any revenues collected from the negative housing tax net of the slope tax portion owed equally to all qualifying households be redistributed to local governments as a supplemental CDBG. The CDBG would be allocated in proportion to revenues generated so that areas paying the highest negative housing tax would receive the highest CDBG allocations. Under current income tax law, coastal states with the highest housing costs generate the largest tax expenditures per capita from the mortgage interest deduction (Keightley 2014). Under my proposal, local governments in these states would receive the largest CDBG allocations to offset housing costs.

I propose that local governments have the flexibility to choose the appropriate mix of compensation and equalization approaches and have flexibility to choose an appropriate mix of supply-side and demand-side housing subsidy approaches, subject to a few constraints. Local governments would have discretion to spend supplemental CDBG allocations on (1) supplements to the national guaranteed monthly housing allowance for residents with very low income who choose to live within their jurisdictions, (2) affordable housing production subsidies, or (3) local public good provision, subject to the following constraints: (a) all recipients of supplemental CDBG allocations must remove local regulatory barriers to the production of affordable housing, and (b) jurisdictions with high housing prices may only use supplemental CDBG allocations to expand affordable housing opportunities (expenditure items 1 and 2), whereas jurisdictions with low housing prices may rely on supplemental CDBG allocations for these same purposes in addition to subsidizing expenditures on local public goods and services (expenditure items 1, 2, and 3). Constraint (b) is designed to ensure that wealthy jurisdictions do not use supplemental CDBG allocations to exacerbate geographic inequalities in the capitalized value of local public goods.

The Color of Housing Justice

As documented in previous chapters, US housing inequalities often cause, and are caused by, racial and ethnic injustices. Does the racial and ethnic dimension of US housing inequality raise distinct housing justice concerns, and if so, does housing justice call for policies designed to promote the integration of neighborhoods by race and ethnicity? In this section, I argue that the ideal of civic equality justifies a variety of policies that combat racial and ethnic housing market injustices. Still, the front lines of the fight against racial and ethnic injustice extend beyond the sphere of housing justice. Furthermore, while civic equality does not require the realization of perfectly integrated residential outcomes, it is consistent with the procedural aim of removing certain housing market barriers that perpetuate segregated living conditions.

From the standpoint of housing justice, the racial and ethnic dimension of US housing inequality is a concern for several reasons. First, it often results from unjust discriminatory treatment in housing transactions, which is a concern from the standpoint of virtually any conception of justice. Housing discrimination is also a direct concern for housing justice because it constrains housing choices and compromises the tenure security of those facing discrimination. Second, given the special social and economic significance of housing, racial and ethnic housing inequalities often produce, and are produced by, unjust group-based inequalities in social status and economic and political power. Third, housing inequality arising from the residential segregation of households by race and ethnicity is a distinct form of injustice because it reinforces group-based inequalities across space.

The housing reform strategies discussed so far do not directly target the racial and ethnic dimension of US housing inequality. Still, the ideal of civic equality is consistent with policies such as the FaHA that are designed to eliminate unjust forms of housing discrimination. The ideal of civic equality is also compatible with measures that aggressively target predatory lending. Although the elimination of racial and ethnic discrimination in all aspects of a housing market transaction would remove the injustice associated with allocating housing on the basis of race or ethnicity, antidiscrimination laws do not directly target the racial and ethnic gap in housing wealth or racial and ethnic segregation.

Racial and ethnic gaps in housing wealth arise from three separate factors. First, historic inequalities created by de jure segregation have limited the ability of families of color to accumulate housing wealth and transfer it to future generations. The legacy of past discrimination robs young families of color of resources that could have been applied to a down payment on a mortgage. This down payment constraint directly contributes to racial and ethnic gaps in homeownership rates. A second factor arises from the combined influence of racial and ethnic segregation and spatial differences in home price appreciation between majority-white communities and communities of color. Because of redlining, discrimination, and whites' aversion to minority-majority neighborhoods, homes located in communities of color often do not appreciate as rapidly as homes located in majority-white communities. Finally, people of color are more likely to be victimized by predatory lending practices and ownership tenures that end in foreclosure, as discussed in the introduction (Asante-Muhammad et al. 2017; Bocian et al. 2010; Shapiro 2004; Wolf 2014).

The negative housing tax and property law reforms discussed so far offer a partial solution to the racial and ethnic gap in housing wealth. The negative housing tax is designed to eliminate housing wealth inequalities that arise from the disproportionately high number of low-income people of color who experience housing instability. Furthermore, the capital gains tax incentives to place homes sold under affordability deed restrictions are designed to expand the supply of affordable homes. The justification for a secure tenure property regime offered in chapter 7 provides a rationale for policies designed to reduce the likelihood of foreclosure for those who are currently struggling to meet mortgage payments.

Above the floor of sufficiency, the negative housing tax and property law reforms discussed so far do not directly target the racial and ethnic gap in housing consumption or wealth. Instead, the negative housing tax discourages extremely high levels of housing consumption and housing wealth accumulation for all racial and ethnic groups. Leveling down the disproportionately high levels of white housing wealth may reduce the racial and ethnic housing wealth gap to some extent, but the negative housing tax does nothing to elevate the housing wealth of Black or Hispanic households. Even so, the ideal of civic equality is consistent with a variety of measures that target opportunity hoarding. If majority-white communities rely on exclusionary land-use policies to prop up the collective value of their homes, civic equality justifies eliminating these policies.

A deeper problem arises from the persistence of historical injustices created by generations of discriminatory and exclusionary housing policies. Even if current housing policies are just, the nonideal world of injustice echoes across generations. As discussed in previous chapters, policies such as exclusionary zoning, exclusionary private covenants, and discriminatory FHA underwriting criteria have constrained the housing choices of people of color for generations. Even though de jure forms of housing discrimination are now prohibited by law, the housing wealth robbed from previous generations that could not be passed on to current generations constrains the housing choices of young families of color. With fewer (and in some cases zero or negative) resources being transferred between generations, families of color are often more likely than white families to rely on their own savings rather than on family assistance to purchase a home (Shapiro 2004). These issues raise questions of "corrective justice," which Tommie Shelby (2016, 13) describes as follows: "Theorizing about corrective justice is more than laying down principles for compensating the victims of past injustice or reducing their disadvantages. It also includes the philosophical aim of collective efforts to establish a society regulated by a mutual commitment to justice. Reformers and revolutionaries should be aiming to create a society in which the principles of justice are fully realized in its institutions and in which citizens comply with institutional rules because these are in accord with their shared conception of justice. It is in this way that ideal theory serves as a guide for nonideal theory."

Does housing justice call for additional corrective justice measures beyond those discussed so far? According to Shelby (2016), corrective justice requires compensating the current generation for unjust inherited disadvantages, transforming historically unjust distributive arrangements, and reorienting society toward justice. A difficult problem from the standpoint of corrective justice is that capitalism and the institution of private property permit the commodification of race by creating economic value or disvalue from a person's racial identity (Leong 2013; Robinson 1983). Prejudiced white households contribute to the commodification of race by paying more for housing located in majority-white neighborhoods, a phenomenon that David Cutler, Edward Glaeser, and Jacob Vigdor (1999) describe as "decentralized racism." Antigentrification advocates characterize the displacement of communities of color as a form of "racial banishment" that is equivalent to apartheid and racial cleansing (Roy 2017, A8).

Do civic equality and the public justification for private property address the commodification of race within private housing markets? To some extent, yes. The solution to tenure security consists in viewing private property in terms of its contribution to civic equality while attenuating the right to earn income from the sale or rent of residential property. If white home seekers avoid minority-majority neighborhoods because of a perception that such neighborhoods are less likely to appreciate over time, decoupling wealth from housing consumption eliminates the economic incentive to engage in this form of decentralized racism. Similarly, by reducing the incentive to engage in collective action to protect the investment value of the home, majority-white communities no longer have a purely economic reason to adopt exclusionary local land-use policies. Racist whites may still act on their individual prejudices when seeking homes. Still, as society at large becomes more diverse, racists will incur a personal cost by acting on their prejudices when making residential location decisions, because their housing choices will be constrained by their reluctance to live in racially and ethnically diverse neighborhoods.

Even with structural institutional reforms designed to eliminate the vestiges of de jure discrimination and reorient private property around the ideal of civic equality, prejudiced households may still consider the racial and ethnic composition of neighborhoods a relevant stick in the housing bundle, even if neighborhood racial and ethnic composition only proxies for other neighborhood conditions. To the extent that households sort into neighborhoods on the basis of race or ethnicity and a sufficient number of home seekers view minority-majority neighborhoods negatively, majority-white neighborhoods may still appreciate more rapidly than minority-majority neighborhoods, thereby perpetuating the racial and ethnic housing wealth gap and the commodification of race in housing markets. This points to one additional advantage of the previously discussed equalization approach to addressing spatial inequalities in housing costs: equalization of the capitalized value of local public expenditures will tend to lift the value of homes in many minority-majority neighborhoods. Even with full equalization of the capitalized value of local public expenditures, however, neighborhood gaps in home price appreciation may persist if decentralized racism remains.

The persistence of race and ethnicity as factors shaping housing market decisions has led some to conclude that racial and ethnic equality can only be achieved by eliminating residential segregation. According to David Rusk (2001), segregation imposes a tax on people of color that is priced into the value of their homes. From the standpoint of moral equality, racial segregation is a concern because segregation often produces unequal access to local public goods and amenities. Segregation is a concern from the standpoint of relational equality if segregation results from discriminatory treatment, stigmatizes certain racial or ethnic groups through place-based stereotyping, or contributes to unequal social, political, or economic relations between groups. Segregation may also be a concern if it compromises the social solidarity needed to support social citizenship in the first place.

Elizabeth Anderson (2010) provides the most comprehensive philosophical case for promoting residential integration. Her defense of prointegrative policies rests on many of the same arguments that follow from the ideal of civic equality, with the exception that she assigns a more prominent role for democracy than the ideal of civic equality that I have defended would support. In the conception of social citizenship that I defended in chapter 6, democracy has instrumental value as a way to evaluate political arguments, reach consensus, protect civic freedom, and promote social solidarity. Still, democracy has no intrinsic value apart from its instrumental role in promoting civic equality. Anderson (2010) is saying something more: that democracy has an intrinsic value that cannot be realized within a racially segregated society. I reject both the intrinsic value of democracy and the claim that democracy is only possible in a world where neighborhoods are integrated by race and ethnicity.

Anderson's (2010) democratic justification for prointegrative housing policy violates the principle of moral equality because not everyone would accept the controversial claim that the good life consists of active participation in public life. In this book, I have defended the alternative view that the good life often consists of being able to retreat from the public realm from time to time. According to Arendt, "The four walls of one's private property offer the only reliable hiding place from the common public world, not only from everything that goes on in it but also from its very publicity, from being seen and being heard. A life spent entirely in public, in the presence of others, becomes, as we would say, shallow" (Arendt 1958, 71). In addition to appealing to a controversial conception of the good life, grounding a conception of housing justice in the intrinsic value of democracy ignores the unequal burdens of democratic participation that often fall on those who do not currently receive their fair share of the benefits of citizenship. There is an essential unfairness associated with requiring residents of disadvantaged communities to constantly fight for the provision of basic services through democratic mobilization when residents of advantaged communities enjoy the privilege of retreating to the private realm with the assurance that such matters are being adequately addressed by public institutions.

Even if democracy is a value worth promoting from the standpoint of justice, it does not necessarily require integrated living patterns. Iris Marion Young (1990; 2002) argues that democracy is a core ingredient of justice that requires the inclusion of underrepresented groups in democratic decision-making processes. Still, her conception of democratic inclusion does not require members of different racial and ethnic groups to live near one another. Instead, Young favors a spatial pattern of "differentiated solidarity" defined by voluntarily formed racial and ethnic enclaves with open borders that allow residential mobility between communities and a regional governance structure that promotes a flow of resources across communities (Young 1999; Young 2002). Even if all neighborhoods are perfectly integrated by race and ethnicity, propinquity does not guarantee solidarity, nor does it necessarily produce bridging social ties across racial and ethnic lines (Shelby 2016).

Even if integration is not required for democracy, does housing justice require prointegrative housing policies? In many ways, this question gets to the heart of the distributive tensions inherent in the pluralist conception of housing justice that I have defended. The injustice of segregation from the standpoint of tenure security is that segregation may limit the availability of housing options for those whose tenure is insecure. From the standpoint of civic equality, segregation is a concern if it is associated with moral or relational inequalities, even if everyone is adequately housed. Whereas moral equality discourages policies that privilege particular ways of living, relational equality is consistent with some measures that privilege a conception of the good life favored by those who are currently disadvantaged by segregated living patterns. The distributive tensions within the ideal of civic equality arise primarily from the antiperfectionist principle of state neutrality implied by moral equality.

Policies that aim to achieve a particular spatial pattern of households by race or ethnicity risk violating moral equality while compromising tenure security. For example, mixed-income housing programs such as HOPE VI often displace low-income residents of color while favoring mixed-income living arrangements. Similarly, prointegrative residential mobility programs such as MTO favor housing located in particular areas while reducing the resources available to meet urgent housing needs, given that subsidies designed to encourage prointegrative moves could have been allocated to a larger number of households seeking housing in less expensive locations. The same critiques can be applied to some antigentrification policies that reinforce existing patterns of residential segregation by race and ethnicity. Policies designed to spatially fix segregated living patterns by discouraging new housing investment in segregated areas may compromise the tenure security of those who are currently homeless while promoting a controversial conception of the good life that is premised on the superiority of segregated living patterns.

Although racial and ethnic segregation is often unjust for a variety of reasons, segregation patterns also result from a variety of morally benign reasons, and perfectly integrated living patterns are neither a sufficient nor a necessary condition for the realization of housing justice. Achieving a balance between housing justice and racial justice is much easier if the emphasis on particular spatial outcomes is abandoned in favor of an emphasis on the decommodification of race within the American private property regime. This approach resembles George Galster's (1992) recommendation to promote a "stable integrative process" rather than a perfectly integrated spatial outcome. Galster (1992, 271) defines a stable integrative process as a "dynamic in which home seekers representing two or more races actively seek to occupy the same vacant dwellings in a substantial proportion of a metropolitan area's neighborhoods over an extended period."[8] Such a process assumes that individuals are not denied (or awarded) housing on the basis of their race or ethnicity nor financially penalized (or rewarded) because they happen to live in neighborhoods where certain racial or ethnic groups are in the majority. An emphasis on the realization of a stable integrative process is consistent with the aim of respecting the diversity of legitimate ways of living that may entail segregated or integrated living patterns. The conception of housing justice offered in this book suggests that the aim of promoting tenure security should take priority over the aim of promoting integration, and when housing resources are scarce, the aim of housing those with the greatest housing needs should take priority over the goal of encouraging those in need to move to integrated neighborhoods.

Another way of approaching the question of residential segregation is to ask whether those most disadvantaged by segregation patterns—people of color—might reasonably object to prointegrative policies. Many prointegrative policies would be reasonably rejected by people of color who would be forced to take on a larger share of the burden to realize integrated living patterns. Programs such as *Gautreaux* that require people of color to move to majority-white areas to achieve integration restrict the liberty of people of color, not whites, and measures that foster mixed-income communities by displacing people of color compromise, rather than promote, tenure security. Just as homeowners and residential property owners should shoulder a larger share of the burden of expanding tenure security, whites should shoulder the majority of the burden of realizing more integrated living patterns (Goetz 2018).

This section only scratched the surface of the complex relationships between housing justice and racial justice, but civic equality is a robust ideal that justifies a range of antiracist policy reforms beyond those discussed in this section. Because racist attitudes are a direct manifestation of the injustice associated with citizens not viewing one another as equal participants in the social order, the ideal of relational equality justifies a range of policies that attack racism at its core, including reforms that are designed to eliminate exclusionary land-use regulations, housing market discrimination, and race-based predatory lending.

Attacking the injustices that arise from racist beliefs embedded within society at large requires a response that is broader than the sphere of justice occupied by housing alone. Still, the ideal of civic equality and the public justification for private property can provide the foundation for sweeping reforms of property-based institutions. For example, calls to "defund the police" grew louder in the wake of George Floyd's brutal death at the hands of the Minneapolis police. Local police departments protect property owners from unwanted trespassing and theft of owned property, but if police officers violate a person of color's basic right to life and right to be treated as an equal under the law, this property-based justification for police protection falls apart. If the justification for police protection derives instead from the security of tenure that police protection safeguards, it seems justifiable to reallocate a portion of the police budget to affordable housing provision when the police fail in their duties to protect the social rights of citizenship.

Gentrification and the Right to the City

As discussed in chapter 5, a new alliance appeals to the idea of human rights to housing and the city to justify measures designed to fight gentrification. This understanding of housing justice raises two questions. First, is the right to housing, understood as a right to secure tenure, complementary to or in conflict with the right to the city? Second, is the fight against gentrification a cause that aligns with principles of housing justice? The right to housing I described in chapter 7 is an incident of private property, stripped of the right to earn income. This is an individual right, which suggests that it may come into conflict with the right to the city, which is often understood as a collective right. As I argue in this section, there is no conflict between the right to housing and the right to the city if the right to the city is understood as an individual right that supports the right to inhabit. In this case, the right to housing provides ammunition in the fight against gentrification. When the right to the city is interpreted as a collective right, there are potential conflicts between the right to the city and the right to housing. I argue that when faced with these conflicts, housing advocates should prioritize the right to housing over the right to the city.

Henri Lefebvre (1968) understands the right to the city as encompassing two distinct rights: the right to participation, or the right to contribute to the production of urban space, and the right to appropriation, or the right to physically access, occupy, and use urban space (Purcell 2002). According to David Harvey (2008, 23), "The right to the city is far more than the individual liberty to access urban resources: it is a right to change ourselves by changing the city. It is, moreover, a common rather than an individual right since this transformation inevitably depends upon the exercise of a collective power to reshape the processes of urbanization. The freedom to make and remake our cities and ourselves is, I want to argue, one of the most precious yet most neglected of our human rights."

As Don Mitchell (2003) suggests, the right to housing protects one form of appropriation. It is a right to *inhabit* space: "a place to sleep, a place to urinate and defecate without asking someone else's permission, a place to relax, a place from which to venture forth" (Mitchell 2003, 19). Mitchell (2003) goes on to argue that the right to inhabit is distinct from the right to own private property. Still, it is not clear how the right to inhabit differs from the right to use and occupy property, which is among the bundle of rights assigned to property owners. Arguably, anything less than the rights to use and occupancy enjoyed by owner-occupants would fail to provide secure tenure. It seems more appropriate to say that the right to housing, understood as a right to inhabit, is an incident of the right to own property that possibly conflicts with other ownership incidents when ownership is understood in terms of the bundle of rights associated with full liberal ownership.

Lefebvre's right to inhabit is not a collective right unless it is interpreted as a right that is exercised by a group of individuals who collectively inhabit urban space. Exercising the right to "a place to sleep, a place to urinate and defecate without asking someone else's permission, a place to relax, a place from which to venture forth" (Mitchell 2003, 19) requires the opposite. It requires having the civic freedom that is protected by private property. Another sense in which the right to inhabit may be considered a collective right is when homeless persons are treated as a distinct class of citizens who are defined by their lack of residential property and who have special claims to exist and be afforded the rights of citizenship despite their lack of property. This conception of the right to inhabit essentially transforms the right to housing into a right to exist in a civilized manner without housing. For example, as discussed in chapter 5, those advocating on behalf of the homeless have called for the adoption of homeless bills of rights, which protect the homeless from laws that criminalize sleeping in public and afford homeless persons the same civil rights enjoyed by those with homes. This understanding of the right to inhabit actually *denies* the right to housing, seeking instead to recognize, on the grounds of citizenship, the rights of the homeless to equal protection under the law despite their propertylessness. Thomas Dumm (1994) goes one step further to suggest that homelessness is the embodiment of the spiritual freedom of the nomad, and a just society is one in which homelessness is supported and made possible.

Another way of understanding the right to inhabit as a collective right is to interpret it as a collective "right to stay put" and not be displaced by gentrification (Hartman 2002). The right to stay put is an expression of the "right not to be excluded," which C. B. Macpherson (1987) argues is a corollary claim implied by the liberal right to exclude. The right to stay put is generally characterized in one of two ways. If the right is interpreted as a right not to be arbitrarily displaced from one's residence, it is hard to see how this is any different from the individual right to secure tenure, where the right to secure tenure is justified, in part, by the home's contribution to one's place-based sense of identity and personhood (Radin 1993).

Alternatively, the right to stay put may be interpreted as a collective right that a place, and all of its sociohistorical and cultural attributes, continue to exist. Nicholas Blomley, in his study of antigentrification activism in Vancouver, observes that the ownership claims of private property investors often "ignore the collective constitution of the 'community,' and its moral right not only to continue as an entity, but to remain *in situ*. For activists, the injustices wrought by gentrification and displacement extend beyond the denial of the property rights of individual residents to the use of their hotel rooms. Development pressures challenge the collective entitlement of poor community members to the use and occupation of the *neighborhood as a whole*" (Blomley 2004, 52; italics in the original). This is a reasonable way of understanding the right to inhabit as a collective right because place has meaning independently of the individuals living there. Still, one can easily imagine how this collective right may conflict with an individual right to housing, particularly if the place in question lacks adequate and affordable housing for those who wish to call the place home.

This collective understanding of the right to stay put, or "right to place," may also justify exclusionary measures designed to protect the aesthetic qualities of the place at the expense of those who wish to become inhabitants. Historic district designations that increase the cost of housing and large-lot zoning measures that restrict housing supply to preserve rural character are two examples. Given these two possible interpretations of the right to stay put, the individual right to stay put is a more attractive basis for a right to housing than a collective right to place and a more defensible basis for one's right not to be displaced by gentrification.

Another way of viewing the right to stay put as a collective right to place is to define it as a right that only protects those places inhabited by groups who have been marginalized by majoritarian institutions and whose place-based identity has been threatened. This is a more defensible conception of the collective right to place because it cannot be evoked to defend exclusionary policies that contribute to opportunity hoarding in majority-white communities. Still, the potential for conflict with the individual right to secure tenure remains, particularly if the collective right to place justifies exclusionary prohibitions on affordable housing investment within marginalized communities.

The collective nature of the right to the city may also derive not from the right to inhabit but rather from the right to participation or the right to contribute to the production of urban space. If this is the case, the question then becomes whether the right to participation conflicts with the right to inhabit. Setting aside the question of how the right to participation is distinct from other democratic rights, a collective right to participation can be understood in several ways. First, it may refer to the right to exercise voice in collective decision-making bodies that play a role in shaping the built environment. If this is how the right to participation is understood, it is difficult to see how it necessarily supports the right to housing, because collective land-use decision-making bodies have more often relied on their collective authority to exclude rather than approve low-income housing. If the collective right to participation is meant as a collective right to produce affordable housing for those who lack it, it can only be interpreted as a right that trumps collective efforts to adopt exclusionary land-use policies. If this is how the right to participation is understood, this right is no different from an individual right to housing, understood as an individual immunity against collective decisions to exclude housing provision.

Another way of understanding the right to participation as a collective right is to interpret the right as one held by tenants to collectively organize to secure rights to the homes that they inhabit or seek to inhabit. For example, the Washington, DC, TOPA law recognizes tenants' collective rights of first refusal to purchase rental buildings prior to the building's sale as a condominium (Huron 2018; Gallaher 2016). Shared-equity ownership arrangements such as limited-equity cooperatives and community land trusts are other examples of collective rights to property that provide tenure security to individual inhabitants. While these alternative tenure arrangements can be understood in terms of collective rights, the right to collectively organize or collectively manage common space should not be confused with the individual right to housing that collective action secures. Collective forms of ownership may or may not enhance security of tenure for individual inhabitants. In some cases, the time and resources required to organize collectively and the coordination costs of making collective decisions may compromise tenure security for individual occupants, particularly if common property is not managed effectively or agents hired to represent collective interests engage in rent-seeking behavior and act in ways that are contrary to the interests of tenants. The litmus test for these forms of collective rights is whether, in the end, they support tenants' individual rights to secure tenure.

Completing the Arc of Housing Justice

This chapter completed the book's conception of housing justice by examining several concrete proposals designed to extend tenure security to all while promoting housing equality. The negative housing tax is a tax on housing consumption and the capital gains from home sales that provides revenues to fund a guaranteed monthly housing allowance. Revenues exceeding the amount needed to cover the cost of extending a location-invariant monthly housing allowance to all those experiencing insecure tenure would be allocated as a supplemental CDBG designed to alleviate spatial inequalities in housing costs.

I also examined the connection between housing justice, racial justice, and the right to the city. The conception of housing justice offered in this book provides an indirect way to decommodify race from housing markets by eliminating the institutional mechanisms that translate racial prejudice into housing market inequalities. I argued that housing justice does not require the realization of integrated residential patterns but is consistent with certain measures that promote the progressive realization of stable integrative processes. I also argued that the right to housing should be interpreted as an individual right, and this understanding of the right to housing provides a justification for measures designed to mitigate the harms of gentrification. To the extent that the right to the city is understood as a collective right, it may conflict with the right to housing, and in the face of this conflict, housing justice may require prioritizing the right to housing over the right to the city.

Conclusion

Charity begins at home, and justice begins next door.
—Charles Dickens, *Martin Chuzzlewit* (1908 [1844], 462)

Tigg Montague was wrong.[1] Justice begins at home, the place of refuge, reflection, repair, and repose, where flourishing lives take root. When next doors disappear, and neighbors have no place to call home, justice moves next door. Housing justice is an architect's plan for a property regime that delivers shelter in accordance with fundamental moral values. This book constructed a conception of housing justice from housing's distinctive contextual features, the social meanings of the American home, the material ingredients of social citizenship, and America's federal housing policy framework. In this final chapter, I recap the book's main arguments by revisiting several questions about housing justice that were introduced in part I.

What is housing justice? Housing justice is an application of distributive justice that addresses moral questions about the production, distribution, occupancy, and ownership of housing. Conceptions of housing justice differ according to how each assembles the materials of justice—conceptions of value, principles, grounds, and bases—to account for housing's moral significance. Nineteenth-century land reformers proposed that everyone has a natural right to enough privately owned land to establish a functioning homestead, and this idea echoed through generations, culminating in the homeownership tier of the federal housing policy apparatus. Late nineteenth- and early twentieth-century progressive and utilitarian reformers rejected right-based approaches to housing justice in favor of regulatory reforms designed to promote collective goals. Franklin D. Roosevelt tried to reconstruct a right-based conception of social citizenship from the fragments of liberalism and progressivism, but in the end, social rights became secondary to the goals of expanding access to homeownership and providing a "decent home and suitable living environment" (Housing Act of 1949, 42 U.S.C. § 1441) for a small proportion of America's low-income renters. Right-based reforms returned with renewed force during the 1960s, but by this time the moral foundations of the rights being asserted rested on new claims to positive freedoms and collective self-determination. The right-based social movements of the 1960s coevolved during the contemporary neoliberal era, at times clashing over the issues of gentrification and racial segregation. The right-based conception of housing justice offered in part III of this book embodies the spirit of Roosevelt's unrealized social right to housing, the right-based egalitarianism of the radical land reform tradition, the pragmatism of the Progressive Era, and the republican emphasis on freedom from domination.

Why is housing "special" from a moral standpoint? Certain contextual features of housing influence how it is distributed and valued, and these features call for an approach to justice that considers housing's unique moral qualities. American housing has a distinctive social meaning, but this meaning has been contested throughout American history, and the social meaning of housing does not tell us how housing should be distributed. At the same time, the social meaning of American housing, particularly as embodied in the ideal of the owned single-family detached home, has been evoked in defense of a variety of American housing reforms. I argued in this book that housing's moral significance ultimately stems from its connection to social citizenship. Housing provides access to America's common culture and has come to define what it means to live a dignified and civilized life. To the extent that American citizenship and social status have been defined in terms of access to decent housing, denying adequate shelter is to deny what is equally owed to everyone by right.

What are the grounds of housing justice? The grounds of housing justice provide the reasons that individuals and government agents should support institutions that deliver housing in particular ways. This book proposed a conception of housing justice that appeals to the ground of citizenship. Compared to other grounds, citizenship does not require an appeal to a controversial view of human nature or human excellence. Instead, it grounds a practical, relational conception of what citizens owe one another as moral equals. I defended a liberal-republican conception of citizenship that acknowledges the morally significant link between housing and social citizenship, is right based rather than virtue based, values a physical and deliberative distinction between the public and private realms, and values equality of civic freedom. I also defined citizenship broadly and inclusively, arguing that everyone living on US soil has a right to be housed justly, regardless of their legal citizenship status.

What moral principles regulate the distribution of housing? Social citizenship, as I understand it, can be expressed in terms of the principles of moral equality and relational equality, which together constitute the ideal of civic equality. Moral equality refers to the commitment to show equal concern and equal respect for all citizens. Relational equality implies a commitment to policies designed to ensure that all citizens view one another as equal participants in the social order. These two principles are complementary but are in tension with moral equality's emphasis on state neutrality, which constrains the scope of state actions and the morally acceptable justifications for them.

Civic equality's two moral principles support a pluralist distributive ideal that combines sufficientarianism with egalitarianism. At the most basic level, civic equality is consistent with a distribution of housing where everyone has access to shelter that would be recognized by society as providing a minimum level of security and comfort. This sufficientarian aim can be understood as a goal that is lexically prior to the realization of other distributive goals. This means that if federal housing resources are scarce, the aim of alleviating homelessness should be prioritized over the goal of reducing the cost burdens or improving the housing quality of those who are currently housed.

Above the floor of sufficiency, civic equality has procedural and substantive implications for the distribution of housing. Procedurally, civic equality requires that housing be distributed in a manner that respects the variety of ways that individuals value and assign meaning to housing. Civic equality is consistent with policies designed to promote a variety of housing styles and living arrangements and is inconsistent with policies that promote certain housing styles on the basis of the moral superiority of particular ways of living. Civic equality is also consistent with the procedural aim of ensuring that public policies and private housing market agents do not unfairly discriminate against particular racial or ethnic groups. Substantively, civic equality calls for measures that reduce extreme housing inequalities, even if everyone's basic housing needs are met.

What is the right to housing? This book offered a right-based conception of housing justice. In contrast to other bases, rights structure democratic deliberation, shape expectations and incentives, and give official recognition to a nation's constitutive commitments to its citizens. The right to housing, defined in this book as the right to secure tenure, is an individual right that is constitutive of, structures, and provides a justification for the right to own private property. If the private property regime is not structured to deliver secure residential tenure to everyone, private property fails to function in accordance with its most compelling justification. The right to housing is a right that is constitutive of a private property regime that delivers tenure security to all, allows the incidents of private property to be flexibly assembled to promote tenure security, and creates incentives that are compatible with the tenure security justification for private property.

What are the implications of housing justice for US federal housing policy reform? The ideal of civic equality and public justification for private property provide the materials to defend a secure tenure property regime that is structured around the primary aim of securing and extending the right to housing and the secondary aim of reducing housing inequality through the taxation of housing consumption and housing wealth accumulation. The proposed negative housing tax can be implemented through the federal income tax code by treating income spent on owner occupancy and rental occupancy equivalently. The proceeds from the tax would fund a guaranteed monthly housing allowance and a supplemental block grant designed to reduce spatial inequalities in housing costs.

The conception of housing justice offered in this book has implications for racial justice and the fight against gentrification. Civic equality is consistent with proactive measures designed to reduce racial and ethnic inequalities arising from housing injustices, but housing justice does not necessarily require that neighborhoods be integrated by race or ethnicity.

Conclusion

Civic equality is consistent with various antigentrification measures, but given that the right to housing I have defended is an individual right, antigentrification measures that appeal to collective rights to the city may conflict with the right to housing. When the two collide, I argued that the right to housing should be prioritized over the right to the city.

The policy proposals discussed on the preceding pages are offered as hypotheses to be tested in the real world of policy reform and implementation. Much empirical, theoretical, and advocacy work remains to determine whether private property and the right to housing can coexist alongside a housing policy infrastructure designed to reduce housing inequality. I conclude with a call to the next generation of housing justice theorists and practitioners to investigate the lingering questions that remain while transforming the American dream into a just American reality.

Housing justice should nurture, not neglect, social justice. More work is needed to understand the relationship between housing justice and social justice writ large. Housing's special moral significance does not mean that housing occupies an autonomous distributive sphere that is isolated from the distribution of other goods and resources. Housing directly distributes access to social and economic opportunities, natural amenities, and local public goods. Principles of justice that are too narrowly tailored to the in-kind distribution of housing risk ignoring the trade-offs that households make to consume their most preferred bundle of goods. Housing justice is also intimately connected to racial justice, spatial justice, and environmental justice. I have scratched the surface of these connections, but more work remains to elucidate the relationships among different spheres of justice. Several important questions about housing justice still need answers. I hope that the conception of housing justice introduced in this book provides a place to begin the search.

Notes

Introduction

1. The US Department of Housing and Urban Development defines a severe housing problem as an expenditure on rental housing costs that exceeds 50 percent of a household's income or the condition of living in homes with severely inadequate plumbing, heating, electrical systems, or upkeep (Watson et al. 2020).

2. The US Department of Housing and Urban Development defines a family as very low income if it earns an income that does not exceed 50 percent of the median family income for the surrounding metropolitan area (US Department of Housing and Urban Development 2019). As this book goes to press, rents have begun to decline within the largest US cities, as many of the most mobile urban workers have abandoned urban living to reduce their exposure to COVID-19 (Salviati, Popov, and Warnock 2020). The long-term effects of this trend on urban housing affordability are unclear, particularly given that the least mobile urban workers have also been hit the hardest by unemployment.

3. The term "manifesto right" comes from Joel Feinberg (1973).

Chapter 1

1. Refer to Risse (2012) for a discussion of these and other grounds of justice.

2. According to Jeremy Waldron (1988, 64), "In any but the most intuitionistic moral or political theory, it is possible to distinguish between judgements or propositions that are more or less basic in the sense that less basic judgements are derivable from or justified by more basic ones (perhaps with the help of premises concerning matters of fact)."

3. Ronald Dworkin (1978) assumes that right-based and duty-based theories are grounded in an individualistic morality. As I discuss later in the book, right-based theories may also be grounded in a collectivistic morality.

4. The term "impartial spectator" comes from Adam Smith (2000 [1759]).

5. I draw inspiration for the inquiry into housing's special moral qualities from Shlomi Segall (2010), who asks a similar question in defense of his conception of justice in health and health care.

6. Another way of saying the same thing is to say that housing's value to an owner reflects both an investment value and a consumption value (Ioannides and Rosenthal 1994).

7. The view that value diversity has intrinsic rather than instrumental value is itself a controversial conception of value on which to ground distributive principles.

8. Adams (1932, 404) defines the American dream as a "dream of a land in which life should be better and richer and fuller for every man, with opportunity for each according to his ability or achievement."

9. This book's definitions of *liberalism* and *republicanism* draw from the standard definitions given by political philosophers and should not be confused with the definitions often given by contemporary American politicians and pundits. In contemporary political discourse, the term *liberal* typically describes political views that are consistent with left-leaning welfare-state liberalism, whereas the term *republican* typically describes the conservative views advanced by the Republican political party. Contemporary Democrats in the United States often hold republican views of civic life, while Republicans often favor economic policies that are consistent with classic liberalism.

Chapter 2

1. The legal protections for home under ancient Roman law were not based on the idea of homeownership as it is understood today. The idea of ownership, or dominium, did not emerge until the end of the Roman republic, after the time of Cicero (Domingo 2017).

2. The idea of home and property as a physical domain of privacy and exclusion traces back to the English practice of enclosing land to improve the efficiency of sheep grazing. Until the mid-1500s, land for grazing was owned by feudal lords and available for common use by tenant farmers. Farmers soon learned that by enclosing a portion of the commons, through a process known as "engrossment," sheep could be more closely monitored, and the concentration of sheep manure deposits helped to fertilize the soil (Linklater 2013).

3. A similar conception of the "right to necessity," or "subsistence right," can be found in the writings of Thomas Aquinas, Hugo Grotius, Samuel Pufendorf, and Francis Hutcheson (Mancilla 2016).

4. Richard Dagger (1997) offers a contemporary political theory that fuses liberalism and republicanism.

5. Despite early experimentation with communal systems of land ownership, most land in the American colonies would eventually be privately owned fee simple or through a similar system known as "free and common socage" (Price 1995).

6. John Stuart Mill (1965 [1848]) made a similar argument years earlier, referring to the increased value of land attributable to collective improvements as the "unearned increment" of land value. Mill argued that the unearned increment of land value should be taxed, whereas Henry George argued that land value minus the value of property improvements should be taxed.

7. The connection between labor and land reform in New York is somewhat unique, given the historical ties between these two movements since the early 1800s. In Chicago, for example, labor leaders sought to improve workers' housing conditions by boosting wages. In their call for a citywide strike in July 1881, labor reformers conflated employers with landlords, urging workers to strike against both. Chicago labor activist Joseph Gruenhut regularly attacked employers and landlords, arguing that higher wages and the expansion of homeownership opportunities were the keys to improving workers' living conditions (Garb 2003).

8. While the building and loan industry was in its infancy in the early nineteenth century, it was well developed, albeit local, after the 1870s (D. Mason 2004).

Chapter 3

1. In *Trustees of Dartmouth College v. Woodward* (1819), the court held that corporations enjoyed the right to enter into contracts, and in *Pembina Consolidated Silver Mining Company v. Pennsylvania* (1888), the court held that the rights of due process applied to corporations.

2. Unlike the property and contract clauses of the Constitution, which limit the government's ability to interfere with private property rights, the police power doctrine justifies government restrictions on private property rights, provided those restrictions are designed to enhance public health, safety, and welfare. Police powers are not explicitly enumerated but are implied by the Tenth Amendment, which reserves certain powers to state governments.

3. Some scholars argue that despite its radical intent, the abolitionist movement ironically laid the groundwork for the liberty of contract doctrine by providing rhetorical ammunition for an expansive reading of free labor ideology to include protections against any government-imposed constraints on employment contracts, including government measures designed to improve working conditions (Ely 1998).

4. "By Utilitarianism is here meant the ethical theory, that the conduct which, under any given circumstances, is objectively right, is that which will produce the greatest amount of happiness on the whole; that is, taking into account all whose happiness is affected by the conduct" (Sidgwick 1890, 411).

5. Although not always acknowledged by the progressives, American land reformers made this same argument but from a natural rights perspective. Thomas Skidmore argued for a stronger state role in limiting the amount of land that could be owned, and anarchists such as Benjamin Tucker, Ezra Heywood, and Joshua Ingalls argued that property rights should be limited to the rights of occupancy and use only. Similarly, Henry George's single tax constrained the right to earn income from land.

6. Homer Hoyt questioned Burgess's assertion that cities grew outward in well-defined circles of activity. His "sector theory" was based on the idea that activities tended to concentrate in sectors that extended outward radially from the center (Gottdiener, Hutchison, and Ryan 2014).

7. Simon Patten criticized the negative understanding of freedom because it "put the freedom of person above group welfare" (Schafer 2000, 53).

8. Baltimore's 1910 law was preceded by a report commissioned by the city's Charity Organization Society that proposed a dual regulatory system that differentiated between tenement and alley house districts. Within the alley house districts, which housed a large concentration of Baltimore's Black population, the report recommended the adoption of stringent regulatory measures that included mandated reductions in housing density, condemnation of uninhabitable dwellings, a ban on sleeping in basements, and prohibitions on the construction of new alley housing. The report also singled out the city's Black alley house residents for criticism, condemning the "gregarious, light-hearted, shiftless, irresponsible alley dwellers" and their "low standards and absence of ideals" (Power 1983, 297).

9. In Boston, Benjamin Flower applied Georgist reasoning to the slum problem. He wrote that the landlord has no incentive to improve his dwellings, because "he will have his taxes doubled or tripled for his pains." Facing these disincentives to improve the "death-dealing atmosphere" of rented dwellings, the landlord enjoys an "enormous per cent on his investment" (Kersten 1973, 22).

10. Robert Wiebe (1967, 176) argues that New York State housing regulations succeeded "primarily out of upstate Republican antagonism to Tammany Hall."

Chapter 4

1. The characterization of American federal housing policy in terms of its "two tiers" comes from Gail Radford (1996).

2. In New York, the number of persons per dwelling unit declined from 20.4 persons per dwelling in 1900 to 12.3 in 1930 (Barrows 1983).

3. In the manufacturing sector, real wages fell by 15 percent between 1929 and 1932 (Wolman 1933).

4. Catherine Bauer changed her name to Catherine Bauer Wurster in 1940, when she married architect William Wurster.

5. Richard T. Ely described American homebuilding as a process where the family would first "buy the site, gradually pay for it, then . . . mortgage it through a building and loan association or otherwise . . . construct the home with the aid of the mortgage and gradually . . . extinguish the mortgage" (Harris 2009, 526).

6. Whereas in *Muller* Brandeis appealed to social science evidence to argue in favor of the disparate treatment of women working in factories, in *Shelley* NAACP lawyers relied on social science evidence to argue against the disparate treatment of Black home seekers.

7. The Douglas Commission's report was not released until after the adoption of the Fair Housing Act.

8. The "right to community" should not be confused with Lefebvre's (1968) "right to the city." I discuss the right to the city in later chapters.

9. The Back-of-the-Yards district had earned notoriety when Upton Sinclair described the deplorable living and working conditions of its residents in *The Jungle* (1906).

10. The Back-of-the-Yards Council was known for its slogan, "We, the people, will work out our own destiny" (Jacobs 1961, 297).

11. Earlier in 1947, philosophers had been asked to reflect on the question, "How is an agreement conceivable among men who come from the four corners of the earth and who belong not only to different cultures and civilizations, but to different spiritual families and antagonistic schools of thought?" (Glendon 2002, 222).

12. Appeals to republican values could only be taken so far. Because most republicans believed that those without property lacked the civic virtues to govern themselves, republican arguments often justified exclusionary restrictions on political enfranchisement.

Chapter 5

1. In the US Court of Appeals case *Williams v. Barry* (1983), Judge Robert Bork made a similar argument, writing that "no one has plausibly maintained that there is a Constitutional or other legal right to city-provided shelter" (Berger 1991, 325).

2. The push for a reform of relations among federal, state, and local governments was initiated by the establishment of the Advisory Commission on Intergovernmental Relations in 1959 under President Dwight Eisenhower. During the 1960s, scholars such as Vincent Ostrom, Charles Tiebout, and Robert Warren took an interest in questions related to the appropriate scale of governance for local public goods when citizens have heterogeneous preferences for the level and mix of goods (Ostrom, Tiebout, and Warren 1961).

3. The federal government only allowed savings and loan (S&L) institutions to pay interest rates on deposits that were substantially below the interest rates on deposits paid by banks. Also, the federal government allowed S&Ls to originate only mortgages, not any other lending products. In short, S&Ls funded their long-term, fixed-rate mortgages with short-term deposits. This strategy became increasingly risky in the late 1970s and early 1980s, when inflation and interest rates dramatically increased, creating a funding crunch for most S&Ls. Although regulators responded by deregulating the S&L industry in the early 1980s, a vast number of S&Ls collapsed, were bailed out by taxpayers, or were absorbed by banks in the late 1980s and early 1990s (Hays 2012; D. Mason 2004).

4. Fannie Mae was created as a government agency in 1938 to purchase FHA-insured loans and was chartered as a GSE in 1968. In response to growing concerns about Fannie Mae's visible public debt liability, in 1968 Congress split Fannie Mae into two units: the Government National Mortgage Association (Ginnie Mae), which remained a government entity that bought government-issued affordable housing loans that were sold to investors, and the privatized Fannie Mae, henceforth owned by stockholders while retaining its public mission. When Fannie Mae was converted from a government agency to a regulated GSE, it was authorized to purchase non-FHA-insured conforming mortgages that met certain loan size requirements (Hays 2012).

5. I participated in several research symposia sponsored by the PATH regulatory barriers initiative.

6. The Housing and Community Development Act of 1974 resurrected the rhetoric of the nineteenth-century land reform movement to expand homeownership opportunities for the urban poor under the newly repackaged label of "urban homesteading." Section 810 authorized HUD to transfer repossessed residential properties to localities for use in a HUD-authorized urban homesteading demonstration program, building on the local successes of earlier programs in Baltimore, Philadelphia, and Wilmington (Blackburn, Millman, and Schnare 1981, 1).

7. The community land trust movement arose from the efforts of civil rights leaders Robert Swann and Slater King to establish New Communities, Inc., a large land trust in Lee County, Georgia.

8. In *Village of Arlington Heights v. Metropolitan Housing Development Corp.* (1977), for example, the finding that Arlington Heights was overwhelmingly white led

the court to override a local zoning ordinance that precluded the construction of low-income housing that "would be a significant step towards integrating the community" (Gordon 2006, 444). In this case, disparate impact was defined in terms of "the effect which the decision has on the community involved; if it perpetuates segregation and thereby prevents interracial association" (Gordon 2006, 443–444). At issue in the *TDHCA v. ICP* case was whether allocating too many LIHTCs to majority-Black inner-city neighborhoods and too few to predominantly white suburban neighborhoods constituted a disparate impact. To support its prima facie case, it was shown in a lower district court decision that "from 1999–2008, [TDHCA] approved tax credits for 49.7% of proposed non-elderly units in 0% to 9.9% Caucasian areas, but only approved 37.4% of proposed non-elderly units in 90% to 100% Caucasian areas. " Second, it found "92.29% of [LIHTC] units in the city of Dallas were located in census tracts with less than 50% Caucasian residents" (*TDHCA v. ICP*, 576 U.S. ___ 2015, 3). Thus, unlike individual instances of discrimination, where it must be shown that an individual was denied a single housing opportunity because of the individual's membership in a protected class, litigants of disparate impact cases typically rely on statistical evidence to demonstrate that a given policy or practice has the effect of perpetuating the spatial segregation of protected class members.

Chapter 6

1. Nussbaum argues that if one has a right to shelter, it is better to understand this right in terms of capabilities, rather than in terms of resources or utility, because

> giving resources to people does not always bring differently situated people up to the same level of capability to function. The utility-based analysis also encounters a problem: traditionally deprived people may be satisfied with a very low living standard, believing that this is all they have any hope of getting. A capabilities analysis, by contrast, looks at how people are actually enabled to live. Analyzing economic and material rights in terms of capabilities thus enables us to set forth clearly a rationale we have for spending unequal amounts of money on the disadvantaged, or creating special programs to assist their transition to full capability. (Nussbaum 2000, 99)

2. Some liberals interpret the public-private distinction as an order of justification for public action that assumes a presumption in favor of private liberty (Gaus 2011). Other liberals interpret the public-private distinction as an assumption about the scope of justice. In the Lockean conception of justice, for example, justice pertains only to the laws governing relations outside the private realm. Contemporary "public reason" liberals such as Rawls (1971) interpret the public-private distinction as a constraint on the reasons that may be presented in defense of public laws and institutions.

3. The distinction between moral equality and relational equality is inspired by, but subtly different from, Rondel's (2018) distinction between horizontal and vertical equality.

4. Refer to Wall (1998) for an elaboration on the tensions between perfectionism, state neutrality, and the promotion of autonomy.

5. Refer to Raz (1986) for an argument supporting the view that the promotion of autonomy is consistent with Mill's (1978 [1859]) harm principle.

6. As discussed in chapter 1, utilitarianism also provides a justification for being concerned about extreme levels of housing inequality, because the positionality of housing and the law of diminishing marginal utility imply that extreme inequalities in housing consumption may reduce aggregate utility.

7. The argument that choice justifies certain inequalities has been the focus of a sustained critique by many relational egalitarians. "Luck" egalitarians such as Ronald Dworkin (2000), Richard Arneson (1989), and G. A. Cohen (1989) argue that as long as any morally arbitrary conditions arising from luck or other circumstances beyond one's control have been neutralized, any remaining inequalities that arise from free choice are just. Furthermore, as long as everyone faced an acceptable range of opportunities prior to making a choice, any inequalities resulting from choice are just. This argument has intuitive appeal as an answer to the question of why equality matters, but it also has perverse implications for housing justice. First, some may make poor choices that render them without any housing whatsoever. Second, one's choices are often influenced by relations of social domination or oppression. Third, the choice between two equally bad alternatives is arguably not a free choice. Fourth, extreme housing inequalities, particularly those caused by prejudice or discrimination, may be unjust from a relational equality perspective even if the inequalities resulted from free choice. Fifth, the sufficientarian objection still applies. If all that matters from the standpoint of justice is everyone having their most basic housing needs met, housing inequalities above the threshold of sufficiency are not a concern of justice. Elizabeth Anderson (1999) elaborates on these and other objections to luck egalitarianism.

8. Theorists have traditionally understood rights in one of two ways. Interest-based theorists understand rights as morally weighty interests that obligate some other party to take action to satisfy that interest, where interests are defined in terms of the aims of each rightholder, taken one at a time (Raz 1986). Choice-based theorists understand rights not in terms of the interests that they serve but in terms of the zone of decision-making autonomy within which the rightholder has discretion to act (Hart 1955). Both conceptions have limitations. The interest-based theorist must respond to the challenge that the value of the interests justifying rights is agent-relative and incommensurable with the value of the same interest for other agents. The choice-based theorist must provide an account of rights that does not require the rightholder to possess the power to waive others' duty to satisfy rights (Mack 2000). Eric Mack (2000) offers a third "jurisdictional" conception of rights that responds to both these challenges.

9. The term "predistribution" comes from Jacob Hacker (2011).

Chapter 7

1. According to G. W. F. Hegel (1967 [1821]), individuals possess free will independently of any relation to material objects, but full development of the autonomous will is only possible through the embodiment of the will in external objects. Embodiment includes both the possession and use of an object, and it is through embodiment that people's subjective conception of themselves becomes concrete and recognizable to themselves and others (Waldron 1988).

2. According to Allan Gibbard (1976, 77), "If a person owns a thing, his ownership enhances his liberty, but it does so at the expense of the liberty of others. Ownership of a thing gives a person the right to exclude others from its use, and that right, though it adds to the freedom of the owner, detracts from the freedom of those others."

3. The pervasiveness of propertylessness in a world where others own property has led some to conclude that private property cannot be justified. During the English Civil War, various revolutionary groups argued that unless everyone had access to some property, the institution of property was illegitimate. The Diggers denied that God had granted land to man for exclusive appropriation, and they sought to return to a state of communally owned land. The Levellers took a different approach and argued that property rights are legitimate only if everyone has the same amount of property (Linklater 2013). Pierre-Joseph Proudhon (1876) famously equated private property with robbery. For Karl Marx, the right of private property "leads every man to see in other men not the realization, but rather the limitation, of his own liberty" (Tucker 1978, 42). Marx believed that private property institutionalizes the illusion that freedom consists in the separation among human beings.

4. Homeowners who are unable to stay current on their mortgages face the threat of foreclosure and lack secure control rights. For these homeowners, the tenure security requirement justifies a variety of foreclosure prevention and mediation measures that help homeowners remain in their homes.

5. Under LEC arrangements, occupants' ownership shares are tied to a long-term lease, and the occupant enjoys a durable right of occupancy that includes the rights to exchange and alienate ownership shares upon residential mobility.

Chapter 8

1. Homeownership tax expenditures in the 2020 tax year are lower than in previous years due to reductions in homeowners' tax benefits following the Tax Cuts and Jobs Act of 2017.

2. Milton Friedman (1962) popularized the negative income tax idea.

3. One concern with a housing wealth increment tax is that it may reduce homeowners' willingness to sell homes, creating supply shortages in tight housing markets. An alternative approach that is less likely to have negative supply-side impacts is an annual tax on the stock of housing wealth or a tax on those who own homes that are more expensive (Dawkins 2020a).

4. If the tax on imputed rental income is equal to some fraction of estimated housing value and housing capital gains are also taxed, the full annual negative housing tax obligation for those who sell their homes at the end of the tax year is equivalent to a tax on the stock of housing wealth.

5. Another critique of the negative housing tax is that it is likely to encounter political resistance, particularly among elderly homeowners, who may not have the financial means to pay the housing consumption tax. One simple solution to this problem is to exempt low-income seniors from negative housing tax obligations. Another approach is to award low-income seniors who "age in place" a tax credit equal to the housing wealth increment tax revenue that would have been generated from the sale of a home (Dawkins 2020a).

6. Complex equality is not the only distributive principle that considers the interrelations among different goods. Standard neoclassical economic models, for example, assume that utility is maximized when the marginal utility per dollar spent on each good is equal across all goods consumed. The question that remains is whether the distributive relationships among different goods are best understood through the lens of complex equality or an approach that aims to achieve complementarity between the distributive principles of different distributive spheres.

7. For example, if local public education is a good that should be distributed to everyone at a minimum level of adequacy, but adequate education can only be accessed in areas where housing is expensive, the source of the injustice is the dominance of the sphere of housing over the sphere of education, irrespective of how housing or education should be distributed.

8. Galster (1992) argues that a stable integrative process does not require restrictions on housing choice to promote integration but is consistent with choice-expanding options such as race-based affirmative marketing strategies and the provision of information to those seeking to make prointegrative moves. Race-based marketing strategies potentially improve relational equality, but they also risk perpetuating the commodification of race within housing markets, only in a prointegrative fashion.

Conclusion

1. Tigg Montague is a loan shark who announces that "charity begins at home, and justice begins next door" in Charles Dickens's novel *Martin Chuzzlewit*.

References

Acharya, Viral V., Matthew Richardson, Stijn Van Nieuwerburgh, and Lawrence J. White. 2011. *Guaranteed to Fail: Fannie Mae, Freddie Mac, and the Debacle of Mortgage Finance*. Princeton, NJ: Princeton University Press.

Adams, Charles Francis. 1865. *The Works of John Adams, Second President of the United States, Vol. 2*. Boston: Little, Brown.

Adams, James Truslow. 1932. *The Epic of America*. Boston: Little, Brown.

Adams, John. 1965. *Legal Papers of John Adams, Vol. 1*, edited by L. Kinvin Wroth and Hiller B. Zobel. Cambridge, MA: Belknap Press of Harvard University Press.

Adams, John, and William Tudor. 1819. *Novanglus, and Massachusettensis; Or, Political Essays, Published in the Years 1774 and 1775, on the Principal Points of Controversy, between Great Britain and Her Colonies*. Boston: Hews and Goss.

Adams, Willi Paul. 1980. *The First American Constitutions: Republican Ideology and the Making of the State Constitutions in the Revolutionary Era*. Chapel Hill: University of North Carolina Press.

Akimoto, Fukuo. 2009. The Birth of "Land Use Planning" in American Urban Planning. *Planning Perspectives* 24 (4): 457–483.

Albouy, David, and Mike Zabek. 2016. Housing Inequality. NBER Working Paper 21916, National Bureau of Economic Research, Cambridge, MA.

Alinsky, Saul D. 1971. *Rules for Radicals: A Pragmatic Primer for Realistic Radicals*. New York: Vintage Books.

Allen, Anita. 1988. *Uneasy Access: Privacy for Women in a Free Society*. Totowa, NJ: Rowman and Allanheld.

Allgeyer v. Louisiana, 165 U.S. 578 (1897).

Anderson, Carol. 1996. From Hope to Disillusion: African Americans, the United Nations, and the Struggle for Human Rights, 1944–1947. *Diplomatic History* 20 (4): 531–563.

Anderson, Carol. 2003. *Eyes off the Prize: The United Nations and the African American Struggle for Human Rights*. Cambridge: Cambridge University Press.

Anderson, Carol. 2008. A "Hollow Mockery": African Americans, White Supremacy, and the Development of Human Rights in the United States. In *Bringing Human Rights Home, Vol. 1: A History of Human Rights in the United States*, edited by Cynthia Soohoo, Catherine Albisa, and Martha F. Davis, 75–101. Westport, CT: Praeger.

Anderson, Elizabeth. 1999. What Is the Point of Equality? *Ethics* 109 (2) (January): 287–337.

Anderson, Elizabeth. 2010. *The Imperative of Integration*. Princeton, NJ: Princeton University Press.

Anderson, Hannah L. 2011. That Settles It: The Debate and Consequences of the Homestead Act of 1862. *History Teacher* 45 (1): 117–137.

Arendt, Hannah. 1958. *The Human Condition*. Chicago: University of Chicago Press.

Arendt, Hannah. 1968. *The Origins of Totalitarianism*. San Diego: Harcourt.

Arendt, Hannah. 2018. Public Rights and Private Interests: A Response to Charles Frankel. In *Thinking without a Banister: Essays in Understanding 1953–1975*, edited by Jerome Kohn, 506–512. New York: Schocken Books.

Argersinger, Jo Ann E. 2010. Contested Visions of American Democracy: Citizenship, Public Housing, and the International Arena. *Journal of Urban History* 36 (6): 792–813.

Arneson, Richard J. 1989. Equality and Equal Opportunity for Welfare. *Philosophical Studies* 56 (1) (May): 77–93.

Aronovici, Carol. 1934. *America Can't Have Housing*. New York: Museum of Modern Art.

Arrington, Benjamin T. 2012. "Free Homes for Free Men": A Political History of the Homestead Act, 1774–1863. PhD diss., University of Nebraska-Lincoln.

Asante-Muhammad, Dedrick, Chuck Collins, Josh Hoxie, and Emanuel Nieves. 2017. *The Road to Zero Wealth: How the Racial Wealth Divide Is Hollowing Out America's Middle Class*. Washington, DC: Prosperity Now and the Institute for Policy Studies. http://prosperitynow.org/files/PDFs/road_to_zero_wealth.pdf.

Aurand, Andrew, Dan Emmanuel, Daniel Threet, Ikra Rafi, and Diane Yentel. 2020. *The Gap: A Shortage of Affordable Homes*. Washington, DC: National Low Income Housing Coalition. http://reports.nlihc.org/sites/default/files/gap/Gap-Report_2020.pdf.

References

Axel-Lute, Miriam. 2019. YIMBYs: Friend, Foe, or Chaos Agent? *Shelterforce: The Voice of Community Development*, February 19, 2019. http://shelterforce.org/2019/02/19/yimbys-friend-foe-or-chaos-agent/.

Bachelard, Gaston. 1969. *The Poetics of Space*. Boston: Beacon Press.

Badger, Emily. 2019. Renters Are Mad. Presidential Candidates Have Noticed. *New York Times*, April 23, 2019. http://www.nytimes.com/2019/04/23/upshot/2020-democrats-court-renters.html.

Bailyn, Bernard. 1967. *The Ideological Origins of the American Revolution*. Cambridge, MA: Harvard University Press.

Baiocchi, Gianpaolo. 2018. *Communities over Commodities: People-Driven Alternatives to an Unjust Housing System*. Brooklyn, NY: Right to the City Alliance.

Banzhaf, H. Spencer, and Kyle Mangum. 2019. Capitalization as a Two-Part Tariff: The Role of Zoning. NBER Working Paper 25699, National Bureau of Economic Research, Cambridge, MA.

Barker, Charles Albro. 1955. *Henry George*. New York: Oxford University Press.

Barros, D. Benjamin. 2006. Home as a Legal Concept. *Santa Clara Law Review* 46 (2): 255–306.

Barrows, Robert G. 1983. Beyond the Tenement: Patterns of American Urban Housing, 1870–1930. *Journal of Urban History* 9 (4): 395–420.

Bauer, Catherine. 1934. *Modern Housing*. Cambridge, MA: Riverside Press.

Becker, Lawrence C. 1977. *Property Rights: Philosophic Foundations*. London: Routledge and Kegan Paul.

Beckett, Andy. 2015. The Right to Buy: The Housing Crisis That Thatcher Built. *The Guardian*, August 26, 2015. http://www.theguardian.com/society/2015/aug/26/right-to-buy-margaret-thatcher-david-cameron-housing-crisis.

Bentham, Jeremy. 1843. *The Works of Jeremy Bentham, Vol. 1*, edited by John Bowring. Edinburgh: William Tait.

Berger, Curtis. 1991. Beyond Homelessness: An Entitlement to Housing. *University of Miami Law Review* 45 (2): 315–335.

Berlin, Isaiah. 1971. *Four Essays on Liberty*. London: Oxford University Press.

Bieri, David S., and Casey J. Dawkins. 2016. Quality of Life, Transportation Costs, and Federal Housing Assistance: Leveling the Playing Field. *Housing Policy Debate* 26 (4–5): 646–669.

Bietz, Charles R. 2009. *The Idea of Human Rights*. Oxford: Oxford University Press.

Billington, Ray Allen. 1974. *Westward Expansion: A History of the American Frontier.* New York: Macmillan.

Bischoff, Kendra, and Sean F. Reardon. 2014. Residential Segregation by Income, 1970–2009. In *Diversity and Disparities: America Enters a New Century*, edited by John Logan, 208–233. New York: Russell Sage Foundation.

Bishop, Bill. 2009. *The Big Sort: Why the Clustering of Like-Minded America Is Tearing Us Apart.* New York: Houghton Mifflin Harcourt.

Blackburn, Anthony J., Molly Beals Millman, and Ann B. Schnare. 1981. *Evaluation of the Urban Homesteading Demonstration Program: Final Report, Vol. 1.* Washington, DC: US Department of Housing and Urban Development.

Blackmar, Elizabeth. 1989. *Manhattan for Rent, 1785–1850.* Ithaca, NY: Cornell University Press.

Blackstone, William. 2016 [1765]. *Commentaries on the Laws of England, Book 2: Of the Rights of Things.* Introduction, Notes, and Textual Apparatus by Simon Stern. Oxford: Oxford University Press.

Blau, Joel. 1992. *The Invisible Poor: Homelessness in the United States.* New York: Oxford University Press.

Block v. Hirsch, 256 U.S. 135 (1921).

Blomley, Nicholas. 2004. *Unsettling the City: Urban Land and the Politics of Property.* New York: Routledge.

Bocian, Debbie Gruenstein, Wei Li, and Keith S. Ernst. 2010. Foreclosures by Race and Ethnicity: The Demographics of a Crisis. CRL Research Report, Center for Responsible Lending, Durham, NC. http://www.responsiblelending.org/mortgage-lending/research-analysis/foreclosures-by-race-and-ethnicity.pdf.

Borgwardt, Elizabeth. 2005. *A New Deal for the World: America's Vision for Human Rights.* Cambridge, MA: Harvard University Press.

Bradizza, Luigi. 2013. *Richard T. Ely's Critique of Capitalism.* New York: Palgrave Macmillan.

Brettschneider, Corey. 2007. *Democratic Rights: The Substance of Self-Government.* Princeton, NJ: Princeton University Press.

Brettschneider, Corey. 2012. Public Justification and the Right to Private Property: Welfare Rights as Compensation for Exclusion. *Law and Ethics of Human Rights* 6 (1): 121–146.

Brighouse, Harry, and Adam Swift. 2006. Equality, Priority, and Positional Goods. *Ethics* 116 (3): 471–497.

Brown v. Board of Education, 347 U.S. 483 (1954).

References

Brueckner, Jan K. 2014. Eliminate the Mortgage Interest Deduction or Tax Imputed Rent? Leveling the Real-Estate Playing Field. *Cityscape: A Journal of Policy Development and Research* 16 (1): 215–218.

Bryson, Phillip J. 2011. *The Economics of Henry George: History's Rehabilitation of America's Greatest Early Economist*. New York: Palgrave Macmillan.

Buchanan v. Warley, 245 U.S. 60 (1917).

Buhle, Paul, and Alan Dawley. 1985. *Working for Democracy: American Workers from the Revolution to the Present*. Champaign: University of Illinois Press.

Bulosan, Carlos. 1943. Freedom from Want. *Saturday Evening Post*, March 6, 1943. http://www.saturdayeveningpost.com/2017/12/carlos-bulosans-freedom-want/.

Burroughs, William S. 1998. From the Job. In *Word Virus: The William S. Burroughs Reader*, edited by James Grauerholz and Ira Silverberg, 289–292. New York: Grove Press.

Byrne, Thomas, and Dennis P. Culhane. 2011. Right to Housing: An Effective Means for Addressing Homelessness. *University of Pennsylvania Journal of Law and Social Change* 14 (3): 379–390.

Callahan v. Carey, No. 79-42582 (Sup. Ct. N.Y. County, Cot. 18 1979).

Capek, Stella, and John I. Gilderbloom. 1992. *Community versus Commodity: Tenants and the American City*. Albany: State University of New York Press.

Case, Karl E. 1991. Investors, Developers, and Supply-Side Subsidies: How Much Is Enough? *Housing Policy Debate* 2 (2): 341–356.

Castells, Manuel. 1979. *The Urban Question: A Marxist Approach*. Cambridge, MA: MIT Press.

Ceraso, Karen. 1999. Whatever Happened to the Tenants Movement? *Shelterforce: The Voice of Community Development*, May 1, 1999. http://shelterforce.org/1999/05/01/whatever-happened-to-the-tenants-movement/.

Chadwick, Edwin. 1965 [1842]. *Report on the Sanitary Condition of the Labouring Population of Great Britain*, edited by M. W. Flinn. Edinburgh: Edinburgh University Press.

Chapple, Karen, and Edward G. Goetz. 2011. Spatial Justice through Regionalism? The Inside Game, the Outside Game, and the Quest for the Spatial Fix in the United States. *Community Development* 42 (4): 458–475.

Chastleton Corp. v. Sinclair, 264 U.S. 543 (1924).

Chetty, Raj, Nathaniel Hendren, and Lawrence F. Katz. 2016. The Effects of Exposure to Better Neighborhoods on Children: New Evidence from the Moving to Opportunity Experiment. *American Economic Review* 106 (4): 855–902.

Christman, John. 1991. Self-Ownership, Equality, and the Structure of Property Rights. *Political Theory* 19 (1): 28–46.

Christman, John. 1994. *The Myth of Property: Toward an Egalitarian Theory of Ownership*. Oxford: Oxford University Press.

Cicero, Marcus Tullius. 1900. *The Orations of Marcus Tullius Cicero*, translated by Charles Duke Yonge. London: George Bell and Sons.

Claeys, Eric R. 2004. Euclid Lives? The Uneasy Legacy of Progressivism in Zoning. *Fordham Law Review* 73 (2): 731–770.

Clark, Kenneth B. 1965. *Dark Ghetto: Dilemmas of Social Power*. New York: Harper and Row.

Cloward, Richard, and Francis Fox Piven. 1966. The Weight of the Poor: A Strategy to End Poverty. *The Nation*, May 2, 1966.

Coase, Ronald H. 1960. The Problem of Social Cost. *Journal of Law and Economics* 3 (October): 1–44.

Cohen, G. A. 1989. On the Currency of Egalitarian Justice. *Ethics* 99 (4): 906–944.

Cohen, G. A. 1995. *Self-Ownership, Freedom, and Equality*. Cambridge: Cambridge University Press.

Cohn, Jan. 1970. *The Palace or the Poorhouse: The American House as a Cultural Symbol*. East Lansing: Michigan State University Press.

Colburn, Ben. 2010. *Autonomy and Liberalism*. New York: Routledge.

Commission on Race and Housing. 1958. *Where Shall We Live? Report of the Commission on Race and Housing*. Berkeley: University of California Press.

Committee on Economic, Social and Cultural Rights (CESCR). 1991. CESCR General Comment No. 4: The Right to Adequate Housing (Art. 11 (1) of the Covenant). United Nations Office of the High Commissioner for Human Rights, Geneva.

Committee on Economic, Social and Cultural Rights (CESCR). 1997. CESCR General Comment No. 7: The Right to Adequate Housing (Art. 11 (1) of the Covenant): Forced Evictions. United Nations Office of the High Commissioner for Human Rights, Geneva.

Commons, John R. 1893. *The Distribution of Wealth*. New York: Macmillan.

Cooley, Thomas M. 1868. *A Treatise on the Constitutional Limitations Which Rest upon the Legislative Power of the States of the American Union*. Boston: Little, Brown.

Cooper, Thomas Valentine, and Hector Tyndale Fenton. 1890. *American Politics (Non-partisan) from the Beginning to Date: Embodying a History of All the Political Parties, with Their Views and Records on All Important Questions, Book 2*. Boston: B. A. Fowler.

CoreLogic. 2017. *United States Residential Foreclosure Crisis: 10 Years Later*. Irvine, CA: CoreLogic. http://www.corelogic.com/research/foreclosure-report/national-foreclosure-report-10-year.pdf.

Craven, Matthew C. R. 1995. *The International Covenant on Economic, Social, and Cultural Rights: A Perspective on Its Development*. Oxford: Clarendon Press.

Crimmins, James E. 2017. Jeremy Bentham. In *Stanford Encyclopedia of Philosophy*, edited by Edward N. Zalta. Metaphysics Research Lab, Center for the Study of Language and Information, Stanford University. http://plato.stanford.edu/entries/bentham/.

Crowder, George. 2002. *Liberalism and Value Pluralism*. London: Continuum.

Cutler, David M., Edward L. Glaeser, and Jacob L. Vigdor. 1999. The Rise and Decline of the American Ghetto. *Journal of Political Economy* 107 (3): 455–506.

Dagger, Richard. 1997. *Civic Virtues: Rights, Citizenship, and Republican Liberalism*. New York: Oxford University Press.

Davis, David Brion. 1997. *Antebellum American Culture: An Interpretive Anthology*. University Park: Pennsylvania State University Press.

Dawkins, Casey J. 2017a. Autonomy and Housing Policy. *Housing, Theory and Society* 34 (4): 420–438.

Dawkins, Casey J. 2017b. Putting Equality in Place: The Normative Foundations of Geographic Equality of Opportunity. *Housing Policy Debate* 27 (6): 897–912.

Dawkins, Casey. 2018. Toward Common Ground in the U.S. Fair Housing Debate. *Journal of Urban Affairs* 40 (4): 475–493.

Dawkins, Casey. 2020a. Realizing Housing Justice through Comprehensive Housing Policy Reform. *International Journal of Urban Sciences* 25 (S1): 266–281.

Dawkins, Casey. 2020b. The Right to Housing in an Ownership Society. *Housing and Society* 47 (2): 81–102.

Dawkins, Casey, and Mark Miller. 2017. The Characteristics and Unmet Housing Program Needs of Disabled HUD-Assisted Households. *Housing Policy Debate* 27 (4): 499–518.

DeLuca, Stefanie, and Peter Rosenblatt. 2017. Walking Away from the Wire: Housing Mobility and Neighborhood Opportunity in Baltimore. *Housing Policy Debate* 27 (4): 519–546.

Demographia. 2001. City of New York & Boroughs: Population & Population Density from 1790. http://www.demographia.com/dm-nyc.htm.

Desmond, Matthew. 2016. *Evicted: Poverty and Profit in the American City*. New York: Crown.

de Vita, Alvaro. 2007. Inequality and Poverty in Global Perspective. In *Freedom from Poverty as a Human Right*, edited by Thomas Pogge, 103–132. Oxford: Oxford University Press.

Dewilde, Caroline, and Richard Ronald. 2017. *Housing Wealth and Welfare*. Cheltenham: Edward Elgar.

Dickens, Charles. 1908 [1844]. *Martin Chuzzlewit, Volume I with Introduction, Critical Comments, Argument, Notes, etc.* New York: University Society.

Dillon, John. 1872. *Treatise on the Law of Municipal Corporations*. Chicago: James Cockcroft.

Domingo, Rafael. 2017. The Law of Property in Ancient Roman Law. Social Science Research Network working paper. http://ssrn.com/abstract=2984869.

Donohue, Kathleen G. 2003. *Freedom from Want: American Liberalism and the Idea of the Consumer*. Baltimore: Johns Hopkins University Press.

Dorsey v. Stuyvesant Town Corp., 299 N.Y. 512 (1949).

Drier, Peter. 1984. The Tenants' Movement in the United States. *International Journal of Urban and Regional Research* 8 (2): 255–279.

Du Bois, W. E. B. 1947. *An Appeal to the World: A Statement of Denial of Human Rights to Minorities in the Case of Citizens of Negro Descent in the United States of America and an Appeal to the United Nations for Redress*. New York: National Association for the Advancement of Colored People.

Du Bois, W. E. B. 2007 [1899]. *The Philadelphia Negro: A Social Study*. Oxford: Oxford University Press.

Dumm, Thomas L. 1994. *United States (Contestations)*. Ithaca, NY: Cornell University Press.

Dunn, John. 1990. *Interpreting Political Responsibility*. Cambridge: Cambridge University Press.

Dworkin, Ronald. 1978. *Taking Rights Seriously*. Cambridge, MA: Harvard University Press.

Dworkin, Ronald. 2000. *Sovereign Virtue*. Cambridge, MA: Harvard University Press.

Dworkin, Ronald. 2008. *Is Democracy Possible Here? Principles for a New Political Debate*. Princeton, NJ: Princeton University Press.

Eldredge v. Koch, 118 Misc.2d 163 (1983).

Elliott, Rebecca. 2018. Housing Advocates Sue HUD, Seek to Block Houston from Receiving Harvey Aid. *Houston Chronicle*, March 20, 2018. http://www.houstonchronicle.com/news/article/Austin-housing-advocates-sue-HUD-seek-to-block-12768774.php.

Ellis, Richard J. 1992. Radical Lockeanism in American Political Culture. *Western Political Quarterly* 45 (4): 825–849.

Elster, Jon. 1992. *Local Justice: How Institutions Allocate Scarce Goods and Necessary Burdens*. New York: Russell Sage Foundation.

Ely, James W., Jr. 1998. *The Guardian of Every Other Right: A Constitutional History of Property Rights*. New York: Oxford University Press.

Ely, Richard T. 1886. Constitution By-Laws and Resolutions of the American Economic Association. *Publications of the American Economic Association* 1 (1): 35–46.

Ely, Richard T. 1914. *Property and Contract in Their Relations to the Distribution of Wealth*. New York: Macmillan.

Ely, Richard T. 1917. Landed Property as an Economic Concept and as a Field of Research. *American Economic Review* 7 (1): 18–33.

Engels, Friedrich. 1975 [1872]. *The Housing Question*. Moscow: Progress.

Eshet, Dan. 2010. *Fundamental Freedoms: Eleanor Roosevelt and the Universal Declaration of Human Rights*. Brookline, MA: Facing History and Ourselves National Foundation.

Essert, Christopher. 2016. Property and Homelessness. *Philosophy and Public Affairs* 44 (4): 266–295.

Evans, George Henry. 1844. *Workingman's Advocate*, October 5, 1844.

Faherty, Duncan. 2007. *Remodeling the Nation: The Architecture of American Identity, 1776–1858*. Durham: University of New Hampshire Press.

Fair Housing Act, 42 U.S.C. 3601 et seq. (1968).

Farley, Reynolds. 2008. The Kerner Commission Report Plus Four Decades: What Has Changed? What Has Not? Report 08–656, University of Michigan Institute for Social Research, Ann Arbor.

Feinberg, Joel. 1973. *Social Philosophy*. Englewood Cliffs, NJ: Prentice Hall.

Feldman, Leonard C. 2004. *Citizens without Shelter: Homelessness, Democracy, and Political Exclusion*. Ithaca, NY: Cornell University Press.

Fischel, William A. 2005. *The Homevoter Hypothesis: How Home Values Influence Local Government Taxation, School Finance, and Land-Use Policies*. Cambridge, MA: Harvard University Press.

Fish, Gertrude S. 1979. *The Story of Housing*. New York: Macmillan.

Fisher, Robert. 1994. *Let the People Decide: Neighborhood Organizing in America*. Updated ed. New York: Twayne.

Fishman, Robert. 1987. *Bourgeois Utopias: The Rise and Fall of Suburbia*. New York: Basic Books.

Flaherty, Jordan. 2010. *Floodlines: Community and Resistance from Katrina to the Jena Six*. Chicago: Haymarket Books.

Foglesong, Richard E. 1986. *Planning the Capitalist City: The Colonial Era to the 1920s*. Princeton, NJ: Princeton University Press.

Foner, Eric. 1990. *A Short History of Reconstruction*. New York: Harper and Row.

Foner, Eric. 1995. *Free Soil, Free Labor, Free Men: The Ideology of the Republican Party before the Civil War*. Oxford: Oxford University Press.

Foner, Philip S. 1998. *History of the Labor Movement in the United States, Vol. 2: From the Founding of the A. F. of L. to the Emergence of American Imperialism*. New York: International.

Foscarinis, Maria. 2004. Homelessness, Litigation and Law Reform Strategies: A United States Perspective. *Australian Journal of Human Rights* 10 (2): 105–132.

Foscarinis, Maria. 2006. Advocating for the Human Right to Housing: Notes from the United States. *NYU Review of Law and Social Change* 30 (3): 447–481.

Fox Piven, Frances, and Richard A. Cloward. 1967. Rent Strike: Disrupting the Slum System. *New Republic*, December 2, 1967.

Fox Piven, Frances, and Richard A. Cloward. 1971. *Regulating the Poor: The Functions of Public Welfare*. New York: Vintage Books.

Frank, Robert H. 2007. *Falling Behind: How Rising Inequality Harms the Middle Class*. Berkeley: University of California Press.

Frankfurt, Harry. 1987. Equality as a Moral Ideal. *Ethics* 98 (1) (October): 21–43.

Fraser, Nancy, and Axel Honneth. 2004. *Redistribution or Recognition? A Political Philosophical Exchange*. London: Verso.

Freeden, Michael. 1978. *The New Liberalism: An Ideology of Social Reform*. Oxford: Clarendon Press.

Freund, Ernst. 1904. *The Police Power: Public Policy and Constitutional Rights*. Chicago: Callaghan.

Friedman, Lawrence M. 1968. *Government and Slum Housing: A Century of Frustration*. Chicago: Rand McNally.

Friedman, Milton. 1962. *Capitalism and Freedom*. Chicago: University of Chicago Press.

Friefeld, Jacob K., Mikal Brotnov Eckstrom, and Richard Edwards. 2019. African American Homesteader "Colonies" in the Settling of the Great Plains. *Great Plains Quarterly* 39 (1): 11–37.

Frost, Robert. 1917. *North of Boston*. New York: Henry Holt.

Frug, Gerald E. 1980. The City as a Legal Concept. *Harvard Law Review* 93 (6): 1057–1154.

Fullilove, Mindy Thompson. 2004. *Root Shock: How Tearing Up City Neighborhoods Hurts America, and What We Can Do About It*. New York: One World, Ballantine Books.

Gaffney, Mason, and Fred Harrison. 1994. *The Corruption of Economics*. London: Shepheard-Walwyn.

Galbraith, John Kenneth. 1958. *The Affluent Society*. New York: Houghton Mifflin.

Gallaher, Carolyn. 2016. *The Politics of Staying Put: Condo Conversion and Tenant Right-to-Buy in Washington, D.C.* Philadelphia: Temple University Press.

Galster, George C. 1992. The Case for Racial Integration. In *The Metropolis in Black and White: Place, Power, and Polarization*, edited by George C. Galster and Edward W. Hill, 270–285. New Brunswick, NJ: Center for Urban Policy Research.

Galston, William. 2002. *Liberal Pluralism: The Implications of Value Pluralism for Political Theory and Practice*. Cambridge: Cambridge University Press.

Garb, Margaret. 2003. Health, Morality, and Housing: The "Tenement Problem" in Chicago. *American Journal of Public Health* 93 (9): 1420–1430.

Gates, Paul Wallace. 1941. Land Policy and Tenancy in the Prairie States. *Journal of Economic History* 1 (1): 60–82.

Gaus, Gerald F. 1996. *Justificatory Liberalism: An Essay on Epistemology and Political Theory*. Oxford: Oxford University Press.

Gaus, Gerald F. 2011. *The Order of Public Reason: A Theory of Freedom and Morality in a Diverse and Bounded World*. Cambridge: Cambridge University Press.

Gaus, Gerald F. 2012. Property. In *The Oxford Handbook of Political Philosophy*, edited by David Estlund, 93–112. Oxford: Oxford University Press.

George, Henry. 1942 [1879]. *Progress and Poverty: An Inquiry into the Cause of Industrial Depressions and of Increase of Want with Increase of Wealth*. New York: Walter J. Black.

George, Henry. 1999 [1871]. *Our Land & Land Policy: Speeches, Lectures, and Miscellaneous Writings*, edited by Kenneth C. Wenzer. East Lansing: Michigan State University Press.

Gerstle, Gary. 2015. *Liberty and Coercion: The Paradox of American Government from the Founding to the Present*. Princeton, NJ: Princeton University Press.

Gibbard, Allan. 1976. Natural Property Rights. *Noûs* 10 (1) (March): 77–86.

Glaeser, Edward L. 2011. Rethinking the Federal Bias towards Homeownership. *Cityscape: A Journal of Policy Development and Research* 13 (2): 5–37.

Glaeser, Edward L., and Joseph Gyourko. 2008. *Rethinking Federal Housing Policy: How to Make Housing Plentiful and Affordable*. Washington, DC: American Enterprise Institute for Public Policy Research.

Glendon, Mary Ann. 1982. The Transformation of American Landlord-Tenant Law. *Boston College Law Review* 23 (3): 503–576.

Glendon, Mary Ann. 2002. *A World Made New: Eleanor Roosevelt and the Universal Declaration of Human Rights*. New York: Random House Trade Paperbacks.

Godkin, E. L. 1890. The Rights of the Citizen: To His Own Reputation. *Scribner's Magazine*, July 1890.

Goering, John M. 1986. *Housing Desegregation and Federal Policy*. Chapel Hill: University of North Carolina Press.

Goering, John, and Judith D. Feins. 2003. *Choosing a Better Life: Evaluating the Moving to Opportunity Social Experiment*. Washington, DC: Urban Institute.

Goetz, Edward G. 2003. *Clearing the Way: Deconcentrating the Poor in Urban America*. Washington, DC: Urban Institute Press.

Goetz, Edward G. 2013. *New Deal Ruins: Race, Economic Justice, and Public Housing Policy*. Ithaca, NY: Cornell University Press.

Goetz, Edward G. 2018. *The One-Way Street of Integration*. Ithaca, NY: Cornell University Press.

Goetz, Edward G., and Karen Chapple. 2010. You Gotta Move: Advancing the Debate on the Record of Dispersal. *Housing Policy Debate* 20 (2): 209–236.

Goetz, Edward G., Anthony Damiano, and Rashad A. Williams. 2019. Racially Concentrated Areas of Affluence: A Preliminary Investigation. *Cityscape* 21 (1): 99–123.

Gold, Roberta. 2014. *When Tenants Claimed the City: The Struggle for Citizenship in New York City Housing*. Champaign: University of Illinois Press.

Goldberg v. Kelly, 397 U.S. 254 (1970).

Gordon, Adam. 2006. Making Exclusionary Zoning Remedies Work: How Courts Applying Title VII Standards to Fair Housing Cases Have Misunderstood the Housing Market. *Yale Law and Policy Review* 24 (2): 437–469.

Gottdiener, Mark, Ray Hutchison, and Michael T. Ryan. 2014. *The New Urban Sociology*. 5th ed. New York: Routledge.

Government of Canada. 2017. *Canada's National Housing Strategy: A Place to Call Home*. www.placetocallhome.ca/pdfs/Canada-National-Housing-Strategy.pdf.

Gray, John. 1993. *Post-Enlightenment Liberalism*. London: Routledge.

Grey, Thomas. 1980. The Disintegration of Property. In *Ethics, Economics and the Law of Property*, edited by J. Roland Pennock and John W. Chapman, 69–85. New York: New York University Press.

Griffin, James. 2008. *On Human Rights*. Oxford: Oxford University Press.

Griscom, John H. 1845. *The Sanitary Conditions of the Laboring Population of New York with Suggestions for Its Improvement*. New York: Harper and Brothers.

Griswold v. Connecticut, 381 U.S. 479 (1965).

Grotius, Hugo. 2005 [1625]. *The Rights of War and Peace, Book 1*, edited by Richard Tuck. Indianapolis: Liberty Fund.

Gyourko, Joseph. 2009. Housing Supply. *Annual Review of Economics* 1:295–318.

Habermas, Jürgen. 1996. *Between Facts and Norms: Contributions to a Discourse Theory of Law and Democracy*. Cambridge, MA: MIT Press.

Hacker, Jacob. 2011. *The Institutional Foundations of Middle-Class Democracy*. London: Policy Network.

Hackworth, Jason. 2007. *The Neoliberal City: Governance, Ideology, and Development in an American Urbanism*. Ithaca, NY: Cornell University Press.

Hadden, Sally E., and Patricia Hagler Minter. 2013. *Signposts: New Directions in Southern Legal History*. Athens: University of Georgia Press.

Hafetz, Jonathan L. 2002. "A Man's Home Is His Castle?": Reflections on the Home, the Family, and Privacy during the Late Nineteenth and Early Twentieth Centuries. *William and Mary Journal of Women and the Law* 8 (2): 175–242.

Hall, Robert E. 1997. Potential Disruption from the Move to a Consumption Tax. *American Economic Review, Papers and Proceedings of the Hundred and Fourth Annual Meeting of the American Economic Association* 87 (2): 147–150.

Halpern, Robert. 1995. *Rebuilding the Inner City: A History of Neighborhood Initiatives to Address Poverty in the United States*. New York: Columbia University Press.

Hamilton, Bruce W. 1976. The Effects of Property Taxes and Local Public Spending on Property Values: A Theoretical Comment. *Journal of Political Economy* 84 (3): 647–650.

Harrington, James. 1992 [1656]. *The Commonwealth of Oceana and a System of Politics*, edited by J. G. A. Pocock. Cambridge: Cambridge University Press.

Harrington, Michael. 1962. *The Other America: Poverty in the United States*. Baltimore: Penguin Books.

Harris, Richard. 2009. The Birth of the Housing Consumer in the United States. *International Journal of Consumer Studies* 33 (5): 525–532.

Hart, H. L. A. 1955. Are There Any Natural Rights? *Philosophical Review* 64 (2): 175–191.

Hartman, Chester. 1998. The Case for a Right to Housing. *Housing Policy Debate* 9 (2): 223–246.

Hartman, Chester W. 2002. The Right to Stay Put. In *Between Eminence and Notoriety: Four Decades of Radical Urban Planning*, edited by Chester W. Hartman, 120–133. New Brunswick, NJ: Center for Urban and Policy Research.

Hartz, Louis. 1955. *The Liberal Tradition in America: An Interpretation of American Political Thought since the Revolution*. New York: Harcourt, Brace.

Harvey, David. 1989. *The Condition of Postmodernity*. Oxford: Blackwell.

Harvey, David. 2005. *A Brief History of Neoliberalism*. Oxford: Oxford University Press.

Harvey, David. 2007. Neoliberalism and Creative Destruction. *Annals of the American Academy of Political and Social Science* 610 (March): 22–44.

Harvey, David. 2008. The Right to the City. *New Left Review* 53 (September–October): 23–40.

Hayden, Dolores. 1984. *Redesigning the American Dream: The Future of Housing, Work, and Family Life*. New York: W. W. Norton.

Hays, R. Allen. 2012. *The Federal Government and Urban Housing*. Albany: State University of New York Press.

Hegel, G. W. F. 1967 [1821]. *The Philosophy of Right*, translated by T. M. Knox. Oxford: Oxford University Press.

Henry, Meghan, Rian Watt, Anna Mahathey, Jillian Ouellette, Aubrey Sitler, and Abt Associates. 2020. *The 2019 Annual Homeless Assessment Report (AHAR) to Congress*. Washington, DC: US Department of Housing and Urban Development, Office of Community Planning and Development. http://files.hudexchange.info/resources/documents/2019-AHAR-Part-1.pdf.

Herbert, Frank. 1979. *The Great Dune Trilogy*. London: Gollancz.

Heskin, Allan David. 1983. *Tenants and the American Dream: Ideology and the Tenant Movement*. New York: Praeger.

Hills v. Gautreaux, 425 U.S. 284 (1976).

Hirt, Sonia. 2013. Home, Sweet Home: American Residential Zoning in Comparative Perspective. *Journal of Planning Education and Research* 33 (3): 292–309.

Hirt, Sonia A. 2014. *Zoned in the USA: The Origins and Implications of American Land-Use Regulation*. Ithaca, NY: Cornell University Press.

Hobbes, Michael. 2019. Progressive Boomers Are Making It Impossible for Cities to Fix the Housing Crisis. *Huffington Post*, July 6, 2019. http://www.huffpost.com/entry

/as-cities-try-to-fix-housing-boomers-are-radicalizing-to-stop-progress_n_5d1bcf0ee4b07f6ca58598a9.

Hofstadter, Richard. 1960. *The Age of Reform*. New York: Vintage Books.

Hohfeld, Wesley Newcomb. 1919. *Fundamental Legal Conceptions as Applied in Judicial Reasoning*. Westport, CT: Greenwood Press.

Hohmann, Jessie. 2014. *The Right to Housing: Law, Concepts, Possibilities*. Oxford: Hart.

Honoré, A. M. 1961. Ownership. In *Oxford Essays in Jurisprudence*, edited by A. G. Guest, 107–147. Oxford: Oxford University Press.

Horne, Thomas A. 1990. *Property Rights and Poverty: Political Argument in Britain, 1605–1834*. Chapel Hill: University of North Carolina Press.

Housing Act of 1937, 42 U.S.C. § 1437 (1937).

Housing Act of 1949, 42 U.S.C. § 1441 (1949).

Howe, Frederic C. 1913. The Remaking of the American City. *Harper's Monthly Magazine*, July 1913.

Hunt, D. Bradford. 2005. Was the 1937 U.S. Housing Act a Pyrrhic Victory? *Journal of Planning History* 4 (3): 195–221.

Huron, Amanda. 2018. *Carving Out the Commons: Tenant Organizing and Housing Cooperatives in Washington, D.C.* Minneapolis: University of Minnesota Press.

Igo, Sarah E. 2018. *The Known Citizen: A History of Privacy in Modern America*. Cambridge, MA: Harvard University Press.

Imbroscio, David L. 2004. Can We Grant a Right to Place? *Politics and Society* 32 (4): 575–609.

Imbroscio, David. 2012. Beyond Mobility: The Limits of Liberal Urban Policy. *Journal of Urban Affairs* 34 (1): 1–20.

Immergluck, Dan. 2009. *Foreclosed: High-Risk Lending, Deregulation, and the Undermining of America's Mortgage Market*. Ithaca, NY: Cornell University Press.

Immerwahr, Daniel. 2015. *Thinking Small: The United States and the Lure of Community Development*. Cambridge, MA: Harvard University Press.

Indritz, Tova. 1971. The Tenants' Rights Movement. *New Mexico Law Review* 1 (1): 1–142.

Ioannides, Yannis M., and Stuart S. Rosenthal. 1994. Estimating the Consumption and Investment Demands for Housing and Their Effect on Housing Tenure Status. *Review of Economics and Statistics* 76 (1) (February): 127–141.

Jackson, Kenneth T. 1980. Race, Ethnicity, and Real Estate Appraisal: The Home Owners Loan Corporation and the Federal Housing Administration. *Journal of Urban History* 6 (4): 419–452.

Jackson, Kenneth. 1985. *Crabgrass Frontier: The Suburbanization of the United States*. New York: Oxford University Press.

Jacobs, In Re, 98 N.Y. 98 (1885).

Jacobs, Jane. 1961. *The Death and Life of Great American Cities*. New York: Vintage Books.

Jefferson, Thomas. 1954 [1787]. *Notes on the State of Virginia*. Chapel Hill: University of North Carolina Press.

Johnson, Senator [Andrew], Cong. Globe, 36th Cong., 1st Sess. 1653 (1860).

Joint Center for Housing Studies of Harvard University. 2019. *The State of the Nation's Housing 2019*. Cambridge, MA: President and Fellows of Harvard College.

Kain, John F. 1992. The Spatial Mismatch Hypothesis: Three Decades Later. *Housing Policy Debate* 3 (2): 371–392.

Kant, Immanuel. 2012 [1785]. *Groundwork of the Metaphysics of Morals*, edited by Mary Gregor and Jens Timmermann. Revised ed. Cambridge: Cambridge University Press.

Kantor, Harvey A. 1974. Benjamin C. Marsh and the Fight over Population Congestion. *Journal of the American Institute of Planners* 40 (6): 422–429.

Katz, Michael B. 1996. *In the Shadow of the Poorhouse: A Social History of Welfare in America*. 10th anniversary ed. New York: Basic Books.

Katz, Stanley N. 1997. Thomas Jefferson and the Right to Property in Revolutionary America. In *Property Rights in the Colonial Era and Early Republic*, edited by James W. Ely Jr., 187–208. New York: Garland.

Katznelson, Ira. 1981. *City Trenches: Urban Politics and the Patterning of Class in the United States*. New York: Pantheon.

Keating, W. Dennis, Michael B. Teitz, and Andrejs Skaburskis. 1998. *Rent Control: Regulation and the Rental Housing Market*. London: Routledge.

Keeling, Brock. 2018. Are You a PHIMBY? *Curbed*, April 13, 2018.

Keightley, Mark P. 2014. *An Analysis of the Geographic Distribution of the Mortgage Interest Deduction*. Washington, DC: Congressional Research Service.

Kelley, Florence. 1906. The Settlements: Their Lost Opportunity. *Charities and the Commons* 16 (April): 79–81.

Kelly, Kristen A. 2002. Private Family, Private Individual: John Locke's Distinction between Paternal and Political Power. *Social Theory and Practice* 28 (3): 361–380.

References

Kent, James. 1826. *Commentaries on American Law, Vol. 2*. New York: O. Halsted.

Kerr, Gavin. 2017. *The Property-Owning Democracy: Freedom and Capitalism in the Twenty-First Century*. New York: Routledge.

Kersten, Stephen A. 1973. Housing Regulation and Reform in Boston, 1822–1924: Antecedents of Zoning. Studies in Political Economy Working Paper 7, Brandeis University, Waltham, MA.

King, Peter. 2003. *A Social Philosophy of Housing*. Aldershot: Ashgate.

Knafo, Saki. 2015. Is Gentrification a Human Rights Violation? *The Atlantic*, September 2, 2015.

Kwak, Nancy H. 2015. *A World of Homeowners: American Power and the Politics of Housing Aid*. Chicago: University of Chicago Press.

Kymlicka, Will. 2002. *Contemporary Political Philosophy: An Introduction*. Oxford: Oxford University Press.

Ladd, Brian. 1990. *Urban Planning and Civic Order in Germany, 1860–1914*. Cambridge, MA: Harvard University Press.

Lamb, Robert. 2015. *Thomas Paine and the Idea of Human Rights*. Cambridge: Cambridge University Press.

Larmore, Charles. 1987. *Patterns of Moral Complexity*. Cambridge: Cambridge University Press.

Larmore, Charles. 2003. Patterns of Moral Complexity, Selections. In *Perfectionism and Neutrality: Essays in Liberal Theory*, edited by Steven Wall and George Klosko, 47–60. Lanham, MD: Rowman and Littlefield.

Lause, Mark A. 2005. *Young America: Land, Labor, and the Republican Community*. Urbana: University of Illinois Press.

Lawson, Ronald. 1984. The Rent Strike in New York City, 1904–1980: The Evolution of a Social Movement Strategy. *Journal of Urban History* 10 (3): 235–258.

Lawton v. Steele, 152 U.S. 133 (1894).

Leepson, M. 1979. *Rental Housing Shortage*. Editorial Research Reports 1979 (Vol. 2). Washington, DC: CQ Press.

Lefebvre, Henri. 1968. *Le droit à la ville*. Paris: Anthropos.

Lehrer, Joseph D. 1973. Housing and Land Use—Lindsey v. Normet: A Supreme Court Refusal to Federalize Oregon's Landlord-Tenant Procedure. *Urban Law Annual* 1973 (1) (January): 309–318.

Leishman, Chris. 2001. Housing Building and Product Differentiation: An Hedonic Price Approach. *Journal of Housing and the Built Environment* 16 (2): 131–152.

Leonard, Thomas C. 2005. Retrospectives: Eugenics and Economics in the Progressive Era. *Journal of Economic Perspectives* 19 (4): 207–224.

Leonard, Thomas C. 2016. *Illiberal Reformers: Race, Eugenics, and American Economics in the Progressive Era*. Princeton, NJ: Princeton University Press.

Leong, Nancy. 2013. Racial Capitalism. *Harvard Law Review* 126 (8): 2151–2226.

Lessig, Lawrence. 1995. The Regulation of Social Meaning. *University of Chicago Law Review* 62 (3): 943–1045.

Lewis, Hope. 2008. "New" Human Rights: U.S. Ambivalence toward the International Economic and Social Rights Framework. In *Bringing Human Rights Home, Vol. 1: A History of Human Rights in the United States*, edited by Cynthia Soohoo, Catherine Albisa, and Martha F. Davis, 103–144. Westport, CT: Praeger.

Light, Jennifer. 2011. Discriminating Appraisals: Cartography, Computation, and Access to Federal Mortgage Insurance in the 1930s. *Technology and Culture* 52 (3): 485–522.

Lindsay, Matthew J. 2010. In Search of "Laissez Faire Constitutionalism." *Harvard Law Review* 123 (5): 55–78.

Lindsey v. Normet, 405 U.S. 56 (1972).

Linklater, Andro. 2013. *Owning the Earth: The Transforming History of Land Ownership*. New York: Bloomsbury.

Linmark Associates, Inc. v. Willingboro, 431 U.S. 85 (1977).

Lippmann, Walter. 1914. *Drift and Mastery: An Attempt to Diagnose the Current Unrest*. New York: Mitchell Kennerley.

Lippmann, Walter. 1938. *An Inquiry into the Principles of the Good Society*. Boston: Little, Brown.

Lochner v. New York, 198 U.S. 45 (1905).

Locke, John. 1895 [1689]. *Of Civil Government and Toleration*. London: Cassell.

Locke, John. 1980 [1690]. *Second Treatise of Government*, edited by C. B. Macpherson. Indianapolis: Hackett.

Logan, John R., and Brian Stults. 2011. The Persistence of Segregation in the Metropolis: New Findings from the 2010 Census. Census brief prepared for Project US2010, Brown University.

Lough, Alexandra Wagner. 2013. The Last Tax: Henry George and the Social Politics of Land Reform in the Gilded Age and Progressive Era. PhD diss., Brandeis University, Department of History.

Lubove, Roy. 1961. Lawrence Veiller and the New York State Tenement House Commission of 1900. *Mississippi Valley Historical Review* 47 (4): 659–677.

Lubove, Roy. 1962. *The Progressives and the Slums: Tenement House Reform in New York City, 1890–1917*. Pittsburgh, PA: University of Pittsburgh Press.

Lung-Amam, Willow S. 2017. *Trespassers? Asian Americans and the Battle for Suburbia*. Oakland: University of California Press.

Lyons, David. 1982. Utility and Rights. *Nomos* 24:107–138.

Macedo, Stephen. 1990. *Liberal Virtues: Citizenship, Virtue, and Community in Liberal Constitutionalism*. Oxford: Clarendon Press.

Mack, Eric. 2000. In Defense of the Jurisdiction Theory of Rights. *Journal of Ethics* 4 (1–2): 71–98.

MacKinnon, Catherine A. 1987. *Feminism Uncommodified: Discourses on Life and Law*. Cambridge, MA: Harvard University Press.

Macpherson, C. B. 1987. *The Rise and Fall of Economic Justice and Other Essays*. New York: Oxford University Press.

Madden, David, and Peter Marcuse. 2016. *In Defense of Housing*. London: Verso.

Mancilla, Alejandra. 2016. *The Right of Necessity: Moral Cosmopolitanism and Global Poverty*. London: Rowman and Littlefield.

Mandell, Betty Reid. 2012. The Rise and Fall of ACORN. *New Politics* 13 (4) (Winter): http://newpol.org/review/rise-and-fall-acorn/.

Manduca, Robert A. 2019. The Contribution of National Income Inequality to Regional Economic Divergence. *Social Forces* 98 (2): 622–648.

Maness, David L., and Muneeza Khan. 2014. Care of the Homeless: An Overview. *American Family Physician* 89 (8): 634–640.

Marcuse, Peter. 1980. Housing in Early City Planning. *Journal of Urban History* 6 (2) (February 1): 153–173.

Marsh, Benjamin Clarke. 1953. *Lobbyist for the People: A Record of Fifty Years*. Washington, DC: Public Affairs Press.

Marshall, T. H. 1950. *"Citizenship and Social Class" and Other Essays*. Cambridge: Cambridge University Press.

Martin, James J. 1957. *Men against the State*. New York: Libertarian Book Club.

Marx, Karl. 1978 [1843]. On the Jewish Question. In *The Marx-Engels Reader*, 2nd ed., edited by Robert C. Tucker, 26–52. New York: W. W. Norton.

Maslow, A. H. 1943. A Theory of Human Motivation. *Psychological Review* 50 (4): 370–396.

Mason, Andrew. 2004. Just Constraints. *British Journal of Political Science* 34 (2): 251–268.

Mason, David L. 2004. *From Buildings and Loans to Bail-Outs: A History of the American Savings and Loan Industry, 1831–1995*. Cambridge: Cambridge University Press.

Masquerier, Lewis. 1877. *Sociology: Or, the Reconstruction of Society, Government, and Property*. New York: Published by the author.

McCabe, Brian J. 2016. *No Place like Home: Wealth, Community & the Politics of Homeownership*. Oxford: Oxford University Press.

McClure, Kirk. 2019. The Allocation of Rental Assistance Resources: The Paradox of High Housing Costs and High Vacancy Rates. *International Journal of Housing Policy* 19 (1): 69–94.

McDonnell, Timothy L. 1957. *The Wagner Housing Act: A Case Study of the Legislative Process*. Chicago: Loyola University Press.

Meehan, James. 2014. Reinventing Real Estate: The Community Land Trust as a Social Innovation in Affordable Housing. *Journal of Applied Social Science* 8 (2): 113–133.

Michelman, Frank I. 1970. The Advent of a Right to Housing: A Current Appraisal. *Harvard Civil Rights–Civil Liberties Law Review* 5 (2): 207–226.

Mill, John Stuart. 1965 [1848]. *Principles of Political Economy*, edited by J. M. Robson. London: Routledge and Kegan Paul.

Mill, John Stuart. 1978 [1859]. *On Liberty*. Indianapolis: Hackett.

Miller, David. 1999. *Principles of Social Justice*. Cambridge, MA: Harvard University Press.

Miller, Kenneth E. 2010. *From Progressive to New Dealer: Frederic C. Howe and American Liberalism*. University Park: Pennsylvania State University Press.

Mink, Gwendolyn, and Alice O'Connor. 2004. *Poverty in the United States: An Encyclopedia of History, Politics, and Policy*. Santa Barbara, CA: ABC-CLIO.

Mirowski, Philip, and Dieter Plehwe. 2009. *The Road from Mont Pèlerin: The Making of the Neoliberal Thought Collective*. Cambridge, MA: Harvard University Press.

Mitchell, Don. 2003. *The Right to the City: Social Justice and the Fight for Public Space*. New York: Guilford Press.

Moses, Julia. 2019. Social Citizenship and Social Rights in an Age of Extremes: T. H. Marshall's Social Philosophy in the *Longue Durée*. *Modern Intellectual History* 16 (1): 155–184.

References

Moyn, Samuel. 2018. *Not Enough: Human Rights in an Unequal World*. Cambridge, MA: Belknap Press.

Moynihan, Daniel P. 1969. *Maximum Feasible Misunderstanding*. New York: Free Press.

Mugler v. Kansas, 123 U.S. 623 (1887).

Muller v. Oregon, 208 U.S. 412 (1908).

Murphy, Liam, and Thomas Nagel. 2002. *The Myth of Ownership: Taxes and Justice*. New York: Oxford University Press.

National Advisory Commission on Civil Disorders. 1968. *Report of the National Advisory Commission on Civil Disorders*. Washington, DC: National Institute of Justice.

National Commission on Urban Problems. 1968. *Building the American City*. Washington, DC: Government Printing Office.

National Law Center on Homelessness and Poverty (NLCHP). 2014. *Human Rights to Human Reality: A 10 Step Guide to Strategic Human Rights Advocacy*. Washington, DC: National Law Center on Homelessness and Poverty.

Nedelsky, Jennifer. 1990. *Private Property and the Limits of American Constitutionalism: The Madisonian Framework and Its Legacy*. Chicago: University of Chicago Press.

Nelson, Eric. 2008. From Primary Goods to Capabilities: Distributive Justice and the Problem of Neutrality. *Political Theory* 36 (1): 93–122.

New York City Housing Authority v. Muller, 1 N.E.2d 153 (N.Y. 1936).

New York Constitution, Article XVII, § 1.

New York Times. 1971. Tenants Prepare a National Drive. *New York Times*, November 7, 1971.

Nightingale, Carl H. 2012. *Segregation: A Global History of Divided Cities*. Chicago: University of Chicago Press.

North, Douglass C. 1966. *The Economic Growth of the United States 1790–1860*. New York: W. W. Norton.

Nozick, Robert. 1974. *Anarchy, State, and Utopia*. New York: Basic Books.

Nussbaum, Martha C. 2000. *Women and Human Development*. Cambridge: Cambridge University Press.

Nussbaum, Martha C. 2006. *Frontiers of Justice: Disability, Nationality, Species Membership*. Cambridge, MA: Harvard University Press.

Oberlander, Peter H., and Eva Newbrun. 1999. *Houser: The Life and Work of Catherine Bauer*. Vancouver: University of British Columbia Press.

O'Donnell, Edward T. 2015. *Henry George and the Crisis of Inequality: Progress and Poverty in the Gilded Age*. New York: Columbia University Press.

Office of Management and Budget (OMB). 2019a. *A Budget for a Better America. Promises Kept. Taxpayers First*. Washington, DC: US Government Publishing Office.

Office of Management and Budget (OMB). 2019b. *A Budget for a Better America. Promises Kept. Taxpayers First. Analytical Perspectives*. Washington, DC: US Government Publishing Office.

Okin, Susan Moller. 1979. *Women in Western Political Thought*. Princeton, NJ: Princeton University Press.

O'Neill, Onora. 2016. *Justice across Boundaries: Whose Obligations?* Cambridge: Cambridge University Press.

Ostrom, Vincent, Charles M. Tiebout, and Robert Warren. 1961. The Organization of Government in Metropolitan Areas: A Theoretical Inquiry. *American Political Science Review* 55 (4): 831–842.

Otsuka, Michael. 2003. *Libertarianism without Inequality*. Oxford: Clarendon Press.

Paine, Thomas. 1995 [1797]. *Rights of Man, Common Sense, and Other Political Writings*, edited by Mark Philp. Oxford: Oxford University Press.

Pateman, Carole. 1988. *The Sexual Contract*. Oxford: Polity.

Patrick, John J. 1995. The Virginia Declaration of Rights (June 12, 1776). In *Founding the Republic: A Documentary History*, edited by John J. Patrick, 52–55. Westport, CT: Greenwood Press.

Pembina Consolidated Silver Mining Company v. Pennsylvania, 125 U.S. 181 (1888).

Pennsylvania Coal Co. v. Mahon, 260 U.S. 393 (1922).

Perlman, Selig. 1923. *A History of Trade Unionism in the United States*. New York: Macmillan.

Pessen, Edward. 1954. Thomas Skidmore, Agrarian Reformer in the Early American Labor Movement. *New York History* 35 (3): 280–296.

Pestritto, Ronald J., and William J. Atto. 2008. *American Progressivism: A Reader*. Lanham, MD: Lexington Books.

Peterson, Jon A. 2009. The Birth of Organized City Planning in the United States, 1909–1910. *Journal of the American Planning Association* 75 (2): 123–133.

Pettit, Philip. 1997. *Republicanism: A Theory of Freedom and Government*. Oxford: Oxford University Press.

Phillips, Anne. 1999. *Which Equalities Matter?* Oxford: Polity.

Pieper, Josef. 2009. *Leisure: The Basis of Culture*. San Francisco: Ignatius Press.

Piketty, Thomas. 2014. *Capital in the Twenty-First Century*. Cambridge, MA: Belknap Press.

Pocock, J. G. A. 2003. *The Machiavellian Moment: Florentine Political Thought and the Atlantic Republican Tradition*. Princeton, NJ: Princeton University Press.

Poe, Edgar Allan. 1984 [1849]. *Poetry and Tales*. New York: Library of America.

Pogge, Thomas. 2002. *World Poverty and Human Rights*. Cambridge: Blackwell.

Polikoff, Alexander. 1986. Sustainable Integration or Inevitable Resegregation: The Troubling Questions. In *Housing Desegregation and Federal Policy*, edited by John M. Goering, 43–71. Chapel Hill: University of North Carolina Press.

Pollock v. Farmers' Loan & Trust Co., 157 U.S. 429 (1895).

Ponder, Emily. 2016. Gentrification and the Right to Housing: How Hip Becomes a Human Rights Violation. *Southwestern Journal of International Law* 22 (2): 359–383.

Popkin, Susan J., Bruce Katz, Mary K. Cunningham, Karen D. Brown, Jeremy Gustafson, and Margery A. Turner. 2004. *A Decade of HOPE VI: Research Findings and Policy Challenges*. Washington, DC: Urban Institute.

Post, Louis F., and Fred C. Leubuscher. 1961 [1887]. *Henry George's 1886 Campaign: An Account of the George-Hewitt Campaign in the New York Municipal Election of 1886*. New York: Henry George School of Social Science.

Pottinger v. City of Miami, 720 F. Supp. 955 (S.D. Fla. 1989).

Powell, Catherine. 2008. *Human Rights at Home: A Domestic Policy Blueprint for the New Administration*. Washington, DC: American Constitution Society for Law and Policy.

Power, Garrett. 1983. Apartheid Baltimore Style: The Residential Segregation Ordinances of 1910–1913. *Maryland Law Review* 42 (2): 289–328.

Power, Garrett. 1989. The Advent of Zoning. *Planning Perspectives* 4 (1): 1–13.

Price, Edward T. 1995. *Dividing the Land: Early American Beginnings of Our Private Property Mosaic*. Chicago: University of Chicago Press.

Proudhon, Pierre-Joseph. 1876. *What Is Property?*, translated by Benjamin Tucker. Princeton, MA: Benjamin R. Tucker.

Purcell, Mark. 2002. Excavating Lefebvre: The Right to the City and Its Urban Politics of the Inhabitant. *GeoJournal* 58:99–108.

Purcell, Mark. 2013. Possible Worlds: Henri Lefebvre and the Right to the City. *Journal of Urban Affairs* 36 (1): 141–154.

Quinn, Sarah Lehman. 2010. Government Policy, Housing, and the Origins of Securitization, 1780–1968. PhD diss., University of California, Berkeley.

Radford, Gail. 1996. *Modern Housing for America: Policy Struggles in the New Deal Era.* Chicago: University of Chicago Press.

Radin, Margaret Jane. 1993. *Reinterpreting Property.* Chicago: University of Chicago Press.

Rankin, Sara. 2015. A Homeless Bill of Rights (Revolution). *Seton Hall Law Review* 45 (2): 383–434.

Ratcliff, Richard U. 1949. *Urban Land Economics.* New York: McGraw-Hill.

Rawls, John. 1971. *A Theory of Justice.* Cambridge, MA: Harvard University Press.

Rawls, John. 1975. Fairness to Goodness. *Philosophical Review* 84 (4): 536–554.

Rawls, John. 1993. *Political Liberalism.* New York: Columbia University Press.

Rawls, John. 1997. The Idea of Public Reason Revisited. *University of Chicago Law Review* 64 (3): 765–807.

Raz, Joseph. 1986. *The Morality of Freedom.* Oxford: Clarendon Press.

Reich, Charles. 1964. The New Property. *Yale Law Journal* 73 (5): 733–787.

Reeves, Richard V. 2017. *Dream Hoarders: How the American Upper Middle Class Is Leaving Everyone Else in the Dust, Why That Is a Problem, and What to Do About It.* Washington, DC: Brookings Institution Press.

Revell, Keith D. 1999. The Road to Euclid v. Ambler: City Planning, State-Building, and the Changing Scope of the Police Power. *Studies in American Political Development* 13 (1): 50–145.

Right to the City Alliance. 2015. *Block by Block: Renter Nation Assembly Toolkit.* New York: Right to the City Alliance.

Riis, Jacob A. 1890. *How the Other Half Lives: Studies among the Tenements of New York.* New York: Charles Scribner's Sons.

Risse, Mathias. 2012. *On Global Justice.* Princeton, NJ: Princeton University Press.

Robinson, Cedric. 1983. *Black Marxism: The Making of the Black Radical Tradition.* Chapel Hill: University of North Carolina Press.

Rodgers, Daniel T. 1998. *Atlantic Crossings: Social Politics in a Progressive Age.* Cambridge, MA: Belknap Press of Harvard University Press.

Roemer, John E. 1998. *Equality of Opportunity.* Cambridge, MA: Harvard University Press.

Rognlie, Matthew. 2015. Deciphering the Fall and Rise in the Net Capital Share: Accumulation or Scarcity? Brookings Papers on Economic Activity, Brookings Institution, Washington, DC.

Rohe, William. 1991. Expanding Urban Homesteading. *Journal of the American Planning Association* 57 (4): 444–455.

Rondel, David. 2018. *Pragmatist Egalitarianism*. New York: Oxford University Press.

Roosevelt, Theodore. 1924. *Theodore Roosevelt: An Autobiography*. New York: Charles Scribner's Sons.

Rosen, Sam. 2017. Atlanta's Controversial "Cityhood" Movement. *The Atlantic*, April 26, 2017. https://www.theatlantic.com/business/archive/2017/04/the-border-battles-of-atlanta/523884/.

Rothstein, Richard. 2017. *The Color of Law: A Forgotten History of How Our Government Segregated America*. New York: Liveright.

Roy, Ananya. 2017. Dis/possessive Collectivism: Property and Personhood at City's End. *Geoforum* 80:A1–A11.

Rubinowitz, Leonard, and James E. Rosenbaum. 2000. *Crossing the Class and Color Lines*. Chicago: University of Chicago Press.

Rusk, David. 2001. *The "Segregation Tax": The Cost of Racial Segregation to Black Homeowners*. Washington, DC: Brookings Institution Program on Metropolitan Policy.

Salviati, Chris, Igor Popov, and Rob Warnock. 2020. Apartment List National Rent Report. *Apartment List*, December 28, 2020. https://www.apartmentlist.com/research/national-rent-data.

San Antonio School District v. Rodriguez, 411 U.S. 1 (1973).

Sandel, Michael J. 1998a. *Democracy's Discontent: America in Search of a Public Philosophy*. Cambridge, MA: Harvard University Press.

Sandel, Michael J. 1998b. *Liberalism and the Limits of Justice*. 2nd ed. Cambridge: Cambridge University Press.

Sanders, Bernie. 2007. Remarks before the U.S. Senate, September 4, 2007. User-created video clip from C-SPAN, July 15, 2015, 11:42. https://www.c-span.org/video/?c4544522/user-clip-sen-bernie-sanders-dream-turned-nightmare.

Scanlon, T. M. 1998. *What We Owe to Each Other*. Cambridge, MA: Belknap Press.

Scanlon, T. M. 2018. *Why Does Inequality Matter?* Oxford: Oxford University Press.

Schafer, Axel R. 2000. *American Progressives and German Social Reform, 1875–1920*. Stuttgart: Steiner.

Schneider, Benjamin. 2018a. Meet the PHIMBYs. *CityLab*, April 13, 2018. http://www.citylab.com/equity/2018/04/nimbys-yimbys-and-phimbys-oh-my/557927/.

Schneider, Benjamin. 2018b. The American Housing Crisis Might Be Our Next Big Political Issue. *Citylab*, May 16, 2018. http://www.citylab.com/equity/2018/05/is-housing-americas-next-big-political-issue/560378/.

Schneider, Tatjana, and Jeremy Till. 2007. *Flexible Housing*. London: Routledge.

Schwartz, Alex F. 2015. *Housing Policy in the United States*. 3rd ed. New York: Routledge.

Segall, Shlomi. 2010. *Health, Luck, and Justice*. Princeton, NJ: Princeton University Press.

Sen, Amartya. 1985. *Commodities and Capabilities*. Amsterdam: North-Holland.

Sen, Amartya. 2009. *The Idea of Justice*. Cambridge, MA: Belknap Press.

Shannon v. HUD, 305 F. Supp. 205 (E.D. Pa. 1969).

Shapiro, Thomas M. 2004. *The Hidden Cost of Being African American: How Wealth Perpetuates Inequality*. Oxford: Oxford University Press.

Shapiro v. Thompson, 394 U.S. 618 (1969).

Shelby, Tommie. 2016. *Dark Ghettos: Injustice, Dissent, and Reform*. Cambridge, MA: Belknap Press.

Shelley v. Kraemer, 334 U.S. 1 (1948).

Sheppard, Steve, ed. 2003. *The Selected Writings and Speeches of Sir Edward Coke, Vol. 1*. Indianapolis: Liberty Fund.

Shue, Henry. 1996. *Basic Rights: Subsistence, Affluence, and U.S. Foreign Policy*. 2nd ed. Princeton, NJ: Princeton University Press.

Sidgwick, Henry. 1890. *The Methods of Ethics*. 4th ed. London: Macmillan.

Silver, Christopher. 1997. The Racial Origins of Zoning in American Cities. In *Urban Planning and the African American Community: In the Shadows*, edited by June Manning Thomas and Marsha Ritzdorf, 23–42. Thousand Oaks, CA: Sage Publications.

Sinclair, Upton. 1906. *The Jungle*. New York: Doubleday, Page.

Sitaraman, Ganesh. 2017. *The Crisis of the Middle-Class Constitution: Why Economic Inequality Threatens Our Republic*. New York: Alfred A. Knopf.

Skidmore, Thomas. 1829. *The Rights of Man to Property!* New York: Printed for the author by Alexander Ming Jr.

Skinner, Quentin. 1998. *Liberty before Liberalism*. Cambridge: Cambridge University Press.

References

Slack, Paul. 1995. *The English Poor Law, 1531–1782.* Cambridge: Cambridge University Press.

Slaughterhouse Cases, 83 U.S. 36 (1873).

Smith, Adam. 1827 [1776]. *An Inquiry into the Nature and Causes of the Wealth of Nations.* Edinburgh: Thomas Nelson and Peter Brown.

Smith, Adam. 2000 [1759]. *The Theory of Moral Sentiments.* Amherst, NY: Prometheus Books.

Smith, Henry E. 2004. Exclusion and Property Rules in the Law of Nuisance. *Virginia Law Review* 90 (4): 965–1049.

Smith, Neil. 2010. Building the Frontier Myth. In *The Gentrification Debates*, ed. Japonica Brown-Saracino, 113–117. New York: Routledge.

Speek, Peter Alexander. 1915. The Singletax and the Labor Movement. PhD diss., University of Wisconsin.

Steil, Justin. 2018. Antisubordination Planning. *Journal of Planning Education and Research.* Published online December 7, 2018. https://doi.org/10.1177/0739456X18815739.

Stobo, J. R. 2008. Organized Labor, Housing Issues, and Politics: Another Look at the 1886 Henry George Mayoral Campaign in New York City. Working paper, Columbia University.

Sunstein, Cass. 2004. *The Second Bill of Rights: FDR's Unfinished Revolution and Why We Need It More Than Ever.* New York: Basic Books.

Swyngedouw, Erik. 1997. Neither Global nor Local: "Glocalization" and the Politics of Scale. In *Spaces of Globalization: Reasserting the Power of the Local*, edited by K. Cox, 137–166. New York: Guilford Press.

Syrett, Harold C., and Jacob E. Cooke, eds. 1962. *The Papers of Alexander Hamilton, Vol. IV: January 1787–May 1788.* New York: Columbia University Press.

Tax, Sol. 1959. Residential Integration: The Case of Hyde Park in Chicago. *Human Organization* 18 (1): 22–27.

Texas Dept. of Housing and Community Affairs v. Inclusive Communities Project, Inc. No. 13-1371, 576 U.S. ___, slip op. at 23 (2015).

Tiberius, Valerie. 2015. Prudential Value. In *The Oxford Handbook of Value Theory*, edited by Iwao Hirose and Jonas Olson, 158–174. Oxford: Oxford University Press.

Tiebout, Charles. 1956. A Pure Theory of Local Expenditures. *Journal of Political Economy* 64 (5): 416–424.

Tilly, Charles. 1999. *Durable Inequality.* Berkeley: University of California Press.

Trenchard, John. 1755. *Cato's Letters: Or, Essays on Liberty, Civil and Religious, and Other Important Subjects, Vol. 3.* London: J. Walthoe, T. and T. Longman.

Trustees of Dartmouth College v. Woodward, 17 U.S. 518 (1819).

Tucker, Robert C. 1978. *The Marx-Engels Reader.* 2nd ed. New York: W. W. Norton.

United States v. Certain Lands in the City of Louisville, 78 F.2d 684 (6th Cir. 1935).

US Bureau of the Census. 1949. *Historical Statistics of the United States 1789–1945.* Washington, DC: US Department of Commerce, Bureau of the Census, and the Social Science Research Council.

US Department of Housing and Urban Development (HUD). 2015. *24 CFR Parts 5, 91, 92, 570, 574, 576, and 903. Affirmatively Furthering Fair Housing, Final Rule, July 16.* Washington, DC: US Department of Housing and Urban Development.

US Department of Housing and Urban Development (HUD). 2016. *PD&R: A Historical Investigation at (Almost) 50: A HUD 50th Anniversary Publication.* Washington, DC: US Department of Housing and Urban Development, Office of Policy Development and Research.

US Department of Housing and Urban Development (HUD). 2019. *Methodology for Determining Section 8 Income Limits.* Washington, DC: US Department of Housing and Urban Development. http://www.huduser.gov/portal/datasets/il//il19/IncomeLimits Methodology-FY19.pdf.

US Government Accountability Office (GAO). 2010. *Housing and Community Development Grants: HUD Needs to Enhance Its Requirements and Oversight of Jurisdictions' Fair Housing Plans.* Washington, DC: US Government Accountability Office.

US House of Representatives. 2020. Yes in My Backyard Act. H.R. 4351. 116th Cong., 2nd Sess.

Vale, Lawrence J. 2000. *From the Puritans to the Projects.* Cambridge, MA: Harvard University Press.

Vale, Lawrence J. 2007. The Ideological Origins of Affordable Homeownership Efforts. In *Chasing the American Dream: New Perspectives on Affordable Homeownership,* edited by William H. Rohe and Harry L. Watson, 15–40. Ithaca, NY: Cornell University Press.

Vanhorne's Lessee v. Dorrance, 2 U.S. 304 (1795).

Van Parijs, Philippe, and Yannick Vanderborght. 2017. *Basic Income: A Radical Proposal for a Free Society and a Sane Economy.* Cambridge, MA: Harvard University Press.

Veblen, Thorstein. 1912 [1899]. *The Theory of the Leisure Class: An Economic Study of Institutions.* New York: Macmillan.

References

Veiller, Lawrence. 1914. Housing Reform through Legislation. *Annals of the American Academy of Political and Social Science* 51 (1): 68–77.

Village of Arlington Heights v. Metropolitan Housing Development Corp., 429 U.S. 252 (1977).

Village of Euclid v. Ambler Realty Company, 272 U.S. 365 (1926).

Vincent, Carol Hardy, Laura A. Hanson, and Carla N. Argueta. 2017. *Federal Land Ownership: Overview and Data*. Washington, DC: Congressional Research Service.

von Hoffman, Alexander. 1998a. The Origins of American Housing Reform. Working Paper W98-2, Harvard University Joint Center for Housing Studies, Cambridge, MA.

von Hoffman, Alexander. 1998b. Like Fleas on a Tiger: A Brief History of the Open Housing Movement. Working Paper W98-3, Harvard University Joint Center for Housing Studies, Cambridge, MA.

von Hoffman, Alexander. 2000. A Study in Contradictions: The Origins and Legacy of the Housing Act of 1949. *Housing Policy Debate* 11 (2): 299–326.

von Hoffman, Alexander. 2008. Enter the Housing Industry, Stage Right: A Working Paper on the History of Housing Policy. Working Paper W08-1, Harvard University Joint Center for Housing Studies, Cambridge, MA.

von Hoffman, Alexander. 2009. Let Us Continue: Housing Policy in the Great Society, Part One. Working Paper W09-3, Harvard University Joint Center for Housing Studies, Cambridge, MA.

von Hoffman, Alexander. 2012a. History Lessons for Today's Housing Policy: The Political Processes of Making Low-Income Housing Policy. Working Paper W12-5, Harvard University Joint Center for Housing Studies, Cambridge, MA.

von Hoffman, Alexander. 2012b. The Past, Present, and Future of Community Development in the United States. Working Paper W12-6, Harvard University Joint Center for Housing Studies, Cambridge, MA.

Waldron, Jeremy. 1987. *"Nonsense upon Stilts": Bentham, Burke and Marx on the Rights of Man*. London: Methuen.

Waldron, Jeremy. 1988. *The Right to Private Property*. Oxford: Clarendon Press.

Waldron, Jeremy. 1991. Homelessness and the Issue of Freedom. *UCLA Law Review* 39 (1) (October): 295–324.

Waldron, Jeremy. 2009. Dignity, Rank, and Rights. Tanner Lectures on Human Values, delivered at the University of California, Berkeley, April 21–23, 2009. http://tannerlectures.utah.edu/_documents/a-to-z/w/Waldron_09.pdf.

Wall, Steven. 1998. *Liberalism, Perfectionism, and Restraint.* Cambridge: Cambridge University Press.

Wallace, John William. 1873. *Cases Argued and Adjudged in the Supreme Court of the United States, December Term, 1872, Vol. 16.* Washington, DC: W. H. and O. H. Morrison.

Wallis, Allan D. 1991. *Wheel Estate.* Oxford: Oxford University Press.

Walzer, Michael. 1983. *Spheres of Justice: A Defense of Pluralism and Equality.* New York: Basic Books.

Walzer, Michael. 1985. Interpretation and Social Criticism. Tanner Lectures on Human Values, delivered at Harvard University, November 13–14, 1985. http://tannerlectures.utah.edu/_documents/a-to-z/w/walzer88.pdf.

Ware, Leland B. 1989. Invisible Walls: An Examination of the Legal Strategy of the Restrictive Covenant Cases. *Washington University Law Review* 67 (3): 737–772.

Warren, Samuel D., and Louis D. Brandeis. 1890. The Right to Privacy. *Harvard Law Review* 4 (5): 193–220.

Watson, Nicole Elsasser, Barry L. Steffen, Marge Martin, and David A. Vandenbroucke. 2020. *Worst Case Housing Needs: 2019 Report to Congress.* Washington, DC: US Department of Housing and Urban Development, Office of Policy Development and Research. https://www.huduser.gov/portal/sites/default/files/pdf/worst-case-housing-needs-2020.pdf.

Weinstein, David. 2007. *Utilitarianism and the New Liberalism.* Cambridge: Cambridge University Press.

Weiss, Marc A. 1989. Richard T. Ely and the Contribution of Economic Research to National Housing Policy, 1920–1940. *Urban Studies* 26 (1): 115–126.

Welfeld, Irving. 1992. *HUD Scandals: Howling Headlines and Silent Fiascoes.* New Brunswick, NJ: Transaction.

Wells, Katy. 2016. The Right to Personal Property. *Politics, Philosophy and Economics* 15 (4): 358–378.

Wells v. Commissioners of Hyattsville, 77 Md. 125, 26 A. 357 (1893).

West, Thomas G. 2017. *The Political Theory of the American Founding: Natural Rights, Public Policy, and the Moral Conditions of Freedom.* Cambridge: Cambridge University Press.

Wheelock, David C. 2008. Changing the Rules: State Mortgage Foreclosure Moratoria during the Great Depression. *Federal Reserve Bank of St. Louis Review* 90 (6): 569–583.

Wheildon, L. 1946. *National Housing Emergency, 1946–1947*. Editorial Research Reports 1946 (Vol. 2). Washington, DC: CQ Press.

Whitman, Walt. 1856. New York Dissected. *Life Illustrated*, July 19, 1856.

Whitman, Walt. 1964 [1892]. *Prose Works 1892, Vol. 2: Collect and Other Prose*, edited by Floyd Stovall. New York: New York University Press.

Wiebe, Robert H. 1967. *The Search for Order, 1877–1920*. New York: Hill and Wang.

Williams v. Barry, 708 F.2d 789, 793 (D.C. Cir. 1983).

Williamson, Chilton. 2019. *American Suffrage: From Property to Democracy, 1760–1860*. Princeton, NJ: Princeton University Press.

Williamson, Thad. 2010. *Sprawl, Justice, and Citizenship: The Civic Costs of the American Way of Life*. Oxford: Oxford University Press.

Wilson, James Q. 1966. *Urban Renewal: The Record and the Controversy*. Cambridge, MA: MIT Press.

Wilson, William Julius. 1990. *The Truly Disadvantaged: The Inner City, the Underclass, and Public Policy*. Chicago: University of Chicago Press.

Winthrop, Robert C. 1869 [1629]. *Life and Letters of John Winthrop, Governor of the Massachusetts-Bay Company at Their Emigration to New England, 1630*. Boston: Little, Brown.

Wolf, Edward N. 2014. Household Wealth Trends in the United States, 1962–2013: What Happened over the Great Recession? NBER Working Paper 20733, National Bureau of Economic Research, Cambridge, MA.

Wolman, Leo. 1933. Wages during the Depression. *National Bureau of Economic Research Bulletin* 46:1–5.

Wood, Edith Elmer. 1931. *Recent Trends in American Housing*. New York: Macmillan.

Wood, Gordon. 1998. *The Creation of the American Republic: 1776–1787*. Chapel Hill: University of North Carolina Press.

Woolf, Virginia. 1929. *A Room of One's Own*. Orlando, FL: Harcourt.

Wright, Gwendolyn. 1981. *Building the Dream: A Social History of Housing in America*. Cambridge, MA: MIT Press.

Yinger, John. 1995. *Closed Doors, Opportunities Lost: The Continuing Costs of Housing Discrimination*. New York: Russell Sage Foundation.

Young, Arthur Nicholas. 1916. *The Single Tax Movement in the United States*. Princeton, NJ: Princeton University Press.

Young, Iris Marion. 1990. *Justice and the Politics of Difference*. Princeton, NJ: Princeton University Press.

Young, Iris Marion. 1999. Residential Segregation and Differentiated Citizenship. *Citizenship Studies* 3 (2): 237–252.

Young, Iris Marion. 2002. *Inclusion and Democracy*. New York: Oxford University Press.

Zundel, Alan F. 2000. *Declarations of Dependency: The Civic Republican Tradition in U.S. Poverty Policy*. Albany: State University of New York Press.

Index

Abrams, Charles, 106
ACORN (Association of Community Organizations for Reform Now), 140–141
Adams, John, 37–38, 173, 250n7
Adams, Willi Paul, 39
Advisory Commission on Intergovernmental Relations, 254n2
Affordable housing. *See also* Housing policy reform proposal
  affordability crisis, 4, 5, 6–7, 146, 249n1
  California crisis, 6–7
  COVID-19 and, 249n2
  Dudley Street Neighborhood Initiative (DSNI), 147
  filtering process and, 136, 220–221
  foreclosure crisis and, 4
  gentrification and, 6
  homebuilding industry and, 89–90, 127, 134–136
  housing market segmentation and, 3–4, 212
  LIHTC program, 6–7, 128, 149, 223, 225, 255
  modern housing and, 89, 95–96, 122, 137, 145–146, 153–154
  New Deal federal housing policy, 90–98
  NIMBY (not in my back yard), 5–6, 7, 146
  postwar homeownership, 98–101
  private-sector housing and, 7
  public housing and, 6, 89–90, 94–97, 100, 101, 127, 133–134, 139
  supply-side housing assistance, 134–136, 145–146
  tenant-based housing assistance, 6, 112–113, 131–134, 225
  tenants' rights organizing and, 53–57, 142–148
  YIMBY (yes in my back yard), 5–6, 143, 145–146
Age of Reform (Hofstadter), 61
Agrarian economics, 42, 203. *See also* Jefferson, Thomas; Paine, Thomas
Agrarian Justice (Paine), 203
Aid to Dependent Children (ADC), 100
Albouy, David, 137
Alienation, 86, 195–196, 197, 203, 207
Alinsky, Saul, 108
Allen, Anita, 176
Allgeyer v. Louisiana (1897), 64
American Dream, the
  use of term, 3, 27–28, 250n8
American Economic Association (AEA), 72, 79, 82
Anarchism, 57–58, 203, 252n5
Anderson, Elizabeth, 19, 180, 233, 256n7
Antipoverty initiatives, 100, 107, 112, 140–142

Appeal to the World, An (Du Bois), 116–117
Arneson, Richard, 256n7
Asian American households, 28–29, 78
Association for Improving the Condition of the Poor (AICP), 67
Associationism, 69
Autonomy
  citizenship and, 182–183
  civic equality and, 182–183, 183
  control rights and, 203
  eviction and, 25, 166, 196, 197
  harm principle and, 183, 256n5
  heteronomy vs., 195
  normative agency, 166–167, 169, 182
  perfectionism and, 183
  private property rights and, 198, 204
  security of tenure and, 195
  state neutrality and, 182–183, 186–187, 189
  sufficientarianism and, 25–26
  value of housing and, 25–26, 27, 166, 168–169, 174, 182–183

Bailyn, Bernard, 43
Baiocchi, Gianpaolo, 159
Banzhaf, Spencer, 225–226
Bartholomew, Harland, 79, 92
Basis of justice. *See also* Right-based theories
  duty-based, 17, 44, 64–65, 75, 119–120, 168, 189, 201, 236, 249n3
  goal-based, 16–17, 23–27, 51, 62, 106, 120, 142, 186–187, 189, 243–244
  right-based, 8, 16–17, 119–120, 189–190, 243–244, 246, 249n3
  use of term, 9, 16–17, 32, 188–192, 192
  virtue-based, 17, 44, 189
Bassett, Edward M., 74
Bauer, Catherine (Catherine Bauer Wurster) 89, 95–96, 98, 119, 129, 146, 253n4
Beecher, Catherine, 53

Bentham, Jeremy, 65–66, 67, 190–191, 207
Berlin, Isaiah, 30–31, 72–73, 193
Bietz, Charles R., 114, 163
Black households
  alley house districts and, 9, 252n8
  citizenship rights and, 58–59, 84
  homeownership and, 4
  homesteader communities, 58–59, 105
  household wealth and, 4, 230
  housing segregation and, 102–104, 148–149, 185, 254n8
  MINDIS and, 116
  Reconstruction and, 58–59, 105
  right to community and, 105–109
  single Black woman households, 100
  tenants' movement and, 11, 113–134, 116
Blackstone, William, 30
Block v. Hirsch (1921), 110
Blomley, Nicholas, 238–239
Bork, Robert, 253n1
Boston, MA, 45, 49–50, 52, 59–60, 68, 147, 252n9
Bowditch, Henry, 68
Bradizza, Luigi, 44
Bradley, Joseph, 64
Brandeis, Louis, 71, 74, 87, 102
Breckinridge, Sophonisba, 84
Brettschneider, Corey, 170–171, 202
Buchanan v. Warley (1917), 78–79, 102
Building and loan industry, 59, 70, 99, 251n8, 253n5
Building the American City (Douglas Commission), 103–104
Burger, Warren, 124
Burgess, Ernest, 77, 252n6
Burroughs, William S., 3
Bush, George H. W., 129, 131, 136
Bushnell, Horace, 53

California, 6, 78, 113, 144–146
Callahan v. Carey (1979), 140

Index

Canada, 191
Capabilities approach, 24–25, 169
Capital gains, 218, 222–223, 230, 240, 258n4
Castle doctrine, 36–38
Chadwick, Edwin, 65–66, 67
Chastleton v. Sinclair (1924), 110
Chicago
  Back-of-the-Yards district, 10, 107, 253n9
  Chicago Housing Authority lawsuit, 133–134
  Hyde Park-Kenwood Urban Renewal Plan, 106–107
  labor reform/land reform and, 251n7
  sanitary reform, 67–68
  TWO (The Woodhull Organization), 109
Christman, John, 203, 205, 207
Cicero, Marcus Tullius, 36, 38, 43, 250n1
Citizenship. *See also* Civic equality; Human status; Social citizenship
  autonomy and, 182–183
  Black households and, 58–59, 84
  civic equality and, 11, 159–160, 177–178
  civil rights and, 120, 163–164
  equal citizenship, 177–182
  gender and, 84
  ground of citizenship, 16, 159–160, 163–164, 170, 182, 188, 244–245
  homeownership and, 99–100, 173–174
  horizontal equality and, 180–181, 255n3
  housing justice and, 163–164, 170–173
  human dignity and, 159–160
  human status and, 159–160, 162–164
  legal citizenship and, 187–188
  liberalism and, 170–172, 244–245
  liberal-republican conception of, 244–245
  public/private functions of, 171–177
  republicanism and, 244–245
  state neutrality and, 182–183
  women and, 84
Civic equality. *See also* Moral equality; Relational equality
  autonomy and, 182–183, 183
  citizenship and, 11, 159–160, 177–178
  defund the police, 236
  discriminatory housing polices and, 185–187, 229–236, 246
  distribution of housing and, 183–187, 245
  egalitarianism and, 186–187, 245
  gentrification and, 246–247
  global housing equality and, 184
  guaranteed housing allowance and, 11, 215, 216–219, 220
  housing finance reform, 216
  housing inequalities and, 184–187
  housing markets and, 246
  human status and, 177, 183–184
  legal citizenship and, 187–188
  public justification and, 216, 219, 231–232, 236, 246–247
  racial justice and, 228–236, 246–247
  right to the city and, 247
  state neutrality and, 182–183
  sufficientarianism and, 183–187, 186–187, 245–246
  taxation and, 219–221, 258n5
  tenure insecurity and, 11
  use of term, 11, 178, 245–246
Civil rights
  citizenship and, 120, 163–164
  human rights and, 113–118, 122, 188–189
  human rights frameworks and, 113–118, 122, 188–189
  legal reform and, 148
  natural right to property and home, 38–40
  Reconstruction and, 58–59

Civil rights (*continued*)
  right-based housing reform and, 17
  right to community and, 105–109, 119, 122, 143–144, 146–148
  right to fair housing, 6–7, 101–104
  tenants' rights movement and, 111–113
Claeys, Eric, 75
Clark, John Bates, 82
Cleveland, Ohio, 82, 105, 111
Clinton, William (Bill), 129, 131, 136
Coalition for the Homeless, 139, 140, 141–142
Cohen, G. A., 256n7
Colburn, Ben, 182
Cold War era, 10, 100–101, 117, 187
Commission on Race and Housing, 103
Common culture, 162, 168, 170, 196, 244
Common good, the
  homeownership and, 119–120, 131, 173–174
  natural rights doctrine and, 66, 138–139
  private property and, 76–80, 85
  progressivism and, 8, 65, 71–72, 76–80, 88, 138–139
  republicanism and, 31, 44–45, 46, 76–80, 88
  social citizenship and, 119–120
  utilitarianism and, 66, 76, 78, 88
Commons, John R., 72, 75, 76, 82
Commonwealth of Oceana, The (Harrington), 43–44, 88
Communitarianism, 28, 57
Community action agencies (CAAs), 107–109
Community-based advocacy
  discriminatory housing polices and, 105–109
  homelessness and, 140–142
  nonprofit housing organizations and, 95–96, 107, 124, 126, 139, 151
  tenants' rights, 142–148

Community Development Block Grants (CDBG), 125, 146, 227–228, 246
Community development corporations, 109, 126, 139
Community land trust movement, 83, 138, 147, 240, 254n7
Comparative justice, 19
Conception of value, 13–15, 15–16
Contract doctrine. *See* Liberty of contract doctrine
Control rights, 203, 207, 209–210, 257n4
Cornfield, Gilbert, 111–112
Corporate rights, 64
Croly, Herbert, 76, 78
Cushman, Robert, 45
Cutler, David, 231

Dagger, Richard, 30, 251n4
Darwinism, 76–77
De Forest, Robert, 81–82
Desmond, Matthew, 4–5
De Vita, Alvaro, 188
Devyr, Thomas, 54
Dewey, John, 73–74
De Wolf, Oscar Coleman, 67
Dickens, Charles, 243, 258n1
Dillon, John, 63
Dillon's Rule, 63, 65, 82, 105
Discriminatory housing polices. *See also* Civic equality; Fair housing; Racial segregation; Residential segregation
  civic equality and, 185–187, 229–236, 246
  community-based advocacy and, 105–109
  corrective justice and, 231
  disparate impact doctrine and, 74, 149–151, 181, 253n6, 254n8
  distribution of housing and, 15
  Hills v. Gautreaux (1976), 133–134
  historical discriminatory policies, 230–231
  housing justice and, 229–236

housing markets and, 6, 13, 24, 79, 101–104, 246
housing wealth and, 228–232
redlining, 93–94
relational equality and, 185–186, 256n7
residential segregation and, 10, 101–104, 148–151, 232–236, 258n8
right to community and, 105–109
Disparate impact doctrine, 74, 149–151, 181, 253n6, 254n8
Displacement, 5–6, 13, 105 106–107, 131, 139. *See also* Gentrification
Distribution of housing
  civic equality and, 183–187, 245
  discriminatory housing polices and, 15
  egalitarianism and, 245, 256n7
  homelessness and, 142
  leisure and, 26
  natural rights doctrine and, 38–42
  predistribution and, 191
  republicanism and, 43–45
  right to redistribution, 200–201
  sufficientarian distribution and, 27, 142, 170, 183–187, 200–201, 215, 223–224
Distributive justice
  housing justice and, 13–14, 15–20
  social meaning of goods and, 15, 20, 28–32, 86
  social practices and, 16, 19, 27–28, 161, 168
  use of term, 13–14, 15–20
Dorsey v. Stuyvesant Town Corp. (1949), 106, 111
Douglas Commission (National Commission on Urban Problems), 103–104
Du Bois, W. E. B., 79, 116
Dudley Street Neighborhood Initiative (DSNI), 147
Dumm, Thomas, 238
Dunn, John, 17

Duty-based theories, 17, 44, 64–65, 75, 119–120, 168, 189, 201, 236, 249n3. *See also* Basis of justice
Dworkin, Ronald, 14–15, 16–17, 165, 178, 190, 249n3, 256n7

Egalitarianism. *See also* George, David Lloyd
  agrarian economics and, 42, 203
  civic equality and, 186–187, 245
  distribution of housing and, 245, 256n7
  equal concern and, 178–180, 182, 184, 185, 224, 245
  homeownership and, 60
  labor theory of property and, 39–40
  land reform movement and, 244
  natural rights doctrine and, 35–36, 40
  progressive republicanism and, 57
  slavery trade and, 42
  sufficientarianism and, 170
Eldredge v. Koch (1983), 140
Ely, Richard T., 72–74, 78, 79, 82, 85, 92, 253n5
Engels, Friedrich, 62
Enlightenment ideals, 10, 115, 163
Equal concern, 178–180, 182, 184, 185, 224, 245. *See also* Autonomy; State neutrality
Equal respect, 66, 178–80, 182, 245. *See also* Autonomy; Relational equality; State neutrality
Essert, Christopher, 193, 205–206, 207, 208
Evans, George Henry, 48, 49–51, 54, 105
Evicted (Desmond), 4–5
Eviction. *See also* Homelessness
  autonomy and, 25, 166, 196, 197
  environmental conditions and, 55
  housing justice and, 5–6, 210
  human rights frameworks and, 151, 152–153
  root shock and, 196

Eviction (*continued*)
  tenants' rights and, 113, 146, 147–148, 152–153, 191
Existing Housing Program, 132

Fabian Society, 83
Fair housing. *See also* Discriminatory housing policies
  as civil right, 6–7, 101–104
  Fair Housing Act (FaHA), 104, 148–151, 181, 229, 253n7
  federal housing policy and, 101–104, 148–151
  gentrification and, 149
  Hills v. Gautreaux (1976), 133–134
  housing market discrimination and, 6, 13, 24, 148
  human rights frameworks and, 151–154
  racial segregation and, 103, 232
  renter advocacy and, 142–148
  residential segregation and, 103–104, 106, 122, 131–134, 148–151, 149–151, 228–236, 258n8
  right-based reform and, 101–104
  right to community and, 149–151
  subsidized housing and, 148–149
  suburbs and, 130, 133–134, 135, 148, 254n8
Fair Housing Act (FaHA), 104, 148–151, 181, 229, 253n7
Federal Experimental Housing Allowance Program (EHAP), 132
Federal Housing Administration (FHA)
  exclusionary policies and, 79
  Fannie Mae and, 254n4
  housing segregation and, 93–94, 98, 230–231
  mortgage underwriting and, 93–94, 254n4
  Roosevelt and, 95
  single-family housing and, 98–99, 230–231

Federal housing policy
  community development policy and, 125–126
  exclusionary policies, 79
  fair housing and, 101–104, 148–151
  Fannie Mae, 254n4
  homelessness and, 140–142
  homeownership and, 60, 98–101
  homesteading and, 243
  HOPE VI demonstration program, 129–131
  housing justice and, 246–247
  laissez-faire constitutionalism, 63–65
  low-income housing and, 126–128, 129
  middle-income households and, 89–90
  mortgage finance industry, 128–129
  natural right to property and, 243
  neoliberalism and, 122–125
  New Deal era, 90–98
  new federalism and, 125–126, 132–133, 135
  public housing reform, 129–131
  savings and loan industry and, 60
  supply-side housing policy reform, 134–136, 145
  tenant-based housing assistance, 112–113, 131–134, 134–136, 145–146
  use of term "two-tier," 89–90, 252n1
Feinberg, Joel, 249n3
Feminism, 28, 53, 175–176
Filtering process, 136, 220–221
Financial Institutions Reform, Recovery, And Enforcement Act (FIRREA), 128
Fino, Paul A., 131
Flaherty, Jordan, 215
Flower, Benjamin, 252n9
Floyd, George, ix, 236
Foglesong, Richard, 67, 78, 84–85
Foner, Philip, 57
Foreclosure crisis, 4, 92, 138, 147, 194, 230

Frankfurt, Harry, 142
Freedman's Bureau, 58
Freedom (liberty)
 civic freedom, 176–177
 domination vs., 30, 43, 176, 186, 197
 freedom from domination, 30, 244
 moral foundation of rights and, 244
 negative liberty, 30–31, 77, 114, 252n7
 positive freedom, 77–78, 97–98, 188–189, 244
 privacy/private sphere and, 176–177
 social citizenship and, 245
 use of term, 252n7
Free Soil (Free Democratic) Party, 35, 51
Freestanding Voucher Program, 132–133
Freund, Ernst, 73, 74, 77, 78, 84
Friedman, Milton, 123, 153, 257n2
Frost, Robert, 13, 31
Fullilove, Mindy, 196

Galbraith, John Kenneth, 100–101
Galster, George, 235, 258n8
Gaus, Gerald F., 189–190, 204, 255n2
Gender
 disparate impact doctrine and, 74, 253n6
 feminist critiques of housing, 28, 53, 175–176
 gendered labor in the home, 52–53
 homelessness and, 140
 privacy/private sphere and, 175–176
 progressive maternalism and, 84
 public-private distinction and, 175–176
 single Black woman households, 100
 social meaning of home and, 28, 53, 175–176
Gentrification
 affordable housing and, 6
 civic equality and, 246–247
 displacement and, 5–6, 13, 146, 149, 153, 231
 fair housing and, 149
 housing justice and, 246–247

 housing policy reform proposal and, 236, 238–239
 racial banishment, 231
Geography of housing justice, 224–228
George, David Lloyd, 83
George, Henry
 community land trust movement and, 83, 147
 income rights, 203, 206–207, 251n6, 252n5
 labor movement and, 54, 56–57
 natural rights doctrine and, 35–36
 New York housing reform and, 53–57
 progressivism and, 80–83
 single-tax proposal and, 36, 53–54, 56–57, 62, 80–83, 203, 222–223, 251n6, 252n5
Gibbard, Allan, 257n2
Glaeser, Edward, 231
Glendon, Mary Ann, 115, 253n11
Glocalization, 123
Goal-based theories, 16–17, 23–27, 51, 62, 106, 120, 142, 186–187, 189, 243–244. *See also* Basis of justice
Godkin, E. L., 87
Goldberg v. Kelly (1970), 112, 177
Gray, John, 190
Greeley, Horace, 51
Green, Thomas Hill, 77, 83, 122
Griffin, James, 168
Griscom, John H., 67
Griswold v. Connecticut (1965), 175
Gropius, Walter, 134–135
Grotius, Hugo, 38–39, 40, 199–200, 250n3
Ground of citizenship, 16, 159–160, 163–164, 170, 182, 188, 244–245
Grounds of justice
 citizenship and, 162–164, 187–188
 human status and, 162–164, 187
 local grounds of justice, 164
 nonrelational grounds, 16, 162–164

Grounds of justice (*continued*)
  relational grounds, 16, 163–164, 177, 180–181, 185–187, 244–245
  use of term, 16–17
Gruenhut, Joseph, 251n7
Guaranteed housing allowance, 11, 215, 216–219, 220
Gyourko, Joseph, 218

Habermas, Jürgen, 198
Hale, Edward E., 59
Hale, Sara Josepha, 53
Hamilton, Alexander, 44, 173
Hamilton, Bruce, 100
Harlan, John Marshall, 64
Harm principle, 183, 256n5
Harrington, James, 43–44, 88
Harrington, Michael, 101
Hartman, Chester, 200
Hartz, Louis, 43
Harvey, David, 122, 123, 161, 237
Hayek, Friedrich von, 123
Hegel, G. W. F., 204, 257n1
Herbert, Frank, 13
Heteronomy, 195
Hewitt, Abram, 57
Heywood, Ezra, 57–58, 203, 252n5
Higher-income households
  filtering process and, 136, 220–221
  homeownership republic and, 100–101
Hills v. Gautreaux (1976), 133–134
Hirt, Sonia, 86
Hispanic households, 4, 11, 230
Hobhouse, Leonard T., 77, 83, 119, 122
Hobson, John A., 77, 122
Hofstadter, Richard, 61, 71, 85–86
Hohfeld, Wesley Newcomb, 75, 201
Hohmann, Jessie, 117, 175
Holmes, Oliver Wendell, 71
Home. *See also* Social meaning of home
  castle doctrine and, 36–38
  use of term, 250n2

Homebuilding industry
  affordable housing and, 89–90, 127, 134–136
  building and loan industry and, 59–60, 70, 99, 251n8, 253n5
  use of term, 253n5
Homelessness
  alienation and, 197
  antihomelessness movements, 140–142
  community-based advocacy and, 140–142
  domestic violence as, 175
  domination and, 197
  economic stability and, 4–5
  federal housing policy and, 140–142
  gender and, 140
  housing inequality and, 3–4
  marginalization and, 197
  National Housing Strategy (Canada), 191
  neoliberalism and, 140–142
  private property rights and, 205–206
  propertylessness vs., 238, 257n3
  public sphere and, 161
  right to community and, 154
  Seattle tax proposal and, 7
  secure tenure and, 210–211
  sufficientarianism and, 142, 245
  tenure insecurity and, 205–206
Homeownership. *See also* Housing wealth; Land-use policies; Single-family housing ideal; Social meaning of home
  Black households and, 4
  Boston and, 59–60
  building and loan industry and, 59–60, 70, 99, 251n8, 253n5
  capital gains and, 218, 222–223, 230, 240, 258n4
  citizenship and, 99–100, 173–174
  common good and, 119–120, 131, 173–174

community land trust movement and, 83, 138, 147, 240, 254n7
control rights, 203, 207, 209–210, 257n4
deregulation and, 128–129
distributive justice and, 15
egalitarianism and, 60
federal housing policy and, 60, 98–101
foreclosure crisis and, 4, 92, 138, 147, 194, 230
housing consumption tax and, 221–224, 230, 240–241, 258n5
housing production and, 89–90, 127, 134–136
legal protections of, 35–36, 87, 141–142, 193–194, 250n1
postwar homeownership, 98–101
relational equality and, 181
savings and loan institutions and, 59–60, 89, 92, 126, 128, 254n, 254n3
secure tenure and, 246
social rights and, 244
urban poor and, 254n6
yeoman republic and, 45–46, 51, 105
Homeownership republic, 90, 98–101, 101–102, 119, 160. *See also* Homeownership; Single-family housing ideal
Home Owners Loan Corporation (HOLC), 92–94
Homestead Act (1862), 51
Homesteads
  Black households and, 58–59, 105
  Boston and, 59–60
  federal housing policy frameworks and, 243
  homestead exemptions and, 50
  land reform and, 46–53, 243
  natural right to property and, 243
  slavery and, 50–51
  urban homesteading, 59, 140, 152–153, 254n6
Honoré, A. M., 203

Hoover, Herbert, 31, 91–92
Housing. *See also* Home; Social meaning of home
  common culture and, 162, 168, 170, 196, 244
  feminist critiques of, 28, 53, 175–176
  public/private functions of, 160–162
  security and, 166
  social and cultural life and, 161–162
  social citizenship and, 64–65, 244
  social meaning of, 27–32
  as special, 20, 35–36, 244, 247, 250n5
  use of term "home," 250n2
Housing Act of 1937, 5, 95–96, 131
Housing Act of 1949, 5, 97, 98, 101, 129–130, 244
Housing and Community Development Act (1974), 125–126, 132–133, 254n6
Housing assistance
  supply-side assistance, 134–136, 145–146
  tenant-based assistance, 112–113, 131–134
Housing Choice Voucher (HCV) programs, 133, 216, 224–225
Housing construction. *See* Housing assistance; Housing production; Savings and loan (S&L) industry
Housing consumption tax, 219–221, 230, 240–241, 258n5
Housing finance reform
  civic equality and, 216
  compensation approach, 226
  equalization approach, 226
  geography of housing justice and, 224–228
  guaranteed housing allowance, 216–219
  housing consumption tax, 219–221, 258n5
  housing wealth increment tax, 215, 216, 221–224, 258n3, 258n5

Housing finance reform (*continued*)
  negative housing tax and, 5, 11, 215, 216, 221–224, 226, 227–228, 230, 240, 246, 258n4
Housing justice. *See also* Basis of justice; Housing policy reform proposal
  citizenship and, 163–164, 170–173
  defund the police and, 236
  distributive justice and, 13–14, 15–20
  gentrification and, 246–247
  geography of housing justice, 224–228
  global housing equality and, 184
  human dignity and, 165–170
  human rights and, 162–163
  human status and, 165–170
  human well-being and, 165–170
  overview of, 5–9, 13–14
  privacy and, 160–161
  racial justice and, 215, 228–236, 246–247
  right-based approach to, 11, 188–192
  right to the city and, 215
  secure tenure property regime and, 206–212
  social citizenship and, 244–245
  social meaning of home and, 28–32, 159–160
  sufficientarianism and, 170
  use of term, 13–14, 240–241, 243–244, 247
Housing markets
  affordable housing and, 3–4, 212
  civic equality and, 246
  discriminatory housing polices and, 6, 13, 24, 79, 101–104, 246
  homeownership republic and, 99–100
  housing inequalities and, 246
  housing justice and, 21–22
  incentive compatibility and, 212
  local obligations/collective subnational rights, 164
  market segmentation, 3–4, 212
  spatial inequality and, 164–165, 224–227, 229–230
  stable integrative process and, 235, 258n8
Housing policy reform proposal
  community development block grants, 215, 227–228
  compensation approach, 226–227
  equalization approach, 226–227
  gentrification and, 236, 238–239
  geography of housing justice and, 215, 224–228
  guaranteed housing allowance, 215, 216–219
  housing consumption tax, 219–221, 258n5
  housing production subsidies, 225
  housing wealth increment tax, 215, 216, 221–224, 258n3, 258n5
  racial justice and, 228–236
  right to the city and, 236–238, 236–240
  tenant-based subsidy programs and, 224–228
Housing production
  affordable housing construction and, 89–90, 127–128
  building and loan industry, 59, 70, 99, 251n8, 253n5
  homebuilding industry and, 89–90, 127, 134–136
  homeownership and, 89–90, 127, 134–136
  incentive compatibility, 212
Housing reform
  land reform movement and, 58–60
  modern housing and, 89, 95–96, 122, 137, 145–146, 153–154
  New York housing reform, 53–58
  social meaning of home and, 29–30
  utilitarian origins of, 65–70
Housing segregation. *See* Racial segregation; Residential integration; Residential segregation

Housing wealth
  Black household wealth, 4, 230
  discriminatory housing polices and, 228–232
  housing wealth increment tax, 215, 216, 221–224, 258n3, 258n5
  human well-being and, 221, 229–232
  negative housing tax and, 225–228
  racial and ethnic housing wealth gap, 221, 229–232
Housing wealth increment tax, 215, 216, 221–224, 258n3, 258n5
Houston, TX, 6–7
Howard, Ebeneezer, 83
Howe, Frederic C., 76, 78, 81, 84, 85
How the Other Half Lives (Riis), 69
Hoyt, Homer, 77, 79, 94, 252n6
HUD (US Department of Housing and Urban Development)
  budget authority cuts, 7, 126–128
  Clinton administration and, 136
  community development corporations and, 126
  Fair Housing Act and, 104, 148–151
  Houston fair housing violations, 6–7
  HUD Code, 136
  low-income housing programs, 219
  manufactured housing industry and, 135–136
  mortgage subsidy programs, 7, 121
  Nixon administration and, 125–126, 132–133, 135
  Reagan administration and, 7, 121, 126–129
  supply-side housing policy reform, 134–136, 145
  tenant-based subsidies and, 6, 131–134, 225
  urban homesteading programs, 140, 254n6
Human dignity, 23, 24, 159–160, 165–170, 196–197

Human rights frameworks
  capabilities approach and, 24–25, 169
  civil rights and, 113–118, 122, 188–189
  eviction and, 151, 152–153
  fair housing and, 151–154
  housing justice and, 162–164
  ICESCR, 117–118, 151, 153, 163, 187, 200
  right to housing and, 113–118
  right to inhabit and, 152, 199–200, 210, 237–240
  right to necessity and, 200
Human status
  citizenship and, 16, 159–160, 162–164, 187
  civic equality and, 177, 183–184, 183–187
  housing justice and, 165–170
  human dignity and, 23, 24, 159–160, 165–170, 196–197
  preemptory rights to necessity and, 199–200
  use of term, 16, 177
Human well-being
  citizenship and, 159–160
  homelessness and, 5
  housing justice and, 165–170
  housing value and, 23–27
  housing wealth and, 221, 229–232
  human dignity and, 5, 22, 23–27, 122–123, 159–160, 165–170, 196–197
  human status and, 16, 159–160, 162–164, 165–170
  indignity vs., 196–197
  positionality and, 23, 26–27, 256n6
  sanitary reform and, 5, 9–10, 55, 65–68, 70
Hurricane Harvey, 7

Ideal theory, 17–18, 231
Impartial spectator, the, 19, 199, 250n4
Ingalls, Joshua, 57–58, 203, 252n5

Inquiry into the Principles of the Good Society, An (Lippmann), 71, 123
International Covenant on Economic, Social, and Cultural Rights (ICESCR), 117–118, 151, 153, 163, 187, 200

Jacobs (1885), 64–65
Jefferson, Thomas, 39, 42, 45–46, 48, 49, 57, 63, 105
Johnson, Andrew, 51, 58
Johnson, Lyndon B., 104, 107–108, 125, 131–132
Johnson, Tom, 82
Justice. *See* Basis of justice; Grounds of justice; Housing justice

Kain, John, 134
Kaiser Commission (President's Committee on Urban Housing), 132
Kant, Immanuel, 165, 166
Katznelson, Ira, 85
Kelley, Florence, 71–72, 81
Kennedy, John F., 101
Kent, James, 63
Kentucky, 102
Kerner Commission (National Advisory Commission on Civil Disorders), 103–104
King, Martin Luther, Jr., 104, 111, 118, 120
King, Slater, 254n7
King v. Steward (1774), 37
Kohn, Robert D., 61, 71, 85–86
Kwak, Nancy, 187
Kymlicka, Will, 176

Labor reform
  feminists and, 28, 53, 175–176
  homestead ideal and, 47–53, 59–60
  labor theory of property and, 39–40
  land reform and, 251n7
  urban housing reform movement and, 53–57

Laissez-faire constitutionalism, 63–65, 72
Land reform
  anarchism and, 57–58, 203
  Boston and, 59–60
  communitarianism and, 57
  egalitarianism and, 244
  federal land and, 46–47
  Freedman's Bureau and, 58
  homestead ideal and, 46–53, 59–60, 243
  labor theory of property and, 39–40
  natural rights doctrine and, 243, 252n5
  property rights limitations, 252n5
  radical Lockeanism, 58–59
  Radical Republicanism, 59
  Reconstruction and, 59
  slavery and, 50
Land-use policies. *See also* Zoning
  progressivism and, 70–73
  racial zoning and, 78–79, 102
  state neutrality and, 210
Lawton v. Steele (1894), 64
Le Corbusier, 134
Lefebvre, Henri, 152, 237–238, 253n8
Leisure, 26, 207
Liberalism
  citizenship and, 170–172, 244–245
  egalitarianism and, 57
  fusion with republicanism, 44–45, 251n4
  liberal consensus theory, 43
  public-private distinction and, 171–172, 174–175, 255n2
  right to housing, 97, 98, 101, 129–130, 244
  social citizenship and, 244
  social meaning of home and, 30
  use of term, 250n9
Liberty. *See* Freedom (liberty)
Liberty of contract doctrine
  abolitionism and, 251n3
  corporate rights and, 64

laissez-faire constitutionalism and, 63–65
private property rights and, 251n2
Limited equity cooperatives (LEC), 210, 257n5
Lindsey v. Normet (1972), 124
Linmark Associates, Inc. v. Willingboro (1977), 104
Lippmann, Walter, 71, 123
Lochner v. New York (1905), 64
Locke, John, 10, 39–42, 163
Low-income households. *See also* Public housing
  COVID-19 and, ix, 5, 249n2
  filtering process and, 136, 220–221
  low-income seniors, 258n5
  Moving to Opportunity program (MTO), 134, 149, 234
  public housing and, 6, 89–90, 94–97, 100, 101, 127, 133–134, 139
  racial and ethnic bias and, 94
  tenant-based rental subsidies, 6, 131–134, 225
Low-income housing. *See also* Housing policy reform proposal
  community development corporations, 109, 126, 139
  dismantling of, 126–128
  LIHTC programs, 6–7, 128, 149, 223, 225, 255
  low-income seniors, 258n5
  opposition to, 7–8
  postmodern housing landscape and, 137–138
  supply-side housing policy reform, 134–136, 145
  tenant-based housing assistance, 6, 112–113, 131–134
  use of term, 249n2
Village of Arlington Heights v. Metropolitan Housing Development Corp. (1977), 254n8

Low-Income Housing Tax Credit (LIHTC) program, 6–7, 128, 149, 223, 225, 255. *See also* Supply-side housing policy reform
Lubove, Roy, 67
Lung-Amam, Willow S., 28–29

Macedo, Stephen, 15
Mack, Eric, 256n8
MacKinnon, Catherine, 176
Macpherson, C. B., 238
Madden David, 196
Madison, James, 42, 44–45, 173
Malik, Charles, 114, 163
Mancilla, Alejandra, 195, 199, 250n3
Mangum, Kyle, 225–226
Marcuse, Peter, 196
Marginalization, 175, 197
Marsh, Benjamin, 72, 73, 81–82
Marshall, Thomas Humphrey, 119–120, 159–160
Marshall, Thurgood, 103
Marx, Karl, 163–164, 165, 196, 257n3
Maryland
  Baltimore, 78–79, 97, 99, 134, 225, 252n8, 254n6
  Columbia, 99
  Hyattsville, 81
Masquerier, Lewis, 48–49, 105
Materials of justice, 9, 13–14, 159–160, 243–244
McKenzie, Roderick, 76–77
"Mending Wall" (Frost), 13, 31
Middle-class households, 10, 69, 71, 85–86, 93, 98
Middle-income households
  federal housing policy and, 89–90
  homeownership republic and, 90, 98–101
Mill, John Stuart, 183, 221, 251n6
Mises, Ludwig von, 123
Mitchell, Don, 237

Modern housing, 89, 95–96, 122, 137, 145–146, 153–154
Modern Housing (Bauer), 89, 95–96, 122, 137, 145–146, 153–154
Montague, Tigg, 243, 258n1
Moral equality. *See also* Civic equality
  civic equality, 178–180
  comparative justice and, 19
  constitutive commitments and, 191
  duty-based theories and, 249n3
  equal concern and, 178–180, 182, 184, 185, 224, 245
  equal respect and, 66, 178–180, 182, 245
  horizontal and vertical equality and, 178, 180–181, 255n3
  perfectionism and, 18, 181, 183, 189, 234, 256n4
  public justification and, 15, 179–180, 184–185
  racial segregation and, 232
  right-based reforms and, 188–192
  social citizenship and, 245
  spatial inequality and, 234–235
  state neutrality and, 180, 225, 234, 245–246
  use of term, 178–180, 245
Morris, George Sylvester, 74
Moyn, Samuel, 142
Moynihan, Daniel Patrick, 132
Mugler v. Kansas (1887), 64
Muller v. Oregon (1908), 74, 102, 253n6
Murphy, Liam, 219

Nagel, Thomas, 219
National Advisory Commission on Civil Disorders (Kerner Commission), 103–104
National Association for the Advancement of Colored People (NAACP)
  racially restrictive covenants and, 102–103, 106, 115–116, 253n6
  United Nations and, 116–117, 118

National Association of Real Estate Boards (NAREB), 91, 131
National Commission on Urban Problems (Douglas Commission), 103–104
National Housing Strategy (Canada), 191
National Reform Association (NRA), 49, 50–51, 54
Native American households, 45, 105–106, 144
Natural rights doctrine
  British law and, 36–38, 43–44
  civil rights and, 38–40
  the common good and, 66, 138–139
  conditional justifications for private property and, 201–202
  distribution of housing and, 38–42
  due process and, 36, 38, 58
  egalitarianism and, 35–36, 40
  federal housing policy frameworks and, 243
  home as castle and, 36–38
  homestead ideal and, 46–53, 59–60, 243
  human rights and, 163–164
  inequality and, 40, 44–45
  labor theory of property and, 39–42
  laissez-faire constitutionalism and, 63–65
  land reform and, 46–53, 243
  New York housing reform and, 53–58
  overview of, 38–42
  public land and, 46–47
  right-based reform and, 83–88
  single-tax proposal and, 36, 53–54, 56–57, 80–83
  spoliation proviso and, 40–41
  sufficiency limitation and, 40–41
  use of term, 35–36
  utilitarianism and, 66
Nedelsky, Jennifer, 44

Negative housing tax
  block grants and, 227–228, 246
  filtering process and, 221
  geography of housing justice and, 225–228
  guaranteed housing allowance and, 11, 216–219
  housing consumption tax and, 219–221, 230, 240–241, 258n5
  housing inequality and, 229–236
  housing subsidies and, 246
  housing wealth increment tax and, 221–224, 225–230
  spatial inequality and, 246
  use of term, 11
Neoliberalism
  federal housing policy and, 122–125
  glocalization and, 123
  homelessness and, 140–142
  housing finance deregulation, 123–124, 128–129, 154
  housing justice and, 138–139
  low-income housing policy and, 129
  postmodern housing landscape and, 137–138
  privacy/privatization and, 160–161
  right-based social movements and, 244
  spatial manifestations of, 71, 123
  use of term, 122–123
New Communities, Inc. (Georgia), 254n7
New Deal era, 89–90, 90–98, 243–244
Newton, Huey, 108
New York, 53–57, 67, 68–69, 95, 251n7, 252n10
New York City Housing Authority v. Muller (1936), 95
NIMBY (not in my back yard), 5–6, 7, 146
Nixon, Richard, 109, 121, 124, 125–126, 132, 135
Nonideal theory, 17–18, 231

Nonprofit housing organizations, 95–96, 107, 124, 126, 139, 151. *See also* Community development corporations
Notes on the State of Virginia (Jefferson), 46
Nozick, Robert, 20, 189
Nussbaum, Martha, 24–25, 165, 168–170, 255n1

Obama, Barack, 141, 150–151, 153
Occupancy rights
  anarchism and, 57–58, 203
  negative housing tax and, 215, 246
O'Connor, Thomas, 52
O'Donnell, Edward, 57
Office of Economic Opportunity (OEO), 107–109, 125, 127
Ostrom, Vincent, 254n2
Otis, James, 37–38
Otsuka, Michael, 202
Owen, Robert, 47, 48, 57
Owen, Robert Dale, 48

Paine, Thomas, 42, 48, 49, 54, 57, 163, 202, 203
Park, Robert, 76–77
Pateman, Carole, 175
Patten, Simon, 72, 73, 252n7
Patterson, William, 62
Pease, Edwin, 83
Pembina Consolidated Silver Mining Company v. Pennsylvania (1888), 251n1
Pennsylvania Coal Co. v. Mohan (1922), 71
Perfectionism, 18, 181, 183, 189, 234, 256n4
Personhood, 25–26, 195–196, 210, –211, 238
Pettit, Philip, 176
Philadelphia, 47, 79, 148–149, 254n6
Philadelphia Negro, The (Du Bois), 79
Phillips, Anne, 161–162, 168, 170, 196, 244
Philosophy of Right (Hegel), 204

PHIMBY (public housing in my backyard), 6, 145–146, 153
Pink, Louis, 94
Pitt, William, 37
Pocock, J. G. A., 43
Poe, Edgar Allen, 121, 154
Police power doctrine, 63–65, 73, 74, 77–78, 83, 190, 251n2
Pollock v. Farmers' Loan & Trust Co, (1895), 81
Positionality, 23, 26–27, 256n6
Pottinger v. City of Miami (1989), 142
Poverty
  affluent society vs. 100–101
  antipoverty initiatives, 100, 107, 112, 140–142
  community action agencies (CAAs), 107–109
  homeownership republic and, 100–101
  sanitary reform and, 5, 9–10, 55, 65–68, 70
  urban reform and, 60
Pragmatism, 19–20, 68, 84, 244. *See also* New Deal era
President's Committee on Urban Housing (Kaiser Commission), 132
Principles of justice, 16, 17–18, 19, 29, 163, 164, 189, 247
Privacy/private sphere. *See also* Public-private distinction
  civic freedom and, 176–177
  gender and, 175–176
  housing justice and, 160–161
  property rights and, 30
  public/private functions of housing, 160–162
  social citizenship and, 171–172, 174–175, 245, 255n2
Private property rights. *See also entries under* right to
  anarchism and, 57–58, 203, 252n5
  autonomy and, 198, 204

common good and, 76–80, 85
conditional justifications for, 201–202
contract law and, 2, 3, 251n1
control rights and, 203–204, 207–208
English Civil Wars and, 43–44, 257n3
Enlightenment ideals and, 10
general rights to private property, 204–206
homelessness and, 205–206
housing justice and, 20–21
income rights and, 203–204, 207–208
landlord-tenant laws and, 21
land reform and, 46–53
legal protection and, 35–36, 87, 141–142, 193–194, 250n1
propertylessness and, 238, 257n3
public justification and, 193–194, 198–199, 216, 219, 231–232, 236
right to necessity, 199–200
right to redistribution, 200–201
secure tenure and, 246
tenure insecurity and, 198–199, 205–206
use of term, 30–31, 250n2
Production of housing. *See* Housing production
Progress and Poverty (George), 35, 53–58
Progressivism
  bundle-of-rights concept, 73–76
  Chicago School and, 76–77
  city planning and, 57, 73, 76, 81–82
  common good and, 8, 65, 71–72, 76–80, 88, 138–139
  progressive maternalism and, 84
  racial inequalities and, 79, 116
  regulatory reform and, 243–244
  social citizenship and, 244
  society-as-organism, 76–77
  tax reform and, 80–83
  zoning and, 70–73
Proudhon, Pierre-Joseph, 257n3

Public housing
    affordable housing and, 6, 89–90, 94–97, 100, 101, 127, 133–134, 139
    affordable housing construction and, 89–90, 127–128
    federal housing policy, 129–131
    HOPE VI demonstration program, 129–131
    Housing Act of 1937, 95–96
    Housing Act of 1949, 97, 98, 101, 129–130, 244
    PHIMBY (public housing in my backyard), 6, 145–146
    public housing reform, 129–131
    race and, 100, 103, 130, 133–134
    suburban public housing, 130, 133–134
    supply-side housing assistance, 127–128, 134–136, 145–146
    tenant-based housing assistance, 112–113, 131–134
Public justification
    civic equality and, 184–185, 193, 219, 231, 236, 246–247
    global housing equality and, 184
    moral equality and, 179–180, 184–185
    race and, 231–236
    state neutrality and, 180
    tenure insecurity and, 193, 198–199
    use of term, 15, 198–199
Public-private distinction. *See also* Privacy/private sphere; Public sphere
    domestic violence and, 175
    feminist critiques of, 175–176
    gender and, 175–176
    liberalism and, 171–172, 174–175, 255n2
    public sphere and, 160–162
    social citizenship and, 171–172, 174–175, 245, 255n2
Public sphere
    homelessness and, 161
    housing justice, 161–162
    property rights and, 30
    public-private distinction, 160–162
    social citizenship and, 245
Puerto Rican households, 11

Quality Housing and Work Responsibility Act (1998), 133

Race and ethnicity. *See also* Black households; Racial justice; Racial segregation; Residential integration
    Asian Americans and, 28–29
    fair housing rights and, 101–105
    foreclosure crisis and, 4, 230
    Freedman's Bureau and, 58
    gentrification and, 231
    Hispanic households, 4, 11, 230
    historical discriminatory policies, 230–231
    homeownership republic and, 101–104, 119
    housing inequalities and, 246–247
    housing wealth gaps, 221, 229–232
    Native American households, 45, 105–106, 144
    negative housing tax and, 229–236
    public justification and, 231–236
    racial banishment, 231
    racially restrictive covenants, 28
    racial zoning ordinances, 28, 78–79, 102, 139, 173, 185, 230–231
    right to community and, 105–109
    single Black woman households, 100
    stable integrative processes, 235, 258n8
Racial justice. *See also* Housing policy reform proposal
    civic equality and, 228–236, 246–247
    defund the police and, 236
    housing justice and, 215, 228–236, 246–247

Racial segregation. *See also* Discriminatory housing polices; Residential integration
Black households and, 102–104, 148–149, 185, 254n8
Buchanan v. Warley (1917), 78–79, 102
differentiated solidarity and, 233–234
fair housing and, 103, 132, 149–151, 232
FHA exclusionary policies, 79
Hills v. Gautreaux (1976), 133–134
moral equality and, 232–234
racial zoning ordinances and, 28, 78–79, 102, 139, 173, 185, 230–231
relational equality and, 232, 234
residential segregation and, 10, 101–104, 148–151, 232–236, 258n8
right-based social movements and, 232, 244
urban neighborhoods and, 10, 101, 106–107, 254n8
Radford, Gail, 252n1
Radin, Margaret, 25, 195–196, 210
Rawls, John, 17, 20, 40, 171, 174, 198–199, 200–201, 205, 207, 255n2
Raz, Joseph, 167–168, 256n5, 256n8
Reagan, Ronald, 7, 109, 121, 126–129
Relational equality. *See also* Civic equality
choice and, 256n6
civic equality and, 180–181, 185–187, 192, 232–234, 236, 245–246, 255n3, 256n7, 258n8
discriminatory housing polices and, 185–186, 256n7
homeownership and, 181
horizontal and vertical equality and, 178, 180–181, 219, 255n3
housing inequality and, 185–186
moral equality and, 181, 234
racial segregation and, 232, 234
social citizenship and, 245

stable integrative process and, 235, 258n8
use of term, 178, 180–181, 245
Republicanism
citizenship and, 172–173, 244–245
civic republicanism, 43–44, 45–46, 130
common good and, 31, 44–45, 46, 76–80, 88
distribution of housing and, 43–45
domination and, 30, 43, 176, 186, 197
egalitarianism and, 57
freedom from domination, 30, 244
fusion with liberalism, 44–45, 251n4
progressive republicanism, 57
property ownership and, 253n12
Reconstruction and, 58
single-family detached homes, 69–70
social meaning of home and, 30–31, 45–46
use of term, 250n9
utilitarianism and, 69–70, 80, 88
yeoman republic and, 45–46, 51, 105
Residential integration. *See also* Racial segregation
Black households and, 102–104, 148–149, 185, 254n8
FHA and, 93–94, 98, 230–231
Hills v. Gautreaux (1976), 134
Kerner Commission and, 103–104
low-income housing programs and, 254n8
Residential segregation
differentiated solidarity and, 233–234
discriminatory housing polices and, 10, 101–104, 148–151, 232–236
fair housing and, 103–104, 106, 122, 131–134, 148–151, 149–151, 228–236, 258n8
housing policy reform and, 232–236
racial segregation and, 10, 101–104, 148–151, 232–236, 258n8
stable integrative process and, 235, 258n8

Right-based theories. *See also* Basis of justice
  choice-based rights, 8, 256n7
  civil right to fair housing, 101–104
  collectivistic morality and, 249n3
  constitutive commitments and, 191
  demise of, 83–88
  duty-based theories and, 16–17, 39, 45, 87, 120, 178, 181, 189, 199, 201, 249n3
  housing justice and, 192
  human right to housing, 113–118
  jurisdictional view of rights, 190, 256n8
  land reform and, 16
  moral reasoning and, 188–192, 249n3
  neoliberalism and, 244
  predistribution and, 191
  racial segregation and, 232, 244
  right to community, 105–109
  social citizenship as, 244–245
  social reform and, 61–63
  tenants' rights, 109–112
  urban reform and, 83–88
  use of term, 16–17
  utilitarianism and, 189
  virtue-based theories and, 96, 174, 177, 189, 245
  welfare rights, 112–113
Rights of Man to Property! (Skidmore), 48
Right to community, 45–46, 51, 105–109, 119–122, 143–144, 146, 149–151, 154
Right to housing
  human rights frameworks and, 113–118
  right to inhabit and, 152, 199–200, 210, 237–240
  right to redistribution, 200–201
  right to secure tenure, 246
  right to the city vs., 159, 236–240, 247
  use of term, 8, 13, 246
Right to inhabit, 152, 199–200, 210, 237–240

Right to necessity, 199–201, 250n3
Right to redistribution, 200–201
Right to shelter, 140–142, 199–200, 255n1
Right to the city
  civic equality and, 247
  right to community vs., 253n8
  right to housing vs., 159, 236–240
  right to inhabit and, 152, 199–200, 210, 237–240
  right to private property and, 159
Right to the City Alliance, 152, 159
Robbins, Ira, 94
Robinson, Charles Mulford, 82
Rockwell, Norman, 113
Rondel, David, 18, 19, 178, 255n3
Roosevelt, Eleanor, 114, 116, 177
Roosevelt, Franklin D., 10, 89, 92–93, 113–114, 115, 155, 188, 244
Roosevelt, Theodore, 57, 64–65
Rosenthal, Tracy Jeanne, 145
Ross, Edward, 79
Rouse, James, 99, 126
Rüstow, Alexander, 123

San Antonio School District v. Rodriguez (1973), 124–125
Sanders, Bernie, 3
Sanitary reform movement, 65–70
Savings and loan (S&L) industry, 59–60, 89, 92, 126, 128, 254n3
Scanlon, T. M., 14, 178–179, 198–199
Seattle, Washington, 7
Second Bill of Rights, 96–97, 119
Second Treatise of Government (Locke), 39
Secure tenure. *See also* Control rights; Tenure insecurity
  bundle flexibility and, 208, 211
  environmental conditions and, 167–168, 194–195
  homelessness and, 3, 205–206, 210–211
  incentive compatibility, 208, 211–212

Secure tenure (*continued*)
  income rights and, 206–207
  private property ownership and, 246
  right to housing and, 212–213, 246
  right to secure tenure, 11
  secure tenure property regime, 206–212
  state neutrality and, 209–210
  use of term, 11, 194–195, 208–211, 246
Segall, Shomi, 250n5
Seligman, Edwin R. A., 72, 73, 82
Sen, Amartya, 17–18, 19, 24
Shannon v. HUD (1969), 148
Shapiro v. Thompson (1969), 113
Shaw, George Bernard, 83
Shelby, Tommie, 231
Shelley v. Kraemer (1948), 93, 102–103, 253n6
Sidgwick, Henry, 252n4
Sinclair, Upton, 253n9
Single-family housing ideal
  autonomy and, 31
  critiques of, 160
  feminist critiques of, 28, 53, 175–176
  FHA and, 98–99, 230–231
  low-income households and, 10
  moral frameworks and, 14, 32, 160
  progressivism and, 160
  social meaning of home and, 31–32
  urbanization and, 60, 160
  utilitarian reform and, 160
Skidmore, Thomas, 47–49, 204
Skinner, Quentin, 43
Slaughterhouse Cases (1873), 64
Smith, Adam, 123, 161–162, 167–168, 199, 250n4
Smith, Henry, 75
Smith, Neil, 144
Social citizenship
  civic equality and, 11, 159–160
  the common good and, 119–120
  consumer-voters and, 99, 171

  critical right of citizenship, 84
  freedom and, 245
  housing and, 64–65, 244
  housing justice and, 244–245
  liberalism and, 244–245
  marginalization and, 175, 197
  moral equality and, 245
  progressive reform and, 244
  public-private distinction and, 171–172, 174–175, 245, 255n2
  relational equality and, 245
  as right-based, 244–245
  social meaning of home and, 159–160
  social rights and, 244
  use of term, 119–120, 159–160, 177, 245
Social meaning of home. *See also* Value of housing
  civic republicanism, 45–46
  common culture and, 162
  distributive justice and, 15, 20, 28–32, 86
  domesticity and, 28–29
  feminists and, 28, 53, 175–176
  gender and, 28, 53, 175–176
  housing and, 27–32
  housing justice and, 159–160
  inequality and, 137–138
  liberalism and, 30–31
  moral principles and, 29
  positionality and, 23, 26–27, 256n6
  private property and, 29–30
  racial hierarchies and, 28–29
  social movements and, 29–30
Social practices, 16, 19, 27–28, 161, 168
Spatial inequality
  geography of housing justice and, 215, 224–228
  glocalization and, 123
  housing markets and, 164–165, 224–227, 229–230
  jurisdictional view of rights, 190, 256n8

liberalism and, 30–31
moral equality and, 234–235
negative housing tax and, 246
neoliberalism and, 71, 123
private sphere and, 30–31
racial and ethnic inequalities and, 246
spatial justice, 247
urban renewal initiatives and, 97, 106–107, 137, 139, 140
Spencer, Herbert, 76
Stable integrative process and, 235, 258n8
State neutrality
autonomy and, 182–183, 186–187, 189
citizenship and, 182–183
civic equality and, 182–183
harm principle and, 183
housing justice and, 186–187
housing wealth increment tax and, 221
land-use policy reform and, 210
moral equality and, 180, 225, 234, 245–246
perfectionism and, 189, 234
public justification and, 180
secure tenure and, 209–210
tenant-based subsidies, 6, 131–134, 225
tenure security and, 209–210
use of term, 27, 180
zoning and, 210
Stewart B. McKinney Homeless Assistance Act (1987), 141
Stockman, David, 126
Storey, Moorfield, 102
Sub-commission on Prevention of Discrimination and Protection of Minorities (MINDIS), 116
Subsistence rights, 49, 96, 115, 143–144, 166, 177, 250n3
Suburbs
affluent society and, 100–101
fair housing and, 130, 133–134, 135, 148, 254n8

homeownership and, 59, 90, 93–94, 95, 98–101, 172–173, 181
housing production and, 99–100, 99–101
housing wealth and, 185
racial segregation and, 103–104, 106, 130, 133–134, 185, 255n8
suburban public housing, 130, 133–134
Sufficientarianism
autonomy and, 25–26
civic equality and, 183–187, 245–246
conditional justifications and, 201–202
difference principle and, 200–201
egalitarianism and, 142, 170, 245, 256n7
homelessness and, 142, 245
housing justice and, 170
tenure security and, 167, 205, 215, 216–217, 223–224
use of term, 27, 142
Sumner, William Graham, 76
Sunstein, Cass, 191
Supply-side housing policy, 134–136, 145. See also Low-Income Housing Tax Credit (LIHTC) program
Supply-side housing policy reform, 223, 225–228
Sutherland, George, 78
Swann, Robert, 254n7
Swyngedouw, Erik, 123

Taxation
block grants and, 227–228, 246
capital gains and, 218, 222–223, 230, 240, 258n4
civic equality and, 219–221, 258n5
guaranteed housing allowance, 216–219
homelessness and, 7
housing consumption tax, 219–221, 230, 240–241, 258n5

Taxation (*continued*)
  housing wealth increment tax, 215, 216, 221–224, 258n3, 258n5
  increment tax, 83
  LIHTC program, 6–7, 128, 149, 223, 225, 255
  low-income seniors and, 258n5
  municipal reform movement and, 82
  negative housing tax and, 11, 215, 216, 221–224, 227–228, 230, 240, 246, 258n4, 258n5
  progressive tax reform and, 80–83
  rental income and, 258n4
  single-tax proposal and, 36, 53–54, 56–57, 80–83
  state neutrality and, 221
  Tax Cuts and Jobs Act (2017), 257n1
  tenement housing and, 54–57, 252n8, 252n9
Tenant-based subsidy programs
  geography of housing justice and, 224–228
  guaranteed housing allowance, 216–219
  Housing Choice Voucher (HCV) program, 132–133, 216, 224–225
  housing policy reform proposal and, 224–228
  low-income households, 6, 131–134, 225
  Moving to Opportunity program (MTO), 134, 149, 234
  National Association of Real Estate Boards (NAREB), 91, 131
Tenant Opportunity to Purchase Act (Washington, DC), 144, 211, 240
Tenants' rights
  California affordable housing, 6
  eviction and, 113, 146, 147–148, 152–153
  Lindsey v. Normet (1972), 124
  private property rights and, 21
  renter advocacy and, 53–57, 142–148
  right to community and, 119, 122, 143–144, 154
  tenants' rights organizing and, 142–148
  urban housing reform movement and, 53–57
Tenement housing
  labor and, 55–56, 64–65
  regulations and, 54, 64–65, 65–70, 67, 70–71, 75, 80, 83, 252n8
  sanitary reform movement and, 65–70
  taxation and, 54–57, 252n8, 252n9
  urban poor and, 56–57, 59–60, 62, 65–70, 86–87, 131
  zoning and, 70–71, 75, 80
Tenure insecurity
  alienation and, 195–196
  civic equality and, 11
  environmental conditions and, 167–168, 194–195
  heteronomy and, 195
  homelessness and, 205–206
  indignity and, 196–197
  marginalization and, 175, 197
  private property rights and, 198–199, 205–206
  right to necessity and, 199–200
  use of term, 194–195
Tenure security. *See also* Control rights
  justification for private property and, 246
  sufficientarianism and, 167, 205, 215, 216–217, 223–224
  tenure neutral housing security, 11
Texas, 6–7, 50, 149–150
Texas Department of Housing and Community Affairs v. The Inclusive Communities Project, Inc. (2015), 149–150, 254n8
Tiebout, Charles, 99–100, 254n2
Truman, Harry, 96–97, 117, 135
Trump, Donald J., 6, 150–151
Trustees of Dartmouth College v. Woodward (1819), 251n1

Tucker, Benjamin, 164, 252n5, 257n3
TWO (The Woodlawn Organization), 109

Underwriting Manual (Babcock), 93–94
United States Constitution, natural rights doctrine and, 43–45
United States v. Certain Lands in the City of Louisville (1935), 94–95
Universal Declaration of Human Rights (UHDR), 117, 151, 163
Urban housing. *See also* Residential segregation
  Boston and, 59–60
  city planning and, 57, 73, 76, 81–82
  displacement and, 106–107, 131
  labor reform and, 53–57
  land reform and, 61–62
  new urbanism and, 130–131
  racial segregation and, 10, 101, 106–107, 254n8
  right-based reform and, 83–88
  sanitary reform and, 5, 9–10, 55, 65–68, 70
  sector theory of, 77, 252n6
  single-family detached homes and, 60
  social reform and, 61–62
  tenants' rights and, 53–57, 142–148
  urban homesteading, 59, 140, 152–153, 254n6
  urban renewal initiatives, 97, 106–107, 137, 139, 140
Utilitarianism
  associationism and, 69
  capabilities approach and, 24–25, 169
  the common good and, 66, 76, 78, 88
  German historical school and, 72
  housing inequality and, 256n6
  housing reform and, 65–70
  income rights and, 207
  natural rights doctrine and, 66
  progressivism and, 70–72
  regulatory reform and, 243–244
  republicanism and, 69–70, 80
  right-based reforms and, 189
  use of term, 252n4
  value and, 23–25, 251n3

Value, conception of, 15–16, 23, 250n7
Value of housing
  alienation and, 196
  autonomy and, 25–26, 27, 166, 168–169, 174, 182–183
  conception of value, 13–15, 15–16, 23, 250n7
  consumption value, 23–25, 86–87, 171, 184–185, 250n6
  filtering process and, 136, 220–221
  homeownership republic and, 99–100
  housing as special, 20, 35–36, 244, 247, 250n5
  housing justice and, 23–28
  human well-being and, 5, 22, 23–25, 23–27, 26
  investment value, 31–32, 231–232, 250n6
  overview of, 23–28
  personhood and, 25–26, 195–196, 210–211, 238
  positionality and, 23, 26–27, 256n6
  prudential value pluralism, 26–27
  sufficientarian distribution of housing, 27, 170, 183–187, 200–201, 215, 223–224
  use of term, 15–16, 32, 250n7
Vanderborght, Yannick, 220
Vanhornes Lessee v. Dorrance (1795), 63
Van Parijs, Philippe, 220
Vaughn, George L., 102–103
Veiller, Lawrence, 68–71, 74, 78, 80–81, 82, 84–87, 88, 92
Vigdor, Jacob, 231
Village of Arlington Heights v. Metropolitan Housing Development Corp. (1977), 254n8
Village of Euclid v. Ambler Realty Co. (1926), 78

Virtue-based theories. *See also* Basis of justice
  perfectionism and, 189
  right-based reforms and, 96, 174, 177, 189, 245

Wagner, Robert, 94
Waldron, Jeremy, 41, 65, 165, 166, 195, 204, 249n2, 257n1
Wall, Steven, 181, 256n4
Walzer, Michael, 18–19, 28–29, 86, 227
Ward, Lester Frank, 76
Warren, Robert, 254n2
Washington, DC, 82, 140, 144–145, 211, 240
Weaver, Robert, 131
Webb, Sidney, 83
Webster, Daniel, 63
Welfare rights, 100, 112–113, 119, 140, 192, 200
Wells, Katy, 204–205
Wells v. Commissioner of Hyattsville (1893), 81
West, Thomas G., 44
White households
  foreclosure crisis and, 4, 137–138
  housing wealth and, 4, 185–186, 229–232
  landownership and, 46–47, 58–59
  low-income households and, 6–7, 94, 106–107, 131–132, 141, 254n8
  majority-white neighborhoods and, 130, 133–134, 137, 185, 185–186, 235–236
  progressivism and, 79
  public housing and, 130, 133–134
  racial segregation and, 6–7, 79, 94, 101–104, 106, 137–138, 235–236
  social meaning of home and, 28–29
Whitman, Walt, 52
Whitten, Robert H., 74
Wiebe, Robert, 252n10
Williamson, Thad, 172

Williams v. Barry (1983), 253n1
Wilson, William Julius, 134
Wilson, Woodrow, 78
Windt, John, 49
Winthrop, John, 38, 40
Woodlawn Organization, The (TWO), 109
Wood, Edith Elmer, 90–91, 94, 136
Wood, Gordon, 43
Woolf, Virginia, 176
Working Men's Party, 48–49
Wright, Frances, 47–49, 204
Wright, Frank Lloyd, 98–99

YIMBY (yes in my back yard), 5–6, 143, 145–146
Young, Iris Marion, 233–234

Zabek, Mike, 137
Zoning. *See also* Land-use policies
  affordable housing and, 6, 254n8
  land-use ordinances, 76–80, 136, 171, 211
  progressivism and, 70–73
  racial zoning, 28, 78–79, 102, 139, 173, 185, 230–231
  single-family home and, 86–88, 91, 98–99
  state neutrality and, 210

Urban and Industrial Environments

Series editor: Robert Gottlieb, Henry R. Luce Professor of Urban and Environmental Policy, Occidental College

Maureen Smith, *The U.S. Paper Industry and Sustainable Production: An Argument for Restructuring*

Keith Pezzoli, *Human Settlements and Planning for Ecological Sustainability: The Case of Mexico City*

Sarah Hammond Creighton, *Greening the Ivory Tower: Improving the Environmental Track Record of Universities, Colleges, and Other Institutions*

Jan Mazurek, *Making Microchips: Policy, Globalization, and Economic Restructuring in the Semiconductor Industry*

William A. Shutkin, *The Land That Could Be: Environmentalism and Democracy in the Twenty-First Century*

Richard Hofrichter, ed., *Reclaiming the Environmental Debate: The Politics of Health in a Toxic Culture*

Robert Gottlieb, *Environmentalism Unbound: Exploring New Pathways for Change*

Kenneth Geiser, *Materials Matter: Toward a Sustainable Materials Policy*

Thomas D. Beamish, *Silent Spill: The Organization of an Industrial Crisis*

Matthew Gandy, *Concrete and Clay: Reworking Nature in New York City*

David Naguib Pellow, *Garbage Wars: The Struggle for Environmental Justice in Chicago*

Julian Agyeman, Robert D. Bullard, and Bob Evans, eds., *Just Sustainabilities: Development in an Unequal World*

Barbara L. Allen, *Uneasy Alchemy: Citizens and Experts in Louisiana's Chemical Corridor Disputes*

Dara O'Rourke, *Community-Driven Regulation: Balancing Development and the Environment in Vietnam*

Brian K. Obach, *Labor and the Environmental Movement: The Quest for Common Ground*

Peggy F. Barlett and Geoffrey W. Chase, eds., *Sustainability on Campus: Stories and Strategies for Change*

Steve Lerner, *Diamond: A Struggle for Environmental Justice in Louisiana's Chemical Corridor*

Jason Corburn, *Street Science: Community Knowledge and Environmental Health Justice*

Peggy F. Barlett, ed., *Urban Place: Reconnecting with the Natural World*

David Naguib Pellow and Robert J. Brulle, eds., *Power, Justice, and the Environment: A Critical Appraisal of the Environmental Justice Movement*

Eran Ben-Joseph, *The Code of the City: Standards and the Hidden Language of Place Making*

Nancy J. Myers and Carolyn Raffensperger, eds., *Precautionary Tools for Reshaping Environmental Policy*

Kelly Sims Gallagher, *China Shifts Gears: Automakers, Oil, Pollution, and Development*

Kerry H. Whiteside, *Precautionary Politics: Principle and Practice in Confronting Environmental Risk*

Ronald Sandler and Phaedra C. Pezzullo, eds., *Environmental Justice and Environmentalism: The Social Justice Challenge to the Environmental Movement*

Julie Sze, *Noxious New York: The Racial Politics of Urban Health and Environmental Justice*

Robert D. Bullard, ed., *Growing Smarter: Achieving Livable Communities, Environmental Justice, and Regional Equity*

Ann Rappaport and Sarah Hammond Creighton, *Degrees That Matter: Climate Change and the University*

Michael Egan, *Barry Commoner and the Science of Survival: The Remaking of American Environmentalism*

David J. Hess, *Alternative Pathways in Science and Industry: Activism, Innovation, and the Environment in an Era of Globalization*

Peter F. Cannavò, *The Working Landscape: Founding, Preservation, and the Politics of Place*

Paul Stanton Kibel, ed., *Rivertown: Rethinking Urban Rivers*

Kevin P. Gallagher and Lyuba Zarsky, *The Enclave Economy: Foreign Investment and Sustainable Development in Mexico's Silicon Valley*

David N. Pellow, *Resisting Global Toxics: Transnational Movements for Environmental Justice*

Robert Gottlieb, *Reinventing Los Angeles: Nature and Community in the Global City*

David V. Carruthers, ed., *Environmental Justice in Latin America: Problems, Promise, and Practice*

Tom Angotti, *New York for Sale: Community Planning Confronts Global Real Estate*

Paloma Pavel, ed., *Breakthrough Communities: Sustainability and Justice in the Next American Metropolis*

Anastasia Loukaitou-Sideris and Renia Ehrenfeucht, *Sidewalks: Conflict and Negotiation over Public Space*

David J. Hess, *Localist Movements in a Global Economy: Sustainability, Justice, and Urban Development in the United States*

Julian Agyeman and Yelena Ogneva-Himmelberger, eds., *Environmental Justice and Sustainability in the Former Soviet Union*

Jason Corburn, *Toward the Healthy City: People, Places, and the Politics of Urban Planning*

JoAnn Carmin and Julian Agyeman, eds., *Environmental Inequalities beyond Borders: Local Perspectives on Global Injustices*

Louise Mozingo, *Pastoral Capitalism: A History of Suburban Corporate Landscapes*

Gwen Ottinger and Benjamin Cohen, eds., *Technoscience and Environmental Justice: Expert Cultures in a Grassroots Movement*

Samantha MacBride, *Recycling Reconsidered: The Present Failure and Future Promise of Environmental Action in the United States*

Andrew Karvonen, *Politics of Urban Runoff: Nature, Technology, and the Sustainable City*

Daniel Schneider, *Hybrid Nature: Sewage Treatment and the Contradictions of the Industrial Ecosystem*

Catherine Tumber, *Small, Gritty, and Green: The Promise of America's Smaller Industrial Cities in a Low-Carbon World*

Sam Bass Warner and Andrew H. Whittemore, *American Urban Form: A Representative History*

John Pucher and Ralph Buehler, eds., *City Cycling*

Stephanie Foote and Elizabeth Mazzolini, eds., *Histories of the Dustheap: Waste, Material Cultures, Social Justice*

David J. Hess, *Good Green Jobs in a Global Economy: Making and Keeping New Industries in the United States*

Joseph F. C. DiMento and Clifford Ellis, *Changing Lanes: Visions and Histories of Urban Freeways*

Joanna Robinson, *Contested Water: The Struggle against Water Privatization in the United States and Canada*

William B. Meyer, *The Environmental Advantages of Cities: Countering Commonsense Antiurbanism*

Rebecca L. Henn and Andrew J. Hoffman, eds., *Constructing Green: The Social Structures of Sustainability*

Peggy F. Barlett and Geoffrey W. Chase, eds., *Sustainability in Higher Education: Stories and Strategies for Transformation*

Isabelle Anguelovski, *Neighborhood as Refuge: Community Reconstruction, Place Remaking, and Environmental Justice in the City*

Kelly Sims Gallagher, *The Globalization of Clean Energy Technology: Lessons from China*

Vinit Mukhija and Anastasia Loukaitou-Sideris, eds., *The Informal American City: Beyond Taco Trucks and Day Labor*

Roxanne Warren, *Rail and the City: Shrinking Our Carbon Footprint While Reimagining Urban Space*

Marianne E. Krasny and Keith G. Tidball, *Civic Ecology: Adaptation and Transformation from the Ground Up*

Erik Swyngedouw, *Liquid Power: Contested Hydro-Modernities in Twentieth-Century Spain*

Ken Geiser, *Chemicals without Harm: Policies for a Sustainable World*

Duncan McLaren and Julian Agyeman, *Sharing Cities: A Case for Truly Smart and Sustainable Cities*

Jessica Smartt Gullion, *Fracking the Neighborhood: Reluctant Activists and Natural Gas Drilling*

Nicholas A. Phelps, *Sequel to Suburbia: Glimpses of America's Post-Suburban Future*

Shannon Elizabeth Bell, *Fighting King Coal: The Challenges to Micromobilization in Central Appalachia*

Theresa Enright, *The Making of Grand Paris: Metropolitan Urbanism in the Twenty-First Century*

Robert Gottlieb and Simon Ng, *Global Cities: Urban Environments in Los Angeles, Hong Kong, and China*

Anna Lora-Wainwright, *Resigned Activism: Living with Pollution in Rural China*

Scott L. Cummings, *Blue and Green: The Drive for Justice at America's Port*

David Bissell, *Transit Life: Cities, Commuting, and the Politics of Everyday Mobilities*

Javiera Barandiarán, *From Empire to Umpire: Science and Environmental Conflict in Neo-liberal Chile*

Benjamin Pauli, *Flint Fights Back: Environmental Justice and Democracy in the Flint Water Crisis*

Karen Chapple and Anastasia Loukaitou-Sideris, *Transit-Oriented Displacement or Community Dividends? Understanding the Effects of Smarter Growth on Communities*

Henrik Ernstson and Sverker Sörlin, eds., *Grounding Urban Natures: Histories and Futures of Urban Ecologies*

Katrina Smith Korfmacher, *Bridging the Silos: Collaborating for Environment, Health, and Justice in Urban Communities*

Jill Lindsey Harrison, *From the Inside Out: The Fight for Environmental Justice within Government Agencies*

Anastasia Loukaitou-Sideris, Dana Cuff, Todd Presner, Maite Zubiaurre, and Jonathan Jae-an Crisman, *Urban Humanities: New Practices for Reimagining the City*

Govind Gopakumar, *Installing Automobility: Emerging Politics of Mobility and Streets in Indian Cities*

Amelia Thorpe, *Everyday Ownership: PARK(ing) Day and the Practice of Property*

Tridib Banerjee, *In the Images of Development: City Design in the Global South*

Ralph Buehler and John Pucher, eds., *Cycling for Sustainable Cities*

Casey J. Dawkins, *Just Housing: The Moral Foundations of American Housing Policy*